The Role of the University in the Preparation of Teachers

The Role of the University in the Preparation of Teachers

Edited by

Robert A. Roth

UK   Falmer Press, 1 Gunpowder Square, London, EC4A 3DE
USA   Falmer Press, Taylor & Francis Inc., 325 Chestnut Street, 8th Floor,
        Philadelphia, PA 19106

First published in 1999

A catalogue record for this book is available from the British Library

ISBN 0-7507-0883-2 cased
ISBN 0-7507-0882-4 paper

**Library of Congress Cataloging-in-Publication Data are available on
request**

Jacket design by Caroline Archer

Typeset in 10/12pt Times by
Graphicraft Limited, Hong Kong

*Printed in Great Britain by Biddles Ltd., Guildford and King's Lynn on
paper which has a specified pH value on final paper manufacture of not
less than 7.5 and is therefore 'acid free'.*

*Every effort has been made to contact copyright holders for their
permission to reprint material in this book. The publishers would be
grateful to hear from any copyright holder who is not here acknowledged
and will undertake to rectify any errors or omissions in future editions of
this book.*

Contents

Contents

Preface

Robert A. Roth was a man of incredible vision who possessed the intelligence, expertise and energy to bring a vision to reality. In the 54 years that he lived, his accomplishments were too numerous to record in this brief tribute. He was a man of exceptional talents. He excelled as an athlete and was inducted into the Hiram College Athletic Hall of Fame. His professional accomplishments included president of the Association of Teacher Educators, NASDTC President, Association of Teacher Educators Distinguished Member, and the State of California Association of Teacher Educators Distinguished Educator. At California State University, Long Beach where he served as Chair of the Department of Teacher Education for 10 years, he was awarded the University Distinguished Scholar. Along with his numerous professional accomplishments, he was the beloved and devoted father of two sons and one daughter, and a respected colleague of many throughout the nation.

Robert Roth was a vibrant, dynamic, and vigorous proponent of excellence for educating America's teachers. A few years prior to his death he shared his belief with selected colleagues that as a profession, we are in process of defining our agenda for the profession and sustaining the role of the university. He became increasingly concerned about the urgency of the task. He believed this to be the time to advance the profession and that there was a danger of sliding backward significantly if we did not take action at this time. He believed the profession was rapidly approaching a major crossroads which would determine the direction and fate of teacher education. Robert Roth, being a man of determination and action launched this movement through conducting a major symposia at the American Association of Colleges of Teacher Education Annual Conference in 1996 and titled it, 'The Ivory Tower Under Siege: The Diminishing Role of the University in Teacher Education.' Some of the leading scholars in education participated. The attendance reflected not only the tremendous interest in the topic, but the enormous respect for those who participated. Dr Roth also co-chaired an Association of Teacher Education National Commission on Quality Standards and Enhancement of Teacher Education. Part of this mission was to enhance the credibility of teacher education, particularly within the university. The overwhelming response to these two commissions inspired Dr Roth to clearly articulate the vision of the role of the university in the education of teachers. He believed this book, which he began the latter part of 1995, would help to launch this initiative to preserve and enhance the profession. The benefits of the book would be to: 1) raise the consciousness level within the teacher education profession by having educators who are highly respected by their colleagues come forth and present their case; 2) present a well-conceived and clearly articulated statement of their case; 3) provide a vision of what an appropriate role of colleges and universities may look like in a best-case scenario, to provide a framework for institutions to review their programs and engage in introspection regarding their practices, relevance, and outcomes; 4) pull together the respected leadership in the profession and engage them in a common cause for the common good. To open up dialogue regarding the nature of the involvement in the enterprise, as well as delineation of future steps that need to be taken as part of a broader plan of action; and 5) present for the role of the university the intellectual contribution it makes to creating a profession. Through this, Dr Roth believed, 'We would be modeling exactly what we are proposing.'

Dr Roth believed that he had brought together the insights of the 'best minds' in teacher education. In discussing his vision for the book with those he believed to be outstanding educators, he invited them to write an original chapter on a particular element of the university's unique contribution to the preparation of teachers in order to sustain and enhance teaching as a profession. Dr Roth would serve as editor of the book. The authors presented in this book are those invited by Dr Roth to contribute a chapter.

Unfortunately, in 1996, Dr Roth was diagnosed with skin cancer. He fought a long and courageous battle until 23 February 1997. In January, 1997 when his energy began to diminish, he discussed his deep concern with me that the book be completed. At that time, he requested that I work with the authors and submit the book for publication. Dr Roth and I had published two books and were acquainted with one another's philosophy of and commitment toward education. It has been an honor for me to have made this small contribution to fulfilling Dr Roth's vision — *The Role of the University in the Preparation of Teachers*, edited by Robert A. Roth. A vision that became a legacy.

Yvonne Gold
California State University, Long Beach

1   Educating Teachers: Getting It Right the First Time

John I. Goodlad

Definitions of education almost invariably contain two components: the individual and the cultural surround. The self is to develop with responsibility to this cultural surround — civility toward others and support to *civitas* (a body of people constituting a politically organized community).[1] The duality of self-realization and sensitive orientation to the culture and others occupying it can take lodging only in individual character. In the United States of America and many other countries, the ideal blending of self and surround is seen to be a democratic symbiosis[2] of free selves aware of and committed to a culture that ensures their freedom. Freedom and responsibility are mutually inclusive.

Assuming the above, the aim of education in the United States becomes the development of democratic character. The meaning of education should not depend on the vagaries of national interests. I argue elsewhere that the best symbiosis so far envisioned for individual humans and the human condition is a democratic one of individual liberty and cultural responsibility (Goodlad, 1997). The future of humankind depends on worldwide education. The underlying premise of what follows is the definition of this education as the development of democratic character.[3] As such, it becomes an inalienable human right, a right that must not be debased by making education instrumental to some lesser end of politics or commerce.

This underlying premise regarding the universal aim of education has profound implications for the education and practice of those whose occupational or professional calling is education. They have in common a mission, a mission that transcends their innumerable specialties: elementary or secondary school teacher; mathematics, biology, history, music, physical education, or special education teacher; guidance counselor, speech therapist, teacher of English as a second language, or school principal. Education surfaces not as a mechanistic process of strengthening ends-means relationships but as an exceedingly risk-laden social responsibility to the human race — *to be counted and accounted for one by one*. The moral implications for educators and their profession abound.[4]

The Differing Natures of Education and Schooling

'Schooling' and 'education' are not words to be used interchangeably. I have endeavored above to raise education above the crosscurrents of political and marketplace symbiotics. In effect, I have implied a nonnegotiable aim for education of sufficient interpretive complexity to ensure endless conversation regarding its full meaning and implications. Schooling, by contrast, is a sociopolitical enterprise subject to all the crosscurrents of multinational, national, state, local, and individual interests. Its purposes are both public and private (Goodlad and McMannon, 1997).

Whereas educators worldwide are bound together in educational mission, the nature of schooling creates enormous circumstantial diversity. Educators coming together internationally in conferences are both surprised and pleased to find in their professional lives so many commonalities. They find even in their differences that most are variations on larger educational themes experienced in common.[5] But, back home, the larger themes of education tend to be overwhelmed by the lesser themes of schooling. The sociopolitical nature of schooling places in jeopardy the aim of education.

Were the aim of education held always above the functions schools are called upon to perform, the preoccupations of schooling would be markedly different from those now characterizing this enterprise in the United States. Education derives its cues from individuals in self-transcendence toward more mature democratic character. The educators' processes derive not from predetermined scripts but from deep understandings of both students' present developmental circumstances and the reservoir of artifacts and concepts potentially relevant to further learning. Schooling derives many of its cues from those instrumentalities for it that dominate in the cultural surround and those systemics and regularities deemed necessary to their efficient fulfillment.[6] What students are to learn is largely prescripted, as are many of the teaching methods to be used (in spite of much rhetoric to the contrary). The narrative of behavioral expectations for both teachers and students is largely already written, the contingencies for teaching and learning preordained.

Given the dominance of efficiency as the criterion of efficacy in our cultural surround, we should not be surprised with the dominance of this criterion in our judging of schools. That which is morally right gains credence in the lexicon of school reform if it is perceived to be simultaneously efficient.[7] Alfie Kohn (1997) provides us with a portrait of students being pulled or pushed toward a predetermined set of behavioral expectations so as to virtually crowd out the deliberative process of critically examining their own behavior and taking personal responsibility for it. This system, as Paul Theobald (1997) points out, promotes a sense of personal failure among the large numbers of losers and creates a self-fulfilling prophecy regarding brisk business in the provision of prison cells. The narrative of economic utility and its god of efficiency, which Neil Postman (1995) sees to be now driving schooling, does not square with the visions for humankind we invariably invoke in defining what education is.

Conflicting Expectations for Schooling

There is plenty of evidence to support the thesis that teachers are torn by the conflict that arises when what they perceive to be the 'right' thing to do clashes with their perceptions of what the systemics and regularities of schooling require that they do. Linda McNeil (1986) has documented the nature and frequency of these 'contradictions of control' and their impact on teachers' decisions. Pressures from the outside complicate the ambiguity of choice-making already present. The most common sources of teachers' curricular and instructional choice-making are textbooks, district courses of study, and their past associations with school-based learning. The natural intrusion of appealing new ideas often runs counter to teachers' customary ways and creates dissonance. Unfortunately, the rather minimal preparation of large numbers of teachers provides professional grounding that is insufficient for confident choice-making (Goodlad, 1990). New ways that appeal create uncertainty in regard to the old ways. When the latter carry with them external authority, only the most confident, autonomous teachers embrace what countervails.

The circumstances described are not absent in the other professions. But they are uniquely severe in their impact on teachers and teaching, in large part because of the uncertain status of teaching as a profession and the tenuous professional grounding of teachers. Strangely, there are many people who would have it no other way. It is culturally convenient to maintain an occupation with some professional trappings but loosely latched gates of entry. It is politically convenient to manipulate at will the ends and means of our major public enterprise without running the gauntlet of a unified profession enjoying strong public credibility. And so teacher education remains a neglected enterprise and teaching a marginal profession.

The Custodial Function of Schools

Ironically, it is a major characteristic of the systemics frustrating the educational purpose of schools that offers the best opportunity for advancing it. One of the most constant regularities of schooling is the daily schedule. Today's parents, more than yesterday's, depend for some order in their lives on school days that begin when many of them are at or are heading for work and end a few hours before they return home — with additional activities often filling up the late afternoon schedule. Absent this regularity, each weekday would place fresh logistical demands on all families with schoolage children.

Jane Roland Martin (1992) begins her book on rethinking schools for changing families by comparing the procession of men moving from private home to public world each day several decades ago with today's procession of men and women crossing this bridge together. She sees this development as increasing, not decreasing, the traditional custodial function of schooling and for this role to be carried out in the fashion of a caring home. It has been said that education sets the human spirit free. But let us not underestimate the degree to which schools have set parents free and, to the degree they are caring places, have provided parents with peace of mind.

There is a vast literature on technology as the quintessential liberator — the force that sets humans free. Even if one were to ignore the less-chronicled downside regarding the bondage accompanying almost all technological advances (Tenner, 1996), as liberator schooling wins hands down.

Imagine today's parental bondage were there no schools. Or, just try to imagine today's workplace in the absence of schools. Schooling is the most comprehensive, least expensive system of childcare ever devised. This is the fact that most retards implementation of those images of a technologically driven system of schooling that have been with us for quite some time. It is, in addition, a fact that should draw our attention even more sharply and critically to the issue of *who*, besides children and youths, should fill up classroom space to ensure that our schools are simultaneously 'places for learning, places for joy' (to borrow the title of one of Theodore Sizer's books[8]).

Schools as Cultural Entities

Educators tend to believe that educational theories and ideas are the dominant vehicles on the road to school improvement. But the roadsides are littered with the wrecks of compelling ideas holding much promise of betterment. Significant though ideology may be in parental expectations for schools, daily circumstances are much more powerful determinants. Not surprisingly, today's parents — frequently, both working or a single, working parent — want assurance that their children are known and safe at school (Johnson and Immerwahr, 1994). What their children bring home and tell them about school ranks high in their views of their own schools' quality. Their negative views of schooling in general are shaped less by personal experience than by the opinion-making role of polls and the popular media.

The 'good' school for many, probably most, parents is the one that creates little dissonance with daily life. This means such things as unchanging school beginnings and endings, ease in getting wanted information, few negative surprises, absence of teacher and school requests that take time, an ethos of a school attending to its business, and so on. Schools soon discover the hazards of scheduling teachers' meetings that cause shortened school days. Alert teachers soon discover the hazards in reporting children's progress to parents who are both 'on the run'. The absence of school–home dissonance transfers to positive parental perceptions in relatively obscure domains of schooling such as curriculum and instruction. The school that takes care of its daily business well and encompasses the home harmoniously in so doing is a far more satisfying place for parents, teachers, and students than one that does not.[9]

There is a powerful message here regarding who is to teach. There exists, even among teacher educators, the view that the competencies required for the good school of the above description are learned on the job. Admittedly, they are honed on the job but their absence at the outset is a major cause of home–school dissonance, of early drop-out from teaching, and perpetuation of the costly business of five or six short-term teachers frequently being required to fill out one career line. Children and society are the ultimate losers.

Teacher education programs have been geared to the culture of the classroom, not the whole school (Goodlad, 1990). The socialization process, in turn, has been geared to the individual teacher, not teams (Su, 1989). Yet, the school, not just individual teachers, attracts community judgment; and it takes the faculty working as a team to engage the school in continuing renewal. Teachers with scant preparation perceive the culture of the school as something beyond their responsibility — something for the principal to worry about, perhaps.

The daily circumstances of schooling do not lend themselves well to easing teachers gradually into their responsibilities, especially those that relate to the whole school. The notion of experienced teachers mentoring new ones is an appealing myth; the experienced teacher down the hallway is fully preoccupied with his or her own responsibilities. As noted above, even modest provision for in-school staff development interferes with family schedules, creating home–school dissonance. New teachers must be off and running at the outset. An ill-prepared beginner is likely to be the ill-prepared experienced teacher.

Integrating the Custodial and Educative Functions

Up to now, this narrative has addressed the potential shortfall in a school's performance of its custodial function when staffed by teachers not prepared to be stewards of whole schools. It has addressed, also, a school's potentially low capacity for renewal when staffed by teachers not prepared for the necessary team work. It is hard to believe that schools performing this custodial function poorly and not engaged in renewal are likely to be, nonetheless, superb or even modestly successful in performing their educational function.

It turns out that schools are bundles of correlating characteristics. A good school is good in virtually everything that matters: class climate, school climate, principal–teacher relationships, home–school relations, hours of instruction each week, teacher–student relationships, and more. A poor school is characterized by showing up far less favorably in these same features. Parents in schools that fit the first of these two descriptions rarely perceive the ongoing program of curriculum and instruction as a problem. Parents in schools for the second description add curriculum and instruction to their list of problems. High teacher and student satisfaction parallels parent satisfaction in the first school and is correspondingly low in the second.

There is a dearth of research on the degree to which academic achievement is a correlate of those correlates of schools taking care of their business. Are schools that are safe and caring and marked by high parent, student, and teacher satisfaction also places of high learning? A common problem with research on school reform reporting no significant improvement in academic achievement is failure to document carefully the actual presence of the conditions that presumably would make a difference. It makes no sense to claim attribution or nonattribution of nonevents! When possibly premature results of the measures taken are announced to show no achievement gains, the reform effort usually closes down. But what might have been the outcome if it had been sustained for an additional three or four years? The research cupboard is disappointingly bare.

There is, however, a highly important issue for which empirical research is irrelevant. Do we not want and value caring schools with good student–teacher–parent–principal relationships? Surely we do not want the opposite. Dare we cast aside as complacency, as some critics do, the high satisfaction with their schools of those closest to them? If claims of owner satisfaction with certain makes of automobiles (and virtually every other commonality) are so sacred in advertising, why do such claims become soft and irrelevant when we turn to our schools? Would evidence of one school taking care of its business in an orderly way and accompanied by high satisfaction on the part of the critical groups of actors involved make no difference in whether we chose it for our children over one absent these characteristics? Not bloody likely. I do not know a parent who would deliberately choose the latter over the former.

The series of studies conducted by the RAND Corporation over a period of years convincingly ruled out the potential of any single variable for producing significant improvement in the performance of schools.[10] Rather, a host of variables creatively orchestrated by the principal and teachers — many of them embedded in the culture of the whole school as well as the classroom — offered promise. Since then, a rash of case studies appearing in the educational literature has added support to this hypothesis. The research of colleagues and me has revealed the degree to which a school faculty, closely connected to homes and community, can positively influence the school's symbiotics — how people *are* with one another, as Donna Kerr expresses the human connection (Kerr, 1997). But it also has revealed the stubborn character of the established curricular and instructional ways — the elements most determined by systemics beyond the schoolhouse and by traditions of schoolteaching that the relatively short, rather unfocused, and not very intensive professional education many teachers experience fails to overcome.

I began an earlier section of this narrative with the observation that the seminal custodial function performed by schools offers a promising opportunity for advancing the educational one. The continuity of teachers, students, and parents that schools seem to require to sustain educational improvement (as measured by academic performance) is most likely to accompany exemplary performance in the custodial domain. I endeavored to make clear that this exemplary performance does not come easily; many schools are far from it. It requires the sustained collaboration of home and school, teachers, parents, and students. It requires teachers prepared at the outset of their careers to work constructively with a diverse array of others.

The attainment of a stable, satisfying school environment is not necessarily accompanied by significant improvement in the educational delivery system, even though parental satisfaction with curricular and instructional matters tends to correlate with their satisfaction in the custodial realm. This suggests that much of the motivation for addressing shortcomings in a school's educational program must arise out of the dissatisfaction of teachers. Rather than basking in the rewards that come from being part of a satisfying school, they must risk and take on the daunting tasks of fundamentally changing what and how they teach. This means doing differently much of what currently is widely regarded as standard. The visions held by most people of what schools should be, even many people wanting reform, are surprisingly similar to the realities of what they remember from the past. The context most favorable to the consideration of needed changes would appear to be the one of considerable satisfaction with and confidence in the current stewardship of the school. The parental satisfaction with this stewardship that carries over into correlating confidence in the educational program is likely to carry over also into support for increased attention to the arts, for example. A constituency perceiving unsatisfactory school performance in mathematics is not likely to see more attention to the arts as a priority.

However, for teachers to advance the need for curricular and instructional improvement, especially if the current ethos tends to support the principle, 'If it ain't broke, don't try to fix it', requires keen sensitivity to what excellence means. And, without solid professional grounding in curricular and instructional domains, teachers are likely to botch the improvement process. Both a supportive context and a well-prepared team of educators are essential to success. Given the longstanding casual neglect of teacher education, we should be thankful for the caring schools we do have and not be surprised that taking even these to a high level of educational performance is not the norm.

Teachers Who Understand and Care

Earlier, I raised the issue of *who* should fill up our schools and classrooms as teachers if parents, more dependent on the custodial role of schools than ever before, are not to be uneasy, as they cross that bridge to work each day, about the care their children are receiving in school. The priorities for most are that their children be known, treated fairly, and safe in the school environment. Even the parents who, at the evening PTA meeting, express concern about the school's reading program have at the top of their list for the next conference with their child's teacher questions about individual attention, relations with peers, and other matters in the caring domain. Few things are more productive of parental satisfaction with their schools than evidences of a bonding relationship with teachers and positive reports of life at school on the part of their children.

Then, I raised implicitly the issue of *who* should fill up our schools and classrooms as teachers if a caring school is to have a good chance of becoming also a place of intense engagement of all students in learning. The development of democratic character must be a goal for more than the few who are the winners in our present system of schooling because we must live with everybody's children. The places of refuge for both winners and losers already are crowded and in much need of civility.

In selecting and even seeking to prepare people for teaching in schools, we have paid scant attention to what teachers are called upon to do there, let alone to what they *should* do there. Commissioned reports on school reform from the early 1890s to the late 1980s omit reference to teachers' education; reports on the reform of teacher education over this same period of time provide no depiction of the demands or expectations of teaching in schools. Failure to make this connection leaves us free to conjure up whatever our biases suggest regarding either or both.

The simplistic often has gained as much or more credibility than the more realistically comprehensive.

And so we have the military model of the ideal teacher, stemming back to the seventeenth century image of schools that would be places of strict discipline, close to the police and the courts (Aries, 1962). Open the gates to teaching for the military retiree. In our own culture of the 1840s, the disciplinary model prevailed still and so came the appeal for *men* to leave their regular work for a spate of teaching in the new schools. The industrial model of the second half of the nineteenth century, grounded in the concept of efficiency, spawned the school model of platooning — a teacher managing with a few 'programmed' aides a graded class of a hundred or more students. Open wide the gates to teaching for male business retirees.

Women answered the call to enroll in the four founding normal schools of Massachusetts. The principals complained of the meager educational backgrounds of their charges and settled for teaching them the subject matter their teaching in grammar schools would require. As in the earlier Dame Schools, these women would ensure some of the nurturing the younger pupils require. Male graduates of the academies, however, presumed to be in command of the subject matter required, remained the ideal for teaching the older students, more in need of discipline than nurturing. Open wide the gates to the scholar and hope he will be spared the fate of Ichabod Crane.

The soldier, the businessman, the modestly schooled woman blessed with the virtue of female caring, the somewhat effete scholar steeped in academic lore — these are the ghosts of perceived teachers past who haunt the paths of attending to teacher education present. These are the ghosts that will haunt the improvement of teacher education future, frustrating attainment of the goal set in 1996 by the National Commission on Teaching and America's Future: all children with access to qualified, caring, competent teachers by the year 2006 (National Commission on Teaching and America's Future, 1996). Unless put to rest, these may well be the ghosts that will prevent us from having schools commonly developing democratic character — a symbiosis of the competent, caring self and the good society.

The recommendations of the National Commission are supported by substantial authenticating scholarly inquiry, particularly that of the preceding decade — inquiry that both lays down an agenda of what must be done to ensure robust, coherent programs of general and professional education and a comprehensive picture of the formidable gap between present and envisioned conditions.[11] What teaching in today's schools demands by way of beginning — not ultimate — efficacy, as sketched in this narrative, embraces a wide range of disciplines in the humanities, natural sciences, and social sciences that pertain to an ecological understanding of our people and our world, as well as to the skills of inter- and intradependence.[12] Teachers must learn not only the subject matters of the human conversation but also the pedagogy for immersing the young productively in this conversation.

Clearly, the foundations and the renewal of a teaching career reside in the university — just as do the foundations and renewal of other professional careers.

But teaching in schools is unique in its use of the intellectual disciplines in enculturating the young. As in the other professions, the necessary principles and skills must be honed in back-and-forth processes of action and reflection that honor the inseparable relationship of theory and practice in human endeavors. Consequently, partner or professional development schools, equivalent in many ways to the teaching hospitals of medical education, are a necessary component of the teacher education program (Clark, 1997).

Curriculum development promises to be demanding work in progress already begun. Some settings are finding it useful to create centers of pedagogy that bring into a single coordinating unit these partner schools and segments of both the arts and sciences and the college of education to ensure the faculty required. Reward systems are undergoing scrutiny and revision to heighten the probability that incentives for participation are in place. Given the time it takes to sunset existing programs and produce graduates of redesigned ones on a large scale, the goal of the National Commission on Teaching and America's Future will not be attained by 2006. It is encouraging to note that, at the time of this writing, the federal department of education is engaged intensively in seeking ways to capitalize on promising work already under way by making funds available to both accelerate it and effect collaboration between interested teacher-preparing settings and those perceived to be further along in the renewing process.

Coda

The preceding narrative presents essentially three interrelated arguments for each beginning corps of schoolteachers to enter practice with the general and specialized knowledge base and pedagogy already sufficiently in place for efficacious fulfillment of the high custodial and educational expectations parents and other citizens set for our schools. The attainment of this condition is our best guarantee that the risk-laden freedom of educating the young will not itself be at risk. It ensures a teaching force prepared to hone its pedagogy through continuing self-renewal.

My first argument pertained to the daunting mission schoolteachers share: the common development of democratic character in the young. My second argument pertained to a major corollary of the changing circumstances of parenthood: the need for a stable, caring daycare environment for their children that alleviates their worry and guilt simultaneously. The increasing significance of education in the lives of all of us heightens parental interest in both the custodial and educational functions of schooling; they expect both. My third argument grew out of an analysis of what it takes to create schools that are both satisfying places for teachers, parents, and students and exemplary places of learning.

Awareness of the incredible significance of those teachers who occupy the daily surround of children and youths for many hours each year over many years is growing, turning attention to their selection and education. I am more optimistic now than I have been in many years regarding the positive influence this awareness is likely to have on support for and the design of solid programs for the education of educators. My major worry is that what appear to many people to be bold and visionary (and costly) recommendations are far too cautious. The legacies of perceived teachers and teaching past temper our expectations and we become timid. To have teachers who are commonly competent and caring and schools that are commonly good is a challenge that equals or exceeds any that has so far tested our vision and competence.

Notes

1 There is at time of this writing growing interest in and concern regarding the need for greater citizen involvement in the infrastructure of their local communities and beyond. Several books include Benjamin R. Barber *An Aristocracy of Everyone: The Politics of Education and the Future of America* (New York: Ballantine, 1992) and Amitai Etzioni *The New Golden Rule: Community and Morality in a Democratic Society* (New York: Basic Books, 1996).

2 In work published between 1603 and 1614, Johannes Althusius wrote of the processes and outcomes of all human associations as symbiotics and symbioses respectively. For a translation and editing of his classic publication, see *Politica*, edited and translated by Frederick S. Carney (Indianapolis, Ind.: Liberty Press, 1995).

3 To emphasize the necessity for responsibility to the habitat, Stephen John Goodlad adds an environmental adjective to democratic character in 'An Ecocentric Environmental Ethic as a Foundation for Schooling, Character, and Democracy.' Unpublished work in progress, 1996.

4 See Roger Soder (ed.) *Democracy, Education, and the Schools* (San Francisco: Jossey-Bass, 1996). Given the risk-laden nature of teaching the young, there are at least equally profound implications for lay teachers as well (particularly those who exclusively home-school). On this issue see Barry L. Bull, 'The Limits of Teacher Professionalization', in John I. Goodlad, Roger Soder, and Kenneth A. Sirotnik (eds) *The Moral Dimensions of Teaching* (San Francisco: Jossey-Bass, 1990), pp. 95–8.

5 These extensive commonalities and circumstantial variations were brought home to me in a conference of participants from 22 nations held in Gränna, Sweden, during the summer of 1971. At the beginning of the six-week workshop, there was much skepticism of having anything of importance sufficiently in common to warrant discourse. After a rather short period, the comments were of combined amazement and satisfaction over the degree to which a common agenda was emerging.

6 Regarding these systemics and regularities, see respectively Gary D. Fenstermacher 'The Absence of Democratic and Educational Ideals from Contemporary Educational Reform Initiatives', Stanley Elam Lecture, Educational Press Association of America, Chicago, 10 June 1994; and Seymour B. Sarason *The Culture of the School and the Problem of Change*, 2d ed. (Boston: Allyn and Bacon, 1982).

7 For documentation of the progression (and deterioration) of school reform proposals from moral persuasion to justification on grounds of efficiency, see Timothy J. McMannon *Morality, Efficiency, and Reform: An Interpretation of the History of American Education*, Work in Progress Series No. 5 (Seattle: Institute for Educational Inquiry, 1995).

8 Theodore R. Sizer *Places for Learning, Places for Joy* (Cambridge, Mass.: Harvard University Press, 1973).

9   The source for this and subsequent observations regarding school satisfaction is the research reported in John I. Goodlad, *A Place Called School* (New York: McGraw-Hill, 1984).

10 A good reference with which to begin perusal of the RAND Corporation's findings over a period of more than a decade of inquiry is Harvey A. Averch et al. *How Effective is Schooling?* (Englewood Cliffs, NJ: Educational Technology Publications, 1974).

11 See, for example, Carnegie Forum on Education and the Economy *A Nation Prepared: Teachers for the 21st Century* (Washington, DC: Carnegie Forum on Education and the Economy, 1986); Holmes Group *Tomorrow's Teachers: A Report of the Holmes Group* (East Lansing, Mich.: Holmes Group, 1986); John I. Goodlad *Educational Renewal: Better Teachers, Better Schools* (San Francisco: Jossey-Bass, 1994).

12 For a penetrating analysis of these worldwide relationships, see Benjamin R. Barber *Jihad vs. McWorld* (New York: Times Books, 1995).

References

ARIES, P. (1962) *Centuries of Childhood*, BALDICK, R. (trans.), New York: Vintage Books, p. 413.

AVERCH, H.A., CARROLL, S.J., DONALDSON, T.S., KIESLING, H.J. and PINCUS, J. (1974) *How Effective Is Schooling? A Critical Review of Research*, Englewood Cliffs, NJ: Educational Technology Publications.

BARBER, B.R. (1992) *An Aristocracy of Everyone: The Politics of Education and the Future of America*, New York: Ballantine.

BARBER, B.R. (1995) *Jihad vs. McWorld*, New York: Times Books.

BULL, B.L. (1990) 'The limits of teacher professionalization', in GOODLAD, J.I., SODER, R. and SIROTNIK, K.A. (eds) *The Moral Dimensions of Teaching*, San Francisco: Jossey-Bass.

CARNEGIE FORUM ON EDUCATION AND THE ECONOMY (1986) *A Nation Prepared: Teachers for the 21st century*, Washington, DC, Author.

CARNEY, F.S. (ed.) (1995) *Politica*, Indianapolis, IN: Liberty Press.

CLARK, R.W. (1997) *Professional Development Schools: Policy and Financing*, Washington, DC: American Association of Colleges for Teaching Education.

ETZIONI, A. (1996) *The New Golden Rule: Community and Morality in a Democratic Society*, New York: Basic Books.

FENSTERMACHER, G.D. (1994, 10 June) *The Absence of Democratic and Educational Ideals from Contemporary Educational Reform Initiatives*, Stanley Elam Lecture, Chicago: Educational Press Association of America.

GOODLAD, J.I. (1984) *A Place Called School*, New York: McGraw-Hill.

GOODLAD, J.I. (1990) *Teachers for Our Nation's Schools*, San Francisco: Jossey-Bass.

GOODLAD, J.I. (1994) *Educational Renewal: Better Teachers, Better Schools*, San Francisco: Jossey-Bass.

GOODLAD, J.I. (1997) *In Praise of Education*, New York: Teachers College Press.

GOODLAD, J.I. and McMANNON, T.J. (eds) (1997) *The Public Purpose of Education and Schooling*, San Francisco: Jossey-Bass.

HOLMES GROUP (1986) *Tomorrow's Teachers: A Report of the Holmes Group*, East Lansing, MI, Author.

JOHNSON, J. and IMMERWAHR, J. (1994) *First Things First: What Americans Expect from the Public Schools*, New York: Public Agenda Foundation.

KERR, D.H. (1997) 'Toward a democratic rhetoric of schooling', in GOODLAD, J.I. and McMANNON, T.J., (eds) *The Public Purpose of Education and Schooling*, San Francisco: Jossey-Bass, p. 78.

KOHN, A. (1997, February) 'How not to teach values: A critical look at character education', *Phi Delta Kappan*, **78**, pp. 428–39.

MARTIN, J.R. (1992) *The Schoolhome*, Cambridge, MA: Harvard University Press.

McMANNON, T.J. (1995) *Morality, Efficiency, and Reform: An Interpretation of the History of American Education*, Work in Progress, Series No. 5, Seattle: Institure for Educational Inquiry.

McNEIL, L.M. (1986) *Contradictions of Control: School Structure and School Knowledge*, New York: Routledge.

NATIONAL COMMISSION ON TEACHING AND AMERICA'S FUTURE (1996) *What Matters Most: Teaching for America's Future*, New York: Teachers College, Columbia University.

POSTMAN, N. (1995) *The End of Education*, New York: Knopf.

SARASON, S.B. (1982) *The Culture of the School and the Problem of Change*, Boston: Allyn and Bacon.

SIZER, T.R. (1973) *Places for Learning, Places for Joy*, Cambridge, MA: Harvard University Press.

SODER, R. (ed.) (1996) *Democracy, Education, and the Schools*, San Francisco: Jossey-Bass.

SU, Z. (1989) *Exploring the Moral Socialization of Teachers: Factors Related to the Development of Beliefs, Attitudes, and Value in Teacher Candidates*, Technical Report No. 7, Seattle: Center for Educational Renewal, College of Education, University of Washington.

TENNER, E. (1996) *How Things Bite Back: Technology and the Revenge of Unintended Consequences*, New York: Knopf.

THEOBALD, P. (1997) *Teaching the Commons: Place, Pride, and the Renewal of Community*, Boulder, Colorado: Westview Press.

2 The Case for University-based Teacher Education

Linda Darling-Hammond

For a number of years, public dissatisfaction with schools has been coupled with dissatisfaction with schools of education as well. Education schools have been variously criticized as ineffective in preparing teachers for their work, unresponsive to new demands, remote from practice, and barriers to the recruitment of bright college students into teaching. In more than 40 states policy makers have enacted alternate routes to teacher certification to create pathways into teaching other than those provided by traditional 4-year undergraduate teacher education programs. Upon his election in 1988, President Bush's only education proposal was the encouragement of alternative teacher certification to allow more flexible teacher recruitment. In 1995, Newt Gingrich proposed the elimination of teacher certification rules, which require preparation for teaching, as his major education initiative.

Voices of dissatisfaction have been raised from within the profession as well. During the past decade, significant critiques of traditional teacher education practices have been raised by the Holmes Group of education deans (Holmes Group, 1986) and the Carnegie Task Force on Teaching as a Profession (1986), along with scholars like John Goodlad (1990), Ken Howey and Nancy Zimpher (1989), and Ken Zeichner (1993), among others. These voices, however, have urged the redesign of teacher education to strengthen its knowledge base, its connections to both practice and theory, and its capacity to support the development of powerful teaching.

Proposals at the far ends of this continuum stand in stark contrast to one another: on the one hand, university-based preparation would be replaced by 'on-the-job' training that focuses on the pragmatics of teaching, while on the other, more extensive professional training would aim to prepare teachers for much more adaptive, knowledge-based practice while tackling the redesign of schools and teacher education in tandem. Which of these routes holds the most promise? What would the implications be for teachers' knowledge, skills, and commitments — and, most important, for the education of children?

While the debates on these questions have been largely ideological, there is a growing body of empirical evidence about the outcomes of different approaches to teacher education and recruitment, ranging from quick alternative routes into the classroom to traditional university-based approaches to newer models that are 5-year extended programs or 5th year postbaccalaureate programs. As I describe in this chapter, the evidence strongly suggests that 'on-the-job' preservice training leaves teachers seriously underprepared. Most alternative routes sponsored by school districts, states, and other vendors have been found to be significantly less effective at preparing and retaining recruits than university-based teacher education programs. Furthermore, these truncated programs tend to feature regressive approaches to teaching practice that are seriously out of synch with new standards for student learning.

Although traditional teacher education programs differ significantly from one another and some have major shortcomings, as a group they produce teachers who are more highly rated and effective with children than are teachers who enter teaching without training or through quick alternate routes. Furthermore, more extensive redesigned programs that have resulted from recent reforms are even more successful than traditional four-year models. In short, teacher education matters, and more teacher education is better than less. In what follows, I discuss why.

What Teachers Need to Know and Be Able to Do

Central to any discussion of teacher preparation is a judgment about what it is teachers must be prepared to do. If teachers are viewed primarily as purveyors of information for students, one could argue that they need little more than basic content knowledge and the ability to string together comprehensible lectures in order to do an adequate job. For this kind of teaching, it is easy to believe that a liberal arts education could be sufficient preparation. But if teachers need to be able to ensure successful learning for students who learn in different ways and encounter a variety of difficulties, then teachers need to be diagnosticians and planners who know a great deal about the learning process and have a repertoire of tools at their disposal. This kind of teaching is not intuitively obvious. And it is this kind of teaching that current social demands increasingly require.

In today's complex society and economy, much greater numbers of students need to be prepared for much more challenging forms of learning than ever before in our history. In order to meet the ambitious standards for student learning currently being developed by states and professional associations, teachers must learn to teach for understanding and to teach for diversity — that is, to teach in ways that enable a wide range of learners to succeed at very demanding intellectual tasks (National Commission on Teaching and America's Future, 1996).

What do teachers need to know to teach all students in the way new standards suggest? First of all, teachers need to understand subject matter in ways that allow them to organize it so that students can create useful cognitive maps of the terrain. They need more than formulaic or procedural understanding of the core ideas in a discipline and how these help to structure knowledge, how they relate to one another, and how they can be tested, evaluated, and extended. Teachers also need to be able to use their knowledge of subject matter flexibly to address ideas as they come up in the course of learning. They need to understand how inquiry in a field is conducted and what reasoning entails — such as what counts as 'proving' something in mathematics as compared with proving something in history (Ball and Cohen, in press). And they need to see ways that ideas connect across fields, and to everyday life, so that they can select and use examples, problems, and applications well.

Understanding subject matter in this way provides a foundation for pedagogical content knowledge (Shulman, 1987), which enables teachers to represent ideas so that they are accessible to others. Knowledge of the domain of study is critical: the teacher needs to understand what ideas can provide important foundations for other ideas and how they can be usefully linked and assembled. The audience is also key: people will understand ideas differently depending on their prior experiences and context. A skillful pedagogue figures out what a particular audience is likely to know and believe about the topic under study, and how learners are likely to 'hook into' new ideas, so as to create productive learning experiences. Knowledge of cognition, information processing, and communication are also important so that teachers can shape lectures, materials, learning centers, projects, and discussions in useful ways.

Interpreting learners' statements and actions and framing productive experiences for them requires knowledge of development — how children and adolescents think and behave, what they are trying to accomplish, what they find interesting, what they already know and what they are likely to have trouble with in particular domains at particular ages in particular contexts. This knowledge includes an understanding of how to support further growth in a number of domains — social, physical, and emotional, as well as cognitive.

Teaching in ways that connect with students also requires an understanding of differences that may arise from culture, language, family, community, gender, prior schooling, or other factors that shape people's experiences, as well as differences that may arise from developed intelligence, preferred approaches to learning, or specific learning difficulties. Teachers need to be able to inquire sensitively and productively into children's experiences and their understandings of subject matter so that they can interpret curriculum through their students' eyes and shape lessons to connect with what students know and how they learn well. To get non-stereotypic information that can help them come to understand their learners, teachers need to know how to listen carefully to students and look at their work as well as to structure situations in which students write and talk about their experiences and what they understand. This builds a foundation of pedagogical learner knowledge (Grimmett and MacKinnon, 1992) which grows as teachers examine how particular learners think and reason, where they have problems, how they learn best, and what motivates them.

An understanding of motivation is critical in teaching for understanding, because achieving understanding is difficult. Teachers must know how to structure tasks and feedback so as to encourage extensive effort without either relinquishing the press for understanding when the going gets tough or discouraging students so that they give up altogether. Motivating students not only requires understanding general principles about how to engage young people and sustain their interest at different ages, but also understanding what individual students believe about themselves and their abilities, what they care about, and what tasks are likely to give them enough success to encourage them to continue to work hard to learn.

Teachers need several kinds of knowledge about learning. Since there are many kinds of learning — for example, learning for recognition or appreciation vs. learning for various kinds of applications or performances — teachers need to think about what it means to learn different kinds of material for different purposes, how to support different kinds of learning with distinctive teaching strategies, and how to make judgments about which kinds of learning are most necessary in different contexts. Not everything can be learned deeply — that is, with opportunities for extensive application — but some things must be deeply understood as foundations for work that is to follow and as a means for developing specific skills and performances. Other ideas may be understood more superficially to create a map of the domain, but learned so that they connect to concepts that are meaningful.

Teachers need to understand what helps children (or anyone) learn in these different ways. They need to be able to construct and use a variety of means for assessing students' knowledge, as well as for evaluating student's approaches to learning. To be effective, they must be able to identify the strengths of different learners while addressing their weaknesses — those who rely more on visual or oral cues; those who tend to reason from the specific to the general or vice-versa; those who use spatial or graphic organizers vs. those who are more text-oriented; those who bring a highly developed logical/mathematical intelligence and those who bring a strong aesthetic sense.

Using this information well requires a command of teaching strategies that address a variety of ways to learn and a variety of purposefully selected goals for learning. Strategies that regularly use multiple pathways to content are one major part of a teacher's repertoire. In addition, more than ever before in the past, all teachers need tools to work with the students in their classrooms who have specific learning disabilities or needs — the estimated 15 to 20 percent of students who are dyslexic or dysgraphic, who have particular visual or perceptual difficulties or difficulties with information processing. There are useful teaching strategies for these relatively commonplace problems, but they have been rarely taught to 'regular' education teachers. And, because language is the gateway to learning, teachers need an understanding of how students acquire language, both native English speakers and students who start from other languages, so that they can build language skills and create learning experiences that are accessible. This may mean strategies ranging from explicit teaching of key vocabulary or use of an array of visual and oral cues and materials to the creation of collaborative learning settings in which students use language extensively.

Teachers need to know about curriculum resources and technologies. They need to be able to connect their students with sources of information and knowledge that extend beyond textbooks, that allow for the exploration of ideas, the acquisition and synthesis of information, and the development of models, writings, designs, and other work products. The teacher's role will be to help students learn to find and use a wide array of resources for framing and solving problems, rather than to remember only the information contained in one source.

And they need to know about collaboration. They need to understand how interactions among students can be structured to allow more powerful shared learning to occur. They need to be able to shape classrooms that sponsor productive discourse that presses for disciplined reasoning on the part of students. They need to understand how to collaborate with other teachers to plan, assess, and improve learning within and across the school, as well as how to work with parents to learn more about their students and to shape supportive experiences at school and home.

Finally, teachers need to be able to analyze and reflect on their practice, to assess the effects of their teaching and to refine and improve their instruction. When teaching for understanding, teachers must maintain two intertwining strands of thought at all times: How am I doing at moving the students toward high levels of understanding and proficient performance and How am I taking into account what students know and care about in the process of moving them toward these curriculum goals and developing their talents and social abilities? Teachers must continuously evaluate what students are thinking and understanding and reshape their plans to take account of what they've discovered as they build curriculum to meet their goals.

These demands that derive from the desire to teach a much wider range of students for much higher standards of performance are new ones for most teachers. With few having experienced this kind of learning themselves, how can it be possible to create a different kind of teaching on a wide scale? The only plausible answer is to develop much more powerful forms of teacher education — both before entry and throughout the teaching career — that systematically provide experience with the kinds of knowledge and forms of practice described above, and then to make that kind of education available to all teachers, not just a few. As Gary Fenstermacher (1992) observes:

> In a time when so many advocate for restructured schools, for greater decision autonomy for teachers, and for connecting the schools more intimately with homes and communities, it is more important than ever that teachers have the capacity to appraise their actions, evaluate their work, anticipate and control consequences, incorporate new theory and research into practice, and possess the skills and understanding needed to explain their work to other teachers, and to students and their parents . . .
>
> These reflective capacities are not innate to human beings, nor are they acquired quickly. They are not acquired during a planning period sandwiched somewhere in between classes, or during evening 'mini-courses' after a full day's work. They are, rather, the outcome of sustained and rigorous study, and of dialogue and exchange with master teacher educators. (35, in manuscript)

Developing the kinds of knowledge I have described requires that most teachers move far beyond what they themselves experienced as students, and thus that they learn in ways that are more powerful than simply reading and talking about new pedagogical ideas (Ball and Cohen, in press). Learning to practice in substantially different ways than one has oneself experienced can occur neither through theoretical imaginings alone, nor on unguided experience alone. It requires a much tighter coupling of the two.

Teachers learn just as students do: by studying, doing, and reflecting; by collaborating with other teachers; by looking closely at students and their work; and by sharing what they see. This kind of learning cannot occur either in college classrooms divorced from engagement in practice or in school classrooms divorced from knowledge about how to interpret practice. Good settings for teacher learning — in both colleges of education and schools — provide lots of opportunities for research and inquiry, for trying and testing, for talking about and evaluating the results of learning and teaching. The 'rub between theory and practice' (Miller and Silvernail, 1994) occurs most productively when questions arise in the context of real students and real work-in-progress where research and disciplined inquiry are also at hand.

Do Education Schools Help Teachers Learn?

Even if one agrees that there are desirable knowledge and skills for teaching, many people sincerely believe that anyone can teach, or, at least, that knowing a subject is enough to allow one to teach it well. Others believe that teaching is best learned, to the extent it can be learned at all, by trial-and-error on the job. The evidence strongly suggests otherwise. Reviews of research over the past 30 years summarizing hundreds of studies have concluded that, even with the shortcomings of current teacher education and licensing, fully prepared and certified teachers are better rated and more successful with students than teachers without this preparation (Evertson, Hawley, and Zlotnik, 1985; Ashton and Crocker, 1986; Ashton and Crocker, 1987; Greenberg, 1983; Haberman, 1984; Olsen, 1985). As Evertson and colleagues conclude in their research review:

> The available research suggests that among students who become teachers, those enrolled in formal preservice preparation programs are more likely to be effective than those who do not have such training. Moreover, almost all well planned and executed efforts within teacher preparation programs to teach students specific knowledge or skills seem to succeed, at least in the short run. (Evertson, Hawley, and Zlotnik, 1985, 8)

The importance of full preparation holds across specific subject-matter fields. A review of research on science education, incorporating the results of more than 65 studies, found consistently positive relationships between students' achievement in science and their teacher's background in both education courses and science courses (Druva and Anderson, 1983; see also Davis, 1964; Taylor, 1957). The effects of teacher training are particularly noticeable when achievement is measured on higher-order tasks such as students' abilities to apply and interpret scientific concepts (Perkes, 1967–8). Students' performance in mathematics is also strongly related to their teachers' preparation in teaching methods as well as in mathematics content (Begle, 1979; Begle and Geeslin, 1972; Hawk, Coble and Swanson, 1985). The importance of teachers' education preparation has also been established for teachers of vocational education (Erekson and Barr, 1985), teachers of reading and elementary education (Hice, 1970; LuPone, 1961; McNeil, 1974), teachers in early childhood education (Roupp et al., 1979), and teachers of gifted students (Hansen, 1988).

Other studies point out the differences in the perceptions and practices of teachers with differing amounts and kinds of preparation. A number of studies suggest that the typical problems of beginning teachers are lessened for those who have had adequate preparation prior to entry (Adams, Hutchinson, and Martray, 1980; Glassberg, 1980; Taylor and Dale, 1971). Teachers who are well prepared are better able to use teaching strategies that respond to students' needs and learning styles and that encourage higher order learning (Perkes, 1967–8; Hansen, 1988; Skipper and Quantz, 1987). Since the novel tasks required for problem-solving are more difficult to manage than the routine tasks associated with rote learning, lack of knowledge about how to manage an active, inquiry-oriented classroom can lead teachers to turn to passive tactics that 'dumb down' the curriculum (Carter and Doyle, 1987; Doyle, 1986), busying students with workbooks rather than complex tasks that require more skill to orchestrate (Cooper and Sherk, 1989).

Studies of teachers admitted with less than full preparation — with no teacher preparation or through quick alternate routes — reveal serious shortcomings: Recruits tend to be dissatisfied with their training; they have greater difficulties planning curriculum, teaching, managing the classroom, and diagnosing students' learning needs. They are less able to adapt their instruction to promote student learning and less likely to see it as their job to do so, blaming students if their teaching is not effective. Principals and colleagues rate them less highly on their instructional skills, and they leave teaching at higher-than-average rates. Most important, their students learn less, especially in areas like reading, writing, and mathematics, which are critical to later school success. These feelings undoubtedly contributed to the high attrition rate of TFA recruits. TFA statistics show that of those who started in 1990, 58 per cent had left by the third year, a 2-year attrition rate more than twice the national average for new teachers, including those in cities. The Maryland State Department of Education reported that 62 percent of corps members who started in Baltimore in 1992 had left within two years.

This track record is not unusual for alternative certification programs. Stoddart's (1992) analysis reveals that 53 percent of Los Angeles' alternative certification recruits (prepared in an eight-week summer program run by the district) had left within the first six years of program operation. California's state evaluation found that 20 percent of recruits dropped out before completing the training. Of those who completed the training, 20 percent left during the first two years of teaching, and another 20 percent of the remainder were not deemed ready for employment by the end of year two (Wright, McKibbon, and Walton, 1987).

Of 110 Dallas recruits, only 54 percent had successfully 'graduated' to become full-fledged teachers after their first year as interns (Lutz and Hutton, 1989). Of this group, 24 had the possibility of 'graduating' at some point in time if deficiencies in meeting program requirements were cleared up, along with 14 who were requested to continue as interns for another year in hopes that they could improve their performance sufficiently. Only 40 percent of these alternate route interns said they planned to stay in teaching, as compared to 72 percent of traditionally trained recruits.

Across a range of nontraditional programs reviewed by the RAND Corporation, 75 percent of recruits who had not previously been teachers remained in teaching after two years, while only half planned to make it their career. Among these, candidates admitted through short alternative routes were least likely to say they planned to stay in teaching; mid-career recruits trained in master's degree programs were most likely to plan to stay in teaching (Darling-Hammond, Hudson, and Kirby, 1989).

The Capacity of School Districts to Prepare Teachers

The idea that school districts have the will and the capacity to train and mentor teachers unilaterally and well has been tested repeatedly, without success. The literature of the late 1960s and early 1970s was full of such proposals, and the schools were full of pilots very much like today's short-term alternative routes. The reasons are simple: the districts where most new teachers are hired are poor urban and rural districts with high turnover and few resources. They do not have the level of fiscal or pedagogical resources to take on this job. Neither do they have a strong self-interest in investing thousands of dollars in the preparation of beginners, most of whom will leave for other occupations or suburban schools as soon as they are able. Over and over again, reviews of such district-based efforts find that they leave their candidates underprepared, undersupported, and less effective than candidates who received systematic university-based preparation for teaching.

There are at least three kinds of problems studies have noted with these programs: the amount of time for training, the nature of teaching knowledge conveyed, and the extent and nature of supervision.

School districts are necessarily impatient about the time teachers spend learning rather than covering classes that need to be taught. Virtually all district-run and vendor-provided programs for training teachers are extremely short, generally ranging from three to eight weeks in duration.

Because they are short-term, alternative certification programs provide little pedagogical coursework and no subject matter coursework or extended practicum experience; recruits' 'practicum' consists of their first year(s) of full-time teaching. Pedagogical training tends to focus on generic teaching skills rather than subject-specific pedagogy, on singular techniques rather than a range of methods, and on specific, immediate advice rather than research or theory (see Stoddart, 1992; Bliss, 1992; Zumwalt, 1990). These choices are a necessary consequence of the short period of time available. As one program coordinator in New Jersey's Provisional Teacher program explained: 'The condensed time frame of 200 hours of formal instruction places serious limitations on the amount of curriculum content that can be covered' (Brown, 1990).

These constraints, and the current status of teaching knowledge in many of the districts that mount their own programs or hire teachers with little preparation, lead to a predilection for teacher-proof approaches to training and curriculum that undermine most of the current reforms in teaching and learning. Packaged programs like Distar, ITIP, and Assertive Discipline are frequently used. Although these approaches do not allow teachers to teach diagnostically or in ways that support the acquisition of higher order thinking skills, they can be 'taught' in a day-long workshop and require almost no sophisticated knowledge or skill on the part of teachers. When these programs fail to meet many of the teacher's goals and the students' needs, teachers have no powerful theories or alternative techniques to marshal.

The lack of traditional coursework (and, often, student teaching) in these programs is generally supposed to be compensated for by intensive mentoring and supervision in the initial months of full-time teaching. However, promised mentors do not always materialize. As the RAND report on nontraditional programs noted:

> ...Ironically, given that these (alternative certification) programs presumably emphasize on-the-job training in lieu of standard coursework, the alternative program recruits in our sample received substantially less assistance and supervision than recruits in any of the other types of programs. (Darling-Hammond, Hudson, and Kirby, 1989, 106)

In this study, fewer than a third of alternative certification recruits spent an hour or more each week working with a support person as compared to three-quarters of the recruits in graduate school programs. Other studies have also commented on the unevenness of supervision in AC programs, particularly those that rely on local district resources (Adelman, 1986; Cornett, 1992).

Several studies found that New Jersey's alternate route teachers rarely received the combination of supervision, training, and mentoring services required by the program (Gray and Lynn, 1988; Smith, 1990a; 1990b). For example, 99 percent of AC candidates had no meeting with their support team and 67 percent did not meet with their mentors within the first four weeks of teaching, when their teaching was supposed to be 'intensively supervised'. Over two-thirds did not receive the daily supervision they were to receive, and nearly one-quarter were not observed by anyone at all during this time. By comparison, 96 percent of student teachers were supervised daily (Smith, 1990a, 1990b). School districts were generally unable to provide these services, given the fiscal resources and staff time available to them (Smith, undated).

Even where state resources are available, the promise of serious supervision is not always easy to meet. Despite state funding for mentors, 15 percent of California's alternative certification trainees reported that they had not met with any support person at all during their first year of teaching; fewer than 20 percent had the advantage of meeting at least once a week with a support person (Wright, McKibbon, and Walton, 1987, 82–3).

Reviews of the availability and quality of preparation and supervision offered by university-based programs, on the other hand, have generally been positive (see e.g., Coley and Thorpe, 1985; Darling-Hammond, Hudson, and Kirby, 1989; Sundstrom and Berry, 1989; Smith, 1990b). Many studies have found that, over time, alternative certification programs have added coursework requirements as gaps in teachers' preparation have been identified, and states and districts have increasingly turned to universities to provide coursework and supervision (Hudson et al., 1988; Carey, Mittman, and Darling-Hammond, 1988; Cornett, 1992).

Programs launched by states, districts, and other non-university sponsors have also been unstable. One recent study of nontraditional programs for preparing mathematics and science teachers found that during the year in which a survey was being conducted, 8 out of 64 programs had already disappeared, while several others were unsure as to whether they would continue in the following year (Carey, Mittman, and Darling-Hammond, 1988). Discontinuation was related to funding, reputation, availability of recruits, and stability of the agency operating the program. Programs that survived had broadened their target recruitment pools, refined their programs, and had become attached to university-based teacher education programs, if they were not already part of such programs.

Similarly, Lutz and Hutton (1989, 251) point out the dramatic shrinkage over several years in the alternative certification programs operated by the Houston and Dallas Independent School Districts, speculating that the decline may be attributed 'to a shrinking pool of qualified applicants or the high financial cost of such programs, which are carried by the local school district'. For these and other reasons — including a preference for traditionally trained and certified candidates —, most districts in states that allow alternative certification programs do not participate in them (Cray and Lynn, 1988; Wright, McKibbon, and Walton, 1987; Mitchell, 1987).

Recent Responses to Critiques of Traditional Teacher Education

Lest schools of education become sanguine, however, there are grounds for concern about traditional preparation programs as well. One major aspect of the critique of teacher education is that, particularly in the years after normal schools were abandoned for university departments, and in the places where lab schools or other kinds of partner schools never emerged, many teacher education programs seemed to separate theory and application to a large extent. In some places, teachers were taught to teach in lecture halls from texts and teachers who frequently had not themselves ever practiced what they were teaching. Students' courses on subject matter topics were disconnected from their courses on teaching methods, which were in turn disconnected from their courses on foundations and psychology. Students completed this coursework before they began student teaching, which was a brief taste of practice typically appended to the end of their program with few connections to what had come before. Many encountered entirely different ideas from those they had studied in the classrooms where they did their student teaching, because university and school-based faculty did little planning or teaching together. Sometimes, their cooperating teachers were selected with no regard for the quality or kind of practice they themselves engaged in. When new teachers entered their own classrooms, they could remember and apply little of what they had learned by reading in isolation from practice. Thus, they reverted largely to what they knew best: the way they themselves had been taught.

The often-repeated critiques of traditional teacher education programs include:

- Inadequate time: The confines of a four-year undergraduate degree make it hard to learn subject matter, child development, learning theory, and effective teaching strategies. Elementary preparation is considered weak in subject matter; secondary preparation, in knowledge of learning and learners.
- Fragmentation: Elements of teacher learning are disconnected from each other. Coursework is separate from practice teaching; professional skills are segmented into separate courses; faculties in the arts and sciences are insulated from education professors. Would-be teachers are left to their own devices to put it all together.
- Uninspired teaching methods: For prospective teachers to learn active, hands-on and minds-on teaching, they must have experienced it for themselves. But traditional lecture and recitation still dominates in much of higher education, where faculty do not practice what they preach.
- Superficial curriculum: Once-over-lightly describes the curriculum. Traditional programs focus on subject-matter methods and a smattering of educational psychology. Candidates do not learn deeply about how to understand and handle real problems of practice.
- Traditional views of schooling: Because of pressures to prepare candidates for schools as they are, most prospective teachers learn to work in isolation, rather than in teams, and to master chalkboards and textbooks instead of computers and CD-ROMS (National Commission on Teaching and America's Future, 1996, p. 32).

Over the past decade, many schools of education and school districts have begun to change these conditions. Stimulated by the efforts of the Holmes Group and the National Network for Educational Renewal, more than 300 schools of education have created programs that extend beyond the confines of the traditional 4-year bachelors degree program, thus allowing more extensive study of the disciplines to be taught along with education coursework that is integrated with more extensive clinical training in schools. Some are one- or two-year graduate programs that serve recent graduates or mid-career recruits. Others are 5-year models that allow an extended program of preparation for prospective teachers who enter teacher education during their undergraduate years. In either case, because the 5th year allows students to devote their energies exclusively to the task of preparing to teach, such programs allow for year-long school-based internships that are woven together with coursework on learning and teaching.

These approaches resemble reforms in teacher education abroad. Countries like Germany, Belgium, and Luxembourg have long required from two to three years of graduate level study for prospective teachers on top of an undergraduate degree — sometimes with two disciplinary majors — in the subject(s) to be taught. Education courses include the study of child development and learning, pedagogy and teaching methods, plus an intensively supervised internship in a school affiliated with the university. Many other nations have recently launched similar reforms.

In 1989, both France and Japan undertook major teacher education reforms to extend both university- and school-based training. In France, all candidates must now complete a graduate program of teacher education in newly created University Institutes for the Preparation of Teachers that are closely connected to schools in their regions. In Japan, although most candidates still prepare in undergraduate programs, they have lessened responsibilities in their first year of teaching and continue to engage in significant study through a highly structured induction program. Recent reforms in Taiwan include graduate-level preparation for teachers plus a yearlong induction program.

A number of recent studies have found that graduates of extended (typically five year) programs are not only more satisfied with their preparation, they are viewed by their colleagues, principals, and cooperating teachers as better prepared, are as effective with students as much more experienced teachers, and are much more likely to enter and stay in teaching than their peers prepared in traditional 4-year programs (Andrew, 1990; Andrew and Schwab, 1995; Arch, 1989; Denton and Peters, 1988; Dyal, 1993; Shin, 1994).

Many of these programs have joined with local school districts to create professional development schools where novices' clinical preparation can be more purposefully structured. Like teaching hospitals in medicine, these schools aim to provide sites for state-of-the-art practice which are also organized to support the training of new professionals, extend the professional development of veteran teachers, and sponsor collaborative research and inquiry. Programs are jointly planned and taught by university-based and school-based faculty. Cohorts of beginning teachers get a richer, more coherent learning experience when they are organized in teams to study and practice with these faculty and with one another. Senior teachers report that they deepen their knowledge by serving as mentors, adjunct faculty, co-researchers, and teacher leaders. Thus, these schools can help create the rub between theory and practice that teachers need in order to learn, while creating more professional roles for teachers and building knowledge in ways that are more useful for both practice and ongoing theory-building (Darling-Hammond, 1994).

These new programs typically engage prospective teachers in studying research and conducting their own inquiries through cases, action research, and the development of structured portfolios about practice. They envision the professional teacher as one who learns from teaching rather than one who has finished learning how to teach, and the job of teacher education as developing the capacity to inquire sensitively and systematically into the nature of learning and the effects of teaching. This is an approach to knowledge production that John Dewey (1929) sought — one that aims to empower teachers with greater understanding of complex situations rather than to control them with simplistic formulas or cookie-cutter routines for teaching.

Command of scientific methods and systematized subject matter liberates individuals; it enables them to see new problems, devise new procedures, and in general, makes for diversification rather than for set uniformity (12). This knowledge and understanding render (the teacher's) practice more intelligent, more flexible, and better adapted to deal effectively with concrete phenomena of practice. . . . Seeing more relations he sees more possibilities, more opportunities. His ability to judge being enriched, he has a wider range of alternatives to select from in dealing with individual situations (20–1).

> If teachers investigate the effects of their teaching on students' learning, and if they read about what others have learned, they come to understand teaching 'to be an inherently problematic endeavor, rather than a highly routinized activity' (Houston, 1993, p. 126). They become sensitive to variation and more aware of what works for what purposes in what situations. Access to nuanced knowledge allows them to become more thoughtful decision makers.

Training in inquiry also helps teachers learn how to look at the world from multiple perspectives, including those of students whose experiences are quite different from their own, and to use this knowledge in developing pedagogies that can reach diverse learners. Learning to reach out to students — those who are difficult to know as well as those who are easy to know — requires boundary crossing, the ability to elicit knowledge of others and to understand it when it is offered. As Lisa Delpit (1995) notes, 'we all interpret behaviors, information, and situations through our own cultural lenses; these lenses operate involuntarily, below the level of conscious awareness, making it seem that our own view is simply "the way it is"' (p. 151). Teachers concerned with democratic education must develop an awareness of their perspectives and how these can be enlarged to avoid a 'communicentric bias' (Gordon, 1990) which limits understanding of areas of study as well as of those who are taught.

Developing the ability to see beyond one's own perspective — to put oneself in the shoes of the learner and to understand the meaning of that experience in terms of learning — is, perhaps, the most important role of universities in the preparation of teachers. One of the great flaws of the 'bright person myth' of teaching is that it presumes that anyone can teach what he or she knows to anyone else. However, people who have never studied teaching or learning often have a very difficult time understanding how to convey material that they themselves learned effortlessly and almost subconsciously. When others do not learn merely by being told, the intuitive teacher often becomes frustrated and powerless to proceed. This frequently leads to anger directed at the learner for not validating the untrained teacher's efforts. Furthermore, individuals who have had no powerful teacher education intervention often maintain a single cognitive and cultural perspective that makes it difficult for them to understand the experiences, perceptions, and knowledge bases that deeply influence the approaches to learning of students who are different from themselves. The capacity to understand another is not innate. It is developed through study, reflection, guided experience, and inquiry.

A commitment to open inquiry, the enlargement of perspectives, and the crossing of boundaries are critical features of the ideal of university education. In fact, the basis of the very earliest universities was that they tried to bring together scholars from all over the known world. They sought to create ways to share diverse perspectives from various geographic areas, cultures, and disciplines as the basis for developing knowledge and finding truth. If universities are to continue to make the important contribution to the education of teachers that they can make, they need to pursue these ideals of knowledge-building and truth-finding by creating a genuine praxis between ideas and experiences — by honoring practice in conjunction with reflection and research and by helping teachers reach beyond their personal boundaries to appreciate the perspectives of those whom they would teach.

References

ADAMS, R.D., HUTCHINSON, S. and MARTRAY, C. (1980) 'A developmental study of teacher concerns across time', Paper presented at the American Educational Research Association Annual Meeting, Boston, MA.

ADELMAN, N.E. (1986) *An Exploratory Study of Teacher Alternative Certification and Retraining Programs*, Washington, DC: Policy Study Associates.

ANDREW, M. (1990) 'The differences between graduates of four-year and five-year teacher preparation programs', *Journal of Teacher Education*, **41**, pp. 45–51.

ANDREW, M. and SCHWAB, R.L. (1995) 'Has reform in teacher education influenced teacher performance? An outcome assessment of graduates of eleven teacher education programs', *Action in Teacher Education*, **17**, pp. 43–53.

ARCH, E.C. (1989) 'Comparison of student attainment of teaching competence in traditional preservice and fifth-year master of arts in teaching programs', Paper presented at the annual meeting of the American Educational Research Association, San Francisco, CA.

ASHTON, P. and CROCKER, L. (1986) 'Does teacher certification make a difference?', *Florida Journal of Teacher Education*, **3**, pp. 73–83.

ASHTON, P. and CROCKER, L. (1987) 'Systematic study of planned variations: The essential focus of teacher education reform', *Journal of Teacher Education*, May–June, pp. 2–8.

BALL, D. and COHEN, D. (in press) 'Developing practice, developing practitioners: Toward a practice-based theory of professional education', in DARLING-HAMMOND, L. and SYKES, G. (eds.) *The Heart of the Matter: Teaching as the Learning Profession*, San Francisco: Jossey Bass.

BEGLE, E.G. (1979) *Critical Variables in Mathematics Education*, Washington, DC: Mathematical Association of American and National Council of Teachers of Mathematics.

BEGLE, E.G. and GEESLIN, W. (1972) 'Teacher effectiveness in mathematics instruction', National Longitudinal Study of Mathematical Abilities Reports No. 28, Washington, DC, Mathematical Association of America and National Council of Teachers of Mathematics.

BENTS, M. and BENTS, R. (1990) 'Perceptions of good teaching among novice, advanced beginner and expert teachers', Paper presented at the Annual Meeting of the American Educational Research Association, Boston, MA.

BLISS, T. (1992) 'Alternate certification in Connecticut: Reshaping the profession', *Peabody Journal of Education*, **67**, 3.

BROWN, E.J. (1990) 'New Jersey provisional teacher program: Model of support for beginning teachers', Paper presented at the Annual Meeting of the American Association of Colleges for Teacher Education, Chicago, IL.

CAREY, N.B., MITTMAN, B.S. and DARLING-HAMMOND, L. (1988) *Recruiting Mathematics and Science Teachers through Nontraditional Programs*, Santa Monica: RAND Corporation.

CARNEGIE TASK FORCE ON TEACHING AS A PROFESSION (1986) *A Nation Prepared: Teachers for the 21st century*, Washington, DC, Author.

CARTER, K. and DOYLE, W. (1987) 'Teachers' knowledge structures and comprehension processes', in CALDERHEAD, J. (ed.) *Exploring Teacher Thinking*, London: Cassell, pp. 147–60.

COLEY, R.J. and THORPE, M.E. (1985) *Responding to the Crisis in Math and Science Teaching: Four Initiatives*, Princeton, NJ: Educational Testing Service.

COOPER, E. and SHERK, J. (1989) 'Addressing urban school reform: Issues and alliances', *Journal of Negro Education*, **58**, 3, pp. 315–31.

CORNETT, L.M. (1992) 'Alternative certification: State policies in the SREB states', *Peabody Journal of Education*, **67**, 3.

DARLING-HAMMOND, L. (1992) 'Teaching and knowledge: Policy issues posed by alternative certification for teachers, *Peabody Journal of Education*, **67**, 3, pp. 123–54.

DARLING-HAMMOND, L. (1994) *Professional Development Schools: Schools for Developing a Profession*, NY: Teachers College Press.

DARLING-HAMMOND, L., HUDSON, L. and KIRBY, S. (1989) *Redesigning Teacher Education: Opening the Door for New Recruits to Science and Mathematics Teaching*, Santa Monica: The RAND Corporation.

DAVIS, C.R. (1964) 'Selected teaching–learning factors contributing to achievement in chemistry and physics', Unpublished doctoral dissertation, University of North Carolina, Chapel Hill.

DELPIT, L. (1995) *Other People's Children: Cultural Conflict in the Classroom*, New York: New Press.

DENTON, J.J. and PETERS, W.H. (1988) 'Program assessment report: Curriculum evaluation of a non-traditional program for certifying teachers', Texas A and M University, College Station, TX.

DEWEY, J. (1929) *The Sources of a Science of Education*, New York: Horace Liveright.

DOYLE, W. (1986) 'Content representation in teachers' definitions of academic work', *Journal of Curriculum Studies*, **18**, pp. 365–79.

DRUVA, C.A. and ANDERSON, R.D. (1983) 'Science teacher characteristics by teacher behavior and by student outcome: A meta-analysis of research', *Journal of Research in Science Teaching*, **20**, 5, pp. 467–79.

DYAL, A.B. (1993) 'An exploratory study to determine principals' perceptions concerning the effectiveness of a fifth-year preparation program', Paper presented at the annual meeting of the Mid-South Educational Research Association, New Orleans, LA.

EREKSON, T.L. and BARR, L. (1985) 'Alternative credentialing: Lessons from vocational education', *Journal of Teacher Education*, **36**, 3, pp. 16–19.

EVERTSON, C., HAWLEY, W. and ZLOTNICK, M. (1985) 'Making a difference in educational quality through teacher education', *Journal of Teacher Education*, **36**, 3, pp. 2–12.

FEIMAN-NEMSER, S. and PARKER, M.B. (1990) *Making Subject Matter Part of the Conversation or Helping Beginning Teachers Learn to Teach*, East Lansing, MI: National Center for Research on Teacher Education.

FENSTERMACHER, G.D. (1992) 'The place of alternative certification in the education of teachers', *Peabody Journal of Education*, **67**, 3.

GLASSBERG, S. (1980) 'A view of the beginning teacher from a developmental perspective', Paper presented at the American Educational Research Association Annual Meeting. Boston, MA.

GOMEZ, D.L. and GROBE, R.P. (1990) 'Three years of alternative certification in Dallas: Where are we?', Paper presented at the Annual Meeting of the American Educational Research Association, Boston, MA.

GOODLAD, J. (1990) *Teachers for Our Nation's Schools*, San Francisco, CA: Jossey-Bass.

GORDON, E.W. (1990) 'Coping with communicentric bias in knowledge production in the social sciences', *Educational Researcher*, **19**, p. 19.

GRADY, M.P., COLLINS, P. and GRADY, E.L. (1991) 'Teacher for American 1991 summer institute evaluation report', Unpublished manuscript.

GRAY, D. and LYNN, D.H. (1988) *New Teachers, Better Teachers: A Report on Two Initiatives in New Jersey*, Washington, DC: Council for Basic Education.

GREENBERG, J.D. (1983) 'The case for teacher education: Open and shut', *Journal of Teacher Education*, **34**, 4, pp. 2–5.

GRIMMETT, P. and MACKINNON, A. (1992) 'Craft knowledge and the education of teachers', in GRANT, G. (ed.) *Review of Research in Education*, vol. 18, pp. 385–456, Washington, DC: American Educational Research Association.

GROSSMAN, P.L. (1989) 'Learning to teach without teacher education', *Teachers College Record*, **91**, 2, pp. 191–208.

GUYTON, E. and FAROKHI, E. (1987) 'Relationships among academic performance, basic skills, subject matter knowledge and teaching skills of teacher education graduates', *Journal of Teacher Education* (Sept-Oct.), pp. 37–42.

HABERMAN, M. (1984) 'An evaluation of the rationale for required teacher education: Beginning teachers with or without teacher preparation', Prepared for the National Commission on Excellence in Teacher Education, University of Wisconsin-Milwaukee, September.

HANSEN, J.B. (1988) 'The relationship of skills and classroom climate of trained and untrained teachers of gifted students', Unpublished doctoral dissertation, Purdue University.

HAWK, P., COBLE, C.R. and SWANSON, M. (1985) 'Certification: It does matter', *Journal of Teacher Education*, **36**, 3, pp. 13–15.

HICE, J.E.L. (1970) 'The relationship between teacher characteristics and first-grade achievement', *Dissertation Abstracts International*, **25**, 1, p. 190.

HOLMES GROUP (1986) *Tomorrow's Teachers: A Report of the Holmes Group*, East Lansing, MI, Author.

HOWEY, K.R. and ZIMPHER, N.L. (1989) *Profiles of Preservice Teacher Education*, Albany, NY: State University of New York.

HUDSON, L., KIRBY, S.N., CAREY, N.B., MITTMAN, B.S. and BERRY, B. (1988) *Recruiting Mathematics and Science Teachers through Nontraditional Programs: Case Studies*, Santa Monica: RAND Corporation.

KOPP, W. (1992) 'Reforming schools of education will not be enough', *Yale Law and Policy Review*, **10**, 58, pp. 58–68.

LENK, H.A. (1989) 'A case study: The induction of two alternate route social studies teachers', Unpublished doctoral dissertation, Teachers College, Columbia University.

LUPONE, L.J. (1961) 'A comparison of provisionally certified and permanently certified elementary school teachers in selected school districts in New York State', *Journal of Educational Research*, **55**, pp. 53–63.

LUTZ, F.W. and HUTTON, J.B. (1989) 'Alternative teacher certification: Its policy implications for classroom and personnel practice', *Educational Evaluation and Policy Analysis*, **11**, 3, pp. 237–54.

MCNEIL, J.D. (1974) 'Who gets better results with young children — Experienced teachers or novices?', *Elementary School Journal*, **74**, pp. 447–51.

MILLER, L. and SILVERNAIL, D. (1994) 'Wells junior high school: Evaluation of a professional development school', in DARLING-HAMMOND, L. *Professional Development Schools: Schools for Developing a Profession*, NY: Teachers College Press.

MITCHELL, N. (1987) *Interim Evaluation Report of the Alternative Certification Program* (REA87-027-2), Dallas, TX: DISD Department of Planning, Evaluation, and Testing.

NATIONAL COMMISSION ON TEACHING AND AMERICA'S FUTURE (1996) 'What matters most: Teaching for America's future', NY, Author.

NATRIELLO, G., ZUMWALT, K., HANSEN, A. and FRISCH, A. (1990) 'Characteristics of entering teachers in New Jersey', Revised version of a paper presented at the 1988 Annual Meeting of the American Educational Research Association.

OLSEN, D.G. (1985) 'The quality of prospective teachers: Education vs. non-education graduates', *Journal of Teacher Education*, **36**, 5, pp. 56–9.

PERKES, V.A. (1967–8) 'Junior high school science teacher preparation, teaching behavior, and student achievement', *Journal of Research in Science Teaching*, **6**, 4, pp. 121–6.

POPKEWITZ, T.S. (1995) 'Policy, knowledge, and power: Some issues for the study of educational reform', in COOKSON, P. and SCHNEIDER, B. (eds) *Transforming Schools: Trends, Dilemmas and Prospects*: Garland Press.

ROTH, R.A. (1986) 'Alternate and alternative certification: Purposes, assumptions, implications', *Action in Teacher Education*, **8**, 2, pp. 1–6.

ROTH, R.A. (1993) 'Teach for America 1993 summer institute: Program review', Unpublished report.

ROTTENBERG, C.J. and BERLINER, D.C. (1990) 'Expert and novice teachers' conceptions of common classroom activities', Paper presented at the Annual Meeting of the American Educational Research Association, Boston, MA.

ROUPP, R., TRAVERS, J., GLANTZ, F. and COELEN, C. (1979) *Children at the Center: Summary Findings and Their Implications*, Cambridge, MA: Abt Associates.

SCHORR, J. (1993, December) 'Class action: What Clinton's national service program could learn from "Teach for America"', *Phi Delta Kappan*, pp. 315–18.

SCIACCA, J.R. (1987) 'A comparison of levels of job satisfaction between university-certified first-year teachers and alternatively-certified first-year teachers', Unpublished doctoral dissertation, East Texas State University.

SHAPIRO, M. (1993) *Who Will Teach for America?*, Washington, DC: Farragut Publishing Co.

SHIN, H. (1994) 'Estimating future teacher supply: An application of survival analysis', Paper presented at the annual meeting of the American Educational Research Association, New Orleans, LA.

SHULMAN, L. (1987) 'Knowledge and teaching: Foundations of the new reform', *Harvard Educational Review*, **57**, 1, pp. 1–22.

SKIPPER, C.E. and QUANTZ, R. (1987) 'Changes in educational attitudes of education and arts and science students during four years of college', *Journal of Teacher Education*, May-June, pp. 39–44.

SMITH, J.M. (1990a) 'School districts as teacher training institutions in the New Jersey alternate route program', Paper presented at the Annual Meeting of the Eastern Educational Research Association, Clearwater, FA, February.

SMITH, J.M. (1990b) 'A comparative study of the state regulations for and the operation of the New Jersey provisional teacher certification program', Paper presented at the Annual Meeting of the American Educational Research Association Meeting, April.

SMITH, J.M. (undated) 'Supervision, Mentoring and the "Alternate Route"', Mimeograph.

STODDART, T. (1992) 'An alternate route to teacher certification: Preliminary findings from the Los Angeles unified school district intern program', *Peabody Journal of Education*, **67**, 3.

SUNDSTROM, K. and BERRY, B. (1989) *Assessing the Initial Impact of the South Carolina Critical Needs Certification Program*, Report to the State Board of Education.

TAYLOR, T.W. (1957) 'A study to determine the relationships between growth in interest and achievement of high school students and science teacher attitudes, preparation, and experience', Unpublished doctoral dissertation, North Texas State College, Denton.

TAYLOR, J.K. and DALE, R. (1971) *A Survey of Teachers in the First Year of Service*, Bristol: University of Bristol, Institute of Education.

TEXAS EDUCATION AGENCY (1993) *Teach for America Visiting Team Report*, Austin: Texas State Board of Education Meeting Minutes, Appendix B.

WRIGHT, D.P., McKIBBON, M. and WALTON, P. (1987) *The Effectiveness of the Teacher Trainee Program: An Alternate Route into Teaching in California*, California Commission on Teacher Credentialing.

ZEICHNER, K. (1993, February) 'Traditions practice in US preservice teacher education programs', *Teaching and Teacher Education*, **9**, pp. 1–13.

ZUMWALT, K. (1990) *Alternate Routes to Teaching: Three Alternative Approaches*, NY: Teachers College, Columbia University.

3   No Standards or New Standards? The Future of Teacher Certification

Gary Sykes

Introduction

Across the country today, the university's role in the preparation of teachers is coming under challenge, driven by a combination of old prejudices and new developments. A number of states already have eliminated major requirements to enter teaching and others are considering such a move. Pressures to relax entry standards long have been present in a nation committed to extending so many years of education to its full populace, because the demand for teachers is so great. The sheer size of the schooling enterprise in America has produced twin related difficulties of attracting and paying for the teacher workforce. And these problems are compounded in locales where working and living conditions are regarded as undesirable — mainly schools in the inner city and in rurally isolated communities.

Other countries face similar problems, but they are intensified in the United States because of our greater commitment to mass, public education set within a decentralized system of finance and governance. In countries with education systems operated by central ministries, teachers are 'registered' nationally and assigned to locales of greatest need; then, based on seniority they may eventually transfer to schools of their choice. In this manner, teachers may be deployed where needed as a function of national policy operating within a single employment pool. In the US, however, teacher labor markets are local and salaries vary depending on the state and district revenue base and the push and pull of fiscal politics. All too often locales and teaching specialties (e.g., mathematics, science) facing shortages cannot easily increase salaries to enhance supply.

Other expedients are necessary to produce adequate teacher supply and have become fixtures within our educational non-system. They include increasing class sizes, allowing individuals to teach outside their areas of competence, setting generous cut scores on certification tests, and granting emergency credentials. Teacher supply, then, has become a systemic problem in many communities, coupled to the demographic ebb and flow of the school-age population.

From the perspective of supply — although not of quality — standards for entry to teaching are part of the problem. The more rigorous and rigorously enforced are qualifications to teach, the more difficult it is to generate a sufficient supply of teachers, particularly for hard-to-staff schools. Districts facing perennial shortages may be expected to press states to lower or weaken standards for entry so that enough 'teachers' may be hired. High wealth districts that value education may choose to establish rigorous *hiring* standards, but these contribute to overall inequality of opportunity by inducing the best qualified teachers to migrate to the most desirable districts, rather than to those where good teaching is most needed.

Advocates for teaching standards have always faced an uphill battle, for teaching quality is difficult to measure and to guarantee. Public attitudes historically have regarded teaching as easy work for 'unsaleable men and unmarriageable women' in Willard Waller's (1932) memorable, if painful, phrase. The standard formula — 'know your subject, love children' — grossly oversimplifies the complexities of teaching today, but retains its grip on the public mind. No conclusive proof yet has demonstrated the worth of teaching standards sufficient to break the hold of powerful cultural stereotypes about teaching, so standards may be regarded as luxuries to be dispensed with when shortages loom.

New developments as well are undercutting the rationale for standards. In particular, the movement to introduce choice into public education in such forms as charter schools, vouchers, inter- and intra-district transfer plans, and others creates pressures to deregulate education to promote competition and innovation. To help stimulate invention, choice proponents argue that new schools should be allowed to hire whatever staff they choose, lest ancient regulations retard the progress of innovation and change.

And finally, universities today are themselves coming under increasing scrutiny, facing rising levels of discontent in the face of increased tuition costs, fiscal pressures on state government, and perceptions of indifference to students and their learning. In particular, the education schools that prepare teachers are held in low esteem and are not deemed trustworthy. Proposals to de-emphasize university-based teacher education have gained a favorable hearing in recent years.

Given this new public policy context, the state role in licensing teachers is critical. The market cannot be relied on to produce and equitably distribute an adequate supply of qualified teachers. University-based teacher education relies in part on a state regulatory framework to establish common and acceptable qualifications to teach. Furthermore, and in direct contradiction to the deregulating tendencies just noted, many states in recent years also have developed new and more rigorous standards for entry to ensure that new teachers possess the knowledge, skills, and dispositions that define good teaching. As more than one commentator has noted, state policy has been notably schizophrenic on this matter, both lowering and raising standards for entry to teaching.

At this juncture, it is worth recollecting the rationale for teacher certification which is a key element in the regulatory environment for university-based teacher education. Universities cannot and will not improve the quality of preparation without support and regulation from the public agencies that fund and sanction their work. Consequently, the future of university-based teacher education is closely linked to the future of state licensure for teaching. My argument firmly supports the necessity for strengthening teacher licensure (also called certification in most states) as an integral aspect of improving the profession and practice of teaching.

Why Certify Teachers?

Teacher certification is undergoing scrutiny and change in many states. As policy makers begin close examination of state school codes and other regulations affecting education, they will ask what should be done about qualifications to teach. One answer has been proposed: Let the state do away with them. Let districts or perhaps individual schools determine qualifications for hiring. In the early years of American schooling, teachers served at the pleasure of local communities that hired and paid for them, and states might return to this era. Over the past century, however, states have imposed certification standards for their teachers. Why do states certify teachers? There are several reasons.

- To protect the public, in this case children, from harm. Placing children in the care of unqualified persons is unacceptable in all societies with compulsory education. State requirements establish safeguards about teacher competence as a basic protection for all students required by state law to undertake formal education. The critical consideration here is the compulsory nature of schooling. Because families and children cannot be shielded from harm in schools, there must be public safeguards of various kinds to protect children, primary among which is the certification of adults who work with children.
- To guarantee a common standard across local communities for children's most important learning resource — their teachers. Fairness dictates that *where* a child lives in a state should not determine his or her access to qualified teachers. If teacher qualifications are established entirely through the preferences of individual communities and their ability to pay, an unhealthy variation would disadvantage some children. The state's concern in guaranteeing an adequate education to all children overrides each community's exclusive interest in choosing its teachers.
- To ensure the state's interest in an educated citizenry. Families and local communities have a powerful interest in education, to be sure, but so does the state. The transmission of a shared civic culture together with informed participation in a democracy is essential to the well-being of our society, especially in light of its diversity. Education is a public good with important consequences for society that the state has an obligation to promote. Guaranteeing access to learning resources that meet public standards is a legitimate and necessary state role. But as the founders built an ingenious system of checks and balances into the Constitution, so states delegated the authority for education to seek to balance their interests with those of families and communities. In every state and for the past century and a half, that balance has involved certification of teachers.

Historically, then, state teacher certification arose for these reasons and in the face of hiring practices that abused the public trust. Teaching jobs in many communities went to those with family or other connections to local bosses, to members of the dominant political party, or to those who 'paid' for the job with kickbacks or by accepting below market wages. States intervened not only to establish job-related qualifications, but also to counteract the corruption of treating schools as part of local patronage systems.

Should We Abolish Certification?

Perhaps, however, those days are gone for good and states should strike out boldly in eliminating their certification requirements again, thereby granting full or nearly full authority over teacher qualifications to local communities. What would this mean for teaching?

Sixty to seventy years ago, most states assumed responsibility for licensing teachers along with other occupations where some form of public protection was required (see Sedlak, 1989). Over the years, certification requirements have changed, but today they typically involve undertaking an approved program of preparation that includes attention to subject matter knowledge, professional knowledge, and a course of practice teaching in the schools. Many states also require that aspiring teachers take one or more tests that include basic skills and sometimes professional knowledge (see Darling-Hammond and Berry, 1988, and Roth, 1996 for a review of contemporary standards). Increasingly, many states also have established programs to mentor new teachers and to extend certification into the first years of teaching to provide some base in practice for judgments of teaching competence. Corresponding with the rise of such requirements, states also have developed elaborate classifications of teaching to include all the possible teaching specialties by subject area and grade level. In this manner, the regulation of entry to teaching has become increasingly complex.

Abolishing state certification of teachers eliminates all these requirements. Anyone wishing to teach would not need to demonstrate command of any kind of knowledge — basic skills, subject-related, or professional. They would not need to undertake any professional study or have any prior teaching experience, supervised or otherwise. They would not even need to attend college. Of course localities might choose to include some of these as hiring requirements, but the problems are obvious.

- Communities that sought valid and reliable evidence of teaching competence would have to develop, at substantial cost, their own means for doing so. Costs of evaluating teachers would shift dramatically to the local level. Unless they chose to rely on such weak, fallible measures as grades and test scores, schools or districts would have to plan ways to collect and judge direct evidence of teaching competence, then screen all applicants based on these procedures. To have any value at all, such selection would be time consuming, costly, and burdensome to implement. Without making this considerable, continuing investment, the consumers of education — parents, school boards, citizens, and taxpayers — would have fewer means for determining who is qualified to teach.

- Communities experiencing difficulty in recruiting teachers would respond by reducing qualifications to meet demand, while affluent, attractive locales could maintain high standards and outbid others for teaching talent. Removing the floor of protection would magnify existing inequalities in access to good teachers.
- In the ensuing, chaotic local-market situation, teacher mobility across communities and among states would be seriously compromised. Each move potentially would require some new tests due to variation in qualifications from place to place. No reciprocity agreements among states would be possible, with resulting inefficiencies in teacher labor markets.
- Systematic efforts to organize and improve teacher education could not arise because higher education institutions would have no common standards to direct their efforts. The advancement of standards of professional practice would be slowed to a crawl, at a time when professional standard-setting shows signs of significant pay-off.
- Any locale could require loyalty tests as a condition of hiring, such as allegiance to particular religious, political, or social beliefs, for example, or membership in particular racial, ethnic, or cultural groups. As the state moved to prohibit such practices, an inevitable political and legal battle would commence over needed regulations. In response to lawsuits and the legislative tug-of-war, the state slowly but surely would reassert its control over local practices.

Abolishing state teacher certification is risky public policy that potentially exposes children to many forms of harm. In every profession supplying vital human services, standards of various kinds combine to establish public confidence. Patients want to know that their doctors and nurses are licensed and certified in their specialties. Citizens want to know that bridges and buildings have been designed and constructed by qualified architects and engineers. And parents want to know that the teachers to whom they entrust their children are competent and caring. Parents might all take the time to visit classrooms for extended periods to judge for themselves, but this is unrealistic. Public-professional standards, including those for certification, are a necessary form of consumer information that our society cannot do without. Consider then that if states weaken or selectively eliminate teacher certification, logic demands parallel policy for all other licensed occupations. It would be peculiar, even nonsensical, for a state to license cosmetologists and barbers, not to mention doctors and lawyers, while ignoring the largest class of state employee — school teachers.

Does Certification Work?

Does teacher certification though *actually* supply public confidence in meeting its expressed purposes? Here the critics are on firmer ground, for the measures in place neither represent the best professional thinking nor provide the necessary safeguards that parents should be able to count on. Most of the state tests in use cover basic skills and subject matter knowledge but nothing directly related to education itself — not teaching or learning, curriculum or assessment. The medical equivalent would be a licensure exam that tested a doctor's ability to read and write and measured their grasp of the science underlying practice, but not the practice of medicine itself (in fact, state medical licensure involves a three-part examination that covers basic science, medical knowledge, and clinical practice). Basic skills and subject matter knowledge surely are essential to good teaching, but fall well short of necessary know-how. And, the paper-and-pencil, multiple choice format provides a thin warranty of what individuals know. Test-taking savvy counts as much as any other knowledge, and the pass rates (well over 90 percent in most states) screen out few applicants. The states' tests provide a minimal screen around basic skills and subject knowledge, which is necessary, but do not assess teaching competence itself.

The other strategy common to many states is 'program approval' — require aspiring teachers to complete a program of study approved by the state that includes certain ingredients. The ingredients method makes some sense as a minimal requirement but coupled with weak individual tests is inadequate. The state has no real means to judge the quality of programs, merely their probable existence. Completion of such programs is weakly related to competence in teaching itself. And the requirements are often quite minimal. They stipulate a modest amount of study directly related to education, including brief teaching experience with supervision. Anyone may assume sole responsibility for a classroom with little more than a month and a half of practice, although many universities provide substantially more teaching experience in their programs. Furthermore, most states routinely waive even these requirements in the face of teacher shortages. So-called 'emergency credentials' do signal an emergency, but for children rather than for employing school districts. Standards this low are the policy equivalent of malpractice.

The ingredients method is like judging a meal by glancing at the foodstuffs assembled for its preparation. The real proof is in the tasting, but states currently have few means to 'taste' teaching quality.

What Should States Do?

The critics then have a case against the present system, but they misfire in arguing that the state should move from *current requirements to no requirements*. Instead the debate should be around *current requirements versus different requirements* that would more effectively serve public and professional purposes.

What's the alternative, though? It's this: find out directly whether individuals can teach to some reasonable standard of public confidence. Parents don't care whether a teacher knows mathematics for its own sake; they care whether he or she can teach the subject well to their children. And to meet a public standard, teachers must show they can teach many different children, not just those with a knack. 'One size fits all' is not the motto of good teachers, who combine knowledge of subject, curriculum, and their students to consistently produce learning.

This is ordinary commonsense. To find out if someone is a good golfer, watch them play and get their handicap; don't ask whether they have read a good book on golf or taken lessons. Skeptics, however, seem to doubt that good teaching is very complicated or difficult, an opinion easy to dismiss. Try this test for a week or so: teach reading, writing, math, science, social studies, civics, and the arts to a diverse group of youngsters, while attending as well to their physical and social development. Or try teaching American history to 130 eleventh graders who come into class with widely varying ability to read and write. Such work is neither simple nor easy, as even a brief trial would demonstrate.

Two additional challenges come up. Can people learn to teach well, and, do we have practical, affordable, and trustworthy ways to judge good teaching? The first question harks back to the old adage that 'teachers are born, not made'. We all remember the naturals who taught us, who seemed disposed as much by personality as by any special knowledge and skill to make subjects come alive and to reach their students. This common experience supports the adage but is a half-truth at best. Michael Jordan may be a great natural basketball player, but he is also a highly disciplined student of the game who acquired his knowledge and skill from coaches and mentors, which he then perfected through long practice. A hallmark of all excellence is seemingly effortless performance, making the difficult look easy. Great teachers have undertaken careful study and have learned their craft through both formal education and informal experience. Personality alone does not produce great teaching.

Equally important, the many people who enter teaching without a special gift are even more reliant on professional education and standards to shape their teaching. This is true in all forms of knowledge work in our society today; no enterprise can rely anymore on the few naturals. Expertise must be cultivated among knowledge workers, and professional standards and education are a powerful, indispensable means. The modern adage, and increasingly so, is, 'teachers are born *and* made'.

Evidence is now accumulating that students who undertake strong programs of preparation enter classrooms much better prepared to teach than those who do not. Not only have they acquired such basic skills as classroom management, lesson planning and presentation, assessment of student learning, and mastery of a repertoire of teaching methods, they also possess a deeper understanding of children, of ways of representing and conveying subject matter to diverse learners, and of principles of curriculum. Furthermore, they understand better what they still need to learn and so are better prepared to continue to grow in their knowledge and skill as teachers. Increasingly then, standards of good teaching are emerging in preparation programs, state certification systems, and school-based practices.

Is Teacher Assessment Practical?

But if these truths have any practical consequences for state policy, there must be reasonable ways to judge teaching itself and in relation to student learning. The approach under development nationally and in a number of vanguard states is to create standards for teaching competence that include student learning, then to apply them directly to candidates seeking certification.

The term for this is 'performance-based certification', referring to direct examination of teaching 'performance' as the basis for judgments about qualifications to teach. This principle may be put into practice in a variety of ways including:

- staging judgments of competence over the course of teacher education based on accumulated evidence gathered through portfolios, videotape of teaching, interviews, examination of student learning, and others;
- establishing internship requirements akin to those in medicine, jointly administered by schools and universities, that supply an extended period of classroom teaching under supervision as a basis for direct observation of teaching;
- organizing the collection and scrutiny of student work samples to gauge a novice teacher's capacity to promote learning in a range of students;
- utilizing assessment center methods widely applied in business, government, and other contexts to test candidates' teaching knowledge and skill under controlled conditions;
- drawing on conventional testing methods to develop stronger assessments of knowledge related to teaching, as parts two and three of the medical licensure exam do for medicine; and,
- setting up school district induction programs that include assessment opportunities during the first year of full-time, paid teaching, that may be administered by local schools with assistance from the state in the form of common standards and procedures.

This list illustrates the possibilities that are unfolding in many states today. Oregon is creating a work sample approach. Tennessee is using what they call 'value-added assessment'. Kentucky has invented a school accountability index (for review of these systems that link teacher performance to student achievement, see Millman, in press). Minnesota is identifying a set of schools to serve as sites for internships. Connecticut has created a classroom observation system, applied to all new teachers, as well as special tests of teaching competence. The Educational Testing Service also has developed a classroom observation model that they are marketing in the states. Most importantly, a new organization devoted to the development of advanced standards in teaching has pioneered their first round of assessments, to result in advanced certification for experienced, expert teachers. The National Board for Professional Teaching Standards has created a sophisticated process for the assessment of teaching featuring the assembly of evidence across an entire year, including evidence of student learning, that is evaluated at an assessment center. They have piloted the system with a national sample of teachers, and have begun to issue advanced certificates. And, a national project of state representatives sponsored by the Council of Chief State School Officers (the Inter-State New Teacher Assessment and Support Consortium) is now creating standards for initial certification of teachers that are compatible with and draw on the vanguard work of the

National Board, so that a firm set of standards from beginning to advanced teaching can take shape. Finally, the National Council for the Accreditation of Teacher Education, the professional standard-setting body for teacher education programs, has initiated a new policy that allows institutions to adopt performance-based certification as a means for judging the adequacy of teacher training. The new test for institutions will not be their 'ingredients' but their performance in producing qualified graduates.

Among business, government, and professional leaders nationwide, a consensus has formed that we must take teaching much more seriously than ever before. We must develop standards of good teaching that will direct the preparation and performance of teachers as they supply confidence to the public. This work is decisively launched. All over the country educators and citizens are working together to solve the problems posed by the sophisticated assessment of teaching and learning. Five years ago, there was still reason to doubt these problems could be surmounted. But not today. Progress has been marked, and the pay-off is beginning to emerge. The range of experiments, the energy and creativity already applied, gives full promise of a future in which teaching can be judged by strong, impartial standards. To ignore these developments, to continue the tired old refrain that 'teaching is not brain surgery or rocket science', is to embrace know-nothing policy — we know nothing about teaching, we know nothing about how to prepare teachers, and we know nothing about how to judge teaching. Such an attitude would be scorned in most other fields today. It should be mourned in education, because it retards the progress so promising elsewhere.

In the Meantime . . .

States now have unparalleled resources to draw on in creating new standards for teaching, including most prominently the standards and assessment work of the organizations already mentioned. But choices must be made carefully in the design of new standards, based on experiment and close study. This work should commence immediately, led by leaders from business, government, and the profession, with public and private support.

Too much attention has been paid in the current debate to issues of power and control in education, not enough to competence and standards. It is time to launch a new initiative that will change this. As Casey Stengel once said, 'When you come to a fork in the road, take it.' No standards or new standards? Not a tough call.

In a recent *Newsweek* essay, US House Speaker Gingrich argued to return important public policy decisions to the states then to, 'experiment and if it fails, experiment again, and if that fails, to experiment anew'. This is the spirit that states should adopt. Backward to the future is not the way to go. We need bold experimentation that points ahead. All states should join the vanguard and begin creating world-class standards for teaching related to world-class standards for learning. This is how we move education forward at the dawn of the twenty-first century.

References

DARLING-HAMMOND, L. and BERRY, B. (1988) *The Evolution of Teacher Policy* (JRE-01), Santa Monica, CA: The RAND Corporation.

MILLMAN, J. (in press) *Assuring Accountability . . . ? Using Student Achievement to Evaluate Teachers and Schools*, Thousand Oaks, CA: Corwin Press.

ROTH, R. (1996) 'Standards for certification, licensure, and accreditation', in SIKULA, J., BUTTERY, T. and GUYTON, E. (eds) *Handbook of Research on Teacher Education*, New York: Macmillan, pp. 242–78.

SEDLAK, M. (1989) 'Let us go and buy a schoolmaster: Historical perspectives on the hiring of teachers in the United States, 1750–1980', in WARREN, D. (ed.) *American Teachers: History of a Profession at Work*, New York: Macmillan, pp. 257–90.

WALLER, W. (1932) *The Sociology of Teaching*, New York: Wiley.

4   Teacher Educators and Teachers: The Needs for Excellence and Spunk

Edward R. Ducharme and Mary K. Ducharme

Who Shall Teach the Teachers?

One cannot write of schools, colleges, and departments of education (SCDEs) without writing of faculty, of learning without writing of teaching, and so forth. But we must, from time to time, attempt to isolate any item or issue so as to provide focus. So it is with focus on teacher educators. What kind of teacher educators will be appropriate to work with and develop the teachers of tomorrow? Few have commented on the types of teacher educators necessary and appropriate for the twenty-first century. E. Ducharme and M. Ducharme (1996b) posit a description:

> Perhaps a faculty member composite picture in the year 2,001 might look like this: She is a member of a minority in her mid thirties, tenured at associate professor; she acquired her doctorate while studying full-time, supported by a foundation fellowship promoting educational excellence and equity; she has been at X-University for seven years with one of those years spent in an exchange program in China; she has authored four articles, co-authored six articles with teachers from the schools, developed five media productions on teaching; she spends two days a month at the local middle school working with teachers and children. Prior to working on her doctorate, she taught in a rural youth center for two years and in an inner-city middle school for three years. (p. 299)

The description suggests that teacher educators will have to be competent in technology, in touch with the schools, knowledgeable about differing cultures, and engaged in scholarship. It suggests that they may be part of an interlocked world, one in which scholars from one region work with scholars from other regions and travel and teach in different regions. Complicating the picture of what a twenty-first century teacher educator will look like and do is the recent rush toward site-based teacher education.

Current Demographics

The teacher education faculty are currently a stable lot: largely tenured at associate professor or professor, white, male, and place bound. The Research About Teacher Education (RATE) studies from 1987 through 1994 reveal teacher education faculty average age in the late 40s and early 50s, figures suggesting in 1997 that massive retirements will occur in the early part of the twenty-first century. The RATE studies, one of a few comprehensive data gathering efforts about teacher education faculty, show that the faculty are largely Anglo, between 91 per cent and 93 per cent majority male, particularly at the senior ranks, and there are few minorities in the pipeline (Zimpher and Sherrill, 1996; M. Ducharme and E. Ducharme, 1996b).

Some Views of Teacher Educators

If we could develop a faculty of teacher educators to work with and aid in the development of the nation's future teachers, what would we want that faculty to be like? Surely we would not want the teacher education faculty of the future to resemble those in Howey's (1995) remarks,

> Teaching has not improved because teacher educators, frankly, are limited in their pedagogical abilities, and no major pressures exist to change the nature of their teaching. College classrooms are truly private sanctuaries. These fundamental problems of pedagogy, underestimated by most and ignored by many in the teacher education literature, are nonetheless manifest everywhere. They speak both to how we as educators have failed to authentically engage many bright and materially-rich youngsters in their formal schooling as well as the problem of educating our equally able but less supported youngsters who live in conditions of poverty . . . My perception is that most of us in the teacher education community do not know how to proceed in terms of adapting our programs to meet the demands these developments place upon us. (p. 21)

Howey sees a direct relationship between the quality of teacher educators and the quality of instruction in the schools. Whether or not the cause and effect relationship is as sharp as his words suggest is a debatable point, but that a relationship exists is not debatable. We also wonder about Howey's assertions about the limited pedagogical ability of teacher educators, given his insistence of the privacy of higher education classrooms.

D. Clark (1992) is equally pessimistic about teacher educators from the late twentieth century. He argues that,

> Teacher educators were carrying a history of ineffective program performance and resistance to change into these policy discussions. How difficult it must be for policy makers to understand the extremely negative reaction of the teacher educators to the eighteen-hour cap on education courses when that has been the mode in secondary education teacher preparation for fifty years. If there was a need for expanded life space in the pedagogical instruction in the teacher education curriculum, why had teacher educators been unable to convince their academic colleagues on campus of the need? If teacher educators were concerned about the quality of teachers and teaching why had admission standards to teacher education been set so low? Why had program standards been so low that, almost literally, any college

or university that wished to have a professional curriculum in teacher education could obtain state program approval and national accreditation? If pedagogical instruction was important in classroom performance why did almost all states have a history of meeting teacher shortages by emergency certification that waived teacher training requirements? Why did teacher educators stand on the sidelines in the debate over academic majors and liberal arts education for teachers? (p. 279)

Clark's phrase 'stand on the sidelines' appropriately describes much non-activity of much of teacher education for decades. The voice of teacher education is largely unheard in political circles and generally ignored when heard. Howsam, Corrigan, Denemark, and Nash (1976) addressed issues of 'life space in *Educating a Profession*': Teacher education suffers from serious inadequacies in the 'life space' available to carry out the demanding task of preparing professional teachers. In time, facilities, personnel, instructional and research materials — even in access to quality instruction in other academic units — teacher education programs require greater resources than presently allocated' (p. 98).

Divisive Issues

Many issues appear to preclude teacher educators from effectively participating in reform agendas. Clark (1992) notes some of the contextual characteristics which he believes affected teacher education policy in the 1980s. Among them he includes criticism by clients, low status within the university, and a divided teacher education community (p. 289). The matter of low support by clients is critical. Barr (1992), in describing conditions in Oregon, notes,

Even though critics of teacher education found the results of the surveys to be surprisingly bland, only 10 percent of the teachers surveyed felt they had experienced a truly excellent teacher education program . . . follow-up evaluations of graduates reported a high level of discrepancy between teaching competencies that teachers reported as being important and the adequacy of their teacher education program in helping them achieve these competencies. (pp. 113–14)

It may be lamentable that graduates of teacher preparation programs have had and continue to have a predisposition to point fingers at those who prepared them because they found themselves unready for some of the tasks and expectations that arise during teaching: managing a homeroom, meeting with critical parents, developing effective learning programs for all students, coaching the junior varsity soccer team, advising the debate club, and on and on. Teacher educators must be able to prepare students as well as they can for the unknown, but they must also be able and forthright enough to help prospective teachers understand that no program ever prepared learners for every or even nearly all of the situations that arise. But that realization on students' part, when it occurs, must be accompanied by a feeling and a belief that teacher education as an enterprise is at the ready to assist teachers as they move through their careers.

Edward R. Ducharme and Mary K. Ducharme

Some Aspects of the Future

The teacher educators of tomorrow must be able to teach well and, at the same time, be able to state forthrightly and powerfully that becoming a teacher is not a four-year plan of study, that learning to teach and becoming effective at this very complex task is a lifelong activity. They must be able to articulate the various stages of teacher development, able to prepare individuals for effective survival and growth in the early months and years of teaching, and be knowledgeable and skilled enough to work effectively with teachers in the middle and late stages of their careers. The issue for SCDEs ought not to be how many teachers they prepare for initial certification, but how well they prepare them to *begin* their careers.

In the 1990s, some teacher education is not on campuses. The Teach for America program, alternative certification programs in more than 35 states, increases in local, district-provided inservice education, distance learning inservice programs, and other delivery systems increasingly provide both preserivce and inservice opportunities independent of the traditionally SCDE-based programs.

The issue of where teacher education should occur is international. Grimmett (1995) states that

> Currently, many countries are reintroducing nineteenth century modes of teacher training with the United States, Australia and England in the vanguard. The rush to provide school-based training in these countries indicates scant critical examination of government motives for introducing such measures. Nineteenth century industrialists made no bones about their motives. They wanted a work force skilled enough to operate their machines but not capable of questioning their place in the socio / political system. The idea of teaching children to think critically, to ask questions and solve problems would have seemed to them a recipe for their demise. They made sure that did not happen by their control of the school system and its funding. Have things changed? Does it make any difference where teacher education takes place? (pp. 204–5)

Grimmett's questions are provocative and troubling. What is the appeal of returning to 'nineteenth century modes of teacher training' after so much effort to develop effective ways of introducing young people into the complexities of teaching? Is Grimmett on to something that Americans should attend to, namely, that there is a wish, however *sub rosa* for teacher educators to help prepare teachers who will, in turn, help 'educate' compliant workers? After many years of relative acceptance, teacher educators are having to question their place.

It may be that few professional preparation groups are as hard on themselves as teacher educators are. They are oftentimes the recipient of criticism when they were not the subject of study; for example, *A Nation at Risk* (1983) contained random criticisms and almost 'by-the-way' observations that teacher education must improve so that schools can become better.

Perhaps no group of alleged professionals has been as ill-represented in reform efforts as has been the teacher education community (*community* may be an inappropriate word here; *cacophony* might be better). Teacher education is fond of comparing itself with the professions of law and medicine. However, one recalls that, although drug company representatives, insurance poohbahs and other hangers-on were involved, it was primarily members of the medical profession who rose to address the 1990s attempt by the Clinton Administration to reform health care. Politicians did not and do not tell doctors how to manage medical matters, yet they have no compunction about telling educators how to conduct their affairs. One looks in vain for significant input by teacher educators at national and regional reform agenda meetings. Witness the March, 1996 Education Summit, attended by governors and business executives accompanied by a coterie of educational conservatives largely antagonistic to teacher education.

Merely teaching the future teachers, doing scholarly activity on and off campus, working with teachers in the schools, and whatever else will not suffice if teacher education is, first, to survive and, next, to thrive. Reflection in teacher education, a 1980s and 1990s fixation of teacher educators, may be an appropriate way to grow and study the field, but it is not an effective process for confronting significant issues. Teacher educators must become savvy activists in policy matters. Although many write of policy (e.g., Gideonse, 1992; McBride, 1996; Ginsburg and Lindsay, 1996), few have taken strong, perhaps necessarily adversarial stances on key policy issues. Howey (1995) points out that college classrooms are sanctuaries; one might add that so are college offices. Attracted to the academic life as we have been, we teacher educators may have to take the initiative on confronting the major issues of the day in teacher education and by implication, schooling. The lives of children, the pedagogy appropriate to the age, the necessity for equity — these and a host of other subjects are too important for governors, legislators, business leaders, and others to have not only the major, but often the only say in what must be. Clark (1992) points out how important directions in teacher education such as entry into programs have been the purview of non-educators, how despite the clear growth in knowledge abut teaching and learning from the 1960s through the 1980s the policy results of the 1980s have consistently 'de-emphasized the importance of knowledge about pedagogy in the professional preparation of teachers' (p. 269).

Sheehan and Fullan (1995) comment that

> One result of these critics is powerfully negative myths that persist despite the fact that they are partially, largely and in some cases completely untrue. To say that 'faculties of education are intransigent,' 'teacher education candidates are weak,' 'not enough time is spent in the practicum,' 'schools and teachers are not interested in collaboration,' is to be out of touch with current reality. And yet faculties of education are not able to get their message across . . . Another difficulty with reform of teacher education is the notion prevalent over time and still existing among many in the society today, that teaching requires no special knowledge or skill, the belief that has dogged us for years that teacher education has no knowledge base: that is, that anyone can teach . . . schools are not viewed as learning institutions where the accumulated wisdom of practice is appreciated and disseminated. Schools are still characterized as places with closed classroom doors. There are very few induction programs in schools in Canada and often new teachers are

> saddled with the worst assignments. Furthermore, there is no link between the
> graduates in their first teaching assignments and the programs where they have
> done their preservice teacher education. (pp. 89–91)

When Sheehan and Fullan state that 'faculties of education are not able to get their message across', they hit the mark squarely. The points that teacher education has are of enormous importance, yet they rarely receive any public consideration. Teacher educators must articulate with clarity, force, and decisiveness the values of the profession, the needs for careful preparation for teachers, and the relevancy of powerful research in teaching and learning.

As the twenty-first century approaches, many individuals in a wide range of activities are asking basic questions. Somehow a *fin de siècle* brings out a tendency to ask root questions. One basic question — in various forms — persists: What do teacher educators do or provide that is unique and necessary? A variant form is: How would the world be different — better or worse — if they did not exist? The following are some of the unique and necessary things teacher educators provide:

- Sources of development of new knowledge about teaching, teachers, schools, human development, and learning;
- Sources of counsel and development for those preparing to teach;
- Sources of information for dissemination of knowledge about teaching, teachers, schools, human development, and learning;
- Assistance in prospective teacher inquiry about relationships between education and society, schooling and learning, human development and knowledge and skill acquisition;
- Instances of the union of pedagogy and knowledge. Readers will both argue about the characteristics and thinking of others. Yet how else will such dialogue and study occur? The university-based teacher educators must play a critical role in the development of teachers, but merely saying so will not make it so.

Writing of the value and importance of the university role in teacher preparation, Nash and Ducharme (1974) noted that 'The university's most singular contribution to the preparation of public school educators must be to keep alive in young people a sense of idealism and critical social vision' (p. 107). Taken together, do all of the above and whatever else we might claim satisfy as a *raison d'être* for teacher educators and SCDEs? Smith and his colleagues (1980), arguing the need for a new form of a school of pedagogy, commented, 'The basic program should be shaped by a single overriding purpose; namely, to prepare prospective teachers for work success in the classroom, the school, and the community' (p. 40). How one defines success in the classroom, the school, and the community may have changed dramatically since 1980. Societal changes in population, technology, and cultural divides have affected definitions of what teachers should know and be able to do, changes that in turn affect what teacher educators should be and do.

Much writing recently has focused on the importance of teacher educators and SCDEs as links between teacher education students and the schools; SCDEs without professional development schools (PDSs) are depicted as educational pariahs. Some define the role of teacher education in the future to include systematic, ongoing follow-up and assistance in the careers of teacher education graduates. The Holmes Group (1995) defines the role of schools of education to include:

> The responsibility of the TSE for its graduates continues in another way. The TSE will provide opportunities for them to keep growing. Lifelong professional development will be every bit as much a primary function of the TSE as initial credentialing. In coming years, school districts and individual schools will probably increase their involvement in the on-going development of their professional staff, but the TSE must act whether or not school districts accept this responsibility. (p. 55)

Many have called for this dual responsibility for teacher educators to perform follow-up activities with graduates and to spend time in the schools. Howsam et al. (1976) stated the case clearly:

> Teacher educators must function effectively in the world of higher education. They must be capable of applying the knowledge and research in higher education to the problems of schools and teachers. Teacher educators must relate to both school professionals and to university academicians and be able to cope with the ambiguities and strains this dichotomous relationship generates. (p. 106)

Such responsibilities are germane but rarely rewarded in higher education. The Holmes Group contends, 'The TSE will review and revise its policies and procedures for promotion, tenure, and merit pay in light of high standards for this work, and then negotiate to make appropriate changes in university-wide practices' (p. 64). In this observation, the Holmes Group addresses a perennially unsolved question: How does one reconcile the academy's demands for faculty performance with the need for effective field work?

The Wisdom of Practice

Many would enjoin teacher educators to learn the 'wisdom of practice'. In fact, teacher educators have always found wisdom in the study of teaching, in watching and talking with teachers, in entrusting student teachers to practicing teachers. The rub has come in when there has been, almost inevitably, the clash between the university and school cultures, the one giving precedence to research and scholarship and the other to the day-to-day practice of teaching. Gitlin, Bringhurst, Burns, Cooley, Myers, Price, Russell, and Tiess (1992), writing of the cleavage that developed between practitioners and higher education faculty as teacher education moved from normal schools to the universities, state,

The movement away from practice created some tensions between schools of education and the educational community at large. More and more the interests of the professors were split from the interests of those working in the classroom. Specifically, academics were interested in achieving legitimacy and status within the university, which meant doing research and publishing in high-status journals, while teachers and others in the community were interested in improving schooling, understanding classroom life, and addressing the complex and messy business of learning to teach. Clearly, research can, and has, played a role in addressing some of these concerns. More often than not, however, research didn't find its way to the school level, wasn't related to the problems teachers and others were trying to address, was written for other academics, making it largely inaccessible, and blamed the teacher for school problems. (p. 74)

In reality, there has often been interest from the university in practice in schools and interest from the schools in research and scholarship; but the precise ways of working out the relationships remain unresolved. Proefriedt (1994), reflecting on some of the negative aspects of professors in schools, comments,

None of this is an argument against teacher educators' being involved in schools. There are good reasons why they should be. Schools are the places, after all, where the activities they are inquiring into and teaching about go on. The question is: What sort of work should they be doing there? I am not arguing here that teacher educators can be drawn to the schools if we allow them to pursue their private interest, research and publication, for which they will be rewarded with promotion and tenure. My argument is of a different sort. The roles that teacher educators have developed over the years are those of (1) making inquiries into teaching, schooling generally, and education in a larger sense, and publishing these inquiries, and (2) teaching-specifically, teaching prospective and working teachers. These functions seem valuable. They should not be easily discarded or diminished. (p. 136)

Both university and school faculty can be guilty of *hubris*, the ancient tragic flaw that brings down people of good will. The university can be overly righteous in its view that the development of new knowledge is a primary driving force and is necessary to the successful processes of teaching and learning; the school can be equally righteous in claiming that, without the bind to practice, research and scholarship are for naught. Neither of these views is correct, but the sole belief in either leads only to professional and personal distress. Howsam et al. (1976), in the second of their 24 assertions, noted that 'Teacher education is the preparation and research arm of the teaching profession' (p. 41). Their third assertion states that 'Teacher education is the primary responsibility of (a) the teaching profession and (b) the college or university. Its governance structure should reflect this' (p. 41). These two assertions reflect the conundrum that continues to frustrate the field. The first assertion clearly implies that the campus-based faculty and programs have responsibility for preparation and research in the field while the second implied a shared responsibility. Who does what? Clearly subsequent developments in accreditation reflect the joint responsibility for governance or at least oversight of programs. But what is the role of campus-placed teacher education faculty? Is it in the schools doing a variety of things?

The necessity for the presence of teacher education faculty in the schools has been a repeated mantra of many teacher educators for the past several decades. Wisniewski (1989) argues that 'A normal part of the ideal professor's week regularly would be spent in the schools . . . This expectation should apply to all professors of education with no distinction regarding the area of specialty. The equivalent of one full day each week would be the minimal expectation for this type of activity' (p. 142). Apart from every dean shuddering at the thought of *all* education professors spending a day a week in the schools, the situation relative to SCDE faculty spending much time in the schools raises a host of questions. Should the schools be the primary site of practice-related teacher education? If so, what is the faculty role? What difference will their presence make? How will SCDEs accommodate this time and resource consuming role for full-time faculty? Numerous institutions are beginning to have faculty teach many courses within the schools.

McIntyre (1995) concerned about the process in the United Kingdom whereby so much of teacher education occurs in the schools, notes,

> There are of course many reasons [for opposing school-based teacher education), most but not all of which are, in my opinion, good ones. First, many of us who work in higher education faculties or departments of education understandably feel threatened and justifiably feel deeply resentful. We are resentful because the political campaign which has preceded and accompanied the government initiatives has consisted of scurrilous attacks upon us and our work, and has been based on ludicrously irrational arguments, on grossly uninformed accounts of our practice, and on a view of teaching as an activity which does not require thought except about *what* one is teaching. (p. 30)

Presently, the more powerful view is the primacy of practice. Rice and Richlm (1993) observe that,

> Recently, schools of education in research universities have been called on to learn from the wisdom of practice, to get faculty into this nation's schools, and to focus on the student as client. In particular, more credence is being given to learning from interactions in the classroom and with students who learn in different ways. The quality of our schools depends on our ability to take seriously the scholarship of practice and a different kind of interaction between research and practice. (p. 299)

Practice in and of itself may not mean much. Any of us who has attempted any difficult act such as ballet dancing, playing a musical instrument, hitting a baseball, high diving, and so on has heard the time-honored, but wrong injunction that practice makes perfect. Practice does not make perfect; rather, informed practice leads to improvement.

Teacher educators have the privilege of teaching and working with people of various ages and backgrounds, but largely young, white, and middle class, who are planning or thinking about teaching as a career. These students begin their 'professional' courses while simultaneously fulfilling their general education requirements and, in most cases, requirements for academic majors. Hansen (1995), who sees teaching as a vocation, writes,

> After all, most persons who aspire to teach do not have in mind working in a *particular* school. Rather, they want to teach and have a beneficial impact on the young. To perceive themselves as members of a practice — one, incidentally, as old as civilization itself — can guide them through difficult times. It can help them appreciate that their perspectives and actions need not be determined solely by their specific circumstances. To encounter a series of rough classes; to fail to reach a student; to feel let down by colleagues, administrators, or parents — none of these troubling events so familiar to teachers need demoralize them or lead them to abandon teaching. If they perceive the work in terms larger than their own imme-diate situation, they might discover unexpected resources. (pp. 116–27)

SCDE faculty have unique opportunities to address the senses of idealism and higher purpose in prospective teachers.

A Lost Vision

The past several decades have witnessed teacher education ceding one of its prime venues for addressing these needs in the young as it has largely abandoned founda-tions courses as required parts of teacher preparation programs; in so doing it may have very negatively affected its *raison d'être*. In the 1970s and 1980s, some urged teacher education to do away with these courses.

> Every course should be scrutinized . . . If this were done, a large number of courses would be eliminated at the level of basic preparation. Candidates for deletion would be introduction to education, history of education, philosophy of education, social foundations of education, and host of others including courses in learning and development provided for undergraduate study. Work in these areas can be offered in programs of specialization leading to the doctor's degree. (Smith et al., 1980, p. 40)

Howsam et al. (1976) were less restrictive, 'Foundational studies must be *inter-related*. The more specialized and isolated each of the academic disciplines becomes, the more necessary it will be for foundations faculties to re-integrate the subject matters for educational judgment and action. Educators face a welter of problems and issues too complicated and to be solved within the framework of a single discipline. Not only must preparation programs develop teaching skills and a know-ledge of theoretical and empirical concepts, but they must foster humanistic educa-tional values and attitudes. Indeed, the central task of teacher education is to provide teachers with a philosophy of education that will help them to think seriously and continuously about the purposes and consequences of what they do (pp. 87–9).

Teacher preparation programs and their faculty have nearly carried out Smith's lamentable prescription for reform. Under the guise of alleged irrelevancy of traditional foundations courses to teachers' lives in the schools, programs have frequently substituted variations of An Introduction to Education course which generally occurs during the first years of entry into a program; includes hours of observation and participation in the schools; and provides a quick run through such topics as certification, salaries, school law, methodology, and others. Reporting on his studies of teacher preparation institutions and programs, Goodlad (1990) notes that,

> The major change we saw . . . was in the social foundations component. Whereas in the early 1960s one could virtually count on students' taking a fairly solid course in the history and philosophy of education (or an introduction to American education from a historical and philosophical perspective), this was the minority pattern in our sample . . . the course . . . was devoted to an overview of program requirements, demands and expectations of teaching, and lectures (more than discussions) on selected, rather contemporary topics: AIDS instruction, how to pass a minimum competency test, how to manage a class, and multicultural education, for example — often with one class devoted to each topic. (pp. 203–4)

Hardly the stuff to fulfill visions.
Goodlad (1990) states,

> There is irresponsibility in significantly expanding teachers' authority without educating them to use it well. Using it well requires both knowledge and moral sensitivity. These are acquired, in large part, through critical, disciplined socialization into the full array of expectations and responsibilities a democratic society requires of its teachers. This is unlikely to occur if teaching in schools is seen to require only the generic skills common to all teaching. Nor is it likely to occur if passage through a general undergraduate curriculum and mentoring with an experienced teacher are to be the route to teaching, as is so frequently recommended. Nor is this disciplined socialization commonly occurring in teacher education programs as now conducted. (pp. 26–7)

Butts (1993), long a distinguished professor of foundations at Teachers College, Columbia, makes the case for foundations in the pre-preparation of teachers:

> All teachers and administrators need to develop a coherent and defensible conception of democratic citizenship, an intellectual framework, from which to view the role they play in American democratic society. This is primarily the task of what is known as the foundations of education . . . The foundations of education promote understanding of the role of education in the social, cultural, civic, and ethical life of American society. Here the fundamental purposes, institutions, and policies of education, broadly conceived, are subjected to the scholarly analysis and perspectives of the social sciences and humanities, especially history, political science, political philosophy, law, sociology, anthropology, economics, religion, and comparative and international studies. The fundamental character of a profession is the capacity of its members to make informed judgments about the public good and to engage in those contributions the profession can make to the general welfare as well as to the individual welfare of the persons for whom it has responsibility. (pp. 93–4)

Butts poses a very tall order indeed for the foundations, perhaps too tall an order for completion in a preservice program. But it is not too tall an order to begin in the preservice program and continue throughout the professional lives of teachers. It should be clear to teacher educators that the Smith et al. (1980) prescription, despite the overall appropriateness of much of the rest of *A Design for a School of Pedagogy*, was toxic. The removal of solid foundational studies from teacher preparation took away much spirit and inquiry. The Holmes Group (1995) argues that,

> Foundations courses in education schools bring together perspectives from history, philosophy, sociology, and political science to examine American history. Some educators disparage foundations courses, but we believe these offerings, when taught well, have much to say about why educators do what they do and why public schools are the way that they are ... As taught in the core of professional education, foundations courses ought to be a wonderful vehicle for interdisciplinary knowledge that draws extensively on the humanities and social sciences. This approach should underpin the preparation of all practitioners. (p. 75)

Readers may object that we are arguing too forcefully for the vital nature of foundational studies in teacher preparation. Perhaps. But whether it is foundational studies or another area of inquiry, teacher education students deserve and require the opportunity to reflect in personally enriching ways that ultimately relate to the core of their teaching, to the soul of the nation.

But teacher education has a rich source of wisdom and practice to draw upon to help students continue to develop their sense of vision and purpose. The work of Elliott (1993), Ginsbury (1988), Hargreaves (1994), and a host of others demonstrates how much knowledge teacher education has accrued incrementally over the decades.

Business Talk

Lacking a clear sense of purpose, a solidly developed philosophy, and strategies for accomplishing purposes, teacher education is continually subject to external pressures. Currently, much of education generally and much of teacher education specifically has yielded to the lure of the business community, even adopting the language of buyers and sellers. One wonders about a sense of history, if leaders have read their Tyack and Cremin. Pimm and Selinger (1995) detail how the language of business has infiltrated teacher education conversation in England,

> As ever, one place to start to identify change is through the new rhetoric, particularly as the current discourse stems from other sections of the Thatcher Conservative, consumerist philosophy. Substitution of language in any institutional context is never innocent. Government education documents and reports are now full of the language of the market economy, of *choice* and *competition*; of *consumers* of education (parents or employers apparently rather than the pupils themselves);

of schools forming a *market place* with open enrollment rather than catchment areas, and public performance ranking of schools. The curriculum is now to be *delivered* by teachers (having been decided on and manufactured somewhere elsewhere it would seem). Schools are to *purchase* in-service from *providers*; *management of resources* is to the fore, and *quality assurance* is required for school-based initial education. (p. 48)

Grimmett (1995) says that

> Alongside the myth of educational decline another myth has been cultivated in each of these three countries [US, England, and Australia). This myth is that the so-called business people are capable of solving a variety of problems from the management of publicly funded hospitals to deciding the appropriate curriculum for the different levels of schooling. Such penetration of corporate interests into education is currently popular in the United States, Australia and England. At the same time little opposition has been mounted by teacher educators against such interests. With few exceptions teacher education institutions in these countries appear to have accepted decisions about their place in the education system. In England the reaction by teacher education institutions to political depredation by the national government has been to fall into line and scramble for funds to do things with which they may not agree. (p. 206)

One need only read the reports of recent national meetings of governors and business leaders on the subject of education and some recent writing by educators to see how pervasive the language of the marketplace has become in education. Commenting of the struggles in England over such matters, Ball and Goodson (1985) wrote,

> One outcome of the debate was that attempts were made to make schools and teachers more responsive to and more accountable to the needs of industry and the personal concerns of parents. The force of the latter entered into law through the Education Act of 1981, which required schools to publish their examination results and gave parents the right to choose the school that they wished to send their children to. In other words, schools were to be subject to market forces. The weak would go to the wall. (p. 5)

In some ways, teacher education in America is close to the wall.

The Teachers

Numerous scholars, critics, and pundits have commented on the kinds of teachers necessary for the twenty-first century, the type of skills teachers will require for teaching in the twenty-first century, and the attitudes necessary (Boyer and Baptiste, 1996; Garcia, 1996; Good, 1996; Haberman, 1996). Darling-Hammond (1996) comments that

> If all children are to be effectively taught, teachers must be prepared to address
> the substantial diversity in experiences that children bring with them to school:
> the wide range of languages, cultures, learning styles and challenges, talents, and
> intelligences that require in turn an equally rich and varied repertoire of teaching
> strategies . . . This mission for teaching defies the single, formulaic approach to
> delivering lessons and testing results that has characterized the goals of much
> regulation of teaching, many staff development programs, and a number of teacher
> testing and evaluation instruments. (p. 16)

Darling-Hammond and Cobb (1996) believe that

> The new mission for education requires substantially more knowledge and radic-
> ally different skills for teachers, as well as changes in the ways in which schools
> operate. The kind of teaching required to meet these demands for more thoughtful
> learning cannot be produced through teacher-proof materials or regulated curric-
> ulum. In order to create bridges between common, challenging curriculum goals and
> individual learners' experiences and needs, teachers must understand cognition and
> the many different pathways to learning. They must understand child development
> and pedagogy as well as the structures of subject areas and a variety of alternatives
> for assessing learning . . . There is another challenge as well that requires a more
> knowledgeable and highly skilled teaching force: the social setting for teaching is
> more demanding than ever. Teachers are currently striving to address the needs of
> a growing number of low-income children (one out of four American children now
> lives in poverty), the largest wave of immigrants since the turn of the last century,
> and children who often encounter greater stresses and fewer supports in their
> communities and families . . . teachers must be prepared to address the substantial
> diversity in experiences that children bring with them to school: the wide range of
> languages, cultures, and learning styles and challenges, talents, and intelligences
> that require in turn an equally rich and varied repertoire of teaching strategies.
> (pp. 15–16)

These scholars believe that teachers will require understandings of diversity,
ability to work with varied groups, ability to make careful judgments, ease in varied
cultural groups, good self concepts, willingness to accept and learn about others
different from oneself.

The world of education has never lacked for words describing what various
individuals have thought of as ideal or excellent teachers. Macrorie (1984) produced a text in which he allowed 20 teachers he believed extraordinary to tell their
stories. He noted that 'The idea behind this book is so simple that it may sound at
first like tomfoolery' and went on to note that 'They were not *teachers* in the usual
sense — persons who pass on the accepted knowledge of the world and get it
back from students on tests, but *enablers* who help others to do good works and
extend their already considerable powers' (p. xii). In the remainder of the text,
the 20 teachers present themselves and what Macrorie calls 'the good works done
by students of these enablers' (p. xii), for it is in what their students produce
that Macrorie sees the greatness of the teachers. In the final chapter, after the 20
teachers have presented themselves and the good works of the students, Macrorie
provides 'An Open Letter About Schools'. In it, he states,

Every seven or ten years we read in the papers and hear on TV that education is in crisis. Our schools aren't turning out children competent in math and science. They can't write or read. We are falling behind other countries in high technology. We're hearing these complaints now. In the fifties we heard them about our failure to keep up with the Soviet Union's Sputnik. Now we are hearing about our failure to keep up with Japan in electronics. Old story. In 1893 a writer in the May issue of *The Atlantic Monthly* was discussing the 'great outcry' about the 'inability of the students admitted to Harvard College to write English clearly and correctly'. (p. 233)

Writing of the teachers for the future, Carson (1996) states,

They are responsible for civic education in a society that has grown cynical about politicians and bureaucrats, they are trying to teach international understanding in a world where the threat of nuclear war has receded only to reveal a multitude of virulent ethnic hatreds that have surfaced in many quarters, and they are trying to teach for social justice in a world where the gap between rich and poor continues to grow. Such are the perplexing times facing the aspiring social studies teacher who is still usually white and middle class, but who will probably be teaching in an urban classroom where many of the students will be of different cultures and family backgrounds. (p. 154)

Teacher educators are generally well aware of the failure of the *traits of effective teachers'* approach to teacher preparation. They should also be aware that the failure of the approach as a panacea for the problems of teacher preparation need not necessitate an abandonment of looking at the traits of teachers whom students either admire or disrespect and of seeking to inculcate and develop those attitudes in individuals preparing to teach. The students' comments illustrate, as though the point required further illustration, that teaching is complex and many-sided. Their comments belie the currently popular notion that becoming a teacher means merely acquiring some knowledge. Sheehan and Fullan (1995) note that

Despite the rhetoric about teacher education in today's society, there does not seem to be a real belief or confidence that investing in teacher education will yield results. Perhaps deep down many leaders believe that teaching is not all that dif-ficult. After all, most leaders have spent thousands of hours in the classroom and are at least armchair experts. And they know that scores of unqualified teachers are placed in classrooms every year and required to learn on the job. (p. 89)

Darling-Hammond and Cobb (1996) argue that 'Teachers will need to be prepared to teach in the ways these new standards demand, with deeper under-standings of their disciplines, of interdisciplinary connections, and of inquiry-based learning. They will need skills for creating learning experiences that enable stu-dents to construct their own knowledge in powerful ways' (p. 17). Macrorie (1984) notes, 'There's no way in any country to institute from above a sweeping successful reform of education. Teachers don't like to be handed a new curriculum and told to put it into practice next semester. They don't want to be advised by the teacher next door or the administrator down the hall that they should change their ways radically. They feel they know their job as well as the next person in the field' (p. 250).

C. Clark (1995), writing of the ardor of good teaching, notes that

> Good teaching will never be easy. Nor will it ever be (*sic*) easy to be a good parent, a good nurse, a good scientist, or a good political leader. The essence of these callings is a courageous willingness to form moral relationships, to embrace uncertainty, to do what seems right at the time, to lead but not to control. In those ways, good teaching happens every day in our schools and in our homes, in our workplaces and towns. Perhaps the best preparation for the future of life-long learning, in this culture and elsewhere, is to cultivate and treasure a better appreciation of the present state of good teaching. We cannot change the past, but we can come to understand and cooperate with contemporary goodness more constructively. (p. 16)

Fusion

'The time is out of joint. O cursed spite / That ever I was born to set it right' (Hamlet, I, v, 215–216). Indeed, the times are out of joint, but we were born to help set them right; we are not cursed; we are blessed to 'set it right'. Teacher educators must save themselves at the university level, sustain and develop further their reputation among students and graduates now teaching, and assist in promoting equity and civitas in the nation's schools. No one knows teaching better; no one can fuse teaching and learning as well as teacher educators can. Passion and spunk are the attributes necessary to enter the next century, a century holding the key to a better future for the nation's children in schools where teachers teach them with knowledge, skills, and attitudes wrought in the crucibles of the universities and colleges where teacher educators live and work with dignity and teacher education is . . . writ large on the institutions' agendas.

References

BALL, J. and GOODSON, I. (1985) 'Understanding teachers: Concepts and contexts', in BALL, J. and GOODSON, I. (eds) *Teachers' Lives and Careers*, Philadelphia: Falmer Press, pp. 1–26.

BARR, R. (1992) 'Turmoil in teacher education in Oregon', in GIDEONSE, H. (ed.) *Teacher Education Policy: Narratives Stories and Cases*, Albany, NY: SUNY Press, pp. 111–31.

BOYER, J. and BAPTISTE, H. (1996) 'The crisis in teacher education in America: Issues of recruitment and retention of culturally different (minority) teachers' in SIKULA, J., BUTTERY, T. and GUYTON, E. (eds) *Handbook of Research on Teacher Education*, New York: Macmillian, pp. 779–94.

BUTTS, R.F. (1993) *In the First Person Singular: The Foundations of Education*, San Francisco: Caddo Gap Press.

CARSON, T. (1996) 'Reflective practice and a reconceptualization of teacher education', in WIDEEN, M. and GRIMMETT, P. (eds) *Changing Times in Teacher Education*, Washington, DC: Falmer Press, pp. 151–62.

CLARK, C. (1995) *Thoughtful Teaching*, New York: Teachers College Press.

CLARK, D. (1992) 'Search for a more effective future', in GIDEONSE, H. (ed.) *Teacher Education Policy: Narratives Stories, and Cases*, Albany, NY: SUNY Press, pp. 269–95.

DARLING-HAMMOND, L. (1996) 'The right to learn and the advancement of teaching: Research, policy, and practice for democratic education', *Educational Researcher*, **25**, 4, pp. 5–18.

DARLING-HAMMOND, L. and COBB, V. (1996) in MURRAY, F. (ed.) (1996) *Knowledge Base for Teacher Educators*, San Francisco: Jossey-Bass, pp. 14–62.

DUCHARME, E. and DUCHARME, M. (1996a) 'Development of the teacher education professoriate', in MURRAY, F. (ed.) *The Teacher Educator's Handbook: Building a Knowledge Base for the Preparation of Teachers*, San Francisco: Jossey-Bass, pp. 691–714.

DUCHARME, M. and DUCHARME, E. (1996b) 'A study of teacher educators: Research from the USA', *Journal of Education for Teaching*, **22**, 1, pp. 57–70.

ELLIOTT, J. (1993) 'Professional education and the idea of a practical educational science', in ELLIOTT, J. (ed.) *Reconstructing Teacher Education: Teacher Development*, Washington, DC: Falmer Press, pp. 65–85.

GARCIA, E. (1996) 'Preparing instructional professionals for linguistically and culturally diverse students', in SIKULA, J., BUTTERY, T. and GUYTON, E. (eds) *Handbook of Research in Teacher Education*, New York: Macmillan, pp. 802–12.

GIDEONSE, H. (1992) *Teacher Education Policy: Narratives, Stories, and Cases*, Albany, NY: SUNY Press.

GINSBURG, M. (1988) *Contradictions in Teacher Education and Society: A Critical Analysis*, New York: Falmer Press.

GINSBURG, M. and LINDSAY, B. (1996) *The Political Dimension in Teacher Education: Comparative Perspectives on Policy Formation Socialization and Society*, New York: Falmer Press.

GITLIN, A., BRINGHURST, K., BURNS, M., COOLEY, MYERS, B., PRICE, K., RUSSELL, R. and TIESS, P. (1992) *Teachers' Voices for School Change: An Introduction to Educative Research*, New York: Teachers College Press.

GOOD, T. (1996) 'Teaching effects and teacher evaluation', in SIKULA, J., BUTTERY, T. and GUYTON, E. (eds) (1996) *Handbook of research on teacher education*, New York: Macmillan, pp. 617–65.

GOODLAD, J. (1990) 'The occupation of teaching in the schools', in GOODLAD, J., SODER, R. and SIROTNIK, K. (eds) *The Moral Dimensions of Teaching*, San Francisco: Jossey-Bass, pp. 3–34.

GRIMMETT, P. (1995) 'Reconceptualizing teacher education: Preparing teachers for revitalized schools', in WIDEEN, M. and GRIMMETT, P. (eds) *Changing Times in Teacher Education*, Washington, DC: Falmer Press, pp. 202–25.

HABERMAN, M. (1996) 'Selecting and preparing culturally competent teachers for urban schools', in SIKULA, J., BUTTERY, T. and GUYTON, E. (eds) *Handbook of Research on Teacher Education*, New York: Macmillan, pp. 747–60.

HANSEN, D. (1995) *The Call to Teach*, New York: Teachers College Press.

HARGREAVES, A. (1994) *Changing Teachers, Changing Times: Teachers' Work and Culture in the Postmodern World*, New York: Teachers College Press.

HOLMES GROUP (1995) *Tomorrow's Schools of Education*, East Lansing, MI: The Holmes Group.

HOWEY, K. (1995) 'The United States: The context for restructuring and reconceptualization of teacher preparation', in WIDEEN, M. and GRIMMETT, P. (eds) *Changing Times in Teacher Education*, Washington, DC: Falmer Press, pp. 19–33.

Edward R. Ducharme and Mary K. Ducharme

Howsam, R., Corrigan, D., Denemark, G. and Nash, R. (1976) *Educating a Profession*, Washington, DC: American Association of Colleges for Teacher Education.

Macrorie, K. (1984) *20 Teachers*, New York: Oxford University Press.

McBride, R. (1996) *Teacher Education Policy: Some Issues Arising from Research and Practice*, New York: Falmer Press.

McIntyre, D. (1995) *Initial Teacher Education: An Education that Empowers: A Collection of Lectures in Memory of Lawrence Stenhouse*, Bristol, PA: Cromwell Press.

Nash, R. and Ducharme, E. (1974) 'The university *can* prepare teachers: An unfashionable view', *Educational Forum*, **XXXIX**, 1, pp. 99–109.

National Commission on Excellence in Education (1983) *A Nation at Risk: The Imperative for Educational Reform*, Washington, DC: US Department of Education.

Pimm, D. and Selinger, M. (1995) 'The commodification of teaching: Teacher education in England', in Wideen, M. and Grimmett, P. (eds) *Changing Times in Teacher Education*, Washington, DC: Falmer Press, pp. 47–66.

Proefriedt, W.A. (1994) *How Teachers Learn: Towards a More Liberal Education*, New York: Teachers College Press.

Rice, R. and Richlm, L. (1993) 'Broadening the concept of scholarship in the professions', in Curry, L. and Wergin, J. (eds) *Educating Professions: Responding to New Expectations for Competence and Accountability*, San Francisco: Jossey-Bass, pp. 279–315.

Sheehan, N. and Fullan, M. (1995) 'Teacher education in Canada: A case study of British Columbia and Ontario', in Wideen, M. and Grimmett, P. (eds) *Changing Times in Teacher Education*, Washington, DC: Falmer Press, pp. 89–101.

Smith, B.O., Silverman, S., Borg, J. and Fry, B. (1980) *A Design for a School of Pedagogy*, Washington, DC: US Department of Education.

Wisniewski, R. (1989) 'Ideal professor of education', in Wisniewski, R. and Ducharme, E. (eds) *The Professors of Teaching: An Inquiry*, Albany, NY: State University of New York Press, pp. 134–46.

Zimpher, N. and Sherrill, J. (1996) 'Professors, teachers, and leaders in SCDEs', in Sikula, J., Buttery, T. and Guyton, E. (eds) *Handbook of Research on Teacher Education*, New York: Macmillan, pp. 279–305.

5 The Challenges Teacher Education Presents for Higher Education

Frank B. Murray

The argument against professional teacher education is rooted in the undeniable fact that teaching is a naturally occurring human behavior, a wholly natural act that is an enduring and universal feature of the repertoire of human behaviors. We are, in other words, a teaching species, a species whose young cannot, and do not, survive unless they are taught, invariably by persons with no formal schooling as teachers.

A question of the moment is whether university- and college-based teacher education, coming on the scene only within the last hundred years or so, can offer anything that can take novices much beyond the natural teaching skills all persons have. A further question is — even if formal teacher education improves natural teaching somewhat, can the nation's needs for schooling still be met, less expensively and adequately, by the natural teaching techniques and styles we all possess in varying degrees?

Features of Natural Teaching

J.M. Stephens (1967) catalogued the features of naturally occurring teaching in his theory of spontaneous schooling. His argument was that schooling, a feature of all anthropological groups, was dependent on a set of natural human tendencies that some persons had in greater degrees than others. Those that had these tendencies in generous proportions would be seen, whether they intended to teach or not, as teachers by the members of their communities. Teaching and learning would take place naturally or spontaneously and not necessarily with any particular motive to benefit the pupil. They would occur merely because the tendencies, which fundamentally serve only the teacher's needs, led incidentally and inevitably to learning in those persons in the teacher's company. Teaching, in other words, was spontaneous and non-deliberate. It occurred whenever a person with these tendencies was with any other person for a protracted period and it occurred to satisfy some need of the teacher, not the student.

These tendencies, which sustain natural teaching and schooling, were thought by Stephens to be:

1. a tendency in all of us to collect and manipulate things, classify them, dwell on and play with simple and basic ideas, create systems for grouping things — all done with no immediate payoff;

2 a tendency of a person to talk about what they know because an unshared experience is painful and a burden that must be eased through telling;

3 a tendency to correct others' mistakes, not with any view to making them better persons, but because an error — whether, for example, in a book or spoken on television — must be corrected even when the correction cannot possibly affect or benefit the author, publisher, or actor;

4 a tendency to supply the word that someone else is groping for, not to help the person exactly, but to meet one's own need to provide the answer and to fill the void of silence;

5 a tendency to 'point the moral', to show others how things are related, to show that x leads to y as in 'I told you that would happen'.

The theory of spontaneous schooling, incidentally, is meant to account for two pervasive, and otherwise unexplained, findings in the research literature on schooling: the universality of schooling; and the fact that educational research overwhelmingly finds insignificant differences between educational treatments. It accounts for universality by arguing that wherever there are people, there are these five spontaneous tendencies, and in whomever these reside, there will be a teacher — whether in a formal school or outside one. The pervasive no difference findings in educational research were explained in the theory as the natural outcome of the fact that the tendencies were operating in both the treatment and control groups (e.g., in large and small classes, in TV and conventional instruction, in mixed and segregated ability groups, in classrooms with textbooks A and B, and so forth). The tendencies, by themselves, caused powerful learning effects that swamped any effects that could be attributed to the researcher's treatment. These effects were explained adequately at the time by the prevailing Skinnerian/Thorndike learning theories because the spontaneous tendencies forged the defining stimulus–response learning link. They caused the stimulus to be presented, they permitted the opportunity to respond to it, and they rewarded and shaped the listener's response to the stimulus. At the time, these conditions were thought to be sufficient for all learning.

The theory, like other socio-biological theories, provides a convenient base for arguing that knowledge of subject matter in the company of these tendencies will outfit a person as a teacher, especially in situations where the teacher and the pupil are a lot like each other — as they are in families and other anthropological groups. It is not important whether Stephen's speculations on the specific natural or spontaneous tendencies are correct in every detail, but only whether the natural teaching abilities we all possess, whatever their exact natures, are adequate to support contemporary teaching and schooling.

The Breakdown of Natural Teaching

The theories of spontaneous schooling, sound as it may prove to be in many respects, and the view of teaching that is based on it, have a number of problematical consequences for contemporary schooling because schooling now takes place on larger scales than that found in families and other anthropological groups, and because schooling increasingly takes place in circumstances where the teacher and the pupils are less and less alike. As a result, reliance on the theory of natural teaching can be expected to lead to serious pedagogical mistakes for weak and superior students. Quite apart from the matter of scale and size and the degree of similarity, or commonality, between the teacher and the pupil, the theory promotes a direct mode of instruction that is unduly limiting in terms of modern views of cognition and cognitive development. Finally, the theory provides insufficient guidance for the solution of difficult and novel problems in schooling that go beyond the teacher's reliance on 'telling and showing', the core of the natural style of teaching.

Similarity, Commonality and Expectations

When the teacher and the pupil are not alike and when the teacher has, as a result, lower expectations for the *different* pupil, the natural tendencies lead to very unfortunate consequences (Brophy and Good, 1986; Evertson, Hawley and Zlotnick, 1985). When the teacher and the pupil have dissimilar backgrounds, we can expect the natural teaching mechanisms that support familial instruction will not operate to benefit the student.

American teachers are a relatively homogenous set of lower-middle class suburban white women and the American pupil is increasingly variable with regard to every demographic feature (Howe, 1990; Choy, Bobbitt, Henke, Medrich, Horn and Lieberman, 1993). Thus, the teacher, even if he or she were to rely exclusively on the spontaneous tendencies, would still need to come to terms with the findings in a maturing literature on sexism, racism, bilingualism, cultural and class diversity.

Even if the teacher had acquired this information about the diverse groups in the classroom, and was disposed to act in sympathy with it, there are a predictable number of pedagogical mistakes novices, and regrettably some licensed teachers make unless they also have had the opportunity to practice extensively some counterintuitive and *unnatural* teaching techniques. For example, it is certain that well-meaning and well-read persons with good college grades will still make the following pedagogical mistakes with their pupils for whom they have low expectations, regardless of how they came to have these expectations. They will treat these pupils not as individuals but as a group, seat them further away and outside the classroom zone of frequent teacher–pupil interaction, look at them less, ask them low-level questions, call on them less often, give them less time to respond, give them fewer hints when they are called upon, and give them less praise and more blame than other pupils. And teachers will do all this out of a mistaken sense of kindness that is seemingly oblivious to the pedagogical harm their undisciplined actions have caused their pupils (Hawley and Rosenholtz, 1984; Murray, 1986a).

This untrained and kind person, believing the pupil does not know very much, will not want to embarrass the pupil by calling on the pupil often, will ask *appropriately* easy questions when the pupil is called upon, will give fewer hints and less time when the pupil fails to respond as it would be unkind to prolong the pupil's embarrassment and so on. The professional teacher, like all professionals, and in contrast with the *spontaneous* teacher, must discipline many of his or her kinder instincts and implement an equitable and disciplined professional approach to bring about high levels of achievement from those pupils for whom the teacher would otherwise have low expectations (Oakes, 1985). These professional actions are frequently counterintuitive and as a result require practice, hopefully not on-the-job and at the expense the school's students.

Higher-order Forms of Learning and Knowing

A further limitation of the natural teaching regime, apart from the harm caused to weaker pupils, is that it doesn't take the superior pupil much beyond the kind of information that can be told and demonstrated and conforms to the stimulus-response and imitative forms of learning. While such declarative knowledge is important, the forms of knowledge that are constructed by the pupil, not merely transmitted to the pupil, are increasingly seen as key to the student's performance at the advanced levels of the disciplines (Murray, 1992; Ogle, Alsalam and Rogers, 1991). A pupil can be told and shown that, for example, *A* is greater than *B* and that *B* is also greater than *C*, but the knowledge that *A must* be greater than *C*, and that one could know that without ever looking directly at *A* and *C*, cannot be simply given to the pupil. Not only is *A* truly greater than *C*, but more than that, it has to be greater. That notion of necessity has its origins elsewhere. Showing and telling have not been found, except in very unusual circumstances, to be effective means of 'teaching' necessity (Beilin, 1971; Murray, 1978 and 1990; Smith, 1993). It is one thing to know that a statement is true, but quite another to know that it *must* be true. The origins of necessity, and other pivotal concepts, seem to lie in *dialectical* instruction, which demands intellectual action on the part of the teacher and the student. While more demanding on the student, dialectic is a less direct and more subtle form of instruction than that supported by the natural 'show and tell' teaching tendencies.

The Native Theory of Mind

Along with the natural teaching techniques there often comes a naive and serviceable theory of the human mind (Heider, 1958; Baldwin, 1980). The pupil's school achievement in the naive or common sense theory is tied to four common place factors — ability, effort, task difficulty, and luck. With these four factors, the natural teacher can explain completely the pupil's success or failure by attributing the level of the pupil's work to his ability or effort, or to the difficulty of the school task, or to plain luck. The problem with naive theory, apart from the circularity in the four factors, is that more sophisticated theories have been developed in which it can be shown that ability, to take only one example, is not fixed or stable and that it varies from moment to moment interactively with many other mental factors, not just the few in the naive theory (Baldwin, 1980; Murray, 1991).

Naive theories also yield such maxims as 'practice makes perfect', when it is clearer that 'practice only makes tired' as it is reinforced practice that makes perfect. Moreover, these naive theories give contradictory maxims like 'he who hesitates is lost' and its converse, 'fools rush in where angels fear to tread'. Naive theories, to take another example, see forgetting as the inevitable decay of stored knowledge, when the educated view is that forgetting is an active thinking process of interference and reorganization (Rose, 1993).

Additional Unfortunate Educational Consequences of Naive Views

These naive views of how the mind works coupled with equally naive views about the nature of the academic subject matters as received and objective truth further limits the benefits that can be expected from nonprofessional teaching. The naive view of subject matter shows itself principally in the areas of assessment, academic major policy requirements in teacher education, and ironically in the study of the discipline of education itself.

Classroom Assessment

The teacher's evaluation of the pupil's correct and incorrect responses provides a telling and targeted arena for distinguishing naive and professional teachers. A pupil's reasoning may look illogical to a naive teacher, while the educated teacher will see that the pupil's reasoning is intact, but has operated on different premises from those of the set problem. The naive teacher will be distressed when a pupil who had pluralized *mouse* correctly suddenly pluralizes it as *mouses* while the professional teacher will see the new plural, not as an unfortunate regression, but as a positive sign of cognitive advancement in which the pupil is exhibiting a newly developed appreciation of a linguistic rule that is merely overgeneralized in this instance. Other decrements in performance may also indicate educational progress; for example, the child's identification of the color of the ink in which a color name is printed is affected by whether the color of the ink is the same as the word or not. Readers perform quite poorly when they are asked to identify the red color of the ink in the printed word, *blue*, while nonreaders have little difficulty with the task (the Stroup effect). Along similar lines, some 6-year-old pupils not only maintain incorrectly that the longer row of two rows of five beans has more beans, but also maintain that the longer row must have more beans and would always have more beans. These errors occur even after the pupil has just counted the equal number of beans in each row. It happens that the error ('there *must* be more beans'), which seems the more serious error, is indicative of more developed reasoning than the error ('there are more beans'). Naturally, it is very difficult for the naive or spontaneous teacher to accept any error and poor performance as a marker of progress, yet the failure to see some errors as markers of progress is another serious pedagogical mistake that stems from the naive theory of teaching and learning (Bruner, 1961).

Limitations in the Traditional Academic Majors in Arts and Science

The fact that many liberal arts graduates have succeeded in meeting the expectations of the faculty in their fields of study, should not be taken as evidence that they, having majored in the subject, are ready to take up work as teachers because many of these graduates, despite their high grades, have not mastered many of the fundamental ideas of their disciplines (McDiarmid, 1992; Tyson, 1994). Surprisingly large numbers of undergraduate majors in science and engineering, for example, are simply unable to write an equation to represent the fact that there were six times as many cows in the field as farmers. Their errors are systematic — they write the equation as *6 cows = 1 farmer*, rather than correctly as *1 cow = 6 farmers*. Their mistake reveals a shallow grasp of the logic of the algebraic equation, the core idea in school mathematics.

Harmful Consequences in the Abbreviated Study of Professional Education

While mistakes in the subject matter and its assessment are a problem under any view of teacher employment, there are some who hold that some level of professional knowledge should be acquired, but that a sufficient level can be reached easily and in a short period. Such a view, while a small advance in professional education for teachers, has its own problems, however. For example, on a simple reading of Skinner, prospective teachers will believe that positive reinforcement (or reward) is an effective and preferred way to increase the likelihood of desirable pupil behavior. Without an awareness of the important exceptions and qualifications in which rewards actually weaken a response (*the over-justification phenomenon*), teachers will make mistakes by implementing procedures that run counter to their intentions (Cameron and Peirce, 1994).[1]

Similarly, upon a quick reading, the prospective teacher could get the idea that student grades should be normally distributed or that reliability is a property of a test rather than a property of those who took the test. These professional lessons cannot be easily abridged or rushed because many educational innovations are counterintuitive and subtly tied to hidden factors.

For example, it makes a difference whether addition problems, like $8 + 5 = $ ____, are presented horizontally or vertically. While a 7-year-old girl, to take another example, may understand that the amount of clay in a ball would be unaffected if the ball were flattened into a pancake, she would more than likely believe incorrectly that the same pancake would weigh more and take up less space, despite the fact that the child claims the ball and pancake have the same amount of clay. Furthermore, it is now acknowledged that many research findings are inherently provisional and must be qualified by the cohort or generation of subjects who participated in the study, as different results are obtained from different cohorts on such basic questions as whether intellectual performance decreases after a certain age. Thus, having studied the research literature at one time is not a guarantee that the results can be applied at a later time.

The Limitations in the Discipline of Education

Fortunately, it is possible to perform many routine tasks, even teaching tasks, without the benefit of great theoretical sophistication, but errors of judgment multiply when events in the classroom are not routine and when past practice is an insufficient guide. Even though there are significant gaps in it, over the last 25 years, a body of literature has developed that supports the teacher's reasoning about some educational practices and allows the teacher to evaluate the merits of some educational innovations, techniques, and policies. This literature does provide sound advice about whether a teacher should adopt *ita* (the initial teaching alphabet) that regularizes spelling by having 44 *letters*, one for each of the phonemes of English. The argument is that *ita* facilitates early reading by reducing the discrepancies between English orthography and pronunciation. The teacher who had studied Osgood's transfer surface, unlike the thousands of teachers in the USA and Britain who adopted the innovation in the 1970s or in the 1860s (when the innovation was called *phonotaby*), would know the likely benefits to reading and harm to spelling of the innovation.

Similarly there is a substantial literature on the controversial question of whether failing pupils should repeat a grade or be *socially* promoted to the next grade, or whether a gifted pupil should skip a grade, enter school early, be grouped separately from less gifted pupils. How should the *natural* teacher decide whether or not pupils should use calculators in their arithmetic lessons and homework? How can the naive teacher avoid making mistakes in answering these questions unless they study the relevant research and scholarly literature?

Despite these fragmentary examples, the lack of an encompassing, systematic and authoritative body of scholarly knowledge about teaching, let alone about the education of teachers, presents a formidable obstacle to teaching becoming the genuine profession it aspires to be. While there are many weaknesses in the naive approach to teaching, a strong case for professional education is also difficult to make owing to the failure of educational scholarship to coalesce around any powerful and generative theory of schooling and teaching. Although it is unfortunately a negative example, one test of the tentative and embryonic nature of educational scholarship is that there is still no consensus among educational scholars and practitioners about what would constitute educational malpractice (Collis, 1990).

Apart from teachers' acts which are expressly illegal, there is regrettably no accepted view, except in a few extreme instances (like no longer forcing left-hander to switch hands to write), about what educational practices should never be employed in classrooms. Even competing practices, like *whole word* and *phonic* reading methods, have reasonable levels of current scholarly support and adherents. Without a sure sense of what constitutes educational malpractice, teaching and teacher education are behind other professions which have fairly well-articulated codes of good practice, which by extension define malpractice as the failure to follow good practice.

Surprisingly, the field of teacher education is also held back by the fact that teacher education programs are not clearly connected to the educational needs of children and adolescents. These needs, of course, should be the driving principle in the design of teacher education programs, but the influence of other factors is more clearly seen (Gardner, 1991). The overriding question, whose answer legitimizes any requirement in the program, is — can the requirement be connected, on some line of reasoning, to the teacher's response to an educational need the child or adolescent truly has? The more distant the connection, the less convincing the requirement is to the students and the public. The more distant the connection to the child's needs, the less university-based teacher education is actually warranted because naive or spontaneous teaching would be adequate in this regard as it primarily serves the needs of the teacher, not the pupil's.

Educational scholarship, unfortunately, is not currently organized around the needs of children and adolescents, but rather around the academic disciplines, the separate clinical methods, and the norms of higher education. Were educational scholarship organized around children's needs and the teacher's responses to them, prospective teachers would be guided by the view that the curriculum must be shaped so that it actually solves a problem the student has. The teacher's art is in organizing the activities of the classroom so that the student's academic work solves a genuine problem the student brings to the classroom. As it is now, the problem students have is not brought by the student, but is imposed by the school and is largely artificial — namely the student has to avoid school failure by taking actions that meet the teacher's expectations — whatever they are and no matter how unrelated they are to anything the student directly cares about. To connect the curriculum to problems students truly have is an exceptionally demanding task for the teacher, which is another reason why teachers need specialized knowledge and skill.

Education as a University Subject

Teacher education is probably not warranted at the university level if the teacher is held only to the standard of presenting material truthfully and clearly, to giving students an opportunity to practice, and to testing the student's grasp of the material. The modern teacher's obligation, however, is at a much higher level. It is not enough to have the students simply learn the material, they must *understand* the material (Gardner, 1991).

Understanding, it would appear, cannot be produced by the teacher's art alone, by didactic telling, or by showing and coaching, although the pupil may learn and remember what the teacher said and may imitate what the teacher did. Understanding seems to be dependent upon the student's active investigation and experimentation, guided by *dialectic* — the teacher's skillful questioning and conversation aimed at the student's misconceptions and provoking the student to resolve discrepancy — forging, thereby, a coherent understanding of the events at hand. Unlike *solutions* that are learned, the dialectical outcomes are personal and extraordinarily resistant to forgetting.

Pupils will not understand their lessons if the teacher's role is merely to deliver information, however important information is in high level thinking.

While dialectic requires the pupil to do something overtly — to speak, respond, and question — there are other features of teaching for understanding that require the teacher to abandon the naive and spontaneous techniques as the prime teaching style in which the teacher is more active than the students.

Modern views of intelligence and cognition, for example, are clear that knowing is *negotiated, distributed, situated, constructed, developmental, and affective* — all features of knowing that entail greater degrees of student action and alter traditional schooling based on the naive view. Briefly, these features of knowing have the following characteristics:

Negotiation

The teacher does not in fact have the power, regardless of how well the school is managed, to transfer knowledge to the pupil and this means that the pupil's intellectual cooperation is a precondition of his inventing what he knows and understands. The teacher must begin the lessons with what the pupil brings to the lesson; they must negotiate what is important and privileged and to what aspects of the pupil's prior understanding the lesson will be linked and assimilated.

Distribution

Because the range of things to be known and understood exceeds the cognitive capacities of our minds, knowing must be distributed across technological devices, books, lists, and, increasingly, other people with whom we must cooperate and interact. The amount of mental space available for active processing is severely limited (perhaps to as few as seven simultaneous events), and consequently complex thought is critically dependent upon other devices for assisting the mind in its handling the other factors imbedded in complex problems.

In particular, the use of computer technology in the classroom, not only shifts instruction from the teacher to the student, but shifts the student's activity from learning to understanding (Sheingold, 1991). The Geometric Supposer, a computer program that encourages students to 'do geometry', for example, irrevocably changes the predetermined sequential nature of the school curriculum, the authority for knowledge, and generally forces instruction into a modern format (e.g., Scardamalia and Bereiter, 1991).

Situation

In the last several years the cognitive science literature unequivocally demonstrates that understanding is also dependent upon, and critically shaped by the situation in which it takes place. It proves very difficult to document aspects of thought that transcend particular circumstances and generalize as widely as traditional school pedagogy and curricula assume and hope.

Constructed

Several lines of theory suggest that what we understand is best seen as an invention or construction, provisionally and personally erected to permit sense to be made of a particular set of physical, social, and historical factors. The mind is increasingly seen as a *top down* expectancy driven and meaning seeking system.

Developmental

These mental constructions also seem to be qualitatively different from each other over time and are based upon different mechanisms and logic. It is not simply that the older pupil has more information than the younger one, which of course she does, but rather that the older pupil reasons in a new and novel manner that is not available to the younger pupil. Similarly, and more importantly perhaps, the manner of the younger pupil's and pre-adolescent's reasoning is not available to the adult teacher, especially the *spontaneous teacher*, who would have no reason to suspect that there would be these documented qualitative changes in the student's thinking over the school years.

The older pupil's understanding, in other words, cannot be reduced or decomposed into the intellectual possessions of his younger self. His new understanding emerges from his prior understanding the way *wetness* emerges from the combination of two gasses, oxygen and hydrogen. The later constructions cannot be predicted from any features of the child's prior understanding just as wetness could not be predicted from any feature of a gas.

Affective

Finally, cognition and intellectual functioning are increasingly seen as integrated with the other features of the mind. The systematic and ancient links between knowing, emotion, and motivation, must be respected in pedagogy as knowing is surely in the primary service of pervasive and powerful non-cognitive factors.

Premature Professionalism

Finally, the teaching profession is held back, ironically, by the very fact that it looks like a profession. Teaching seems to have all the attributes of the other professions — accreditation of academic degrees, professional associations, standardized tests, licenses and credentials, advanced degrees, and so forth. Teachers, since the end of the second world war, have been required to have college degrees (in some cases, graduate degrees), pass standardized examinations, meet State licenses standards, fulfill the school district's requirements for tenure, complete annual inservice update courses and show other evidence of professional growth. The irony is that none of these requirements, all demanding in their appearance, has credibility within or outside the profession as each is routinely waived when there are shortages of otherwise qualified persons for the public schools. In the case of the private schools, the States typically set and require no standards at all, a practice that only reinforces the lack of standing the current standards have.

A far better case, in fact, could be made for the waiver of the state driver's license than for the State's teaching license. It is clear, for example, that many persons can drive at a high standard[2] without having passed a particular state's license examination. Yet no State waives its own license requirements, other than on the most short-termed basis, for their residents who wish to drive their automobiles. So strong is the naive view of teaching that these same States, however, willingly and enthusiastically waive teaching license requirements, sometimes even in the name of raising the standards for the teaching profession — perhaps the only instance ever where the waiver of a standard was taken as a sign that it was being raised.

Higher Education's Continuing Role in Preparing Teachers and Educators

It could be tempting to conclude that higher education, and teacher education in particular, has already abdicated its responsibility for the kind of teacher education program that the nation requires (National Commission on Teaching and America's Future, 1996). However, when we turn to the educational reform reports, we find two things: they present very appealing, and easily granted, slogans (*all kids can learn, less is more, student as worker, spiral curriculum*, etc.). And we find the principle thinking and analyses that give these attractive reform slogans any useful meaning are taking place, and have taken place, in the academy and by scholars who, by and large, are employed by the nation's universities.

The work that needs to be done in school reform still requires the participation and leadership of the academic and professional community because the intellectual work that needs to be done, in part, continues to be the unchallenged excellence of the nation's research universities.

As the Holmes Group has pointed out (Holmes Group, 1995), the changes needed in teacher education need to occur in all its components because it could be claimed, with only some hyperbole, that the problem with today's teacher education is simply that the wrong students are studying the wrong things in the wrong places with the wrong people. Consequently, what seems to be called for are improvements in each component of the teacher education programs — the curriculum, the faculty, the site, the students, the faculty, pedagogy, and partners.

New Curriculum

In simple terms, the new curriculum for professional education needs to be *mapped backwards*, so to speak, from the student's intellectual needs to each of the university's degree requirements. There must be some line of reasoning that links each degree requirement in professional education to some need a student truly has. As it is now, the links between what teachers are required to study and what pupils need to know and be able to do are either not evident in the teacher education curriculum, or where there seems to be a reasonable link, the assumptions behind the link are usually not substantiated as either necessary or sufficient for pupil learning and understanding.

The new curriculum extends to the liberal arts component of the teacher education program. Here it focuses on a relatively unexamined, but much needed, area of thought — namely, what are the features of the compelling analogy, metaphor, and explanation of topics and concepts in the curriculum. Of all the ways in which a concept can be represented, which are generative and productive and which do not have these properties?

New Faculty

It is not just a new discipline of academic professional education that is required, but of a new kind of faculty member — a person who is equally at home in the university and public school classroom. A clinical professor, for want of a better term, is needed, who can show and do what education professors would otherwise be lecturing about in university classes on pedagogy, school psychology, counseling, etc. Clinical professors of pedagogy, for example, could be developed from two directions, so to speak — from the university faculty and from the public school faculty. It follows that the clinical faculty would practice what they preached and that criteria would need to be developed by the profession that distinguishes mediocre work in schools from work that makes a contribution to the field.

New Instructional Settings

The Professional Development School (PDS) is the new setting and it is designed to serve itself and professional education the way teaching hospitals serve medical education (Holmes Group, 1990). The PDS is meant to be the site for *as much of* the education of prospective teachers, specialists, counselors, administrators, etc. as can be managed.

The PDS is a regular public school that serves teacher education the way the teaching hospital serves medical education and the way the agricultural extension service serves the agricultural community. The PDS is the place where *all* the elements of educational reform might come together — the community, the school board, the teacher, the pupil, the principal, the social service agencies, the district, the university school of education, and the university academic disciplines.

Although the PDS has some of the attributes of laboratory and demonstration schools, the PDS is neither in the traditional senses. The great university-based laboratory schools, on the whole, failed to bring in some key reform ingredients, such as a diverse student body, an empowered teaching force, a democratic school organization, and the constraints and benefits of membership in a public school district (Nystrand, 1991).

The PDS is more than a site that university-based educational researchers can arrange in accordance with the demands of their research paradigms and designs. Nor is the PDS simply a demonstration school, important as they are, because its purpose is not to demonstrate the utility of a pedagogical or curricular innovation that does not, or could not, exist elsewhere. Apart from the PDS design itself, the Holmes Group and others are not advocating a particular pedagogical model or curriculum scope and sequence.

To understand what the PDS is, it is necessary to understand the problem in American teacher education it was designed to solve, namely the paradoxical problem of the student teaching and clinical experience components of the teacher education program at a research university. The paradox is that while teachers universally praise their student teaching experience as the most valuable part of their teacher education program, university faculties often find it the most distant and intellectually regressive aspect of the program because many student-teachers quickly conform to the traditional and prevailing practices of their supervising teacher (Murray, 1986b).

Until recently, student-teachers rarely have had the opportunity to put into practice a novel, cutting edge, or counterintuitive teaching technique. Student-teachers are no exception to the rule of *regression under stress*, and under the stress of teaching on their own, often for the first time, they invariably fall back on a set of novice teaching behaviors they possessed long before they entered teacher training. The gap between current schooling practices and sites in which ambitious and modern teaching can be practiced is the fundamental problem the PDS is designed to solve.

First and foremost, the PDS must be a modern school. It must have the features of a good school as those have emerged by consensus over the last decade from the scholarly and reform literature, most notably from the work of the Coalition of Essential Schools and the Re: Learning Project, the Effective Schools movement, the Child Development Project, Levin's Accelerated Schools Project, and Comer's School Development Program.

But it is more than a good school; it is a good school that takes on two other assignments that few other schools can take on. It assumes a genuine responsibility for the education of the next generation of educators and it assumes a responsibility to produce the new research and scholarship that is required to build the new discipline of education. The school should be designed to adhere to the following six principles.

Principle 1: Understanding as the Goal of the School

The primary and overriding goal of the school is to have all its pupils understand, not just learn, their lessons. The school must accept nothing less as a goal than students understanding, not just learning algebra, for example, and passing school tests on what he has learned. They must understand algebra and think algebraically. Understanding represents a qualitative change in what is merely learned; it is an 'all or none' event, in other words. A further implication of the principle is that whatever the situation or problem, whether encountered in the school or outside, the student should have the confidence to attack the problem intellectually.

Standards and Rubrics

The school's faculty must clarify their standards for the degree to which each pupil has understood each subject studied in the school. The standards, implicitly applied in the teacher's daily evaluation of each pupil's work, should contain criteria by which all can know whether a student's work meets the standard, is well-below it, or is well-above it. The scoring rubric, by which the student's accomplishments and progress are noted, is at the heart of the matter and is dependent upon the teacher's theory (naive or sophisticated) in two domains: 1 a theory of children's and adolescent's cognitive development and understanding, and 2 a theory of the complexity and sophistication of the subject matter. If a child arrives at the correct answer to a multiplication problem through serial addition, should that response be scored as superior or inferior to the response of a child who arrives at an incorrect answer through multiplication? Do college students, who correctly calculate the mean, median, and mode, operate at scoreably different standards of sophistication if their reasoning is based on a calculation algorithm, a mechanical model of balance, an alegraic deduction, or a special case in the calculus? Upon what theory and by what means would the instructor determine whether some solutions are more sophisticated, elegant, significant, and so forth, than other solutions?

Big Ideas

Because students require more time to understand material than to learn material, the curriculum must be restricted to matters that are truly indispensable to a life of the mind and the life of the nation. Because these matters are important, the teacher must make *complete* provisions for each pupil's understanding and mastery of them.

This feature is sometimes called the *less is more* principle in the sense that while a student will be exposed to less information, he will master what is taught so that he ends up having more. The student, in other words, will understand what he has learned.

Valid Assessment

The commonly used school tests often indicate that the pupil has mastered a subject when it is perfectly plain that in another setting the pupil has very little grasp of it.

The important things that a student has mastered should be apparent in works he can exhibit and in things he can make, compose, and design. It should be evident in the real and personally significant problems he can solve, in the stories he can tell and write, and so forth. The demonstration of recently acquired knowledge through artificial school tasks, tasks that are unlikely to occur elsewhere in life, are not as valid as real-world tasks that reveal what the pupil truly knows and can do.

Recently, this criterion of understanding has been called *authentic assessment* in the sense that the pupil's performance unambiguously indicates that the pupil has understood the true or authentic concept, skill, or disposition.

Principle 2: Creating a Learning Community

None of the other goals will be forthcoming unless the school itself is, in all aspects of its operation, a model of the community values — decency, honesty, integrity, democracy, altruism — that it hopes to have its pupils acquire. More than outcomes in their own right, these values are inherent in, and inseparable from, the negotiated dialectical process that yields understanding.

The tone of the school should make it clear that school is a place where serious and important work takes place, a place where professional people practice their profession, and so forth. The importance of the work conducted in the school is reinforced and enabled by the involvement of other important people in the community, especially parents and other supporters of the pupils, who, along with the teachers, make it clear that they also are learners whose own understanding is enhanced by the interactions with all members of the school community.

All the features of Principle 1, in other words, apply to this principle, and in fact to all the remaining design principles — and vice versa.

Principle 3: Goals of the School Apply to All Pupils

The limits of any pupil's potential achievement in a subject area cannot be predicted in the behavioral sciences with a confidence that would permit the school to have standards for some pupils that were lower than the standards for other pupils. Based upon our current knowledge of cognitive science, there would be no justification in concluding that a child was capable of understanding only some of the algebraic manipulations that needed to be taught. The fact that some children are harder to teach than others does not warrant the school's holding hard-to-teach children to lower standards of learning and understanding.

The entitlement to understand the curriculum, which is embedded in design principle 1, is similar — from a policy perspective — to the American *entitlement* to drive a car. The nation is committed to having a very wide spectrum of natural driving talent accommodated on the highways through training, elaborate and expensive engineering devices in automotive and traffic safety designs, insurance policies, and constant societal intervention and vigilance. Far from an empirical question, the issue of each and every student's understanding, like having all citizens drive, is a matter of commitment to the kind of inclusive society upon which a democratic republic depend.

Principle 4: Career Long Learning and Development

Teaching makes a claim as one of the learned professions to the degree teachers can demonstrate that they can do important things that few other college educated persons can do. Only then will they be afforded the autonomy, compensation, and prestige of the other professions. Teachers, in collaboration with their colleagues, should know enough to be fully responsive to all the demands of the classroom, calling in expert help only in rare instances when a problem exceeds their level of training and skill.

An inevitable consequence of the foregoing features of the PDS is that teachers must continually learn and understand their work differently and more powerfully. Dialectic, being inherently unpredictable in its course, minimizes the teacher's dependence on the routine and the tested. It requires the teacher, novice and expert alike, to continually invent and discover, to be a cognitive apprentice and learn and understand teaching in the same way the student comes to understand algebra.

The professional teacher, especially in the PDS, stands in sharp contrast to the traditional professional who seemingly holds all the knowledge and all the power in the relationship with the client and who, by that fact, is entitled to decide, alone or in consultation with other professionals, what is best for the client. The consequences of the traditional professional role are that knowledge is mystified and made inaccessible, social distance between the professional and client is increased, and there is no reciprocity of effort as it is the professional and not the client who works on the problem.

As these consequences of traditional professionalism clearly would work against the student's understanding, it is no surprise that teachers must have another view of professional work — work in which, by necessity, the client's ability and talent is a determining factor in the outcome of the professional's work. Teaching is the prototypical case for a view of the professional as a catalyst who creates the conditions in which the client achieves understanding, health, justice, salvation — all outcomes of the learned professional's work.

Principle 5: The PDS Research Mission

The engagement in inquiry that contributes to the scholarly literature is perhaps the most novel and distinctive aspect of the PDS mission, as it carries the school beyond the level of inquiry and reflection that is inherent in dialectical teaching for understanding.

Status Enhancement

Engaging in educational research, even as a member of a research team, may increase the teacher's self-esteem and status, increase the teacher's literacy, place the teacher on the cutting edge, and prompt the invention of research-based innovations. Each of these is a worthy outcome of a teacher's participation in a research program, but none is sufficient reason for bringing the research program to the PDS itself because there are more direct ways of raising self-esteem, status, and increasing literacy, and so on.

Research is conducted to solve practical and theoretical problems so that knowledge can be more complete and coherent. The test the PDS must meet is whether educational research is improved by this new collaboration between university researchers and classroom teachers.

Weakness in Traditional Educational Research

Until the last two decades, scholarship in education relied heavily upon findings from other disciplines, particularly the behavioral sciences. The transfer of those findings, collected in non-school settings, to issues of educational practice has been generally unsatisfying. Within the last 20 years, however, the powerful methodologies of the behavioral sciences have been turned on classrooms themselves, not just on distant laboratory simulations of instructional settings with the result that life in classrooms has been studied in such a way that fairly convincing and counter-intuitive conclusions about schooling are now possible. How does the PDS improve upon this trend?

Researchers in the behavioral sciences, as was noted above, are identifying factors and mechanisms that appear to operate uniquely in particular historical periods and contexts. In earlier research paradigms these contextual and cohort-specific factors were controlled experimentally or statistically because they were viewed as uninteresting noise or as factors whose investigation had to be postponed until better research techniques became available.

The pervasive character of these situated factors, however, has meant that consideration of these troublesome factors can no longer be postponed or ignored. Substantial effects can be attributed now to factors that appear to be features of a particular context, social or cultural group, gender, generational cohort, geographic location, historical time period, and so forth (Murray, 1991).

The Particular Case

PDS inquiry is about understanding the particular case, while traditional university-based inquiry seeks more universal explanations and contributions to general theory. PDS research is about a particular student and his or her understanding of a particular idea. At the moment, the powerful mechanisms embodied in the surviving large scale theories (e.g., Piaget, Vygotsky, Skinner, Kohlberg, etc.) provide helpful, but incomplete, accounts of the rich case study documentation of classroom life.

The situation is not unlike Piaget's rejection of traditional behavioral science methods in his pioneering investigations of the young pupil's thinking about basic school subjects in favor of extensive dialectical interviews of individual children. The logic of PDS research is in the tradition of the early Genevan work, and surprisingly, it is also in the Skinnerian tradition of single subject demonstrations of the powerful local and contingent factors that determine the events at hand.

Theoretical Contributions

While the outcome of PDS research is inherently particular, its findings must be accommodated in the end by large scale theories. It is not widely appreciated that cooperative research projects, between developmental psychologists and teachers, have advanced the field at a theoretical level. Throughout the 1960s and early 1970s, for example, researchers all over the world confirmed the young child's inability to take the point of view of another (egocentrism). In fact curriculum and instructional designs routinely accepted the immutability of the young child's limited competence (Cox, 1980).

When teachers and mothers entered graduate programs in substantial numbers in the 1970s and researched these issues, they, based on their unique familiarity with children, devised experiments that showed that young children were able to take the point of view of others. Young children, for example, were found to reduce the complexity of their speech when they spoke with even younger children, and they would select different toys for a younger child than they would select for a peer (Cox, 1980).

These inquiries led to a re-evaluation of the child's cognitive competence that in turn supported the invention of pedagogical techniques, like cooperative learning and reciprocal teaching, that now presuppose the young pupil's competence to take the point of view of another pupil (Murray, 1992). It would not be hard to document other cases where the unique perspectives of school teachers and specialists have shaped the prevailing academic learning and developmental theories (Fosnot, 1989).

Principle 6: Inventing a New Institution

Obviously, the school must be organized and financed in a manner that allows the foregoing principles to be salient features of the school. Like all other professionals, the teacher would need time for reflection, planning, and consultation (Stigler and Stevenson, 1991).

The increase in the proportion of personalized and dialectical instruction means, of course, that teachers will need time to work with all pupils on an individual basis during the school day and to evaluate the pupil's exhibitions of his or her understanding of the curriculum. In time, as increasing professional competence warrants it, and as the teacher's need to rely upon support staff outside the classroom is reduced, class enrollments could be brought in line with the overall funded teacher/ student or unit count ratios.

None of the goals of the school can be accomplished unless the teacher has the time to know each student well. Every goal is compromised when there is insufficient time for a genuine interaction between the teacher and each pupil.

Integrated Support Services

A common coordinated plan of operation, following the principle of distributed intelligence, is essential if the mission of each teacher and each of the separate state agencies that have responsibility for the welfare of children is to be achieved. The school is a sensible central point for the delivery of services that will increase the likelihood that pupils will understand their lessons. A team approach is required in which representatives of each children's service agency coordinate efforts on the child's behalf so that each member of the team is fully aware of the other's activities.

Decision-making in the PDS

The implementation of the PDS rests upon the PDS staff's ability to be thoughtful about the design principles and to make decisions in light of them. Good decisions could be said to have three connected components that, if attended to, should increase the likelihood that the decision will be correct, effective, and wise.

1   Is the decision informed; is it grounded in the pertinent academic literature and a sound reading of the local context?
2   Is the decision rational and coherent? Is there a clear rationale for the decision, a rationale which often must go beyond the scholarly literature on the subject?
3   Is the decision realistic? Is there a feasible plan for the implementation of the decision?

Adherence to the PDS six design principles rests with the school's awareness of what others have thought and written, a clear-headed analysis of the local context, a reasoned formulation of a decision that shows how it flows from the literature and the analysis, and a strategy for implementing the decision that shows how it will bring about the results the decision was meant to accomplish.

Like the six design principles and the criteria that define each, the answers to these three questions presumably influence each other. The answers are not linearly linked in a causal chain in which the former determine the latter. Rather the causal chain between them is reciprocal and interactive. The discussions among the faculty of the school that are needed to formulate a good plan of implementation, for example, can be expected to shape the answers to the other questions — the decision itself may change and evolve differently and the literature that was truly relevant to the decision may be seen differently.

The answers to the three questions are dependent upon the PDS staff's capacity for local inquiry, which is why the PDS research mission distinguishes the PDS from other school reform strategies and why the PDS reform is so critically dependent upon a deep understanding of the PDS design principles by the faculty and administration of the school.

The emergent literature on Professional Development Schools indicates that efforts to create these schools have proceeded to the point at which individual schools and universities have agreed to declare that a PDS has been 222 initiated, but not to the point where there have been documented improvements in student or teacher learning and understanding as a result of the PDS innovation (Abdul-Haqq, 1992; Winitzky, Stoddart, and O'Keefe, 1992). The literature also draws attention to several practical obstacles to PDS reform — increased costs (e.g., $48m for 18–24 PDS's in Michigan), teacher and faculty workload issues (equity, tempo, rewards, autonomy, cultural sensitivity), time constraints inherent in collective bargaining provisions, state inservice regulations, the university rewards structure, equity and access for non-PDS schools, top–down versus bottom–up initiation strategies, and so forth (Nystrand, 1991; Rushcamp and Roehler, 1992).

In the few instances when adequate provisions for these practical matters have been made, successful outcomes are not assured, however, because the obstacles to PDS reform are often deeper. The parties to the reform, even when they adopt a new technique, often do not understand the reform slogans or goals of the reform in a way that allows them to profit from the adoption of an innovation (Brown, 1991). Hampel (1992), for example, has documented a four year state-wide effort in Delaware by 15 schools to take on the attributes of the PDS and found that while some school practices changed (e.g., an increase in team approaches to instruction), the changes were fragile and not conceptually based. Thus, like school subjects learned, but not understood, the reforms are short-lived and deprived of the flexibility that characterizes knowledge.

The very goals of the PDS need to be applied to the reformers themselves because there is a resistance to press the implications of the reform goals to the point where they make a difference in the reformer's understanding (Farnham-Diggory, 1990). Too often these implications are seen in isolation and only in the negative; as what they are not — exhibitions and authentic assessments are not standardized tests (when, of course, they could be), but it is not clear what they are. *Less is more* means only less will be covered with little sense of the *more* that will result, *all kids can learn* means that special education will be eliminated, but not what will replace it. Hard thinking is needed about the practical implications of these innovations; what they are, why they are necessary, and how they *qualitatively* change schooling.

Failure to understand the implications of the *all kids can learn*, reform slogan, for example, proved to be a crippling obstacle to one of the Delaware school's reform aspirations (Hampel, 1992). Should this Delaware school, for example, have implemented fully the research finding, confirmed in hundreds of studies over decades, that student achievement is higher overall when students of different abilities are taught together than when students of differing abilities are taught in separate classrooms? Or is this research flawed because the measures of school success were too modest, or because the most able students were never really challenged, or because the tests of ability were poorly related to the lessons? Or is the research literature largely irrelevant because the issue is about the kind of society we want, not how hard it is to achieve it? Is the issue akin to the nation's goal, mentioned earlier, of having nearly all its citizens drive cars by re-engineering the driving task so that wider bands of the driving-talent spectrum can be accommodated on the roads? The Delaware experience indicates that the implementation of the PDS is critically dependent on the issue of how well the reformers answer the foregoing questions.

Three Tests of Misunderstanding

There are at least three indicators that the reformers have not understood the PDS design principles.

1   One is the failure to see that the principles are interconnected and that none can be implemented without the others. These principles are interrelated and are implications of each other. If any one were truly present, the others would be joined with it, and similarly the denial of any one undermines the others. Less is only more if each student understands; she will not understand if she is not expected to, nor if the principles of active cognition are violated and so forth.

2   A second is that the principles are not new, but have clear antecedents in historical practice and theory (Farnham-Diggory, 1990).

3   The third is the failure to see that the principles are developmental and cannot, as a result, be achieved quickly. The PDS design principles entail qualitative or developmental change on the part of the school. Changes of this sort, in contrast to quantitative or learned changes, cannot be accelerated (Murray, 1991); sudden or effortless changes, in fact, are taken by developmental psychologists as a sign that the change was not developmental or fundamental, but rather a change that is temporary, caused by a peripheral mechanism, and not authentic.

Smith (1989) has shown in another Delaware PDS site that even under ideal teacher-coaching conditions — one on one — highly motivated, knowledgeable, and experienced teachers were still unsure and shaky after 10 months of practice in their efforts to implement a PDS teaching technique. Even though they had practiced the technique in a variety of settings, had video and stimulated recall analysis of their teaching performance, and had personal feedback of their efforts, they were at risk whenever the lesson took an unusual turn (Smith and Neale, 1990).

In summary, each principle for the design of the PDS is derived from the literature, represents a qualitative change in school practice, and can be derived from the other principles. Schools that drive toward understanding (principle 1) cannot set the principle aside for some students (principle 3), nor can they succeed without a school-wide approach (principle 2), or without a *professional* teaching staff (principle 4) that has a capacity for inquiry (principle 5) embedded in a new organization and decision-making system (principle 6). Similarly principle 5 (inquiry) cannot be implemented independently of principles 4 (community) and 6 (new organization) in the service of 1 (understanding) and 3 (same goals for all) by the staff described in 2 (professional teachers). Principle 3 (same goals for all), to take another example, only makes sense, in terms of principle 1 (understanding) and is feasible only if the other principles are in place in the school's design.

Finally, it should be clear that the PDS is connected, not just to the university teacher education program, but to every other stock holder in the reform of schooling. The PDS is the place where all the elements of educational reform come together — the community, the school board, the teacher, the pupil, the principal, the social service agencies, the district, the university school of education, and the university academic disciplines.

New Instructional Arrangement

One of the more far reaching proposals for restructuring teacher education, apart from the invention of the PDS, is the notion that educators should be educated as they would function. Since we increasingly expect that teachers, counselors, school psychologists, curriculum specialists, and administrators should work as a team, it would follow that future educators, despite their delineated roles and licenses, should be grouped as cohorts or teams and be educated with that outcome in mind.

Along the same lines, it follows that as much of the professional curriculum as possible should be common to each of the professional roles. The recommendation is based upon more than the efficacy of team-based problem solutions. It is based also on the fact that each of the professional education roles — teacher, counselor, administrator, etc. — is legitimized by its unique hypotheses and suppositions about the underlying causes of a student's performance. When the student habitually fails to learn his lessons, for example, each professional specialist offers its own group's explanation for the event. The special educator sees the student's chronic failure as a matter of an inappropriate curriculum or pedagogy, the counselor sees the problem as a matter of a cluster of non-school factors (e.g., the student's self-esteem, anxiety over non-school issues, family dynamics, etc.), the school psychologist often sees the problem in terms of the student's tested ability, the administrator may see the difficulty in terms of the school's organization or student grouping or promotion policies, and so on. The point is that each specialist, like the blind discovering the elephant, has an explanation of the student's problem that could benefit from the others' perspectives. The education of each should be arranged so that, *as often as possible*, each has the opportunity to validate and confirm the limitations of his or her own guild's perspectives through the intellectual challenge of other educational specialists' interpretations of the same events.

New Students

Nearly every reform group has seen the need to expand the composition of the cohort of professional educators to include members of several under-represented groups. Special efforts are called for, like the Holmes Scholar initiative, to recruit people of color into the ranks of the next generation of the education professorate. Currently, there are stark under-representations in professional education of people of color, men and women in selected teaching fields and roles, and over-representations of low scorers on academic measures of prior accomplishment everywhere in the system.

New Scholarship

Contemporary educational scholarship is largely derivative and on the margins of theories and research tools developed in other disciplines. What is needed in our field is inquiry about the particular case *in addition to* traditional university-based inquiry that seeks more universal explanations and contributions to general theory. Professionals require research, and research techniques, about a particular student and his or her understanding of a particular idea, for example. This is the reason research in the PDS is directed at local action and the particular child. It is about matters that apparently are not penetrated easily by traditional experimental designs that employ controls for chance and other seemingly irrelevant factors. It is research, in other words, that serves the needs of professionals who work in particular places.

The Need for Partnerships

No matter how successful the ed school would be in creating a new curriculum for new students in new settings working with a new kind of ed school faculty member, and so forth, the problems ed schools and public schools face still might not change very much because there are large-scale factors operating outside the academy that impact the academy's work. For this the problems of American education, let alone teacher education, are beyond the capacity of universities to solve on their own, no matter how well they might conceptualize and administer their teacher education programs.

The problem is that the proper work of the various agents in the profession of education do not intersect or overlap. Each stops short of what is needed — the university gives a degree based upon requirements that are rational only within the academy, the reform organizations and policy-makers publish reports and take no further action on them, commissions announce or assert standards but have neither the will nor the capacity to enforce them, unions write contracts that preserve the current arrangements, school boards and administrators settle for order and peace in their schools, teachers strike Horace's compromises everywhere, and the public has a romantic view of schooling that was forged in childhood memories and storytelling.

Having a problem, such as universities have in a case like this, however, is not a sufficient condition for the formation of a partnership as there are other time-tested ways to solve problems that cannot be solved alone — consultation, or cooperation, or collaboration, for example. In these instances, the parties who seek to solve their problems by consultation, cooperation or collaboration with others, are invariably approaching the problem as they would have approached it alone, but now they have more strength or resources to accomplish what they attempted on their own. Thus, universities, following this line of approach, would improve the quality of their degree programs quantitatively — with more topics, more credits, more clinical experience, more arts and science requirements, better management, and so forth.

In partnerships, however, the parties do not do what they would have done alone, but now do jointly. A partnership is a new entity in which each member's work changes by virtue of its place in the partnership. Successful partnerships depend upon the formulation and acceptance of genuine and important problems that each partner has and cannot solve on its own. It is not just that the parties who have and cannot solve a problem collaborate, pool resources, form a confederation and simply coordinate their work more effectively. In that instance their work is essentially as it was before the confederation, but now it is joint or coordinated.

Some problems are complex and simply will not yield to more and better coordinated effort and in those cases new entities and organizations may need to be created, whose work — collectively — is qualitatively different from what it would have been before the partnership was formed.

The kind of partnership teacher educators seek and require to accomplish their goals is likely to adhere to the following principles:

1 That it be informed and based upon scholarship and research.
2 That it include all parties in the profession.
3 That it include all levels in the field from local schools, through districts, through state and regional groupings to the national level.
4 That the local partnership be a microcosm of the national partnership with all the local counterparts of the national groups actively participating.
5 That it be democratic, i.e., all voices in the partnership at each level have influence in the governance and work of the partnership.
6 That the partnership be a community of inquiry and scholarship, a learning community as it is sometimes put.
7 That it build a consensus for professional action and that its members be committed to taking action.

As an example of the kind of problem that surrounds university degree programs for educators and why university partnerships with the organizations and agencies outside the university are critical to the very design of the degree program, consider the following issues in the mere alignment of academic degrees with other factors in the teacher's career:

1 The BA and/or MAT degree requirements ought to be necessary and sufficient for the State license standards as they might also be embedded in INTASC, NASDTEC, or the Praxis series standards and rubrics. Similarly, the degree requirements would be compatible with accreditation standards (e.g., NCATE) for the institution, the university's promotion and tenure standards for the faculty's work, and the university's standards for the faculty members' own doctoral degree.

2 The school district's hiring and tenure decisions should also be based upon criteria that are connected to the former. These decisions also need to be supported and reinforced by the collective bargaining agreements the district and the professional association negotiate. Further, and more difficult, these decisions need to conform to the public perceptions and expectations of the teacher's duties and performance.

3 The MA or MEd degree requirements, linked as above to the BA/MAT degree, should also be connected to the NBPTS standards. And these in turn need to be connected to the acquisition of skills, knowledge, and dispositions associated with advanced professionals — counselors, psychologists, administrators, specialists, and so forth; that is, they must support the development of complete teachers, who require less and less assistance from experts who work outside the classroom.

4 The PhD/EdD requirements should similarly be linked to the further acquisition of *complete* teacher competence, but now include the research skills of the clinical faculty member, the teacher or the teachers, who has a leadership position in the PDS.

5 Finally, there is the perfection of the clinical faculty/classroom teacher role, which entails an ongoing connection with the university as an instructor in the university's degree programs, particularly in the segments that are located in the PDS. Clearly, the alignment of all these factors requires that all parties with direct responsibility for each factor must be part of an entity devoted to their overlapping interests and has its own responsibility for the intersection of their separate responsibilities. The alignment also entails a reciprocal influence among the factors as each one causes nonlinear changes in the others.

In conclusion, professional decisions have the following interactive and reciprocally caused components. Each evolves over the course of a professional career and each is linked to the mission of the university and its school of education. They are based, for the sake of explication, on three interrelated factors:

1 Professional knowledge — which in turn has at least three components. Scholarship or what is known, research which is devoted to the gap between

what scholarship yields and what is needed for adequate professional knowledge, and experience that serves the professional who has to act before the
research is successfully completed and/or the scholarship is mastered.

2   Intention — a decision or formulation or an idea of what a professional
should or would do.

3   A professional act — which reciprocally interacts with the student's
actions and those of other professionals and is inextricably connected to
the reservoir of professional knowledge and intention.

Each component, presumably, evolves over a career. Teaching actions, for example, that were based initially upon the teacher's assumption of full responsibility
for the student's learning, shift toward more mature and advanced teaching actions
in which the student takes greater responsibility for her learning. Thus, we expect to
see a progression from the naive and spontaneous teaching skill of *show and tell*,
through discussion regimes, and through cooperative and reciprocal learning for-
mats, to dialectic. As these advanced professional actions are often counterintuitive
and rarely found in the naive and spontaneous approaches, they are themselves
dependent upon a program of instruction of the sort called for in the modern
university-based teacher education degree program. In this resides the case for the
continuation and enhancement of professional education programs at the university
and college.

Acknowledgment

This chapter draws on arguments advanced in MURRAY, F.B. (1996) 'Beyond nat-
ural teaching: The case for professional education', in MURRAY, F.B. (ed.) *The Teacher
Educator's Handbook*, San Francisco: Jossey-Bass, pp. 3–13 and in MURRAY, F.B.
(1995) 'Design principles and criteria for professional development schools' in
PETRIE, H. (ed.) *Professionalization, Partnership and Power: Building Professional
Development Schools*, New York: SUNY Press, pp. 23–38.

Notes

1   See further comment on the over-justification phenomenon in the Spring, 1996 issue of
the *Review of Educational Research*, **66**, 1, pp. 1–51.
2   For example, those who have lived in other states or have driven farm machinery on
private lands.

References

ABDAL-HAQQ, I. (1992) 'Professional development schools: An annotated bibliography of
selected ERIC sources', *Journal of Teacher Education*, **43**, 1, pp. 42–5.

BALDWIN, A. (1980) *Theories of Child Development* (2nd ed.), New York: John Wiley.

BEILIN, H. (1971) 'The training and acquisition of logical operations', in ROSSKOPF, M.F., STEFFE, L.P. and TABACK, S. (eds) *Piagetian Cognitive-development Research and Mathematical Education*, Washington, DC: National Council of Teachers of Mathematics, Inc.

BERLINER, D. (1988) 'Implications of studies of expertise in pedagogy for teacher education and evaluation', *New Directions for Teacher Assessment: Proceedings of the 1988 ETS Invitational Conference*, Princeton, NJ: Educational Testing Service, pp. 39–68.

BROPHY, J. and GOOD, T. (1986) 'Teacher behavior and student achievement', in WITTROCK, M. (ed.) *Handbook of Research on Teaching* (3rd ed.) New York: Macmillan, pp. 328–75.

BROWN, R. (1991) *Schools of Thought: How the Politics of Literacy Shape Thinking in the Classroom*, San Francisco: Jossey-Bass Publishers.

BRUNER, J. (1961) *The Process of Education*, Cambridge: Harvard University Press.

CAMERON, J. and PIERCE, D. (1994) 'Reinforcement, reward, and intrinsic motivation: A meta-analysis', *Review of Educational Research*, **64**, 3, pp. 363–423.

CHOY, S.P., BOBBITT, S.A., HENKE, R.R., MEDRICH, E.A., HORN, L.J. and LIEBERMAN, J. (1993) *America's Teachers: Profile of a Profession*, DC: National Center for Education Statistics.

COLLIS, J. (1990) *Educational Malpractice*, Charlottesville, VA: The Michie Co.

COX, M. (1980) *Are Young Children Egocentric?*, New York: St Martin's Press.

EVERTSON, C., HAWLEY, W. and ZLOTNICK, M. (1985) 'Making a difference in educational quality through teacher education', *Journal of Teacher Education*, **36**, 3, pp. 2–12.

FARNHAM-DIGGORY, S. (1990) *Schooling*, Cambridge, MA: Harvard University Press.

FOSNOT, C. (1989) *Inquiring Teachers, Inquiring Learners: A Constructivist Approach for Teaching*, New York: Teachers College Press.

GARDNER, H. (1991) *The Unschooled Mind: How Children Think and How Schools Should Teach*, New York: Basic Books.

HAMPEL, R. (1992) 'Re: Learning: The third year', Unpublished manuscript, Newark, DE: University of Delaware.

HAWLEY, W. and ROSENHOLTZ, S. (1984) 'Good schools: What research says about improving student achievement', *Peabody Journal of Education*, **61**, 4.

HEIDER, F. (1958) *The Psychology of Interpersonal Relations*, New York: Wiley.

HOLMES GROUP (1986) *Tomorrow's Teachers*, East Lansing, Michigan: The Holmes Group.

HOLMES GROUP (1990) *Tomorrow's Schools: Principles for the Design of Professional Development Schools*, East Lansing, Michigan: The Holmes Group.

HOLMES GROUP (1995) *Tomorrow's Schools of Education*, East Lansing, Michigan: The Holmes Group.

HOWE, H. (1990) 'Thinking about the forgotten half', *Teachers College Record*, **92**, pp. 293–305.

McDIARMID, G.W. (1992) *The Arts and Sciences as Preparation for Teaching*, Issue Paper 92-3, E. Lansing: National Center for Research on Teacher Learning.

MURRAY, F. (1978) 'Teaching strategies and conservation training', in LESGOLD, A.M., PELLEGRINO, J.W., FOKKEMA, S. and GLASER, R. (eds) *Cognitive Psychology and Instruction*, New York: Plenum, pp. 419–28.

MURRAY, F. (1986a) 'Goals for the reform of teacher education: An executive summary of the Holmes Group report', *Phi Delta Kappan*, September, pp. 28–32.

MURRAY, F. (1986b) 'Teacher education', *Change Magazine*, September/October, pp. 18–21.

MURRAY, F. (1990) 'The conversion of truth into necessity', in OVERTON, W. (ed.) *Reasoning, Necessity and Logic: Developmental Perspectives*, Hillsdale, NJ: Erlbaum Associates, pp. 183–204.

MURRAY, F. (1991) 'Questions a satisfying developmental would answer: The scope of a complete explanation of developmental phenomena', in REESE, H. (ed.) *Advances in Child Development and Behavior*, (vol. 23), New York: Academic Press, Inc., pp. 39–47.

MURRAY, F. (1992) 'Restructuring and constructivism: The development of American educational reform', in BEILIN, H. and PUFALL, P. (eds) *Piaget's Theory: Prospects and Possibilities*, Hillsdale, New Jersey: Lawrence Erlbaum Associates, pp. 287–308.

NATIONAL COMMISSION ON TEACHING AND AMERICA'S FUTURE (1996) *What Matters Most: Teaching for America's Future*, National Commission on Teaching and America's Future.

NYSTRAND, R. (1991) *Professional Development Schools: Toward a New Relationship for Schools and Universities* (Trends and Issues Paper No. 4), Washington, DC: ERIC Clearinghouse on Teacher Education, pp. 1–25.

OAKES, J. (1985) *Keeping Track: How Schools Structure Inequality*, New Haven: Yale University Press.

OGLE, L., ALSALAM, N. and ROGERS, G. (1991) *The Condition of Education 1991*, DC: National Center for Educational Statistics.

ROSE, S. (1993) *The Making of Memory*, New York: Anchor Books.

RUSHCAMP, S. and ROEHLER, L. (1992) 'Characteristics supporting change in a professional development school', *Journal of Teacher Education*, **43**, 1, pp. 19–27.

SCARDAMALIA, M. and BEREITER, C. (1991) 'Higher levels of agency for children in knowledge building: A challenge for the design of new knowledge media', *The Journal of the Learning Sciences*, **1**, pp. 37–68.

SHEINGOLD, K. (September, 1991) 'Restructuring for learning with technology: The potential for synergy', *Phi Delta Kappan*, **73**, pp. 17–27.

SMITH, D. (1989) 'The role of teacher knowledge in teaching conceptual change science lessons', Unpublished doctoral dissertation, University of Delaware.

SMITH, D. and NEAL, D. (1990) 'The construction of subject matter in primary science teaching', in BROPHY, J. (ed.) *Advances in Research on Teaching Subject Matter Knowledge*, Greenwich, CT: JAI Press.

SMITH, L. (1993) *Necessary Knowledge: Piagetian Perspectives on Constructivism*, Hillsdale, NJ: Erlbaum.

STEPHENS, J.M. (1967) *The Process of Schooling: A Psychological Examination*, NY: Holt, Rinehart and Winston.

STIGLER, J. and STEVENSON, H. (1991) 'How Asian teachers polish each lesson to perfection', *American educator*, **15**, pp. 12–20.

SYNDER, T. (1993) *120 Years of American Education: A Statistical Portrait*, DC: National Center for Education Statistics.

TYSON, H. (1994) *Who Will Teach the Children: Progress and Resistance in Teacher Education*, New York: Jossey-Bass.

WINITZKY, N., STODDART, T. and O'KEEFE, P. (1992) 'Great expectations: Emergent professional development schools', *Journal of Teacher Education*, **43**, 1, pp. 3–18.

6 The Problem of Evidence in Teacher Education

Mary M. Kennedy[1]

The current wave of skepticism about the effects of teacher education is not new. Almost since its inception, the need for, and value of, teacher education has been doubted by non-teacher educators. Some of these doubts stem from beliefs that teachers are born rather than made, some from beliefs that the practice of teaching is not particularly difficult, some from beliefs that teaching can only be learned in the doing. For their part, teacher educators have conducted research on the effectiveness of their efforts, in part to learn how to improve their practices, but also in part to defend themselves from external skeptics.

Several years ago I reviewed these approaches to research on teacher education with an eye toward their potential to help teacher educators understand their practices (Kennedy,1996). My aim in this chapter is to examine the same approaches, this time from the skeptic's point of view.

Five broad strategies, or genres, for research in teacher education have been and are still in widespread use. They are summarized in Table 6.1. Each offers us a glimpse of one aspect of teacher education and one aspect of its influence on teachers, but none is broad enough to capture the entire story. Indeed, if a study were sufficient to capture the entire story, it would be so hopelessly difficult, time-consuming, and expensive to complete that it will probably never exist. As I review each genre, I ask three questions of it. First, what aspects of teacher education does it look at? Second, what outcomes does it look at? And third, on what basis does the research argue that there is a causal relationship between these aspects of programs and these outcomes?

Multiple Regression

The first genre, multiple regression, is most familiar to skeptics of teacher education and least familiar to teacher educators themselves. Researchers working within this genre are not testing any particular theory about teacher education. Instead, they are engaged in a relatively open-ended search for contributions to pupil learning, and one of the possible contributions is teacher education.

These studies were originally stimulated by, and are based on, the *Equality of Educational Opportunity* (EEOS) Study (Coleman, 1966), and many actually used the EEOS data. One of the earliest and best of these studies was conducted by Eric Hanushek (1971, 1972). He began by asking whether teachers differed in their

Table 6.1 Five approaches to research on the contribution of teacher education to teaching

Genre	Argument	Aspect of TE examined	Outcome examined
Multiple Regression	If teachers who have taken more credits in teacher education foster greater gains in student achievement than teachers with fewer credits, then teacher education has made a difference	Number of teacher-education courses or degrees held	Student achievement scores
Follow-up Surveys	If teacher-education graduates claim that their teacher education courses were valuable, then they were	Specific courses	Alumni perceptions
Comparison of credentialed and non-credentialed teachers	If teachers who have received formal teaching certificates teach differently than other teachers, then teacher education has made a difference	Presence or absence of a credential, types of credentials	Classroom behavior
Experiments	If teachers participating in one program approach improve their skill more than other teachers do, then this approach has a greater impact	Discrete course segments or course procedures	Ability to perform specified behaviors on demand
Longitudinal studies of change	If candidates express one view at the beginning of their program and another view later on, and if they refer to their courses to justify their views, then teacher education has made a difference	Whole programs as experienced by candidates	Verbally expressed attitudes and beliefs

ability to increase student achievement, after taking into account the child's initial achievement and various aspects of the child's background. Hanushek found that teachers did make a difference. That is, the teacher a child happened to have could significantly influence the child's achievement growth for the school year. Seeing that this was the case, Hanushek then tried to see which particular teacher characteristics seemed to account for these differences. Among the variables Hanushek examined were the teacher's college major, the number of hours of graduate coursework teachers had taken, and the length of time since the teachers' most recent educational experience. Hanushek found that neither college major nor the number of graduate credits teachers had taken were significantly related to student achievement. Variables that were related, on the other hand, included the teachers' general verbal ability and the recency of their last educational experience. These two variables do not necessarily reflect teacher education courses per se, although verbal ability may reflect the teachers' college education in general. The recency of the teachers' educational experiences may reflect either the nature of the experiences or the teachers' interest in continued professional learning.

Another important study that focused on teacher education was done by Murnane and Phillips (1981). Like Hanushek, they began by testing to see whether teachers made a difference, found that they did, and then tried to see what aspects of teachers seemed to account for these differences. But instead of generating a single equation which included all possible contributions to student achievement, they developed two separate equations, one of which included measures of teacher *behaviors* (e.g. circulating around the room to correct seatwork, use demonstrations, make students repeat poor work, etc.) and the second of which included measures of teacher *characteristics* (e.g. years of experience, possession of a masters degree and prestige of college attended). Their data indicated that teacher behaviors were better predictors of student achievement than were teacher characteristics. Moreover, of those characteristics that Murnane and Phillips examined, neither of their education-related variables — possession of a Masters degree or prestige of college attended — appeared to be relevant to student achievement.

Many skeptics of teacher education reside in the policy community, and they may be more aware of this body of research than of the others that I describe below. If these multiple regressions were the only studies available on the merits of teacher education, it would be easy to conclude that teacher education contributes very little to teaching. But there are some weaknesses in this genre, and these need to be considered before a conclusion is drawn.

Aspects of Teacher Education Examined

The aspects of teacher education that these researchers examine are often relatively crude quantifiable indicators such as whether or not a teacher has a teaching credential, whether he or she has a masters degree, or, occasionally, the number of teacher education courses the teacher took in college. These measures may not be very meaningful, for two reasons.

First, virtually every teacher in these studies *already holds a bachelors degree* and is already certified to teach. The percentage of teachers lacking a bachelors degree was only 7 per cent in 1966, and has since fallen to less than 1 per cent (National Center for Education Statistics, 1989). Presumably, then, virtually all of these teachers have attained the minimum educational background required for teaching. The variations that are measured, therefore, are not variations in the required core of teacher education, but instead variations in what other educational courses teachers have elected to take.

Second, since the United States does not have a centralized curriculum, and since many states give teacher educators considerable leeway in their program designs, teacher education programs can look remarkably different from one institution to the next. One recent study suggested that the number of education credits required by each state ranged from 18 to 90 for elementary teacher candidates (Council of Chief State School Officers, 1988). Not only does the number of education courses taken differ, but their content and character differ as well. These differences reflect different ideas about what teachers need to know and about how teachers learn. By failing to measure the substantive differences among programs, researchers in this genre may miss the very aspect of teacher education that is most likely to make a difference. Moreover, because there is so much variation in the content and character of teacher education programs, measures of the *amount* of teacher education do not measure of a unitary thing. Some teachers may have received extensive education in a mediocre program while others received modest education in a very good program. It should not be surprising, therefore, that these measures generally do not correlate highly with measures of student achievement gains. When a measurement scale does not measure a unitary thing, it is hard to show a relationship between it and other things.

A recent study by Ferguson and Womack (1993) corrects this problem in two ways. First, instead of simply tallying up courses, they document the actual courses students took during their undergraduate preparation and correlated the presence or absence of each course with teaching performance during student teaching. Second, instead of using presence or absence of a disciplinary major as their indicator of subject matter knowledge, they use both grade point average within the subject and score on the subject matter portion of the National Teachers Exam (NTE). With these alterations in method, the researchers found substantial relationships between the teacher education courses that teacher candidates took and the quality of the teaching they demonstrated.

Outcomes

Researchers practicing within this genre take student achievement, or better still, gains in student achievement, as their primary outcome. Since teachers often aim to create benefits to students that extend far beyond those measured by achievement tests, student achievement outcomes measure some, but not all, of the important goals of education. In fact, whether such tests even measure the most important outcomes of schooling is a contentious issue in the current reform rhetoric. Gains in student achievement, then, constitute a very narrow outcome for estimating the contributions of teacher education to teaching.

The Logic of the Argument

The logic of these studies goes something like this: if teachers who have taken more credits in teacher education foster greater gains in student achievement than teachers with fewer credits (after taking into account differences in entering achievement, family background, and so forth) then these teacher education courses have made a difference. Because such differences have rarely been observed, researchers within this genre tend to be skeptics and often argue against policies that require teachers to take certain numbers of credits, or that pay teachers more if they have masters degrees, for instance (see, e.g. Murnane et al., 1991).

Studies in this genre also depend heavily on the ability of complex statistical techniques to ferret out extraneous variables that can influence student achievement — variables such as the child's family background, for instance. The success of each study depends on whether the researcher captures all the relevant variables, and studies can differ substantially in their thoroughness. But there are always influences that cannot be measured. Take, for instance, school climate. There is ample evidence that school climate contributes to student achievement (Brophy and Good, 1986), but less is known about how and why school climate matters. But suppose that the reason school climate contributes to student achievement is because it enables teachers to teach better. If that is the case, then the effects of the teachers' educational background might be masked by variations in school climates. It may be that teachers' educational backgrounds make a difference *within each school climate*, but these effects are not apparent when a wide range of school climates are involved in the study. Or, it is possible that teacher education only makes a difference within reasonably positive school climates, and that teacher education cannot help teachers teach better when they are working in especially difficult schools.

These caveats should not be taken as an excuse for teacher education, however. No doubt a skeptic would respond to these arguments by pointing out that teacher education should have a strong enough impact that it can be seen in any school climate. Still, there are enough limitations in this research genre that it cannot be depended upon to provide unambiguous evidence for the merits of teacher education. The aspects of teacher education that it measures often are degrees, quantities of course work, or courses taken after the bachelors degree, rather than quality or content of these courses. The outcomes it measures represent only a narrow slice of the outcomes teacher educators hope to influence, and to the extent that its arguments about the relationship between teacher education and student achievement are based on incomplete lists of possible influences on student achievement lacks credibility.

Follow-up Surveys

While multiple regression studies are most common outside of the teacher education community, the most common genre within this community is the survey of
graduates. This genre is popular in part because it is relatively inexpensive and
simple to do, and in part because the accreditation system devised by the National
Council for Accreditation of Teacher Education (NCATE) has traditionally required
some form of program evaluation. Adams and Craig (1983) surveyed teacher education programs in 1980 and found that 74 per cent claimed to be conducting some
sort of follow-up of their graduates.

These surveys generally use one of two strategies to estimate the contributions
of teacher education. Either they ask teachers to assess their own knowledge and
skills — that is, to assess their own ability to teach — or they ask the teachers to
assess the merits of particular courses within the program.

Pigge's (1978) survey, though old, is a good example of the genre. Pigge
developed a list of 26 competencies taken from the Bowling Green curriculum on
which the respondents were to rate themselves. On Pigge's five-point scale, most
self-assessments were quite high. The lowest average self-assessment was close
to the mid-point of the scale. Few teachers, then, viewed themselves as seriously
lacking in any of these teaching competencies. Pigge also asked teachers to estimate how important these various competencies were to their work and to indicate
where they learned these competencies. Generally speaking, teachers thought that
the competencies *most* necessary to their work were learned on the job, whereas
those considered *least* necessary were acquired in their teacher education programs.

In an interesting study by Clark, Smith, Newby and Cook (1985), teachers
were observed in their classrooms and then asked where they got the ideas for what
they did. The most frequently cited source for a teaching idea was that the teacher
generated it him- or herself. Second most prominent was the cooperating teacher
with whom the teacher had undergone student teaching. Teacher education faculty
were given credit for only 17 per cent of the practices teachers were asked about.

The vast majority of follow-up surveys are intended for use only within a
particular institution. Many are circulated only within their institutions, and many
others are circulated only through the ERIC (Education Resource Information Center)
system. Only a few are published in journals. This means that policy-makers and
skeptics are not likely to have seen any of these studies. In fact, teacher educators
themselves may not know much about findings from other institutions. However,
occasionally, a non-teacher educator conducts a follow up survey, and these surveys tend to have wider audiences. One such survey was conducted by the National
Education Association (NEA). NEA surveyed its members and asked them to evaluate
the contributions of 14 different sources of knowledge about teaching, one of which
was preservice teacher education (Smylie, 1989). The preservice teacher education
program was ranked by these teachers 13th out of 14 sources of knowledge. The
highest-rated sources of knowledge were direct experience, consultation with other
teachers, and independent study and observations of other teachers, all of which are
entirely in the control of the teacher him or herself. The only source of knowledge

rated less useful than undergraduate teacher education was school district sponsored inservice programs. To the extent that policy-makers and skeptics have any
exposure to this genre of research, their exposure will be to studies like this one
rather than to studies conducted by individual institutions. But this study and others
like it, does not help the cause of teacher education.

Aspect of Teacher Education Examined

Most follow-up surveys ask graduates to assess particular program offerings — the
math methods course, the student teaching experience, or the placement service.
These program features are of less interest to the field as a whole than they are to
the particular institutions which provide them. In fact, the more useful a survey
becomes to its own institution, the less useful it will likely become to others, for local
utility depends on forming questions that are highly specific to the local situation.
The genre was never intended for use beyond the particular institution.

Outcomes

Almost universally, follow-up surveys depend on teachers' judgments of their own
knowledge or skill, or of the value of the courses they took, as their indicator of
program impact. Most surveys provide the teacher with a list of knowledge or
competencies or a list of program courses, and ask the teachers to rate themselves
or their alma mater on something like a five-point scale.

Reliance on teacher judgment is a substantial limitation in these studies, for
several reasons. First, we don't know what *criteria* teachers use when they make
these assessments, or whether their criteria would be the same as an independent
observer's criteria. Koziol and Burns (1986) found that teachers' self-assessments
could be developed to agree more with assessments of independent observers by
focusing the assessment form on specific situations (e.g. first-period social studies
or the teaching of a particular body of content), rather than on teaching in general,
and by using the same set of questions on repeated occasions. In this way, teachers
had a chance to learn to attend to those practices that the researchers were interested in. These conditions, however, are never met in follow-up surveys.

Teacher self-assessments may also be influenced by emotional responses to
the initial difficulties of developing a solid teaching practice. Gaede (1978) found
that teachers' self-assessments gradually increased as teachers moved through their
teacher preparation programs, but decreased substantially during their first year of
teaching. Certainly these teachers did not suddenly know less than they had known
when they were seniors, but just as certainly, they *felt* they knew less once they
encountered the demands of real teaching.

Similarly, when a teacher claims a program has contributed to her knowledge
or skill, or has not contributed to her knowledge or skill, we don't know how
accurate these judgments are. It is highly likely that teachers do not recall what

they knew or were able to do five years earlier. Strang, Badt, and Kauffman (1997) provide some evidence that teachers cannot accurately recall their prior capability. They measured teachers' skills both before and after a program treatment, and they also asked teachers afterward to estimate the degree to which they had changed during the program. The researchers' independent assessment of teacher change showed their proficiency moving from 52 per cent to 87 per cent on their performance scale. However, the *teachers'* assessments of their own change indicated movement from 81 per cent to 85 per cent. Teachers, therefore, may not be good judges of whether they have learned from a program or not.

Generally speaking then, outcome measures employed by follow-up surveys are weakened by their heavy reliance on teachers' judgments of themselves, of their own growth, and of what their programs might have contributed to their growth.

The Logic of the Argument

The logic of 'ask the teacher' studies goes something like this: If teachers who choose to respond to the survey (and this is a big if, for response rates on these surveys are often very low) claim they are competent in certain areas, or if they claim they have (or have not) learned something valuable from their teacher education programs, they are probably correct. Since follow-up surveys rarely directly measure teachers' knowledge or skills, the burden of the argument falls entirely on the teachers' judgments.

These studies are also weak in that, like the multiple regressions, they usually fail to take into account the teaching context. Some teaching situations are far more challenging than others, some provide less assistance to new teachers than others, and some demand different kinds of practices than their programs prepared them for. To the extent that any of these contextual differences might influence teacher judgments, the findings are even more difficult to interpret.

Thus, to make any sense of these data, we have to assume that (a) teachers use the same criteria to judge themselves and their programs as teacher educators, policy-makers, or educational researchers would use; (b) teachers' assessments of their own knowledge and skills, and of their prior knowledge and skills, are not influenced by their emotional states; and (c) the context in which teachers are teaching has no bearing on their assessments of themselves or their teacher education programs. I argued before that these studies are of little use to policy-makers, but I also believe they are also of little use to teacher educators. In fact, the negative evaluations teachers provided in the NEA study could, when combined with multiple regression studies, enhance the skeptics' case.

Comparing Credentialed and Non-credentialed Teachers

Another popular genre, used by both teacher educators and by their critics, consists of comparing teachers with different educational backgrounds. Usually, these researchers focus on a particular school district or geographic region, find all the teachers who have provisional or emergency credentials, and compare them with teachers in the same region who are fully certified. A recent variation on this theme is to compare teachers who received their certifications through alternative routes with those who received traditional certifications. Once two groups of teachers have been identified, the researchers observe the classroom practices of both groups in search of differences. These studies offer several advantages over follow-up surveys: they rely on an independent observer to assess the teachers' practice, they compare two groups who have different kinds of educational backgrounds, and they often control for the influence of context because they sample within limited geographic regions.

The frequency of these studies waxes and wanes with the availability of non-certified teachers. Many such studies were done in the early 1960s, when school districts experienced serious personnel shortages and consequently hired a lot of provisionally certified teachers (e.g. Beery, 1960; Hall, 1964; Gray, 1962; Bledsoe et al., 1967). The recent introduction of alternative routes has spawned a new series of studies that compare traditionally certified teachers and teachers certified via alternative routes (e.g. Cornett, 1984; Brown et al., 1989; Peck, 1989).

One early study in this genre which has often been cited as evidence *against* the value of teacher education, was conducted by Popham (1971). Popham's intent was to develop a performance assessment of teaching. He devised several teaching units and then asking both certified teachers and college students to teach these units. Each unit entailed 9 hours of teaching, and pupils were randomly assigned to teachers. Teachers were not told how to teach the content, but instead were given only the instructional objectives and some materials. (This study differs from most studies in this genre by using student achievement as the outcome rather than teaching practices per se.) Popham found no significant differences between students taught by certified teachers and those taught by college students, and concluded that teacher education had not prepared teachers in a way that made them distinctly different from ordinary, inexperienced, college students.

Dewalt and Ball's (1987) recent study is more typical of the genre, in that it consisted of observing teachers in their regular classrooms. Observers checked an observation form each time they saw a particular behavior, and the behaviors they watched for were taken from research literature on effective teaching strategies. In addition, the observers specifically asked their teachers to demonstrate these competencies. Thus, their observations do not reflect what teachers might normally do in their classrooms, but instead reflected their ability to do these specific things on demand. One group of teachers had taken no teacher education courses, the other had taken at least 12 credit hours in teacher education but had not done student teaching. So the comparison really asks whether taking at least 12 credits in teacher education makes a difference. The two groups were found to differ on several variables, but the differences did not always favor the same group. Behaviors that were more often demonstrated by teachers who had taken at least 12 credits of teacher education were those having to do with creating a non-punitive classroom climate and accommodating individual differences. Those that favored teachers who had taken no courses in teaching had to do with holding students accountable for their work and asking a wide range of questions about the material. These researchers also found, incidentally, a wider variation in practices among the non-prepared teachers than among the prepared teachers.

The studies in this genre are remarkably diverse in the outcomes they measure and in the way they select groups for contrast. Not surprisingly, given this diversity, their findings are mixed as well. Most reviewers of this genre (e.g. Haberman, 1985; Evertson, Hawley and Zlotnik, 1985) perceive the overall pattern of differences as indicating that teacher education does make a difference, though they also point out that these studies do not take account of the content or character of teacher education programs. They share this weakness with multiple regression studies. Now lets consider our three questions.

Aspects of Teacher Education Examined

Instead of examining the particular courses teachers took, researchers in this genre usually focus on entire programs, defining 'teacher education' as whatever set of courses the teacher took in order to receive a certificate. The aspect of teacher education that is of interest to them is the complete program relative to the incomplete, or non-existent, program. Since skeptics are particularly critical of policies that require teachers to complete programs in order to receive certificates, these studies are relevant to their concern. And comparisons among different types of programs — for instance, alternative routes versus traditional programs — are also of interest, particularly in policy climate that encourage alternatives.

Many of these researchers also document the number of undergraduate, as opposed to graduate, education courses taken by teachers in the non-certified group. An important finding from this research is that very few provisionally certified or emergency certified teachers have had absolutely no exposure to teacher education. Instead, they have taken a few courses, but not enough to become certified. Thus, many comparisons are actually between teachers who have taken everything that is required to become certified and teachers who have taken some portion of the requirements. Still, these contrasts are relevant, since both policy-makers and teacher educators expect the completed undergraduate program to make a difference.

A significant weakness of these studies, however, is their failure to document which courses were actually taken, or from which institution. As I noted above, the content and character of teacher education can vary substantially from one institution to the next, so that differences in conclusions among these studies could reflect differences in local teacher education programs from which different samples of teachers are drawn.

Outcomes

Although a few comparison studies use tests of knowledge, such as the NTE or a state-required test (e.g. Cornett, 1984), most depend on observations of teacher for their outcomes. For such observations to be valuable, we would need wide agreement that the practices they document are indeed valued. In fact, because ideas change over time regarding what counts as good teaching, the observation systems change as well, with each reflecting what is fashionable at the time the study was conducted. One could argue, of course, that even though the criteria change over time, each criterion reflects views of good teaching that would also have guided teacher education programs at the time the studies were done. If this is true, it is not unreasonable to expect certified teachers to perform better than non-certified teachers in these studies.

The Logic of the Argument

Studies in this genre actually represent a two-sided argument. On one side, skeptics occasionally conduct such studies to see if teacher education *hinders* teaching. On the other side, advocates conduct such studies to learn whether teacher education *facilitates* teaching. But there is a serious limitation to both sides of this argument, for neither side can be certain that its two groups of teachers did not already differ before they enrolled in their college programs. If those who enroll in teacher education are qualitatively different from those who do not, these differences may still be contributing to teachers' observed pedagogies later on. And there is reason to believe that such prior differences exist. Kennedy (forthcoming), for instance, found that different types of teacher education programs tended to enroll teacher candidates who held different views, even upon entry into the programs, and Skipper and Quantz (1987) found differences between freshmen enrolled in liberal arts programs and those enrolled in teacher education programs.

In fact, even a finding of *no difference* does not avoid this dilemma, for it is possible that different kinds of people enroll in different programs and that the programs washed out the initial differences. Skipper and Quantz (1987) illustrate this point. They followed a group of arts and sciences students and a group of teacher education students from their freshman year through their senior year. They found that substantial differences existed between the two groups as freshmen, but that these differences had disappeared by the time the groups were seniors. No difference at the end of a program, then, means no evidence that teacher education has hindered teaching, no evidence that teacher education has contributed to teaching, and no evidence that different kinds of people enrolled in different programs to start with.

Grossman's (1990) comparisons of six novice teachers with different educational backgrounds improves over many comparison studies in three important ways. First, Grossman interviewed her teachers as well as observing them, and asked them where they got their ideas for teaching. Many referred to specific teacher educators. Second, Grossman visited the teacher education program attended by her sample of certified teachers so that she could test the idea that the program in fact provided content that was consistent with the ideas the novice teachers held. Finally, one of the certified teachers in Grossman's study had actually tried teaching earlier, and, based on this experience, returned to college to obtain a teaching credential. This teacher's recollections of the first teaching experience provided yet another source of evidence to justify the inference that credentialed teachers taught differently because of what they had been taught in their teacher education program.

Overall, then, comparisons of credentialed and non-credentialed teachers focus on a more relevant aspect of teacher education — completed programs versus alternatives or incomplete programs — than do follow-up surveys, and their outcomes are more relevant as well, at least within the era in which they are conducted. But comparison studies suffer a logic problem in that they do not enable researchers to separate the impact of the courses or programs teachers took from the original beliefs or dispositions which may have motivated some teachers to take formal course work in the first place, and motivated others to enter the field later on.

Experiments in Teacher Education

The fourth way to find out whether teacher education makes a difference is to experimentally test the effects of specific approaches to teacher education. This genre has been especially popular among people interested in microteaching, but experiments have also been used to study the effects of hypermedia (Goldman and Barron, 1990), video demonstrations (Winitzky and Arends, 1991), direct instruction (Klesius, Searls and Zielonka, 1990) and a variety of other teacher education strategies. Generally, researchers working within this genre contrast two or more approaches to teacher education in an effort to discern the relative merits of each.

Experiments avoid many of the limitations of the first three genres. They always contrast two or more clearly defined program variations, rather than leaving teacher education undefined; they often assess teachers' knowledge or skill *prior to* their participation in the program as well as after it, so that they can be more sure that whatever differences are eventually observed are due to program differences rather than pre-existing differences; and they usually assess the outcome of interest directly, rather than asking teachers to judge their own performance. In addition, they often randomly assign teacher candidates to program variations to insure that groups receiving different variations do not differ in their prior knowledge or motivations prior to participating. The combination of these features gives experimental researchers a tremendous advantage over those using follow-up surveys, those comparing credentialed and non-credentialed teachers and those looking for predictors of student achievement. Experimental researchers can ascertain how teachers differed both before and after program participation, they know what the program actually did, and they often directly assess the outcomes the program intended to influence.

Recently, as the popularity of microteaching has waned, experiments with other forms of teacher education have begun to appear. One example is a series of studies reported by Nancy Winitzky and Richard Arends (1991). These researchers first contrasted the effects of visiting exemplary classrooms with that of observing videotapes, and found both to be equally effective in helping teachers use cooperative grouping in their own microteaching. In a second study, they contrasted two methods of developing novices' intellectual schemata regarding cooperative grouping, and in the third, they contrasted learning in the exemplary classrooms with learning via microteaching, and found them to be equally effective. Like many such studies, though, these studies did not follow the students into their own student teaching experiences to see the extent to which they carried their new skills into their own teaching practice.

Now let's consider my three questions.

Aspects of Teacher Education Examined

More than any of the other studies, these studies tend to focus on specific approaches to teacher education. Studies in this genre are especially relevant to teacher educators, but are less relevant to policy makers and skeptics, for they do not address the value of entire programs. Even for teacher educators, many of these studies suffer because they are too short in duration. They may contrast relatively small program units — three weeks of one approach versus three weeks of another, or even three hours of one versus three hours of the other. They do this, of course, in part because smaller projects are easier to manage. But evidence from such studies cannot be used to make larger scale changes in the structure of teacher education programs. Nor is it realistic to expect such brief experiences to have lasting effects on teacher candidates.

Outcomes

With respect to outcomes, most of these researchers focus on teacher's ability to perform specific skills. The outcomes are directly relevant to teacher educators who want to develop those skills, but often are limited in that they do not consider the teachers' affective response to the skill. That is, it is possible for teachers to learn what the program intends, and to perform it on demand, but to disapprove of it and never use it again once the teachers are practicing independently. Knowing how to perform does not assure a desire to perform, and many experimental studies have found that teachers learned the target skills but did not practice them once in their own classroom.

The Logic of the Argument

The logic of these studies is persuasive: if teachers participating in one approach improve their skill more than other teachers do, then this approach has a greater impact. Because researchers have assessed their candidates' skills both before and after the candidates participated in these approaches, and because candidates are often randomly assigned to approaches, experimenters can be more sure than other researchers that the outcomes they observe do reflect program influence rather than sampling differences.

Overall, then, these studies are more relevant to teacher educators in the aspects of teacher education they examine, more relevant in the outcomes they assess, and more powerful in their ability to draw unambiguous findings regarding the relative merits of one program approach over another. They do not, however, address the skeptics' concerns, for they do not address the question of whether teacher education as a whole is worthwhile, and they often fail to show whether even the unit they were experimenting with had an influence on teaching practice once teachers graduated and began independent teaching.

Longitudinal Studies of Change

The fifth genre, a relatively new addition to the field, involves following teacher candidates as they proceed through their college education, gathering data on them at several points along the way, to see whether and how their ideas about teaching change over time. Researchers working within this genre want to learn what students are like when they enter their programs, how they change over time in response to their programs, and what they are like when they finish. Like experiments, these studies offer us the advantage of being able to document *change* so that, if differences exist at the end of the study, we can interpret these differences relative to differences that may have existed at the outset. And like experiments, longitudinal studies usually involve looking at the details of the programs in which students participate so that the relationship between student thinking and program content can be examined. Unlike experiments, though, these studies rarely allow us to compare students who participate in different kinds of programs. While we learn more about how they change as they encounter particular aspects of their programs, we cannot say with any confidence how they might have changed if they had participated in some other kind of program.

Longitudinal studies have been especially popular among researchers who are interested in the student teaching component of teacher education (Hodges, 1982; Silvernail and Costello, 1983; Tabachnik and Zeichner, 1984; Goodman, 1986). In the typical study, researchers contrast student-teachers' beliefs or knowledge or skills before and after they participate in student teaching. While these studies are valuable, and have increased our understanding of student teaching, they leave untouched the center of the enterprise — the large, diffuse, complicated web of courses and other events that we call preservice teacher education.

One of the earliest and best examples of an effort to move this genre into the university program is Feiman-Nemser and Buchmann's (1989) study of teacher candidates participating in two different teacher education programs. They followed six students participating in two preservice teacher education programs, interviewing them on several occasions about their understanding of what they were learning and about their views of teaching. They also observed the teacher education courses these students took. Through their descriptions of these students, they were able to demonstrate gradual shifts in views and to demonstrate ways in which program content was sometimes *mis*interpreted by the candidates. The study demonstrated the importance of candidates' initial assumptions and the ways in which they combined their own childhood experiences with the lessons they were being taught to form their ideas about teaching and learning.

Another good illustration of this genre is Hollingsworth's (1989) study of MAT (Masters of Art in Teaching) candidates. She followed candidates through both university courses and teaching internships. Through her investigation, she showed not only the role that prior beliefs played in these teachers' learning, but also how university learning connected to practical experience. She found that candidates' prior beliefs influenced their receptivity to the program, and that they went through several distinct phases in their practice as they tried to accommodate what they had learned in the program with their classroom experiences.

Longitudinal studies range from cases of individuals (e.g. Valli and Agnostinelli, 1992) to large-scale quantitative studies (Galluzzo, 1984). On the quantitative side, Galluzzo gave candidates the National Teaching Examination (NTE) each year during their college program. Interestingly, he found that scores did not change on the general studies portion of the NTE, but did change on the professional knowledge portion. Quantitative studies are particularly popular for assessing the impact of the entire college experience, and Pascarella and Terenzini (1991) provide a remarkably thorough summary of this literature.

Kennedy (forthcoming) presents an example of a large-scale, but qualitative, longitudinal study, the Teacher Education and Learning to Teach (TELT) study. TELT researchers interviewed teachers and teacher candidates multiple times as they participated in different teacher education programs. Her data allow us to see the initial views of teachers entering these different programs, and to see how programs with different content move teachers' thinking in different directions. They also show, however, that different types of programs tend to attract teachers with different initial beliefs. Two findings from that study are especially important. First, nearly every group of candidates changed views as they moved through these programs, and these changes were virtually always in the direction of the program's substantive orientation. However, the changes were not as substantial as teacher educators would probably want to see. Moreover, because different programs had different substantive orientations, the net effect across all programs could appear as if teacher education had not made a difference. That is, some teachers moved in one direction while others moved in the opposite direction.

And now to my three questions.

Aspects of Teacher Education Examined

The aspect of teacher education that longitudinal researchers tend to focus on is the whole program *as it is perceived by the candidates themselves*. That is, longitudinal researchers tend to follow teacher candidates through their coursework, noting how the candidates interpret and respond to the various courses that they take. Further, instead of allowing official program rhetoric to define the courses students take, they often actually attend courses with their sample students. This aspect of teacher education is more relevant than that of experiments, since longitudinal studies tend to examine entire programs. It is not clear whether this aspect of teacher education programs is of interest to skeptics or policy-makers.

Outcomes

With respect to outcomes, longitudinal researchers tend to be more interested in teachers' beliefs and attitudes than in their tested knowledge or their teaching skills. The importance of beliefs has become apparent in microteaching experiments, when teachers learn skills but do not apply them. And the literature indicating the relationship between beliefs and actions is growing as well. Often, however, these studies are limited because they do not follow candidates into practice, to learn whether the changes observed during a program extend into the teachers' classroom practices. Thus, they document changes during preservice teacher education, or during student teaching, but do not tell us whether these changes are sustained later on or whether they actually influence teaching practices.

The Logic of the Argument

Most longitudinal studies are based on the assumption that teacher candidates enter their college programs with a set of initial beliefs that will influence their responses to the courses they take. As candidates participate in teacher education courses, they incorporate some new ideas, but they also reinterpret many of them to make them more consistent with what they already believed.

Studies of change share with multiple regression a tendency to document a wide range of variables, most of which are defined in advance. But whereas multiple regression researchers are measuring various influences on student achievement, longitudinal researchers are measuring a complex of attitudes, values and beliefs and the multitude of experiences that influence these. The success of longitudinal studies, therefore, can depend on the theory of learning that guides data collection.

One difficulty that some such studies encounter is a confusion between change due to normal maturation among college students and change due to program impact. The fact that students are changing and developing over time does not necessarily mean that these changes are a result of a program. College students are still in a highly formative stage in their lives, and may be changing in several ways that have little to do with the particular courses or curricula they encounter as students. Thus, the credibility of longitudinal studies depends either on comparison groups, which permit changes to be contrasted across program types, or on documenting the content of the program so that a clear relationship can be shown between what teachers think and what they have been taught.

Another difficulty that can arise in longitudinal studies derives from the number of observations made on students. Students are often interviewed, or respond to questionnaires, on numerous occasions, and it is highly likely that, over time, they learn not only what they will be asked but also how they are supposed to respond. Thus there is a chance that the researchers themselves are at least partly responsible for the changes they describe.

Overall, then, these studies focus on relevant aspects of teacher education — undergraduate programs and components within those programs, and on relevant outcomes — changes in knowledge and beliefs about teaching. The logic is also sound, provided that attention is given to sorting out natural maturation from program effects. To the extent that longitudinal studies attend to whole programs, and particularly to differences among programs, they may be relevant to policy makers and skeptics. The TELT study, for instance, suggests that programs of teacher education do make a difference, and that different programs make different differences.

Conclusions

Skeptics of teacher education seek evidence that teacher education is sufficiently beneficial to justify that it be required. All five of these research genres are intended to document whether or how teacher education makes a difference, but they examine different aspects of teacher education, they document different types of outcomes, and they employ different forms of logic to establish their case for whether teacher education makes a difference.

Of the five genres reviewed here, findings from multiple regressions are more likely to find their way into the policy community than other findings, for these studies are designed to inform policy decisions. Taken together, these studies do not make a strong case for teacher education. Moreover, the only follow-up surveys to enter the policy making community are those conducted outside of teacher education, such as the NEA study, and that study also does not make a case for teacher education. Some comparisons of credentialed and noncredentialed teachers have entered the policy arena, and these tend to be more favorable toward teacher education. However, even these studies have mixed results, depending on when and where they are done and depending on what outcomes are measured.

All of these genres also have significant weaknesses, however. The first three, for instance, cannot show with certainty that the behaviors, knowledge, or attitudes they document resulted from teacher education programs, rather than from prior dispositions of those who choose to enter teacher education programs. The two remaining genres — experiments and longitudinal studies — offer the strongest possibilities for causal inferences. Both of these genres document changes in teachers, rather than limiting themselves to how teachers respond after they have completed their programs, and both document the content of the program so that they can show the relationship between the changes that were observed and program content. Each, however, is limited in its potential to persuade skeptics and policy makers. Experiments do not address whole programs, and tend to be of very short duration, and longitudinal studies are often case studies, limited to a handful of teacher candidates. And they frequently are limited only to attitudes and beliefs, and do not include teaching practice. So far, neither of these genres has shown that a large group of teachers change in desired ways as a result of participating in teacher education, and continue to practice in improved ways once in the field.

The sad fact is that poorly designed studies are not merely *non*informative. Often, they are *mis*informative: by failing to document the content and character of teacher education programs, they confuse quantity with quality. By failing to consider what teacher candidates know or think prior to participating in teacher education, they may over- or under-estimate the contributions of teacher education. By failing to consider the context in which teachers are teaching, they may confuse the effects of the current teaching context with the effects of the earlier teacher preparation. When they study only handfuls of teachers, they cannot tell us how widespread their observed changes are likely to be. To maximize the potential of their studies, researchers need to address all of these concerns. Until such time as an adequate body of such knowledge exists, teacher education will continue to have a hard time defending itself from skeptics.

Note

1   An earlier version of this paper was presented at the Annual Meeting of the Association of Teacher Educators, February, 1991. Preparation of the paper was supported by the National Center for Research on Teacher Learning under a grant from the US Department of Education, Office of Research. However, the views expressed here are the authors and no official endorsement should be inferred.

References

ADAMS, R.D. and CRAIG, J.R. (1983) 'A status report of teacher education program evaluation', *Journal of Teacher Education*, **34**, 2, pp. 33–6.

ARCH, E.C. (1989) 'Comparison of student attainment of teaching competencies in traditional preservice and fifth-year master of arts in teaching programs', Presented at the annual meeting of the American Educational Research Association, San Francisco, March.

BEERY, J.R. (1960) *Professional Preparation and Effectiveness of Beginning Teachers*, Coral Gables: Graphic Arts Press.

BLEDSOE, C., COX, J.V., and BURNAM, R. (1967) *Comparison between Selected Characteristics and Performance of Provisionally and Professionally Certified Beginning Teachers in Georgia*, ERIC No. ED 015 553.

BROPHY, J. and GOOD, T.L. (1986) 'Teacher behavior and student achievement,' in WITTROCK, M. (ed.) *Handbook of Research on Teaching (Third Edition)*, New York: MacMillan, pp. 328–75.

BROWN, D., EDINGTON, E., SPENCER, D.A., and TINAFERO, J. (1989) 'A comparison of alternative certification, traditionally trained, and emergency permit teachers,' *Teacher Education and Practice*, **5**, 2, pp. 21–3.

BROWNE, D. and HOOVER, J.H. (1990) 'The degree to which student teachers report using instructional strategies valued by university faculty,' *Action in Teacher Education*, **12**, 1, pp. 20–4.

CLARK, D.C., SMITH, R.B., NEWBY, T.J., and COOK, V.A. (1985) 'Perceived origins of teaching behavior,' *Journal of Teacher Education*, **36**, 6, pp. 49–53.

COLEMAN, J.S. (1966) *Equality of Educational Opportunity*, Washington DC: US Department of Health, Education, and Welfare.

COPELAND, W.D. (1975) 'The relationship between micro-teaching and student teacher classroom performance,' *Journal of Educational Research*, **68**, pp. 289–93.

COPELAND, W.D. (1982) 'Laboratory experiences in teacher education,' *Encyclopedia of Educational Research* (V. 2, Fifth Edition), pp. 1008–19.

CORNETT, L. (1984) 'A comparison of teacher certification test scores and performance evaluations of graduates in teacher education and liberal arts and sciences in three southern states,' Atlanta, GA: Southern Regional Education Board.

CORNFIELD, I.R. (1991) 'Microteaching skill generalization and transfer: Training preservice teachers in introductory lesson skills,' *Teaching and Teacher Education*, **7**, 1, pp. 25–56.

COUNCIL OF CHIEF STATE SCHOOL OFFICERS (1988) *State Education Indicators, 1988*, Washington, DC: Author.

CRUICKSHANK, D.R. and METCALF, K.K. (1990) 'Training within teacher preparation,' in HOUSTON, R.W., HABERMAN, M. and SIKULA, J. (eds) *Handbook of Research on Teacher Education*, New York: Macmillan (pp. 469–97).

DEWALT, M. and BALL, D.W. (1987) 'Some effects of training on the competence of beginning teachers', *Journal of Educational Research*, **80**, 6, pp. 343–47.

EVERTSON, C.M., HAWLEY, W.D., and ZLOTNIK, M. (1985) 'Making a difference in educational quality through teacher education,' *Journal of Teacher Education*, **36**, 3, pp. 2–12.

FEIMAN-NEMSER, S. and BUCHMANN, M. (1989) 'Describing teacher education: A framework and illustrative findings from a longitudinal study of six students,' *Elementary School Journal*, **89**, pp. 365–77.

FERGUSON, R. (1990) *Racial Patterns in How School and Teacher Quality Affect Achievement and Earnings*, Cambridge, MA: Kennedy School of Government mimeo.

FERGUSON, P. and WOMACK, S.T. (1993) 'The impact of subject matter and education coursework on teaching performance,' *Journal of Teacher Education*, **44**, 1, pp. 55–63.

GAGE, N.L. (1977) *The Scientific Basis of the Art of Teaching*, New York: Teachers College Press.

GAGE, N.L. (1985) *Hard Gains in the Soft Sciences: The Case of Pedagogy*, Bloomington, IN: Phi Delta Kappa.

GALLUZZO, G. (1984, March) 'An evaluation of a teacher education program,' Paper presented at the annual meeting of the American Educational Research Association, New Orleans.

GALLUZZO, G. and CRAIG, J.R. (1990) 'Evaluation of preservice teacher education programs,' in HOUSTON, W.R., HABERMAN, M. and SIKULA, J. (eds) *Handbook of Research on Teacher Education*, New York: Macmillan (pp. 599–616).

GAEDE, O.F. (1978) 'Reality shock: A problem among first-year teachers,' *The Clearinghouse*, **51**, 9, pp. 405–9.

GLIESSMAN, D.H. (1987) 'Changing complex teaching skills,' *Journal of Education for Teaching*, **13**, 3, pp. 267–75.

GLIESSMAN, D.H. and PUGH, R.C. (1987) 'Conceptual instruction and intervention as methods of acquiring teaching skills,' in TELLEMA, H. and VEENMAN, S.A.M. (eds) 'Developments in training methods for teacher education,' *International Journal of Education*, **11**, pp. 555–63.

GOLDMAN, E. and BARRON, L. (1990) 'Using hypermedia to improve the preparation of elementary teachers,' *Journal of Teacher Education*, **41**, 3, pp. 21–31.

GOODMAN, J. (1986) 'What students learn from early field experiences: A case study and critical analysis,' *Journal of Teacher Education*, **36**, 6, pp. 42–8.

GRAY, H.B. (1962) 'A study of the outcomes of preservice education associated with three levels of teacher certification,' Doctoral Dissertation, Florida State University.

GROSSMAN, P.L. (1990) *The Making of a Teacher: Teacher Knowledge and Teacher Education*, New York: Teachers College Press.

HABERMAN, M. (1985) 'Does teacher education make a difference? A review of comparisons between liberal arts and teacher education majors', *Journal of Thought*, **20**, 2, pp. 25–34.

HALL, H.O. (1964) 'Professional preparation and teacher effectiveness,' *Journal of Teacher Education*, **15**, 1, pp. 72–6.

HANUSHEK, E.A. (1971) 'Teacher characteristics and gains in student achievement: Estimation using micro data,' *American Economic Review*, **61**, 2, pp. 280–8.

HANUSHEK, E.A. (1989) 'The impact of differential expenditures on school performance,' *Educational Researcher*, **18**, 3, pp. 45–51, 62.

HENRY, M. (1987–88) 'The effect of increased exploratory field experiences upon the perceptions and performance of student teachers,' *Action in Teacher Education*, **9**, 4, pp. 93–7.

HODGES, C. (1982) 'Implementing methods: If you can't blame the cooperating teacher who can you blame?' *Journal of Teacher Education*, **33**, 6, pp. 25–9.

HOLLINGSWORTH, S. (1989) 'Prior beliefs and cognitive change in learning to teach,' *American Educational Research Journal*, **26**, 2, pp. 160–89.

KENNEDY, M.M. (1991) 'Some surprising findings on how teachers learn to teach,' *Educational Leadership*, **49**, 11, pp. 14–7.

KENNEDY, M.M. (1996) 'Research genres in teacher education,' in MURRAY, F. (ed.) *The Teacher Educator's Handbook: Building a Knowledge Base for the Preparation of Teachers*, San Francisco: Jossey Bass.

KENNEDY, M.M. (forthcoming) *Defining the Moment: The Contribution of Teacher Education to Teachers' Classroom Decisions*, New York: Teachers College Press.

KLESIUS, J.P., SEARLS, E.F., and ZIELONKA, P. (1990) 'A comparison of two methods of direct instruction of preservice teachers,' *Journal of Teacher Education*, **41**, 4, pp. 34–43.

KOZIOL, S.M., JR., and BURNS, P. (1986) 'Teachers' accuracy in self-reporting about instructional practices using a focused self-report inventory,' *Journal of Educational Research*, **79**, 4, pp. 205–9.

LUPONE, O.J. (1961) 'A comparison of provisionally certified and permanently certified elementary teachers in selected school districts in New York State,' *The Journal of Educational Research*, **55**, 2, pp. 53–63.

MCINTYRE, D.J. and KILLIAN, J.E. (1986) 'Students' interactions with pupils and cooperating teachers in early field experiences,' *The Teacher Educator*, **22**, 2, pp. 2–9.

MCINTYRE, D.J. and KILLIAN, J.E. (1987) 'The influence of supervisory training for cooperating teachers on preservice teacher development during early field experiences,' *The Journal of Educational Research*, **80**, 5, pp. 277–82.

MURNANE, R.J. and PHILLIPS, B.R. (1981) 'Learning by doing, vintage and selection: Three pieces of the puzzle relating teaching experience and teacher performance', *Economics of the Education Review*, **1**, 4, pp. 453–65.

MURNANE, R.J., SINGE, J.D., WILLETT, J.B., KEMPLE, J.J. and OLSEN, R.S. (1991) *Who Will Teach? Policies that Matter*, Cambridge: Harvard University Press.

NATIONAL CENTER FOR EDUCATION STATISTICS (1989) *Digest of Education Statistics 1989*, Washington, DC: Author.

PASCARELLA, E. and TERENZINI, P. (1991) *How College Affects Students: Findings and Insights From Twenty Years of Research*, San Francisco: Jossey-Bass.

PECK, H.I. (1989) 'The effect of certification status on the performance of mathematics teachers: A pilot study,' Paper presented at the annual meeting of the American Educational Research Association, San Francisco, March.

PIGGE, F.L. (1978) 'Teacher competencies: Need, proficiency, and where proficiency was developed,' *Journal of Teacher Education*, **29**, 4, pp. 70–6.

POPHAM, W.J. (1971) 'Performance tests of teaching proficiency: Rationale, development, and validation,' *American Educational Research Journal*, **8**, 1, pp. 105–17.

SILVERNAIL, D.L. and COSTELLO, M.H. (1983) 'The impact of student teaching and internship programs on preservice teachers' pupil control perspectives, anxiety levels, and teaching concerns,' *Journal of Teacher Education*, **36**, 4, pp. 32–6.

SKIPPER, C.E. and QUANTZ, R. (1987) 'Changes in educational attitudes of education and arts and sciences students during four years of college,' *Journal of Teacher Education*, **38**, 3, pp. 39–44.

SMYLIE, M.A. (1989) 'Teachers' views of the effectiveness of sources of learning to teach,' *The Elementary School Journal*, **89**, 5, pp. 543–58.

STRANG, H.R., BADT, K.S., and KAUFFMAN, J.M. (1997) 'Microcomputer-based simulations for training fundamental teaching skills,' *Journal of Teacher Education*, **38**, 1, pp. 20–6.

STRAUSS, R.P. and SAWYER, E.A. (1986) 'Some new evidence on teacher and student competencies,' *Economics of Education Review*, **5**, 1, pp. 41–8.

TABACHNIK, B.R. and ZEICHNER, K.M. (1984) 'The impact of student teaching experience on the development of teacher perspectives,' *Journal of Teacher Education*, **35**, 6, pp. 28–36.

VALLI, L. and AGNOSTINELLI, A. (1992) 'Teaching with and without formal preparation,' Paper presented at the annual meeting of the American Educational Research Association, San Francisco.

WINITZKY, N.E. and ARENDS, R. (1991) 'Translating research into practice: The effects of various forms of training and clinical experiences on preservice students' knowledge, skills and reflectiveness,' *Journal of Teacher Education*, **42**, 1, pp. 52–65.

7 Society's Requirements for K-12 Confront Higher Education

Barry Munitz and Rosemary Papalewis

Introduction

For the *first* time in American higher education dramatic metamorphosis must occur without incremental resources or broad public support, and with the major potential competitors not being other academic institutions. The fundamental transformation may be inevitable, but it is not clear where it will lead, and there is no consistent vision about how higher education ought to look as a result. Without such an overview of the future to structure and insulate a planning process, there can be greater risks than potential rewards to institutional leaders who try to use planning to leverage change, even for those who value the process more than the product. Without the ability to tackle the unknown, planning becomes a technical process of perpetuating past techniques onto future scenarios. To enter an even more treacherous arena, like the reform of K-12 education, is to invite disaster and depression — but society, led by our traditional academic institution, has no choice (Ehrlich, Munitz and Wellman, in press).

Focus on California

> For the reformer has enemies in all those who profit by the old order, and only lukewarm defenders in all those who would profit by the new order. (Machiavelli)

For planning to be effective in stimulating change, it has to be anchored in a forum where planners and their institutions can take some risks to find answers to institutional dilemmas that would otherwise be off-limits. Since the country is so complex and varied when it comes to public school education, this chapter will concentrate on the authors' state, California, and their own institution, the California State University. The chapter begins by concentrating on the intersection of demographics, politics, economic realities, and national reports colliding in California, followed with the CSU response to these internal and external forces, how we are hanging on the cutting edge with the establishment of a nexus for reform and activity. This strategy not only provides the advantage of specific knowledge, but as in many areas of vital social policy, it describes a situation that is, or will soon be sweeping across America.

Economic Trends and Shifting Priorities

The passage of Proposition 13 in 1978 fixed in the California constitution severe limits (impervious even to recent revisionist consideration) on the revenue available for all state expenditures. During these past two decades as income was restricted, priorities for correctional facilities and health and welfare grew, while a subsequent initiative (Proposition 98) guaranteed a minimum of 40 per cent for K-14 (community colleges receive about 10 per cent of that pool).

So what does this mean for the State's likely distribution of funds 10 years hence? By fiscal year 2005, the 18 per cent supporting Higher Education and Other in 1995 decreases to a total of 7 per cent for everything else including Higher Education.

Transforming Demographics

At the same time dollars are increasingly restricted, California is experiencing a unique explosion of population combined with an extraordinary transformation of demographic profiles. If we consider the half-century that we are half-way through (1970–2020), the K-12 student census almost doubles from 4 to 8 million students. Even more dramatically, the relative proportion of major ethnic groups shifts. No state has ever experienced such expansion and demographic transformation.

Higher Education's Master Plan

Almost 40 years ago, Clark Kerr, then President of the University of California led the State through an extraordinary planning process that brought forth the world-respected California Master Plan. It promised access to any Californian seeking post-secondary education, at one of three public segments, with strong quality and a low price. Now the cost is escalating, the quality is under pressure, and given the demographics above the access and opportunity commitments are at severe risk.

In October 1993, Kerr, addressing the only joint meeting of the California State University Board of Trustees and the University of California Board of Regents in the State's history, asked:

> Can we maintain the Master Plan in general and access in particular into the future? I assume that the almost universal answer of the people of this state, that we should if we possibly can, maintain the Master Plan. Access was a promise to the people of the state in which millions of parents, hundreds of thousands of young people have counted. The promise made by the legislature of this state by the time we were through had only one negative plan out of the 120 votes, by the then Governor, unanimously by the UC Board of Regents, unanimously by the state Board of Education, and subsequently endorsed by the new board of CSU Trustees. Access is even more important now, not only because a promise was

made, but also because the labor force required more education in 1960. And because the quality of opportunity is even more important than it was then. To slam the doors now would be, I think, a moral, economic, and political tragedy for this state. (Kerr, 1993)

The worry is not just about colleges and universities. Proposition 98 notwithstanding, concern is even greater at earlier levels. The Business Round Table, Chamber of Commerce and other corporate groups are now increasingly interested in strengthening K-12 because they fear not only for the peaceful social fabric of where they work and live, but also they realize that we will not have a competitive economy in this global market environment if our public schools are not stronger.

In the 1960 Master Plan, one of the great changes for K-12 was that the former teacher colleges, which until then had the same governance as K-12 through the California Department of Education, were merged together into one system and their titles were changed to State Colleges/University. The colleges began to think of themselves less and less as focusing on K-12 teacher preparation, particularly since their colleges of education were at the lowest prestige level on the academic totem pole. They had the highest workload, the lowest salary, their deans had the least political leverage in the system and as all of higher education moved toward the prestige model of advance graduate education and research, it was less and less likely that the former state teachers' colleges would resist the temptation to now present themselves as regional, graduate universities. California State University did *not* escape this trap. Therefore, when we face social pressure from outside agencies telling us that the reform and strengthening of K-12 should be our strongest emphasis, most academic institutions are unable to respond to that priority assignment (even though it promises extraordinary public support and political leverage) without dramatically restructuring their own curricular pattern, prestige and reward system.

Recent Critical Developments: State Capital

The California Governor's budget for 1996–7 (May, 1996) made Education the State's top spending priority, with more than 36.1 cents out of each General Fund dollar dedicated to primary and secondary education in California. Specifically, the Governor's budget message on K-3 class size reduction was, 'The budget provides $771 million to begin an ambitious incentive program to reduce class sizes from 30 to 20 students in early grades. Participating school districts can choose from three consecutive grades — K-1–2 or 1–2–3 — and will have the choice of reducing class sizes for full or half school day' (Wilson, 1996).

In July 1996, the Governor signed AB 1432 a bill to expand the alternative teacher credentialing program to allow more experienced Californians to become public school teachers. Individuals selected to participate in the District Intern Program must have a baccalaureate degree; pass the CBEST (California Basic Educational Skills Test); pass subject matter examinations; have 120 hours of teacher training; be supported by a mentor teacher; and, have a professional development plan. Assembly Bill 1432 removes the requirement that there be a shortage of certified applicants for teaching positions before a district can employ District Interns.

In his July 1995 State of the State Address, Governor Wilson called for alternative credentialing stating, 'Our credentialing system is wasting time and talent which no other state can boast — and which our kids urgently need in their classrooms. We must open the system to that talent now.' The Governor's mention of 'talent' was primarily a reference to the theoretical availability of highly educated displaced aerospace workers; aerospace employment has decreased by 50 per cent since 1989.

Notwithstanding the movement to a more academically prestigious model of higher education, the CSU and the K-12 schools in California remain closely connected. At the heart of the CSU mission is a commitment, to encourage and provide access, to prepare educated, responsible people, to advance and extend knowledge, learning and culture, and to provide public services. The CSU and the K-12 schools in California are closely connected. The schools prepare the students who enroll at the state university and the CSU educates many of the teachers who serve in the state's elementary and secondary classrooms. Given this state of mutual dependency, the CSU is devoting considerable resources and energies to its relationships with the K-12 sector. As of 1995, 21 of the 22 campuses offered approved programs leading to basic teaching credentials, specialist credentials, and services credentials. Every type of teaching, specialist, or services credential could be earned at one or more of the campuses. Seventeen campuses offered one or more credential programs in internship format, as well as, conventional programs. Altogether, CSU campuses offered more than 450 separately approved programs of professional preparation for educators. Nineteen campuses offered master's degree programs in Education. Of the 14 joint doctoral programs (the CSU cannot offer independently the doctoral degree) in which CSU participates, six are in education. In 1994–5 the CSU recommended 10,865 credentials. Of those 4,589 were multiple subject, 2,390 were single subject. The median age of recipients of initial basic teaching credentials was 28.

Recent Critical Developments: Postsecondary National Systems

The members of the National Association of System Heads (personal communication, 15 October 1996) decided at their March, 1995 meeting to give a high priority to deepening the connections between higher education institutions and reform efforts currently underway in the public schools. The reason? Those efforts simply cannot succeed without changes in higher education. Given current demands on state university systems — including pressure to raise standards, reduce remediation, discontinue admission preferences for minority students, while maintaining or increasing the diversity of the student body, shorten time to degree, reduce costs and increase productivity — there are even more reasons to increase connections with K-12. In fact, higher education cannot succeed in meeting the demands on us without their help. It therefore seemed the right time for large public multi-campus systems to reexamine our relationships with K-12 and build a more coordinated improvement strategy, kindergarten through college.

In Maryland, for instance, the University has joined with the Secretary of Higher Education, the State Superintendent of Education, and various business and civic leaders in a joint enterprise aimed at developing a seamlessly integrated elementary, secondary and higher education system based on high standards and rigorous performance assessment against those standards.

> Maryland is not, of course, the only system that has taken steps in this direction. Under their Chancellors' leadership, the University System of Georgia has launched an ambitious and comprehensive effort that they call 'P-16.' This project was featured in the cover story of the September 19 issue of Black issues in higher education.

At least 12 other state systems are also working on one or more aspects of K-16 reform (NASH, 1996). Over the past year, these systems, have been meeting together to think through the pieces of what higher education leaders are coming to regard as a national K-16 reform agenda. Representatives of this group gathered in Baltimore in April, 1996 for a two-day session devoted to aligning admissions with new high school standards, and again during the summer for a three-day institute that looked beyond standards/admissions to issues of teacher preparation and professional development.

Nevertheless, when talking with colleagues across the country distressing signs that those former teachers' colleges which have now become regional universities are reluctant to focus in on K-12 issues for two reasons. First, they fear slipping back into being perceived by the public as 'nothing more than' traditional second-class teachers' colleges; second, they fear that when society discovers that K-12 problems are intractable and impervious to fundamental improvement and positive alteration they will be blamed for failing the K-12 community. However, institutions like the California State University system have realized that their interdependence with public schools is still too great to allow them to alter their traditional commitment to teacher production and K-12 reform. Therefore, the recent recommendations from Darling-Hammond's commission are receiving serious attention.

Recent Critical Developments: Latest Commission

Further, at the national level the just-published *National Commission on Teaching and America's Future* states:

> The Commission is clear about what needs to change. No more hiring unqualified teachers on the sly. No more nods and winks at teacher education programs that fail to prepare teachers properly. No more tolerance for incompetence in the classroom. No more wasting resources on approaches that cannot improve teaching and learning. (Darling-Hammond, 1996, p. 3)

The report suggested that the major problems include inadequate teacher education, slipshod recruitment and hiring, sink-or-swim induction, lack of professional development and rewards for knowledge and skill, and, schools structured for failure. The goals to be reached by 2006 are the following: all children will be taught by competent teachers, all teacher education programs will meet profession standards or be shut down, all teachers will have access to high quality professional development, teachers' salaries will be based on their knowledge and skill levels, and, quality teaching will be the central investment of the school.

Given their awakened sense of connection to K-12, universities are giving serious attention to the recommendations from this commission.

The Voice of California: Board Members

School restructuring, is a topic that school board members view with steely eyed cynicism, because it does not take long to discover that most self-appointed advocates for school reform use the term 'school restructuring' as code words to describe everything from site based management to vouchers (Plotkin, personal communication, September 6, 1996). Plotkin, former President of the California Schools Boards Association, noted,

> Interestingly enough, Charter Schools have really come the closest to actually putting in place what the school reform movement may have really had in mind when 'restructuring' is discussed; changes in delivery systems, innovative curriculum, experimental forms of assessment, changes in the length of the school day and year along with other unique approaches to the traditional calendar, advanced uses of technology for both academic and administrative purposes, and true faculty power over all of the above, including the choice of the 'academic leader', or principal. Few of these approaches have done much to engage parents more directly; the phenomenon of parental involvement in the schools' operation continues to follow the pattern of the younger the child, the greater commitment and participation. And, teachers (with some notable exceptions) continue to shy away from having to confront the realities of having real power — meeting a budget, taking care of everything from the leaky roof to the broken down air conditioning, to dealing with difficult discipline problems and the 'tough' parental interaction that inevitably follows. So, overall, restructuring, like most things in life, comes with some fabulous ideas that are very attractive in the abstract, but a whole different matter in the implementation. Thus, 'school restructuring' has had, at best, a spotty record, with some occasional successes that meet the vision of the school reform movement.

The Voice of California: Policy Leaders

In California, most university undergraduates who intend to become elementary-school teachers major in Liberal Studies, a multidisciplinary curriculum emphasizing breadth in the liberal arts and sciences; most who aspire to secondary-school teaching major in a subject (e.g., English, mathematics, biology) commonly taught in the schools (Service, personal communication, 1996). While acknowledging higher education's commitment to K-12, the current disconnect in California between Schools of Education and Liberal Studies undergraduate degree programs, threaten a healthy interaction between colleges of education and traditional arts and science colleges, and convey a very dangerous message to youngsters who want to consider teaching as a profession. Many key political staff in California argue that, all teacher preparation, according to legislation known as the Ryan Act, occurs in the 'fifth' year after the student has received a Bachelors' degree. Should the Ryan Act be changed? According to several policy experts the approximately 50 pages of statute generally referred to as the Ryan Act certainly warrant revision (Blake, Schwartz, Wilson, Yelverton, personal communications, 1996).

First, the Ryan Act limits traditional teacher preparation to a one-year program and requires that the undergraduate degree be in something other than education. Second, there is an overwhelming perception that the Ryan Act prohibits the integration of education with Liberal Studies, at the undergraduate level. Therefore, the repeal of the Ryan Act would direct attention to the possibility of new education majors/minors configuration, which would be legitimized in legislation.

Some experts argue that nothing in the Ryan Act prohibits the early classroom experiences for undergraduates, nor does it prohibit an education minor. Nothing in the Ryan Act forces university students and faculty to consider education/teacher preparation to be a second-class course of study; in fact, the education major prohibition was in response to that earlier perception. Nothing in the Ryan Act causes Liberal Studies to be an amalgamation of an enormous number of unintegrated classes in the various disciplines — FTES generate for their departments — with no required academic fiscal linkage to a campus's teacher prep program.

Yet other experts would turn their attention to the link between budget structure and the Ryan Act. The politics of Proposition 98, largely which determines how much money the K-14 community receives from the state put all K-12 related moneys in the decentralized control of school districts; nevertheless, they can collaborate — even give higher education cash for long-term mentoring by faculty — if they so choose. However, the historical politics of the academy insisted that support of new public school teachers in the schools by Education faculty or work in schools by faculty is not funded by university nor generally valued by them (Blake, personal communication, 1996). Therefore, serious modification of the Ryan Act, possibly in the development of an education minor, would allow early teaching coursework and clinical experiences within the Liberal Studies program.

The CSU Response

The meaning of good and bad, better and worse, is simply helping or hurting. (Ralph Waldo Emerson)

The Education Round Table and the ICC

The California Education Round Table, a group composed of the leaders of the five educational segments, the University of California, the elected State Superintendent of Public Instruction, the Independent Colleges, California Community Colleges, and the California State University and the California Postsecondary Education, established the Intersegmental Coordinating Committee (ICC) in 1987. The ICC assists the Round Table by overseeing and coordinating the wide range of inter-segmental programs and activities undertaken by the five educational segments to carry out broad policy objectives of the Round Table. The ICC (comprised of faculty, students and policy level staff) ensures a high level of accountability for the success of intersegmental efforts, and a more effective linkage for student progress through California's educational system.

In preparing an intersegmental framework for understanding the various school improvement strategies that have been implemented at the federal, state, and local levels over the last 10 years, the Round Table through the ICC acknowledged that (a) postsecondary faculty are openly critical of public school graduates; (b) efforts to identify specific college prep curriculum and admissions expectation not perceived as successful; (c) perception is that remediation needs are greater than ever before; and, (d) that business and government leaders indicate changes are needed to better prepare high school graduates to enter the workforce.

As they considered the challenges in linking postsecondary education with K-12, the members of the Round Table recognized that the diversity of California's population is increasing daily in terms of age, economic level, racial–ethnic background, native languages, and cultural identification. Because elementary and secondary education in California occurs in the most crowded classrooms in America, our diversity represents an even greater challenge to our ability to provide high quality education. The Round Table and ICC assume that California's increasing diversity has at least two specific implications for our educational systems at all levels:

1   Increasing diversity sharpens the challenge for educators to teach basic skills and complex cognitive abilities to students from groups that the educational system has been least successful with in past years in order that these students may advance to their next educational level and/or succeed in the workplace.
2   Increasing diversity mandates that educators recognize different learning styles and develop curriculum and teaching strategies and design educational experiences that use these differences as a strength in the teaching and learning processes.

There has been considerable cooperation between and among the members of the education community since the California Education Round Table was formed in 1980. It is clear that each education segment's ability to fulfill its mission greatly depends on the success of the other segments. Colleges and universities can educate the full range of students capable of benefiting from higher education only if the elementary and secondary schools effectively prepare those students, and these schools can prepare students only if higher education effectively prepares teachers and college instructors to teach California's diverse students. As a further step in the Round Tables' collaborative efforts, the members issued a joint statement acknowledging the importance of working closely together in key areas of student preparation essential for the collective success of all Californians. It was based upon the following assumptions:

- To reach a consensus on what California students should know, understand, and be able to do in mathematics and English-language arts (reading, writing, speaking and listening) and reflect that consensus in statewide standards.
- To ensure that existing programs structure and resources dedicated to preparing and developing teachers are clearly focused on shared expectations for student achievement and on the recommendations of the Superintendent's Task Forces for reading and mathematics (which were themselves intersegmental in composition).
- To harness powerful technological capacities and advances will be harnessed to (1) improve the teaching of reading, writing, and mathematics; (2) enhance the understanding of university entrance requirements; (3) simplify college admissions and financial aid processes.
- To identify and deploy resources presently in the education systems and the community to improve student preparation and access to college and other postsecondary programs that support a high skills economy.
- To identify and/or develop instruments to assess students' mastery of English and mathematics.

Today, representatives from the Round Table are implementing this comprehensive plan and exploring additional initiatives consistent with the stated priorities and principles. Our institutions already have in place a substantial number of effective program structures that can be built on to address the challenges at hand.

The Round Table objective is to develop several new programs and to link existing ones more effectively to ensure that students who need help will receive special encouragement and support from the elementary grades through college admission and enrollment. They will report periodic progress in implementing this collaborative, integrated, and focused plan for enhancing the quality of education in California and for improving student performance.

The Institute for Education Reform

In November, 1994, CSU announced the formation of the Institute for Education Reform. The Chancellor emphasized that there was an absolutely urgent need to develop and cultivate programs that will improve our public schools. The main focus of the Institutes' work is to improve K-12 pupil academic performance by providing assistance to schools pursuing or contemplating reform efforts (e.g., charter schools, restructured schools, categorical reform, etc.), identifying best practices in K-12 teacher training, finding ways to protect and expand upon those efforts, and actively participating in the education reform debate in California through conferences, papers, and surveys that will be helpful to state policy makers, academics, and K-12 practitioners. Former Senator Gary Hart (who chaired the State Senate Education Committee for 12 years and authored its Charter School and Comprehensive Curriculum Reform bills) who serves as the founding Director of the Institute and his colleague Associate Director Sue Burr (Hart and Blurr, 1996) recommend four primary strategies to address program strengths and weaknesses in teacher preparation. They believe we need to strengthen K-12 and university partnerships through systematic review and recognition, focus on the student teaching experience, establish distinguished teachers in residence, and annually survey graduates for program strengths/weaknesses.

They support systematic reviewing and revising CSU policies to encourage better collaboration between education and arts/sciences faculty, tenure and promotion support for faculty who work within K-12, and a teacher diversity program. Further they recommend revising state laws and regulations for more school based experience for teaching candidates, with emphasis on assessment. These recommendations include:

a   integrated curriculum and early clinical experiences;
b   new models for a five year teacher prep program;
c   repeal of add-on courses;
d   teacher candidate assessment;
e   streamlined credentials;
f   limits on emergency credentials; and
g   expansion of promising state efforts.

Hart and Burr (1996), in the recently released 'The Teachers who Teach our Teachers: Teacher Preparation Programs at the California State University,' insist prospective teachers should be exposed to the theory and practice of teaching early and often in their undergraduate careers while acquiring substantive academic preparation. Likewise, early clinical experience is critical to future teachers. Early identification of those entering freshmen who desire to become teachers encourages early mentoring of the student, as well may influence them to continue to pursue teaching. Lower division undergraduate experiences should place students in the schools for early exposure to the profession. Their focus is on CSU Schools of Education and pre-service teacher preparation. The three primary recommendations made are:

1   Strengthening K-12 and university partnerships:
    a   systematic review and recognition
    b   focus on the student teaching experience

    c   distinguished teachers in residence
    d   survey of graduates for program strengths/weaknesses
2   Systematically reviewing and revising CSU policies to encourage better collaboration between education and arts/sciences faculty:
    a   links between schools of education and liberal studies
    b   support for faculty work with K-12
    c   faculty evaluation–tenure/promotion
    d   teacher diversity program
3   Revising state laws and regulations for more school based experience for teaching candidates, with emphasis on assessment:
    a   integrated curriculum and early clinical experiences
    b   new models for a five year teacher prep program
    c   repeal of add-on courses
    d   teacher candidate assessment
    e   streamlined credentials
    f   limits on emergency credentials
    g   expansion of promising state efforts

Of immediate concern to Hart and Burr are the increasing number of urban school districts in California that are hiring emergency permit holders. These individuals have a bachelor's degree and have passed the California Basic Education Skills Test but are currently being placed in the classroom with little or no previous classroom experience and without preparation in basic teaching methodology. The Institute just released the report (1996) *A State of Emergency. . . . in a State of Emergency Teachers*, which finds emergency teaching permits are valid for no more than one year each, but no limit exists on the number of times they can be renewed, which often results in a temporary circumstance becoming a permanent state of emergency. In theory, statutory and regulatory guidelines on renewal are designed to promote emergency teachers' progress toward a credential. This renewal rule is meant to keep emergency teachers moving toward credentialing. These individuals have a BA/BS degree and have passed the California Basic Educational Skills Test (CBEST). These individuals are currently being placed in the classroom with little or no previous classroom experience and without basic teacher methodology preparation.

While this situation presents a real problem to parents and students within the schools who deserve fully credentialed teachers, it can be rectified to a large extent through the availability of internship programs (Hart and Burr, 1996). With the recommendation and assistance of their school district or combination of school districts, new emergency permit holders may be placed in an internship program in which they will prepare for the MSAT (Multiple Subjects Achievement Test), and they will take classes in basic methodology, classroom management, and curriculum content. This procedure will allow these participants to become interns as soon as they pass the MSAT. Thus the district will be able to assure parents that the teachers of their children are being prepared in a systematic and professional manner. Furthermore, these new teachers will be on a clear path to a full credential, with support and assistance provided while they are completing the prescribed experiences.

The Commitment of External Funds

Selected leaders of the communities (led by CSU/UCLA/USC) comprising Los Angeles County were awarded from The Annenberg Foundation (December, 1994) $53,000,000 over a five-year period to be matched by at least an equal amount of additional funds from other sources, to improve radically the education of local children. This effort, termed the Los Angeles Metropolitan Project (LAAMP), seeks to attack the pathologies of turbulence, transience, and inconsistency which affect the educational lives of many young people in our communities. LAAMP will design schools in which there are consistently high expectations for all children, in which students and faculty know each other as individuals, in which students are achieving at high levels, in which teachers are actively engaged in the educational life of their school including their own professional development, and in which parents and community members actively participate in and receive systematic assessments of work in their school. Numerous school reform efforts throughout the country have made significant progress in this direction, and LAAMP seeks to build on these worthy efforts, extending and enhancing them to the point where such schools are the norm and not the exception. Particular attention will be directed to Families of Schools in which a child can experience a seamless high-quality education from pre-kindergarten through the twelfth grade.

Additionally, the Weingart Foundation (September, 1996), a Los Angeles-based charitable foundation, has awarded an $8.2 million grant to the Los Angeles Annenberg Metropolitan Project (LAAMP) and the Los Angeles Educational Alliance for Restructuring Now (LEARN) in support of a collaborative effort with the California State University system, and the Los Angeles and Long Beach Unified School District to improve teacher preparation, training and professional development for Los Angeles area teachers.

The Weingart Foundation grant (1996), which will be paid over five years, provides for the planning and implementation of a comprehensive professional training and support system for more than 2,000 teachers and administrators in Los Angeles County public schools. The project seeks to transform how universities and school districts prepare future teachers for success in the classroom, provide additional training and support for new teachers, and provide ongoing support and professional development for veteran teachers. The Weingart grant project is systemic and serves as a starting point for fundamentally changing teacher preparation and professional development programs throughout existing educational institutions.

Recognizing the leadership role of the California State University system in preparing new teachers (CSU is the largest teacher training institution in the nation), the new Weingart Foundation funded project establishes the CSU as lead partner with LAAMP and LEARN in a collaborative effort with school districts, teachers, and other institutions of higher education to design and implement a comprehensive teacher professional support system.

The grant also calls on participating school districts to make significant changes in how they provide for the training and professional development needs of educators. School district efforts include the establishment of school site based professional development centers, the recruitment and training of outstanding K-12 teachers to provide training and support for other teachers, and the realignment of salary point credit systems for professional development. It is also intended that this grant will help to create a new and genuine collaboration among Los Angeles area universities, LAAMP, LEARN, school districts, teachers, unions and other organizations to build the capacity of K-12 schools and institutions of higher education to stimulate long term systemic change in public education in Los Angeles County.

The Weingart initiative involves six Los Angeles Basin CSU campuses (Dominguez Hills, Fullerton, Long Beach, Los Angeles, Northridge, Pomona) working together on behalf of systematic reform. To date, most efforts at improvement have not had teachers at the focal point. CSU plans to implement a comprehensive professional training and support system for teachers and administrators jointly developed with K-12 experts. In 1994–5 the CSU issued 10,865 credentials (CSU in the 1990s, 1995), therefore is in an excellent position to lead and build capacity among K-12 schools and other Institutions of Higher Education (IHE). During the fall of 1996 these six campuses are identifying the best possible faculty to partner with K-12 schools and to develop a Professional Development Academy (PDA) collaboratively to revitalize and provide on-site professional development and to support preservice, beginning and inservice teaching efforts. The goal for the PDA is to serve as a mechanism for current and future teachers to create collaborative learning communities. The intent is to raise student achievement driven by student needs and teacher concerns. Assessment will be measured by:

a improvement of student performance;
b quality and match between professional development classroom supplementation and student achievement;
c evidence of better prepared professionals;
d teacher stability; and,
e design and delivery effectiveness of IHE.

The Commitment of Internal Leadership

None of these initiatives will make a difference without the commitment of our internal leadership team. Priorities must be established and understood, messages must be clear, and rewards must be aligned with stated objectives. Recognizing these imperatives, the CSU Deans of Education (1996) issued a statement that stated a plan of action over the next two years. Actions identified are:

1 intensify efforts to recruit teacher candidates;
2 establish regional advising and service centers to support the transition of teachers whose credentials may have lapsed or who have moved to California from other states;

3   expand evening and part-time teacher preparation programs;
4   expand greatly the number and variety of teacher internship credential programs;
5   expand career-ladder opportunities for paraprofessionals to become teachers; and
6   work in partnership with school districts to customize professional development programs for new and experienced teachers.

Their presidents responded quickly and firmly to their Dean's statement. They formed the Presidents' K-18 Committee (June, 1996) to ensure that the strengthening of K-12 education is a key strategic priority for the CSU. Their issued mission is stated as:

> We believe California's future is wedded to the quality of education it provides to its citizens. Our economic prosperity is contingent upon a well-trained and knowledgeable work force. Our ability to respond, whether it be to the revolutionary developments in information technology or the dramatic growth in cultural and linguistic diversity throughout California — depends to no small degree on our schools' ability to provide a dynamic curriculum, offer inspirational teaching, and engage in continuous renewal. Although this responsibility rests with all segments of our educational system — from preschool to post-baccalaureate — the challenges confronting our elementary and secondary schools are particularly compelling given the large number of students and the tremendous range of student backgrounds and interests . . . It is our conviction that the strengthening of K-12 education is of critical importance and must be a key strategic priority of the CSU. We believe that a strong public school system is of vital importance to our state's economy and will ensure the CSU focus of resources on appropriate college-level instruction, scholarly and creative activity, and service. We believe that the central mission of CSU's relationship to K-12 schools ought to be to improve the quality of preparation programs for school site personnel and to insure that the scholarly, pedagogical, technological expertise of the CSU is available to the schools on an ongoing basis.

In pursuit of these goals, the CSU's Presidents' K-18 Committee initial focus will be on internal efforts to improve our own school site personnel preparation programs and their relationship to K-12 education. The ultimate objective, however, is to see that these reform efforts influence K-12 and postsecondary institutions, thus helping to transform educational practices and to affect state education policy.

The following principles guide the Presidents' K-18 Committee designed to strengthen education programs for teachers and other education professionals:

1   The education of teachers is a university-wide responsibility and is of such critical priority that it will influence key decisions regarding faculty recruitment, promotion, tenure, compensation, and workloads. Because prospective teachers are most influenced by the quality of teaching they encounter as students, all university faculty need to demonstrate effective instructional practices and serve as good teaching role models.

2   Students contemplating teaching careers will have opportunities in their undergraduate years to participate in academic majors and other university courses which integrate subject matter and teacher education course work and provide multiple site-based clinical learning opportunities. Such approaches will provide better opportunities to identify high-potential students, recruit exemplary candidates for the teaching profession, and maximize the all-university nature of teacher education and the creation of an integrated five year approach.

3   CSU Schools of Education (SOE) will embody the principles of good professional practice by providing extensive standards to define the characteristics of a well-prepared teacher educated anywhere within the CSU system. In order to complete successfully a CSU preparation program, teacher candidates will be individually assessed based on these established standards, which include competencies such as knowledge in content areas and appropriate instructional planning and presentation skills.

4   SOE as well as other schools and departments within the CSU will develop and maintain partnerships with K-12 schools to facilitate continuous renewal of schools and universities alike. Regular faculty exchanges and other ongoing joint university/school activities will help achieve the simultaneous co-reform of teacher education and of K-12 schools.

5   Regular consultation and collaboration with leaders in the K-12 community is an important all-university responsibility throughout the CSU. In addition, presidential engagement and action will be a high priority regarding recommendations made by groups working to improve education in the state such as the California Education Round Table, the CSU Remedial Education Task Force, the University of California Outreach Task Force, and the SB 1422 Advisory Committee.

6   All CSU Presidents, as campus leaders, have a responsibility to promote the principles articulated above in their personnel practices, academic planning, budget, and public pronouncements. Indeed, for this effort to succeed, leaders throughout the CSU, including the Chancellor, the Board of Trustees, the Presidents, the Academic Vice Presidents, the Academic Deans, and the Academic Senates must also assume this responsibility.

Three committees and an *ad hoc* task force have been formed based on this strategic initiative on teacher preparation and K-18 education:

- *Curriculum/Assessment/Standards Subcommittee* (1) Will develop standards to define the characteristics of a well-prepared teacher educated in any CSU preparation program and identify assessment systems which are currently available or under development which can be used individually to assess teacher candidates to determine if they have attained the standards; (2) Will identify five-year teacher preparation programs (within the CSU or in other IHE's in California) which integrate subject matter and teacher and education coursework and provide multiple site-based clinical learning experiences and recommend means to expand upon such efforts: and (3) Will review existing relationships among Liberal Studies, teacher preparation, and other Arts and Sciences programs and recommend organizational structures to strengthen the link among these programs. Principles 2 and 3 undergird this committee.

- *Rewards/Resources Subcommittee* Will develop reward and recognition systems for faculty which reflect the principle that the education of teachers is a university-wide responsibility and is such a critical priority that it should influence key decisions regarding faculty recruitment, promotion, tenure, compensation and workloads . . . will identify resources needed to implement reward and recognition systems. Principles 1 and 6 undergird this committee.

- *Market Share and CSU Collaboration Subcommittee* Will analyze CSU's decline in credential candidates over the past several years to identify campuses losing these candidates and reasons for the loss . . . will develop strategy to stem the decline of credential candidates prepared in CSU, and identify/develop/sustain partnerships within CSU and with K-12 schools which embody well designed, field-based teacher preparation programs that promote collegiality, reflective practice and continuous improvement. Principles 4 and 5 undergird this committee.

- *Ad Hoc Task Force on Marketing and Resource Development specific to the K-3 Teacher Initiative:* Will secure additional resources and other support needed for CSU to identify and develop new and creative ways to supply the teachers needed to implement the class reduction legislation . . . will set up alliances with partners who share responsibility for meeting the needs of the K-3 Teacher Initiative . . . and will partner with state agencies such as the California State Department of Education, and the Trade and Commerce Department.

Hanging on the Cutting Edge

Tell me and I'll forget; show me and I may not remember; involve me and I'll understand. (Native American Proverb)

The Presidents and Deans Meet the Round Table and the Institute

As the end of the twentieth century approaches, the K-12 reform crisis grows. At CSU the administrative initiatives, supported by dramatic Annenberg and Weingart commitments, and undergirded by the 'Hart Institute' policy leadership, are attracting national attention. All segments in the state are pulling together, and the path to fundamental restructuring is slowly emerging.

In the California Education Round Table document *Collaborative Initiatives to Improve Student Learning and Academic Performance, Kindergarten through College* (1995) they have agreed to take the following steps:

- Agree on high school graduation standards and clarify expected competencies for university admission;
- Strengthen programs and resources for teacher preparation and professional development;
- Use technology to improve the quality of education and streamline access to postsecondary education;
- Bring additional community and professional resources into the teaching and learning process; and
- Assess high school progress more uniformly to determine if the standards have been met.

Partially in response to this intersection of opportunities, the California Department of Education (CDE) has recently allocated $6 million from Goals 2000 funds to 10 County Office of Education service regions to be used to develop partnerships with institutions of higher education that prepare beginning teachers. According to the grant proposal, the intent of these partnerships is to: (1) improve the preservice preparation of K-3 teachers in the area of reading instruction, (2) improve the preservice induction connection and support for beginning teachers, and (3) ensure a supply of well prepared teachers to the districts, particularly to districts that have difficulty in attracting adequately prepared teachers. The grant proposal further states that funds may be spent on curriculum development for preservice instruction, or instruction itself, which addresses a comprehensive list of K-3 reading instruction topics representing a balanced approach to reading instruction that combines explicit direct skills instruction with literature rich comprehension instruction. This approach parallels the mandate contained in AB 3075 (Baldwin), which requires that beginning in 1 January 1997 all multiple subject and single subject credential programs include comprehensive reading instruction that is research-based and includes systematic organized skills and a strong literature, language and comprehension component.

The Institute for Education Reform has created the CSU Center for the Improvement of the Instruction of Reading (1996) to provide a statewide mechanism for faculty professional development in research about effective reading instruction and exemplary classroom practice in beginning reading. The Center has two key missions: (1) to provide professional development opportunities to higher education faculty who teach preservice coursework on language arts or reading and (2) to assist CSU campuses in the development of partnerships with school districts and county offices of education designed to improve the preservice preparation of teachers in reading. The Center is a clearinghouse for research and proven instructional practices in reading. Specific activities of the Center include:

- To provide a series of seminars providing professional development activities for higher education faculty who teach preservice courses in reading or language arts;
- To assemble a group of researchers and exemplary classrooms to serve as resource for higher education faculty and preservice teacher candidates;

- To develop an interactive Internet web site to provide the latest research and classroom practices ideas on the instruction of reading and to serve as the communications hub for individuals involved in professional development activities;
- To promote and coordinate on-site clinical instruction and practice at schools for faculty and prospective teachers; and,
- To create and/or disseminate appropriate instructional materials to university and K-12 educators.

Given the Goals 2000 initiative, CSU campuses are working with local school districts in their regions to develop partnerships which meet the intent of providing improved reading instruction to preservice candidates and beginning teachers.

As noted earlier in this chapter, a specific Hart and Burr (1996) recommendation relating to emergency credentialed teachers is being implemented through the availability of internship programs. A new CSU initiative, Intern 2000 Program, is specifically focused on the six Los Angeles Basin campuses and is linked to the Annenberg-Weingart-Ford grants. With the assistance of their school district new emergency permit holders may be placed in an internship program in which they prepare for the MSAT, and they take classes in basic methodology, classroom management, and curriculum content. These new teachers will be on a clear path to a full credential with support and assistance being provided while they are completing the prescribed experiences.

Credential candidates are not assessed individually to determine their capabilities, which is virtually unlike all other professions, such as, law, medicine. Hart and Burr recommend the establishing of common standards and a system of candidate assessment to ensure the modeling of instructional approaches desired.

There are some items which must be viewed early if we are to break out of traditional molds and have any chance of introducing new concepts. The need to look at existing policies that are both on campuses as well as executive orders at the system level that probably grew out of a need to fix some thing that now has become tradition in practice but may very well impede as we look forward and try to look for innovation. We need to sit down and rethink, put them all back on the table, and determine what we want to keep, what we do not need and then what we might need to be put in its place to help streamline our credentialing process.

Conclusion

Everybody is ignorant, only on different subjects. (Will Rogers)

There is, there can be no question about the legitimacy of higher education's role in the strengthening and reshaping of our nation's K-12 schools.

We start with the following assumptions:

1 For the first time in American history, higher education had to experience fundamental change without incremental resources or widespread public

confidence — therefore, basic transformation had to evolve from painful internal reallocation.

2   The most likely strongest competitors on the horizon — again, for the first time — were *not* other academic institutions. Combined with '1' above, this meant that our institution had to design a variety of strategic alliances with non-university partners to accomplish subtle but inevitable metamorphoses.

3   We must shape a national network of high performance comprehensive university-based consortia devoted to regional human capital and economic development.

4   Higher education's growing hypocritical gap between why patrons send us money and how it is actually spent must be closed through public accountability measures and reward/prestige systems that actually honor the public's priorities.

5   Tied directly to the point immediately above, and with our priority of direct linkage to K-12, we must acknowledge that in the absence of a fundamental revision of the singular prestige and reward system that currently characterizes American higher education, it will be impossible for strong academic institutions to reverse their priority sequence and put a higher emphasis on the value of K-12 reform.

The question then becomes 'What would viable evidence be of a restructured or multi-level status and reward system?' Not just emphasizing undergraduate teaching *vis-à-vis* graduate research, but particularly accruing prestige and tangible value to those faculty and programs that reach into the school system and risk reputations to improve the lives of our nation's youngsters and their families. As we have seen, in California, and particularly at CSU, higher education and prebaccalaureate institutions are reaching out imaginatively and courageously to each other. Fundamental experiments have begun and they have been launched in ways to encourage a planning dialectic between the two levels, each informing and improving the other, and with an abiding commitment to care for lower and middle class anxiety about the future classroom and workplace. Art Levine, the distinguished scholar and new president of Columbia Teachers College, recently told us 'as presidents we talk about the institutions we hope ours will become, not always about the ones ours currently are'. Our goal is to have campus presidents work with faculty leaders to acknowledge the gap, recognize the danger, and move toward matching dream with reality — time, turmoil, and tenacity will tell.

At the core, presidential leadership will be an essential ingredient in the restructuring and reform movement. Their challenge? Let us close with the last paragraphs from Robert Rosenzweig's new manuscript on the Research University soon to be published by Johns Hopkins:

As the university's principal public person, the burden of explaining to the public what it needs from the university and how that may be different from what it thinks it wants, falls most heavily on the president. But the most articulate and persuasive advocate is, in the end, no better than the facts of his case, and in recent years the facts have tended to undermine what should be a strong case. Modern universities, after all, have proven themselves to be the most effective knowledge creating institutions in history. In the process of creating knowledge, and because the process is closely linked with the training of future scholars, they also provide society with its next generation of knowledge producers and transmitters, and they do so at a level of quality that attracts students from all over the world. The values that sustain the university: openness, respect for dissent, commitment to evidence and the proper inference from evidence as the best instrument for settling disputes, integrity, intellectual honesty, these are all the values that also sustain a free society. Moreover, universities are their principal, and in some cases their only, exemplars and practitioners. To change the university fundamentally is to risk the loss of a great deal, indeed. (Rosenzweig, in press)

But it is also true that years of prosperity and preferred treatment have bred elements of carelessness, self-indulgence, a sense of entitlement, and not a little arrogance. Carelessness about faculty misconduct, inattentiveness to the educational needs of undergraduates, disingenuousness about the utility of university research to produce economic benefits, the willingness to accept restrictive conditions in exchange for research funds from industry, the use of political tactics like the pork barrel that undermine the image of universities as something more than another self-interested supper at the public trough, while none of these fairly describes all institutions, all are real and the cumulative effect has produced a level of cynicism about universities that can only be destructive and that, if nothing else, distracts attention from efforts to make the case that is so badly needed.

If those flaws are treated as problems of image, best dealt with by image makers, then the future is bleak. If, however, they are seen as real problems to be addressed by real solutions, then there are grounds for optimism. Indeed, there is no alternative to optimism. The virtual university, like the virtual everything else, is by definition a false university. It may do some things that are now done in universities, but it cannot replace them. Values are given life by institutions. Political theory without political institutions to give it life is mere rhetoric; educational values without educational institutions to live them are mere platitudes. In the end, the health of individual universities, no matter how well managed they may be, will depend on the health of the institution of the university. To attend to the former without attending to the latter is ultimately a failing strategy. That is the challenge modern university presidents face. We should all pray for their success.

References

ANNENBERG FOUNDATION (1994) *Annenberg Challenge Grant for Los Angeles County, CA, School Reform*, St David's, PA: The Annenberg Foundation.

BLAKE, S., Personal Communication, September 4, 1996.

BLAKE, S., SCHWARTZ, H., WILSON, B. and YELVERTON, K., Personal Communications, September 12, 1996.

CALIFORNIA EDUCATIONAL ROUND TABLE (1995) *Collaborative Initiatives to Improve Student Learning and Academic Performance Kindergarten through College*, Sacramento, CA: Intersegmental Coordinating Council.

CSU IN THE 1990s (1995) Unpublished draft document, Long Beach, CA: California State University.

CSU DEANS OF EDUCATION (9 August 1996) Press release, Long Beach, CA: California State University.

DARLING-HAMMOND, L. (1996) *The National Commission on Teaching & America's Future*, James B. Hunt, Jr, Chair, Governor, State of North Carolina.

DEPARTMENT OF FINANCE (June, 1996) *Chart on State Budget Program, 1983–84 to 1995–96*, Sacramento, CA: Department of Finance.

EHRLICH, T., MUNITZ, B. and WELLMAN, J. (in press) *Planning and Policy: Leveraging Change in a Time of Fundamental Transformation*, SCUP Source Book-IDMRP Academy.

HART, G.K. and BURR, S.K. (February, 1996) *The Teachers Who Teach Our Teachers: Teacher Preparation Programs at the California State University*, Sacramento, CA: The CSU Institute for Education Reform.

HART, G.K. and BURR, S.K. (July, 1996) *Center for the Improvement of Reading Instruction*, Sacramento, CA: The CSU Institute for Education Reform.

HART, G.K. and BURR, S.K. (September, 1996) *A State of Emergency. . . . in a State of Emergency Teachers*, Sacramento, CA: The CSU Institute for Education Reform.

KERR, C. (October, 1993) 'Preserving the master plan — What is to be done in a new epoch of more limited growth of resources?', Invited speaker at the Joint Meeting of the California State University Board of Trustees and the University of California Board of Regents, Sacramento, California.

NATIONAL ASSOCIATION OF SYSTEM HEADS (NASH), Personal Communication, October 15, 1996.

PLOTKIN, S., Personal Communication, September 6, 1996.

PRESIDENTS' K-18 COMMITTEE (June 26, 1996) *Mission Statement on K-18 Teacher Preparation*, Long Beach, CA: California State University.

ROSENZWEIG, R. (in press) *The American University: Policy, Politics and Presidential Leadership*, Maryland: Johns Hopkins.

WEINGART FOUNDATION GRANT (September, 1996) *Improving Teacher Preparation, Training and Professional Development*, Los Angeles: The Weingart Foundation.

WILSON, GOVERNOR P. (May, 1996) *Budget Highlights 1996–7 K-12 Education*, Sacramento: Office of the Governor.

WILSON, G. (1996) 'Wilson signs legislation to put more talented dedicated teachers in California classrooms' (26 July), Press release. Sacramento: Office of the Governor.

8   A Grimm Tale

James Raths

Introduction

In my judgment, universities have a key role to play in professional education —
including medicine, law, dentistry, education, and most other professions as well.
Of course there are alternatives. As a matter of policy, it is possible to conceive of
assigning professional preparation programs to night schools, junior colleges, and/
or entrepreneurial consortia in the private sector. Given the fact that practice in
most professions includes a combination of art and science, there is no precise
litmus test to distinguish journeymen from hacks. Advocates for institutions other
than universities would and do argue loud and long that their graduates better serve
the public and are better trained, if not better educated, for the professional roles to
which they aspire.

But there is a missing ingredient in every non-university approach currently
under consideration. There is an urgent need — at every age and in every context
— for universities to criticize (and thus improve) current professional practice. This
obligation holds for all professions, but for the teaching profession certainly. The
profession of Education is a case in point. According to the highly acclaimed report
'A Nation at Risk', the quality of our current schools is so bad, that our enemies
couldn't have designed a worst system for our children (National Commission on
Excellence in Education, 1983). So, massive efforts have been undertaken since
1983 to reform our schools. Does the nation want normal schools or alternative
routes to licensure systems staffed primarily with practicing teachers working to
prepare candidates to 'succeed' in *today's* mediocre (or worse) schools? No, of
course not. Instead, our society needs to prepare teachers for classrooms that don't
exist today and that will serve tomorrow's children after the reforms have taken
hold. The thesis of my 'tale' is that it is becoming more and more difficult for
universities to play this role given current licensing and accreditation trends in the
United States. It is to this new threat that I address my comments.

But first, I want to return to the notion that professional schools' primary
mission is to improve current practice and in so doing become critics of current
practice. There is always a useful tension between practitioners and professors — a
tension that is aroused from one vantage point by an understandable intolerance for
criticism, and from the other a wonderment about the existence of such widespread
bad practice. Let me expand with some examples.

At a midwestern university, there was a program to prepare veterinarians to
care for house pets. Candidates in this program were told explicitly that when a

small dog is brought in with a cut on its leg good practice dictates the use of a sterile mask and gloves to avoid infecting the dog's leg; the use of sterile needle and thread to sew up the cut, and other similar prophylactic measures. Practitioners hearing of these teachings became outraged. It was their position that any veterinarian who practiced in such a mode would go broke in a month. They wrote to the university, asserting that no one in practice could afford such expensive treatments for such a minor injury. The professors responded pridefully, 'Are you interested in implementing good practice or being a hack!'

Of course while healthy in optimum doses, the tensions between the university professional schools and the field can become heated and acrimonious. Some veterinarians were heard to say that the veterinarian professors were only teaching at the university because they couldn't do anything else. Maybe so, but the issue is: How can practice be improved?

Another story about professional school/practitioner tension. Almost 20 years ago during another era of competency based education, medical evaluators at a distinguished medical college were busy writing items that could be given to candidates in clinical medicine to assess their skills and judgments as potential doctors. One of the items on a test developed by the professors was the following:

> You are called in the middle of the night by a woman who says she is a sister of one of your patients. She has a four month old baby girl with an ear ache — and the baby won't stop crying. Which of the following options would you choose?

The options included some obvious ones: (a) give the baby some aspirin and call back if that doesn't work, and (b) take her temperature and call me back with the reading. One of the options, and the one that was keyed as correct by the university-based team was, 'Tell the mother to meet you in the emergency room of the hospital in 15 minutes.' A panel of local doctors who were asked to respond to this item were outraged at the response keyed as correct. They were confident that the response was 'typically academic'. In rather angry tones, the practicing physicians claimed that practitioners could respond in this way because if they did they would never get any sleep. The university team responded by citing medical findings such as the average length of the Eustachian tube in a four month old baby, and how the ear drum itself was at risk in this situation of being severely and irreparably damaged by infection. The local doctors were unconvinced — but the university professors held their ground in the name of 'good practice'.

How likely is it that a normal school faculty or public school teachers moonlighting as teacher educators would have the dispositions or the status to criticize current practice? In my judgment, universities are the current best hope for finding ways to nudge practice along.

Have schools of education criticized current practice? I would said 'yes'. The charge against homogeneous grouping has come mostly from academics; the need to mainstream children was an impetus of parent groups informed and pushed in part by University professors. The changes and improvements in writing instruction and in reading instruction have come in the main from university professors. And without an investment in teacher education and the interaction this process requires between practitioners and researchers/scholars, it seems very unlikely that the university role as critic of current practice and improver of current practice would be played out.

The premise of this collection of essays is that the survival of university-based teacher education is at serious risk. What happened to put university-based teacher education into this precarious situation? I write to share one explanation. The tale I have to tell begins long ago and speaks of a solution that the teacher education establishment developed to address a very pressing problem at the time.[1] The 'solution' was apparently quite successful in the short run. But, as H.L. Menken reminded us: 'For every complex problem, there is a simple solution. And it is usually wrong!' Not only was the solution in this case wrong, but it can also be seen as the seed of disaster for university-based teacher education programs and in the long run the profession itself.

The Tale

Once upon a time, just after World War II, teacher education began to take on increased prominence. Prior to 1940, licensing requirements for teachers were minimal at best — and not taken very seriously. After the war, as populations grew, as professional awareness increased, and as state bureaucracies became more invasive in the lives of citizens, a touchy problem arose that seemed to threaten a principle pillar in the foundation of higher education — namely its autonomy. Universities in the United States had enjoyed for years the privileges of autonomy. Faculties at universities prided themselves in the idea that they alone controlled the University's curriculum and graduation requirements. No royal peer, or political hack, or even wealthy alumnus could dictate curriculum issues to faculty at American universities. This fierce independence on the part of university faculty was recently demonstrated at Yale University when a benefactor donated $20,000,000 to the University to establish a program in western culture. The faculty decided the program proposal was not a good idea and the University returned the money.

On the other hand, state governments are by default assigned responsibility for regulating education by the 10th amendment to the US Constitution, and by almost all of the several state constitutions in the Union. State constitutions, as a rule, assign duties and responsibilities for regulating public schools and for licensing school employees to the legislatures, to the Governor, or to others within State Government, such as a State Board of Education.

In sum, two powerful institutions were on a collision course. The state governments had rights to license teachers and thus to insist on particular forms of professional preparation on the part of candidates prior to licensing. Universities had taken the position that their faculties alone could decide program requirements and graduation requirements.

Our 'elders' in teacher education anticipated the problems that the over-lapping responsibilities foreshadowed. Working through national professional organizations — precursors of today's American Association of Colleges for Teacher Education — teacher educators endorsed and implemented agreements between states and institutions of higher education that would serve to forestall conflict. The agreement was called 'entitlement' or certification by program approval. States would approve teacher education programs at the various institutions of higher education within their jurisdiction, and as a result, any candidate graduating from the institution's approved program would be 'entitled' to a teaching license. As will be illustrated later, the approval process was initially quite informal and deferential. This solution was more generous than 'win/win'. From the vantage point of higher education, it was more nearly 'winner take all'. Or so it seemed.

The fact that higher education had yielded to state governments the authority to review and approve its teacher education programs was lost in the general comity and deference found between state bureaucrats and University officials in the early going. A linchpin in the entitlement process had to do with the program approval process. From the late 1940s through the 1970s the process was far from rigorous. The following description of an exchange of letters between the University of Illinois and the State of Illinois illustrates this point.

Professor J. Marlowe Slater, Associate Dean for Teacher Education at the University, wrote to an official at the Illinois State Board of Education in Springfield who held a title such as 'Supervisor of Teacher Education'. The letter read in its entirety:[2]

Dear Sir:

I am writing to inform you that the University of Illinois has just instituted a new program preparing mathematics teachers for secondary schools. The rationale for the new program and its requirements for admission and graduation are described in the enclosed document. Please enter this program on your list of State-approved programs.

Sincerely,

J. Marlowe Slater
Associate Dean

A reply from Springfield, dated within a week of Professor Slater's original mailing was as follows:

Dear Dean Slater:

Thank you for your letter and description of your new teacher education program in secondary mathematics. Please be assured that I have entered this new program on our list of approved programs. If I can be of further help to you, please let me know.

Sincerely,

J. Arthur Rudd
Supervisor, Teacher Education

Suffice it to say, the state's interest in quality teacher education was delegated, in a sense, to the University.

Sequela

So, as we have seen, higher education ceded in part its claims of program autonomy to negotiate the 'entitlement' compromise. The agreement also in part nullified the need for the state to take the evaluation of candidates as individuals very seriously. In effect, the state delegated the authority to make licensing decisions to the University. Anyone who completed an approved teacher education program successfully was ipso facto eligible for a license. The seeds were now sown for threatening the survival of university based teacher education.

The first threat arose from the university's stepping away from the responsibility of evaluating candidates rigorously in the certification process. It was the rare institution that adopted evaluation procedures for teacher candidates that were different, more rigorous, or more responsible than those found in all other areas of the university. That is, the procedures that were deemed satisfactory for deciding to award a degree to an English major or a history major were seen as sufficient for a teacher education major. And the procedures for making a recommendation to the state involved, in the main, taking into account only grade point average and meeting program course requirements.

Professor Martin Haberman, a distinguished professor of education at the University of Wisconsin at Milwaukee, had challenged his colleagues in teacher education by continually asking:

> Consider a candidate with a B+ average at graduation time. What could this person possibly be or do to prevent his graduating from an approved teacher education program and thus, through the entitlement process, from being licensed as a teacher?

The current answer is, and has been for decades, nothing. Haberman teases (torments) us with examples: 'What if the candidate were an avowed racist? Would he still be allowed to graduate and receive a teaching license?' It is not clear what would happen to such an individual today, but a best guess is that by raising the specter of 'political correctness' and the guarantees of free speech, an avowed racist with a B+ average would be graduated from most approved teacher education programs and be granted a teaching license. Is it unreasonable to anticipate professors saying, 'After all, why should we play God with an individual's career? Let the schools who are making employment decisions sort out those who will be successful teachers from those who would be less successful teachers in their particular contexts' (Haberman and Stinnett, 1973).

As a result, the standard notion that quality control in the professions is composed of a three-legged stool — program accreditation, a realistic and carefully supervised internship experience, and the rigorous evaluation of candidates for teaching licenses — was undercut by the entitlement policy. The state apparently assumed that everyone graduating from approved programs was qualified for a teaching license. The University assumed that what is sufficient rigor for graduating a student in the liberal arts should suffice for graduating a student in teacher education, so nothing beyond the grade point average and number of credits earned was deemed relevant to the decision.

The hypothesis I am advancing is that the decision to implement the 'entitlement' policy — an agreement that brought peace of sorts for the period 1950 through 1970 — was initially successful. But at what costs? Quality control, the rigorous application of high standards, and the accountability for the proficiency of teacher candidates was seriously diluted, leading to high level credibility problems in the 1990s.

The failure of the university to meet its responsibilities in the 'entitlement process' had a significant effect on the credibility of university-based teacher education. But, the other side of the equation, state program approval was also hindering the basic mission of university based teacher education, namely that of critic of current practice. By conceding the right of states to approve and ultimately dictate the content of teacher education programs, the autonomy of higher education, valued and protected over the centuries, was being decimated. When the teacher empowerment movement arrived in the early 1970s, the National Education Association was quick to propose teacher dominated 'teacher education quality control boards' within the various states. These new boards, often created by acts of state legislatures after the powerful prodding of the NEA State affiliates, quickly wrote new regulations requiring Universities to offer early field experiences, as well as courses in special education, parent/community education, multicultural education, and other areas seen as critical — whether or not the University faculty agreed with these priorities or not. Teacher educators, needing to promise their students that they would be eligible for licensure through the entitlement agreements were forced to accept the state regulations as a matter of course. Teacher education programs burgeoned in size — with professional education courses dominating as much as 50 per cent of the graduation requirements.[3]

In sum, Universities ended up with teacher education programs over which their faculties had very little control, graduating teacher candidates who were not evaluated in ways different from degree candidates in the liberal arts. If this scenario is correct, is it any wonder that university-based teacher education is in trouble? What university provost would be willing to invest scarce and precious funds into such an operation? What teacher educator could deny that university based teacher education as we have come to know it is 'at risk'?

But in the 1990s, the problem is becoming even worse. Acting on the recommendations of prestigious commissions, such as that chaired by Darling-Hammond (1996), more and more states are setting requirements for program approval that require candidates to be prepared to teach the state's curriculum in ways the state has mandated. In some states, the teacher quality control boards are even mandating not only what candidates are to be taught, but how they are to learn. A recent standard to be applied to candidates in the State of Delaware states not only that they have specified knowledge, but that they have come to acquire the knowledge through a reflective process. While it is logical for the state government to require teacher preparation programs to prepare candidates for today's schools and to use today's teaching methods and to accept today's ideologies, in the long run this sort of strong arm policy can be disastrous for schools and for educational policy. Criticism of professional practice, now a hallmark of many teacher education programs, will be stifled in the name of 'alignment'.

Moral of the Tale

It would be nice to finish this account with the line, 'And university-based teacher educators lived happily ever after.' Right now, the possibility of any sort of happiness seems remote. What are some policies that universities might adopt to at least ameliorate the problem and reduce the risk that their programs are now experiencing? With full awareness of the danger of 'simple solutions', here are some implications from this tale:

1 Cancel all entitlement agreements. They are seriously flawed and serve to undermine the autonomy of the University. Further, since states are adding increasing requirements for certification beyond mere graduation from an approved program — criminal background checks, attaining passing scores on PRAXIS tests, and similar other mandates — the advantages of graduating from approved programs are diminishing.

2 Deny the right of states to approve teacher education programs. Yield to them the right to license teachers in terms of their experiences, skills, and dispositions. This recommendation is the reverse side of the coin described in Recommendation #1 above. The University should work to insulate itself from the political winds that advance fads and 'common sense' approaches that have little merit.

3 Work with national associations to develop a system of reciprocity for teacher licensure among states that would allow candidates who are graduates from teacher education units accredited by NCATE to seek employment in any state in the Union without undue penalty. There is a slap-dash system now in place, administered in effect by the National Association of State Directors of Teacher Education and Certification (NASDTEC), that allows for a degree of reciprocity. But the agreements negotiated by states through the good offices of NASDTEC are bilateral and complex and continually changing. A better system could be established to the benefit of the profession and the teachers who are its members.

4 To make Recommendation #3 work, the NCATE standards have to be revised once again — to give them more focus on those elements of programs that contribute to quality. That is, some of the politically correct language in the current standards having to do with 'global perspectives' and the idealist expectation that each program (or unit) have an explicit model to give direction to its programs could be omitted. New standards could be written that have to do with resources (human and fiscal) and with program evaluation practices.

5   Finally, states will need to find ways to evaluate individual candidates for licensure. The time-consuming practices of the National Board for Professional Teaching Standards cannot be adopted because they are not feasible. The quick and dirty approach of using PRAXIS examinations should also be shunned because of their problematic validity and because of the negative impacts this practice has on the diversity of the national teaching corps. The profession working together — practitioners, researchers, and policy makers — might design workable procedures that, while not perfect, may be perfectible as our knowledge and technical skills increase over the next century.

Notes

1   Readers should know that this 'story' is not found in the classic histories of teacher education, such as Johnson and Johanningmeier (1972), Haberman and Stinnett (1973), or Clifford and Gutherie (1988). My guess is that the policy originated in the National Commission on Teacher Education and Professional Standards, or its precursors, circa 1950.
2   I am re-constructing these letters from memory since the University of Illinois files are no longer available to me. However, the letters were so brief, and their contents so odd, I am confident that my memory is near perfect on these matters. Also, Professor Slater was indeed the Associate Dean at Illinois at the time; I made up the name of the State official.
3   To be fair, in some states, the Teacher Quality Control Boards took a different tack. Influenced by conservative influences, some states abolished 'education' majors and put a ceiling on the number of education courses that could be required for entitlement programs.

References

CLIFFORD, G.J. and GUTHERIE, J.W. (1988) *Ed school*. Chicago: University of Chicago.
HABERMAN, M. and STINNETT, T.M. (1973) *Teacher Education and the New Profession of Teaching*, Berkeley, CA: McCutchan
JOHNSON, JR.H.C. and JOHANNINGMEIER, E.V. (1972) *Teachers for the Prairie*, Urbana, IL: University of Illinois.
NATIONAL COMMISSION ON EXCELLENCE IN EDUCATION (1983) *Nation at Risk*, Washington, DC: US.
NATIONAL COMMISSION ON TEACHING AND AMERICAN'S FUTURE (1996) *Report*, New York, Author.

9 University Responsibility for a Public Purpose: Institutional Accountability and Teacher Education

Calvin Frazier

Universities tend to treat schools of education and the preparation of teachers like any other department, school, or college. Some variation might be allowed for professionally oriented units such as the schools of journalism, business, architecture, and education but for the most part the same policies and administrative expectations govern all participants in the university culture. The mind set is the same: you are in the university system and you conform to the university rules and culture. Failure to do so means, 'you are not one of us'. Where does this leave those faculty involved in meeting some very critical public expectations relative to the preparation of teachers for America's schools?

From the study of teacher education settings in the 1980s by Goodlad and his colleagues, there were four common themes identified in institutions. Programs for the preparation of educators were characterized by a (Goodlad, Soder and Sirotnik, 1990) 'loss of identity accompanying the shift to a research orientation'; (Soder, 1995) search for prestige; (National Commission on Teaching and America's Future, 1996) intrusion of external forces, and (Soder, 1995) 'market competition' (Goodlad, Soder and Sirotnik, 1990). Loss of identity and search for prestige can generate strong feelings and psychological conflict for teacher educators. One might compare this to an organ transplant rejection by a host body.

Legislators and representatives of state agencies are not seen as having any legitimacy but are external, intrusive forces posing a threat to the university. Roger Soder's wonderful dialogue in the *Record in Educational Leadership* captures the resentment well. 'I don't want the university to have to give up its control of teacher education. Let me tell you, the university already has precious little control over teacher education. We're already little more than a state training institute' (Soder, 1995).

Any consideration of institutional accountability for teacher education quality must recognize the conflict in the two worlds. The external world speaks one language. The university culture speaks another. Teacher educators and their students are caught in the middle. But nested in the one and interacting daily with university policies and expectations, school of education faculty generally are drawn to the research and writing ark and their desire for peer prestige. Off setting this movement, however, is a heightened anxiety caused by the marketing competition from alternative approaches and concern over who, the universities, private vendors or school districts, will prepare the estimated two million teachers projected by the National Commission on Teaching and America's Future to be needed by 2006 (National Commission on Teaching and America's Future, 1996).

This chapter argues for a quality program for the two million new teachers and for the continued involvement of those universities choosing to operate under a new set of accountability guidelines: guidelines that will be seen by some as being even more intrusive than past state approaches but when examined closely will be welcomed by many who will see this as an opportunity to bring a much needed creativity and energy to teacher preparation programs. Such is the price of hosting a program having a very specific and profound public purpose.

Public Purpose versus Institutional Mission

Teacher education has a particular place in the university mission. Unlike other professional development and career programs, teacher education comes into the university culture loaded with public expectations and a sense of urgency. In a community emphasizing academic freedom and faculty designed majors and minors, the teacher preparation program sits as the most heavily regulated offering in the university. Preparing teachers for classroom leadership responsibilities means the institution is assuming a state function and in a very real sense, becoming an agent of the state. But address a school of education faculty as 'agents of the state' and the statement rings as a harsh, dissonant challenge to their role as academicians. However, the state commitment to public education has given birth to schools, local boards of education, state departments of education, and teacher preparation programs. Absent this purpose, education as we know it, may have taken a very different form.

Historically, the well being of our democratic society was seen as resting on the quality of the nation's education undertaking. Again, quoting Soder, 'The purpose of schools, the major purpose of schools in America, is to teach children the moral and intellectual responsibilities for living and working in a democracy' (Soder, 1995). This theme, articulated by Washington, stressed by Jefferson, and advocated by Horace Mann argues persuasively that sustaining a democracy rests on an educated citizenry. The philosophical underpinnings seem undeniable. Yet, the status of schools of education and teacher education would suggest that even faculty members in the school of education, as well as arts and science staff, the campus leadership and governing boards, fail to make the connection between quality schools, quality teachers, and the university's teacher education program. The public ends are regularly displaced by institutional and individual faculty goals and priorities.

The public interest is expressed in state law that in turn is based on constitutional provisions similar to Colorado's Article IX, Section 11, whereby 'the general assembly is granted the power to require, unless educated by other means, that every child shall attend the public school during the ages of six and eighteen years' (Colorado School Laws, 1997). Additionally, state constitutions commonly require that the educational system designed be 'thorough and uniform' (Colorado) or 'thorough and efficient' (New Jersey). Courts have utilized such provisions to require equity in the financing of public schools and uniformity in the preparation of teachers serving the public schools. Absent some common teaching skills and quality by those carrying out the public education mandate, courts have indicated that the equity concept is lost. A state's involvement in preparation programs and teacher licensing is based in large part on some significant and deep-seated constitutional mandates and not the whims of a legislative body. How this equity requirement is met, however, becomes the basis for conflict between the teacher preparation providers and the state.

The university culture and the external forces have become increasingly contentious as legislators and governors have become more determined to address public concerns about elementary and secondary educational quality. Justifiably, lawmakers have revisited their obligation to improve teacher quality as a condition of justifying a compulsory education requirement for all children.

Almost concurrently with the release of the Nation-at-Risk report (National Commission on Excellence in Education, 1983) 11 governors, joined by legislative, educational, and business leaders completed a two year study and issued a bi-partisan report calling for 'a new ethic of excellence in public education' (Task Force on Education for Economic Growth, 1983). One of the key recommendations of the Task Force on Education for Economic Growth was directed to states to 'express a new and higher regard for teachers and for the profession of teaching' acknowledging that this 'will require a substantially restructured and renewed curriculum for teacher training' (Task Force on Education for Economic Growth, 1983).

By the end of the 1980s, the conflict between universities and the legislature over teacher education was evident in legislative sessions across the country. Universities had become acceptant of, and in some cases even encouraged, legislative prescription of courses and content. But frustrated by a reluctance on the part of higher education to explore changes in past approaches, legislators in a number of states opened the doors to alternative routes to certification. In part, legislators did so to respond to a growing number of older, second career applicants wanting access to licensing through routes other than the traditional undergraduate sequence. But it was evident in the state legislative discussions that lawmakers wanted to send a message to higher education to attend to needed change in preparation programs. In alternative certification hearings, higher education was attacked by recent graduates and experienced teachers about perceived program deficiencies. Legislative-higher education rapport was badly damaged during these debates.

The confrontations were curious in one respect. Over the years, teacher education programs had become one of the most regulated of any of the state licensing programs. Although universities bore the brunt of the attack, the criticism voiced by graduates could legitimately have been directed at the lawmakers themselves. Credit hours, courses, content, endorsement areas, number of weeks of student teaching were often topics of detailed state laws and regulations. In their effort to detail the process and inputs, state leaders and campus implementers paid little attention to learning and the quality of the teaching performance. Accountability rested primarily in confirming the presence of the required program components. Legislators, more so than university leaders, moved to address this omission. By 1990, states began to require that candidates for a state license pass a basic skills test to confirm their ability in reading, writing, spelling, and mathematics. From the mid-1980s and a major state confrontation over basic skills testing as proposed by an Arkansas governor named Bill Clinton, 40 states have adopted testing requirements to confirm the basic skills of the prospective teacher (National Association of State Directors of Teacher Education and Certification, [NASDEC], 1996). States didn't stop there. Arguments accelerated for confirmation of the candidate's knowledge of his/her subject area, general studies, and pedagogy. Thirty eight states have set requirements in one or more of these areas (NASDEC, 1996).

By 1996, states were investing heavily in assessment programs aimed at assuring the public that teachers did in fact have a body of knowledge and a minimum level of basic skills as a condition of receiving a state license to teach. From this author's observation, seldom were these proposals initiated or supported by higher education. The accountability train was moving and universities were left protesting at the station. Beyond the testing mania, another far more significant shift occurred in policy making. Universities, still unsure of what to do with the new state assessment data on their graduates, now face a challenge coming from yet another escalation of the accountability thrust.

A Shift in Legislative Policy Making

Parallel to the activity of governors and state policy makers to address shortfalls in teacher education quality, a broader policy shift began unfolding in the early 1980s. President Reagan entered his first term with a theme of reducing government and the massive number of federal regulations. By the time President Clinton entered the White House in 1993, the deregulation theme was now a bi-partisan concern and had expanded to the questioning of long standing assumptions about how government should operate. Public disenchantment with government and politicians had increased. Shortly after the *Time* magazine cover posed the question, 'Is Government Dead?', Osborne and Gaebler answered the question by suggesting this indeed may be the case unless there can be a complete rethinking of how we seek to achieve many of our public goals and ultimately account to the public. To improve public stewardship, the authors, in their book *Reinventing Government*, proposed 10 principles for achieving 'an American Perestroika' (Osborne and Gaebler, 1993). Deregulation was placed in a broader agenda including devolution, customer based and market-oriented approaches, mission-driven operations, and establishment of a results-oriented government. The Osborne and Gaebler treatise is an example of the literature impacting and reflecting a mini-revolution in policy making.

The new approach to policy making is beginning to be seen at all levels of government and in government operations beyond the educational arena. Applied to teacher education, one might make this analysis of the traditional policy approach:

- Centralized control and decision-making to reduce potential for organizational variations;
- Extensive statutory and regulatory mandates to control the process;
- Emphasis on required courses, content, and measurable inputs;
- Rigid adherence to the rules, with little flexibility, less there be a weakening of quality control;
- Quantitative-based evaluation and accountability procedure; and
- Formula driven funding patterns unrelated to the goals desired.

In the last 10 years, governors and legislators have moved to *a* new *policy approach* characterized by:

- Delegation of decision-making to lower levels of government to promote local ownership and leadership;
- Reduced emphasis on rules and regulations;
- Greater specification of desired results and performance;
- Flexibility encouraged to promote identification of solutions to emerging local problems;
- Qualitative-based evaluation and accountability procedures;
- Collaboration across agencies and levels of government to streamline the delivery of services;
- Funds allocated on the basis of results and performance;
- Openness to possible privatization of work previously reserved to federal, state, or local government.

While state policy makers are moving more and more aggressively in this new policy direction, universities seem unaware of the implications of this new configuration. The review of this policy shift is presented in advance of the accountability discussion in the belief that the policy transition offers universities a tremendous opportunity to contribute to this evolution while regaining a greater control of teacher education programs — albeit with a significantly expanded accountability responsibility. Currently universities seem unprepared and often unwilling to assume these responsibilities.

Teacher Education in a Performance-based World

The basis for a performance system begins with the identification of what the state expects of anyone receiving a license to teach. Other than general statements, falling far short of observable and measurable standards by which teacher candidates might be judged, legislatures have been remiss in setting this foundation and, in doing so, undermined a performance-oriented approach to teacher education.

Teacher standards, objected to by some reformists, are a legitimate expression of a public expectation. Less justified is the legislative specification of the program elements. Previously, legislators sought to control the components of the teacher education program and bypassed the professional judgments that should have guided the preparation process. As pressures mounted on the K-12 arena, legislators passed additional laws to control teacher education but the system itself was not pushed to generate creative approaches. The new policy emphasis must have as one of its goals that of energizing a system that has through domination and neglect become passive and uncreative. Setting state expectations and holding institutions responsible for achieving these standards is a constructive approach to achieving organizational change.

In adopting specific expectations, states have found the 10 standards developed by the Interstate New Teacher Assessment and Support Consortium (INTASC) to be a particularly helpful basis for starting a dialogue on standards (Interstate New Teacher Assessment and Support Consortium, [INTASC], 1992). Some states have found reason to consolidate the INTASC standards to a smaller number. For example, Colorado eventually adopted five. Discussions in other states have focused on two additional expectations: the teacher's technology awareness and application and the ability of the teacher to move students to a higher achievement of state adopted learning standards.

A more generic, but nevertheless challenging expectation, has been advocated by John Goodlad in his book, *Educational Renewal: Better Teachers. Better Schools* (Goodlad, 1994). Goodlad argues that it is reasonable to expect that new teachers should enter a school prepared to contribute to the development and maintenance of a responsive and renewing school. Again, acceptance of this or any standard has major program and resource implications. For example, in programs that have traditionally limited their focus to preparing the teacher for classroom responsibilities, learning to work effectively with colleagues, parents, and the community for school change has little chance of being achieved in a 5–10 week student teaching assignment.

The language of the INTASC standards suggest the accountability challenge for universities and teacher education programs:

- Principle #3: The teacher understands how students differ in their approaches to learning, and creates instructional opportunities that are adapted to diverse learners.
- Principle #4: The teacher understands and uses a variety of instructional strategies to encourage students' development of critical thinking, problem solving, and performance skills (INTASC, 1992).

Typically, the standards' statements contain both a cognitive and a performance expectation, i.e., the teacher is aware of or understands, and uses, performs, demonstrates or creates.

States are moving slowly, but steadily into standards for teachers. In the 1996–7 *Manual on Certification and Preparation of Educational Personnel in the United States and Canada*, eight states reported adopting performance standards for teachers and using them in approving programs of preparation and/or the granting of individual licenses. Five had adopted performance standards and were in the process of establishing procedures for applying these standards while 11 states reported studying or moving in this direction (NASDEC, 1996). State adoption of teacher standards has been a steady one in the last five years and there seems to be little countering this trend at this point.

National representatives of the professional community have become more vocal in their support of this approach. 'Get serious about standards, for both students and teachers' (National Commission on Teaching and America's Future, 1996), was the first recommendation to states from the National Commission on Teaching and America's Future in its September, 1996 report. The American Association of Colleges for Teacher Education (AACTE), Association of Teacher Education (ATE), National Council for Accreditation of Teacher Education (NCATE), Council of Chief State School Officers (CCSSO), and the National Association of State Boards of Education (NASBE) have issued statements in favor of teacher standards as the cornerstone of a state's redesign of teacher education. It is reasonable to expect that most if not all states will have standards in place by the year 2000.

Assuming this trend continues, the issue then becomes the assessment of the adopted standards. What is to be measured, how, by whom, and when, are questions states must answer in terms of putting in place an assessment process that is reasonable, efficient, and meets the legal tests of fairness, validity, and reliability. States have developed a track record of sorts in assessment after setting out over 10 years ago to judge the basic skills of applicants for a state license. Litigation has clarified, and continues to do so, state testing practices related to confirming the knowledge base of prospective teachers.

Despite problems over cut-off scores, testing conditions for the disabled, disproportionate failure rates among different populations, connecting the content of tests to the knowledge needed in the classroom, and test availability for all of the state's endorsement areas, states have moved forward in confirming the knowledge base suggested by the adopted standards. Appropriately, legislatures appear ready to leave the problems of performance assessment to the program providers.

Performance and the Challenge to the University

Judging student performance in terms of candidates demonstrating, for example, the 10 principles of INTASC, is not so easily accomplished. Nor is the legal landscape for judging performance clear. For universities, this means going beyond assuring the state that an applicant has completed all required courses, has a BA, and should therefore be considered for a license. Courts have tended to support university decisions in these areas. In grading conflicts, the faculty member is presumed to be qualified based on an academic record that includes the appropriate degrees. Student papers are available for review. And most importantly, courts have been reluctant to substitute their judgment of faculty members for fear of opening a giant litigational box. This protection may not continue as universities move into judgments related to performance.

As Michael Ford suggests, 'performance assessment is a new direction in testing. "It is an effort to access complex skills in a realistic way"' (Ford, 1995). Students must know the standards to be met and the criteria by which they will be evaluated. They must have an opportunity to be trained and to practice the expected performance, and finally, to be judged by qualified judges as they demonstrate these behaviors in appropriate settings. These expectations can be met but the typical teacher education program has not addressed these questions.

The qualifications of the 'judges' become a critical component. The holding of academic degrees may be insignificant to the performance judgments required. The number of qualified observers or raters may be an issue. Again, Ford, in examining the fairness issue, has underscored the value of triangulation or multiple judges, coming from different assignments and backgrounds (Ford, 1995). These components are not new to teacher education programs but they have been done poorly or erratically in many cases. Rather than academic degrees confirming the capacity of a judge to rate performance, other qualifications may be considered more important. In terms of the legal implications, therefore, assessing teacher performance to meet state standards will generally mean meeting a much higher standard of evaluation than universities have been held to in the past.

Most universities must undergo major organizational change to recognize the standards in a world of courses and credits. Faculty know well how to prepare a syllabus; conduct a class; test the students for content, understanding, and awareness; and assign a grade. They are less confident in their performance as a judge affirming that a student can perform consistently in the manner determined by the state to be essential for all teachers. Further, if the tests of validity and reliability are to be met, performance-based assessment means the program must be more field-based in its orientation than what is currently found in most colleges and universities. Faculty and students must spend more time in schools and classrooms where performance judgments must be made, and, as anticipated in triangulation, elementary and secondary personnel must be more actively involved in the preparation and evaluation sequence. Achieving the state goal of a performance-based system and meeting the legal requirements will take a rigorous examination of current university practices and policies.

Can Universities Meet the Challenge?

Implementing the university part of the performance based system will not be easy. In the past, universities met state requirements, but generally in ways that fit nicely into the campus structure. Teacher education didn't disrupt student or faculty routines. Classes in the sequence emphasized the development of the students' knowledge, understanding, and awareness levels. In this area, there may be little reason to adjust the content provided although it will be important to evaluate the offerings in terms of their correlation with the expectations of the standards. Classroom tests and examinations will continue to be important in providing staff and students with feed-back on the progress made toward the knowledge base identified. In addition, the state tests can act as a collective supplement and provide valuable data back to all university faculty in regard to any gaps in the knowledge base of graduates. Closing this last part of the loop may cause some concern if students fail to perform well on the state tests and faculty are unwilling or see no reason to adjust their syllabi. When teacher education students are part of a larger group, there may be some conflict over modifying the course content for one segment, but, for the most part, problems in the knowledge-based realm will be manageable.

University experience in the performance area has been in the capstone experience or the student teaching phase of the program. In this final segment of a quarter or semester of time, the student is expected to bring theory and practice together. The instructors often change during this part of the program. In universities having several hundred students involved in student teaching, the bulk of the student supervision often falls on adjunct faculty and supervising school teachers with neither having much input in or knowledge of the campus preparation content, philosophy or other aspects of the program. There is little chance of universities meeting the legal tests of reliability and validity and the intent of a performance approach if such practices are continued. Major organizational change will be required.

The extent of the change makes this an institutional issue — not just a school of education involvement. Further, the change from a campus-based program to one having significantly more field contacts impacts the local schools of the area as well.

The experience of the National Network for Educational Renewal and the program descriptions provided by Goodlad (1994), suggest the key programmatic conditions that will provide the educational quality and meet the legal tests as well. Examining some of the components suggest how the two come together:

1   Early and supervised contact with classrooms and schools

Students need to enter the teacher education program knowing what is expected of them in terms of the courses, off-campus involvement, and the state standards and assessment requirements of a license. Some universities have found that by providing an orientation and field based contact in the freshmen and sophomore years as many as one out of five students may choose to redirect their study to other careers. Similar gains can be expected by providing these orientation and visitation opportunities in the early weeks of a fifth year or post-BA program.

2   Expanded opportunities for prospective teachers to have experience in schools having racial and income diversity among the students

Preferably every student should have such an experience in an urban setting if at all possible and prior to the internship or student teaching experience. Working with disabled students would be an important consideration as well. Usually, one standard relates to demonstrating one's ability to work effectively with children having diverse backgrounds and abilities.

3   Cohort grouping of students

An important socializing experience through the cohort group approach has helped students reflect on the 'moral, ethical, and enculturating responsibilities to be assumed' (Goodlad, 1994). The cohort group has been an important feed-back opportunity to allow a student to receive comments from staff and students.

4   Partner schools

As field contacts increase, it becomes easier for the university and selected schools to have an ongoing relationship to facilitate understanding, planning, and evaluation of the preparation efforts. Such partnerships, as described more fully by Goodlad (1994), allow the prospective teachers to understand the dynamics of a school and not just the work of a single classroom. Through the partnership, school personnel become informed and, often, are invited to participate as clinical staff in making campus contributions as well as providing school level assistance. The quality of the performance 'judges' is enhanced considerably by such an arrangement.

5   Internships or student teaching experiences providing at least two semesters of school experience

Ideally, this time permits an in-depth experience in two schools having two very different settings and demography. This gives adequate time for the students to practice, revise, and confirm their performance with frequent observations from highly qualified school and campus evaluators.

6   Finally, feed-back and follow-up to allow a formative evaluation of ongoing programs (Goodlad, 1994)

Such a commitment fits well into a field-based program that is routinely gathering data, making qualitative judgments, and adjusting the program to improve the quality of instruction.

Individually or collectively, these programmatic provisions have operational implications that extend beyond the school or college of education. All have implications for arts and sciences faculty. All require the support and involvement of the public schools. A teacher education program buried in the school of education may have trouble gaining the respect and attention of these parties. For this reason, some universities have found it desirable to form a new 'Center for Pedagogy' as recommended by Goodlad (1994) or 'Center for Teaching and Learning' as preferred by some institutions. Here the triad (education, arts and sciences, and local schools) can find equal status. The Center can be a critical vehicle in enabling a university to organize itself to respond to the new demands of a state performance-based approach.

Universities may find value in seeing such a center in a broader context. Assessment findings such as those reported by the National Center on Post-secondary Teaching, Learning, and Assessment in *Realizing the Potential: Improving Post-secondary Teaching, Learning, and Assessment* (National Center on Post-secondary Teaching, Learning, and Assessment, 1995), suggest to this writer that the university efforts to provide a higher quality undergraduate program are not unrelated to the assessment challenges presented by a performance-oriented, teacher education program. Identifying and monitoring the performance indicators of undergraduate student progress and learning can carry one into a similar field of questions and processes.

Additionally, a Center for Teaching and Learning or Pedagogy can be instrumental in improving the overall quality of faculty instruction. Rather than viewing the problems of teacher education assessment as unique and a burden, higher education leaders should see the challenge as running parallel to a broader public accountability concern regarding the university itself.

Underscoring the institutional nature of the changes needed are the findings of a policy study conducted through the National Network for Educational Renewal (Unpublished Summary, 1995). Directors of the Network settings were asked to identify those policies or actions that were most important to the enhancement of university and school collaboration. The most commonly mentioned were these:

1   Critical institutional actions

- Demonstrated support for the simultaneous renewal concept by the institutional governing board and president or chancellor.
- Commitment to a faculty tenure, promotion, reward, and recruitment structure that encourages participation in a field-based program.
- Adoption of formal agreements between the university and the school districts relative to setting the expectations and responsibilities of each party involved in a partnership relationship.
- Acceptance of the idea that teacher preparation is an institutional responsibility. Schools of education have a primary interest but a shared responsibility with arts and sciences faculty who are the recipients of students prepared by the public school teachers.
- Provisions for flexibility in the university calendar and employment contracts that encourage interaction with local schools that have different starting and ending dates.
- Recognition that faculty assignments involving field activities with cohort groups of students take more time than teaching campus based classes.

Often given less attention, but equally important, are the supporting steps to be taken by the local school district.

2   Critical school district actions

- Demonstrated support from the local board and superintendent that school participation in a preparation program is an accepted and valued activity.
- Adoption of formal agreements between the school district and the university relative to setting the expectations and responsibilities of each party involved in the partnership relationship.
- Participation in the selection of the partners schools to take the lead in working with the university.
- Development of a reward system and recognition program for those teachers involved in the preparation of teachers.
- Allowing released time for district faculty to participate in the planning and implementation of the school/university partnership.

- Where applicable, securing collective bargaining provisions that support school/university partnerships.

Each partnership will have its unique policy issues. But universities and school districts are not the only organizations having to rethink their roles. There are significant changes necessary at the state level as well and these must be undertaken in tandem or they will undermine the steps initiated at the campus and school district levels.

State Level Changes to Support Universities

In the state's striving to achieve a state purpose, universities became part of a heavily regulated, top–down system that has sought to control the process and the inputs as a means of maintaining some semblance of quality control. The game and the rules are changing. It is not easy to reverse practices and patterns of relationships that have existed for several decades. Unless the state legislature and state agencies take seriously their rhetoric in support of a more decentralized but accountable system, the next few years will be a dysfunctional mess.

State departments of education, through state boards of education, have traditionally driven the teacher education train. As dissatisfaction built toward teacher preparation and ongoing professional development quality, 15 states created professional standards boards to focus exclusively on educator licensing issues (NASDEC, 1996). Regardless of the state's governance approach, the processes for licensing, program approval, and monitoring of the over-all system must be in sync with performance-based concepts.

The state agency's process of granting a teaching license has revolved around the review of the applicant's transcript. Although agencies have added state assessment results, finger printing, and security checks, the manual review of the applicant's courses and credits has remained the core of the processing sequence. Unless the agency's review acknowledges the performance confirmation of the preparing institution, the new approach is undermined. Applicants coming from state approved programs must be accepted on the basis of institutional recommendation.

Secondly, a revised state program approval process becomes a foundation for building the new performance-oriented, field-based approach. In the past, the state agency has operated much like an accreditation body. The accreditation process and the state program review have similar but distinctly different purposes. The two overlap in respect to examining the process by which the institution monitors the students for achieving the performance standards and the changes implemented from the data compiled. However, the state's program review must examine issues related to:

- the adequacy of state funding;
- K-12/higher education collaboration in establishing partner schools;
- the validity and reliability of the performance assessments being used by the institutions;

- the effectiveness of state statutes and regulations in establishing high quality teacher education programs;
- the recruitment of under-represented groups;
- the use of the state's knowledge-based assessment information and the data from follow-up studies on graduates serving in the state's public schools; and
- the success of the institution in serving troubled K-12 schools such as those commonly found in urban or rural areas serving concentrations of low income families or diversity.

Hopefully, the institution's accreditation findings can be used to expand the state's understanding of the institutional successes and problems, but, in many cases, the accreditation review will involve judgments in areas that are beyond the legitimate interest of the state.

The state must be concerned with the manner in which state moneys are distributed to public institutions. Often, the appropriation of funds is on a formula basis, unrelated to the achievement of specific public goals, and becomes a disincentive to the establishment of good teacher education programs. State leaders have supported the rhetoric of greater emphasis on performance and results but have been unwilling to invest dollars in the added costs of field-based programs and the assessment processes necessary for confirming performance and higher quality programs.

Lastly, the responsible state agency must take the lead in a periodic evaluation of the effectiveness of the state's teacher education program. Do all the changes undertaken make a difference in the quality of instruction taking place in the state's classrooms? Are schools and universities becoming renewing institutions in such a way that they are self-correcting and creative entities? Each university must contribute to this analysis and be ready to change those elements that would improve the system.

Summary

Universities, through their schools of education, have been asked to be central actors in the renewal of the nation's public schools. This has come at a time policy makers have moved to a more decentralized, performance-based policy approach that allows and encourages institutions to bring their best thinking and creativity to a very important public purpose.

Universities have chaffed in the past under the baggage of excessive regulations. They now have an opportunity to control more of the teacher education program, and this should be welcomed by higher education faculty. The challenge — and indeed a threat to some — comes with the added accountability responsibility and the expectation for an expanded relationship with the public schools. In addition to the improvement of teacher education and its graduates, university leaders and many faculty are realizing that accepting the responsibility offers other opportunities. It becomes a means of raising the performance levels of high school graduates seeking entry to post-secondary study. Second, participating and helping to guide the policy transition will raise the image of higher education in the minds of many policy makers.

It is a high stakes challenge. If we believe that education under-girds our democracy and that schools are the footings on which our society rests, universities must undertake the changes necessary to ensure that each candidate for a state teaching license leaves the campus prepared to enhance learning and democracy in our public schools. If that expectation is met, higher education stands to accrue important dividends to the system itself, but will receive as well, accolades from an appreciative and strengthened society.

References

COLORADO SCHOOL LAWS (1997) Article IX, Section 11, Compulsory Education.

FORD, M. (1995) 'Performance assessment and the issue of bias', in *Perspectives in Teacher Certification*, Amherst, MA: National Evaluation Systems, pp. 43–51.

GOODLAD, J.I. (1994) *Educational Renewal: Better Teachers, Better Schools*, San Francisco: Jossey-Bass, pp. 113–94, pp. 235–73.

GOODLAD, J.I., SODER, R. and SIROTNIK, K.A. (1990) *Places Where Teachers Are Taught*, San Francisco: Jossey-Bass, p. 386.

INTERSTATE NEW TEACHER ASSESSMENT AND SUPPORT CONSORTIUM (INTASC) (1992) *Model Standards for Beginning Teacher Licensing and Development: A Resource for State Dialogue*, Washington DC: Council of Chief StateSchool Officers, pp. 14–17.

INTERSTATE NEW TEACHER ASSESSMENT AND SUPPORT CONSORTIUM (1992) *Model Standards for Beginning Teacher Licensing and Development: A Resource for State Dialogue*, Washington DC: Council of Chief StateSchool Officers, p. 64.

NASDEC (NATIONAL ASSOCIATION OF STATE DIRECTORS OF TEACHER EDUCATION AND CERTIFICATION) (1996) *1996–7 Manual on Certification and Preparation of Educational Personnel in the US and Canada*, Dubuque, Iowa: Kendall/Hunt, p. B-4, pp. 1–59, pp. 1–158.

NATIONAL CENTER ON POST-SECONDARY TEACHING, LEARNING, AND ASSESSMENT (1995) *Realizing the Potential Improving Post-secondary Teaching, Learning, and Assessment*, University Park, PA: Pennsylvania State University.

NATIONAL COMMISSION ON EXCELLENCE IN EDUCATION (1983) *A Nation at Risk*, Washington DC: US Government Printing Office.

NATIONAL COMMISSION ON TEACHING AND AMERICA'S FUTURE (1996) *What Matters Most: Teaching for America's Future*, New York: Teachers College, Columbia, p. 4.

NATIONAL NETWORK (1995) Unpublished summary of policy findings from the 16 National Network setting directors, Seattle: University of Washington.

OSBORNE, D. and GAEBLER, T. (1993) *Reinventing Government: How the Entrepreneurial Spirit Is Transforming the Public Sector*, New York: Plume.

SODER, R. (1995) *Record in Educational Leadership*, Centerville, Ohio: Leadership Services International, pp. 13–15.

TASK FORCE ON EDUCATION FOR ECONOMIC GROWTH (1983) *Action For Excellence*, Denver: Education Commission of the States, pp. 3–37.

10 Moving Toward Performance-based Accreditation Systems for the Teaching Profession

Arthur E. Wise

For too long, teacher preparation, licensing, and continuing development have been hostage to the status quo. Some promising reforms have been developed, but they are still not the norm. To ensure quality in teaching, it is time for the profession to embrace a system of quality assurance that is already used by other professions. Such a system is composed of sets of standards within three interconnected mechanisms:

- professional accreditation of institutions that prepare teachers;
- performance-based licensing; and
- certification of accomplished teachers.

As accreditation, licensing, and advanced certification standards are developed to be compatible with one another, a new view of preparation and professional development is emerging. The idea of teacher preparation and development as moving along a continuum, from pre-service preparation to advanced certification, is the basis for a proposed extension of teacher preparation into three phases (see Figure 10.1):

- pre-service preparation;
- extended clinical preparation and assessment; and
- continuing professional development.

The three quality assurance mechanisms serving these three phases of teacher development are now actively at work, developing and implementing standards and assessments which teachers meet along the path of preparation and continuing development. The National Council for Accreditation of Teacher Education (NCATE), as the professional accrediting organization, the Council of Chief State School Officers, through its task force on licensing, and the National Board for Professional Teaching Standards, designed to grant certification to experienced teachers, are working together for the first time to develop a coherent system for quality assurance for the teaching profession. Developing the sets of standards has been the work of the 1980s and continues into the 1990s. Linking them to each other in meaningful ways is the work to be done as we move into the twenty-first century.

Figure 10.1 Teacher preparation: A continuum

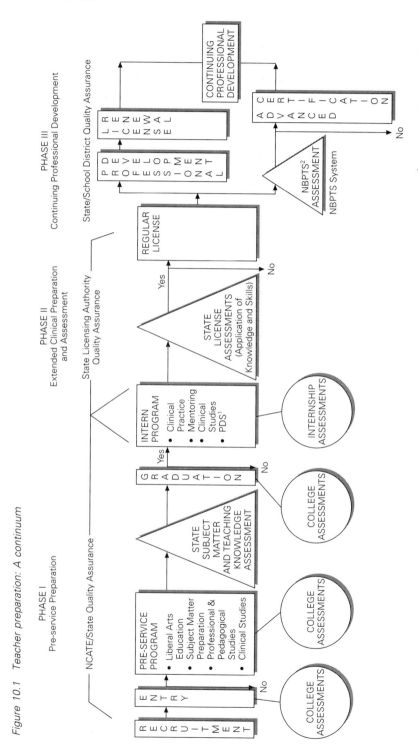

Source: Reprinted with permission National Council for Accreditation of Teacher Education

Linking the standards involves linking the systems that develop them: higher education, state departments of education/standards boards, and the teaching field/ school districts. Working together instead of operating independently involves new sets of meetings, new procedures, and new policies for all entities involved. Attempting change in one part of the system, i.e., strengthening licensing requirements via performance assessments, will work only as well as changes made in other parts of the system, i.e., teacher preparation. States, local districts, and higher education leaders need to work together as new standards are integrated into curriculum frameworks, and as teacher preparation standards and structures change to emphasize teacher performance.

Pre-service preparation is only the *initial portion* of teacher preparation and development, as it is conceived of on the continuum (see Figure 10.1). NCATE, as the accrediting agency for schools of education, functions as the profession's quality assurance mechanism during this phase. Most states also operate approval processes for teacher preparation programs in higher education institutions.

NCATE has 40 partnerships with states as of this writing to conduct joint reviews of schools of education. The purposes of the partnerships are

1   to increase the rigor of review of schools of education;
2   to integrate state and national professional standards; and
3   to reduce or eliminate duplication of effort that occurs when states and NCATE conduct separate assessments.

Schools in partnership states can meet NCATE and state requirements simultaneously. Partnerships vary, but states must agree to the use of national professional standards to participate.

NCATE's influence and strength, and state use of its professional standards, has grown exponentially over the past several years. State/NCATE partnerships have grown in number from 14 in 1989 to 40 in 1996. Through its partnerships, NCATE is affecting state approval and licensing standards and processes. In three states, colleges must meet NCATE standards. In 37 states, colleges must meet NCATE standards or standards that have been substantially shaped by NCATE. Twelve states now use NCATE review only to judge the quality of individual programs, and the schools are free from further state review. What will the future bring in terms of program review and use of NCATE standards?

The next phase of teacher development includes a prolonged clinical phase of teacher preparation, during which the teacher is granted a beginning, or conditional license, and receives extensive clinical assistance. This phase continues initial teacher preparation at least through the first year of teaching, during which the beginning teacher is evaluated for suitability for independent practice. The state plays a dominant role in this phase of a teacher's development. State licensing requirements determine which individuals are permitted to enter the classroom as independent practitioners. Professional development schools, which follow the teaching hospital model in providing the student with a year-long internship, may become the mechanism used for longitudinal assessments of beginning teachers as they move toward licensure. How does this extended phase of preparation impact university programs? What changes in structure and content are taking place?

National Board certification will be an important form of recognition for many teachers, including those who wish to enlarge their roles by becoming mentors to beginning teachers. The creation of the National Board and its development of standards and assessments for excellence in teaching have advanced the entire profession by bringing attention to the inadequacies of licensing and teacher preparation programs, and stimulating change in those quality assurance systems. What role will universities play in preparing teachers for National Board certification?

Pre-service Preparation

One of the hallmarks of a profession is the mastery, by the practitioner, of a body of knowledge that laypersons do not possess, and autonomy in practice based upon application of this knowledge. Professionals in teaching should understand the knowledge base and be able to apply it effectively in their practice. The knowledge base of teaching, and of teaching specific content areas, has exploded in the past 20 years. New research on the teaching of mathematics and science, for example, has propelled the formulation of new K-12 student standards and teacher preparation standards, as well as new methods of teaching mathematics and science.

Being part of a profession involves making judgments every day that relate practice to a knowledge base. Teaching is a profession in which the practitioners must constantly make informed decisions to structure learning experiences in a particular way. There may be no one 'right' answer in a given situation; however, there are approaches that facilitate learning and there are approaches that do not. One does not learn such professional skills or acquire a body of knowledge in a weekend seminar or in a one-day in-service training session. Prospective teachers learn a body of knowledge and develop skills over time through a coherent program of study that includes the liberal arts, as well as professional and clinical preparation.

During the late 1980s and 1990s, the NCATE standards have served as a lever for teacher preparation reform. NCATE's standards and processes were completely redesigned in the 1980s and a new, more rigorous system was implemented in 1987. The centerpiece of the redesign was the development of standards pertaining to the knowledge base for teaching. In order to be accredited, schools of education must now demonstrate that their programs are based on established and current research and best practice, and that students and faculty alike can articulate the framework of the knowledge base.

Almost half of the schools of education that were reviewed in the first three years following the redesign failed to meet the knowledge base standard. Thirty percent were denied accreditation, based in part on the failure to meet this critical standard. Most schools of education that were denied under the new system then made serious efforts to redesign their programs to meet the new, more rigorous standards, and many have since been accredited. Thus, the professional accreditation process has served as an important lever for reform in teacher preparation.

NCATE continually revises its standards to incorporate new knowledge and practice. The 1995 revision emphasizes prospective teacher performance, new forms of assessment, the integration of content and pedagogy, collaboration with K-12 schools, technology and diversity — all in the context of high quality programs and continuous program evaluation. These standards are significantly different than the 1987 standards, in that they focus much more attention on the performance of the graduate of the teacher preparation program — what knowledge and skills the individual possesses and how effective he or she is in the classroom. This shift to performance-oriented standards is just beginning to impact teacher preparation institutions, as they grapple with coming revisions in licensure and new accreditation expectations focusing on performance and assessment.

Emphasis on Performance

NCATE expects schools of education to ensure that prospective teachers have the knowledge and skills they need to work effectively with all students. The indicators to NCATE's standard on professional and pedagogical knowledge are explicit (see Figure 10.2). Teachers should be able to use strategies for developing critical thinking and problem solving. They should be able to use formal and informal assessment strategies to ensure continuous student learning. They should be versed in educational technology, including use of the computer and other technologies for instruction and student assessment. Prospective teachers should be skilled in classroom management and be able to collaborate effectively with parents and others in the community. They should know and use research-based principles of effective practice proven to be effective — in other words, teachers should be able to explain why they decide to use a certain strategy and teach a particular idea in a certain way. In short, teachers should demonstrate competence, needed knowledge, and acceptable proficiency.

The skills and knowledge listed above come directly from a list of 10 principles for new licensing systems developed by the Interstate New Teacher Assessment and Support Consortium (INTASC) task force on licensing reform under the auspices of the Council of Chief State School Officers. NCATE is represented on the task force and has worked diligently to ensure that accreditation standards parallel new, more rigorous expectations for state licensing now under development in several states. In turn, the task force on licensing drew the new licensing principles from the seminal work on standards done by the National Board for Professional Teaching Standards.

In addition, NCATE standards require the school of education to monitor and evaluate the progress of teacher candidates throughout their program of study, and to use performance assessment as a part of the evaluation. Finally, NCATE's standard on 'Ensuring the Competence of Candidates' spells out clearly that the school of education is expected to assess a candidate's competence before the completion of the program and/or recommendation for licensure, and that this assessment should include actual performance.

Figure 10.2 Selected NCATE performance-oriented standards

Standard I.D Professional and Pedagogical Studies for Initial Teacher Preparation

The unit ensures that teacher candidates acquire and learn to apply the professional and pedagogical knowledge and skills to become competent to work with all students.

I.D.2   Candidates complete a well-planned sequence of courses and/or experiences in pedagogical studies that help develop understanding and use of:

- research- and experienced-based principles of effective practice for encouraging the intellectual, social, and personal development of students;
- different student approaches to learning for creating instructional opportunities adapted to learners from diverse cultural backgrounds and with exceptionalities;
- variety of instructional strategies for developing critical thinking, problem solving, and performance skills;
- individual and group motivation for encouraging positive social interaction, active engagement in learning, and self-motivation;
- effective verbal, nonverbal, and media communications for fostering active inquiry, collaboration, and supportive interactions in the classroom;
- planning and management of instruction based on knowledge of the content area, the community, and curriculum goals;
- formal and informal assessment strategies for evaluating and ensuring the continuous intellectual, social, and physical development of the learner;
- collaboration with school colleagues, parents, and agencies in the larger community for supporting students' learning and well-being;
- the opportunity for candidates to reflect on their teaching and its effects on student growth and learning; and
- educational technology, including the use of computer and other technologies in instruction, assessment and professional productivity.

Standard I.E Integrative Studies for Initial Teacher Preparation

The unit ensures that teacher candidates can integrate general, content, and professional and pedagogical knowledge to create meaningful learning experiences for all students.

Standard II.C Monitoring and Advising the Progress of Candidates

The unit systematically monitors and assesses the progress of candidates and ensures that they receive appropriate academic and professional advisement from admission through completion of their professional education programs.

Standard II.D Ensuring the Competence of Candidates

The unit ensures that a candidate's competency to begin his or her professional role in schools is assessed prior to completion of the program and/or recommendation for licensure

II.D.1   The unit establishes and publishes a set of criteria/outcomes for exit from each professional education program.

II.D.2   A candidate's mastery of a program's state exit criteria or outcomes is assessed through the use of multiple sources of data such as a culminating experience, portfolios, interviews, videotaped and observed performance in schools, standardized tests, and course grades.

Source: Reprinted with permission National Council for Accreditation of Teacher Education (NCATE)

NCATE's emphasis on performance assessment requires schools to provide evidence of successful candidate performance. Schools and NCATE are now adjusting to these new expectations. NCATE will ask how the unit knows that its graduates are able to teach effectively. Student portfolios should provide some evidence, but they do not stand alone as complete documentation. Teams are interested in how portfolios are developed, the nature of the feedback from faculty and members of the professional community, and how they are used to improve teaching. Both candidates and faculty should be able to explain how portfolios have been used to improve teaching performance.

Videotapes of teaching performance may be used to document performance, if the performance is analyzed and recommendations for improvement are included. Systematic evaluations of performance from cooperating teachers during the student teaching or internship phase also provide evidence.

The field is just beginning to use performance assessment as a tool to improve teaching and teacher preparation.

Integrating Content and Pedagogy

In the reform-driven 1980s, some states passed legislation eliminating an education major and requiring academic majors for those planning to teach. While it is certainly necessary for teachers to be well-grounded in liberal arts — required in NCATE standards — the academic major is not sufficient. The Project 30 report, *The Reform of Teacher Preparation for the 21st Century*, a collaborative effort of 30 representative higher education institutions to redesign the way prospective teachers are educated, has documented the need to integrate content and pedagogical knowledge.

As the authors of the report note, 'What constitutes the most appropriate academic major for a teacher is not as simple as requiring a regular academic major in some university subject. To require prospective elementary teachers to major in some field may be . . . good, but alone it cannot guarantee that they will acquire competence in the subjects they will teach their pupils' (Murray and Fallon, 1989, p. 17).

Just one of many possible examples that illustrate this point follows: 'We do know that reasonably well-educated college and university graduates find themselves in great difficulty early on in their attempts to answer coherently the questions young children are likely to ask. Sooner or later, an elementary school teacher is going to tell children that the world, despite all appearances, is not flat. Children will inevitably wonder why they don't fall off. Teachers . . . will say something about the power of gravity . . . They have no intellectual resources left to deal with other questions. . . . In fact, there is some risk that gravity will be described as a magnetic force, which it is not, and thus the pupils will be misled about a point that will require correction. . . .' (Murray and Fallon, 1989, p. 16).

In the end, pedagogical content knowledge becomes a discussion of the appropriate ways of organizing information and knowledge (i.e., young elementary school children will be taught one of the algorithms for subtraction — but which one, decomposition, equal additions, rule of nine? Murray and Fallon, 1989, p. 25). It is the search for ways of representing the subject matter, analogies and metaphors, that will take each pupil well beyond what can be held together spatially through rote memorization (Murray and Fallon, 1989, pp. 23–4). It is concerned with an appropriate level of understanding the knowledge — how it can be applied, and how it relates to other phenomena.

The work of Project 30, based in the university, has introduced the issue within the higher education community. Project 30 recommends several approaches to the dilemma, from developing an interdisciplinary major to a pedagogical content minor.

The Project 30 report concludes with the observation that 'the hope of a genuine teaching profession rests [in part] upon the reform of the relations between teacher education and the arts and sciences, as well as on reforms within each' (Murray and Fallon, 1989, p. 34). Teams of faculty from education and the arts and sciences are now working together on these and other campuses to forge new alliances and introduce new collaborative efforts to change the way teachers are prepared. This critical translation of the knowledge itself into a base of understandable pedagogical content knowledge that teachers can use to guide their practice will be a work in progress and should be an integral part of reform efforts as we move into the twenty-first century.

To that end, NCATE has designed a project to strengthen the probability that newly prepared teachers will master content knowledge and effective ways to teach it. The New Professional Teacher Standards Development Project is built upon the proposition that content, and how it is taught effectively, should be given increased emphasis in the accreditation system. This project is designed to assist institutions in implementing the accreditation standards, and move the field forward by integrating content and pedagogy.

In the 1995 standards, NCATE addresses the dilemma identified by Project 30 and includes an expectation that 'the unit ensures that teacher candidates can integrate general content, and professional and pedagogical knowledge to create meaningful learning experiences for all students' (NCATE Standards, 1995, p. 18). Institutions need help with this new standard. Hence, NCATE's Standards Development Project focuses on the development of pedagogical content knowledge that teachers need to know that is not regularly part of the liberal arts disciplines. Using the INTASC principles as a framework and the new K-12 standards as content referents, NCATE will, starting with elementary school, redevelop its teaching content standards.

Developing structures to understand the concepts of a discipline lies at the heart of pedagogical content knowledge. Communicating the content in such a way that the student grasps the concepts and can apply them, rather than simply memorizing facts or equations, has been one of the major 'missing links' in teacher preparation. Other professions do not need to incorporate this step into their professional preparation programs, simply because these professionals communicate the information to other professionals in their daily practice. They do not have the need to translate their knowledge into different forms digestible by a roomful of elementary, middle or high school students. Thus higher education has not, until now, focused on this 'bridge' from sophisticated concept to translation of it into elementary school applications. But if we are to truly transform teacher preparation, this is one bridge that must be built. The higher education community has begun to make a start at this task, which will, when assimilated and acted upon, help ensure better prepared teachers in the nation's classrooms.

Upgrading Clinical Experience: The Professional Development School Movement

Imagine a school designed to help teachers become masters at what they do. Imagine a school where teachers reach out to each other and meet during the day to share ideas. Imagine a school where new teachers are being educated instead of being expected to know everything their first time around. Imagine a school where new teachers share a host of mentors instead of experiencing 'baptism by fire'. Imagine a school devoted to the clinical education of beginning teachers and to research aimed at continuous improvement of practice.

Some of these places already exist, in the new structure of professional development schools. A professional development school, or PDS, is a partnership between a college or university and one or more K-12 schools. These partnerships have a four-pronged mission:

1 the preparation of new teachers;
2 the continuing development of teachers in practice;
3 the support of student learning; and
4 the support of research directed at the improvement of practice.

PDSs are a key strategy for redesigning schools of education while at the same time restructuring elementary, middle, and secondary schools. PDSs link teacher preparation reform to school reform in a powerful way. They build in continuous performance assessment of the beginning intern/teacher; thus, they provide a comprehensive evaluation of a beginning teacher's competence. And since professional development schools are partnerships between higher education institutions and school districts/K-12 schools, they inextricably link standards for preparation to standards for licensure. The Council of Chief State School Officers has prepared briefing materials for states that contain a flow chart connecting comprehensive assessment to preparation, induction, and professional development. It is a historic step, as policymakers are acknowledging that a system of standards and assessments should be developed in each phase of preparation and development. Acknowledging induction as a phase of preparation demonstrates recognition that teacher preparation must be connected to practice, and that standards for each must be aligned.

NCATE is engaged in supporting the growth of professional development schools by initiating a PDS Standards Project that is designed:

1   to establish a consensus about quality and good practice in professional development schools;
2   to develop a policy framework that can sustain and nurture them; and
3   to develop initial standards that might eventually become the basis for making judgments about quality for purposes of accreditation.

The 1987 NCATE standards were based in part on an emerging concept of professional community. Hendrick Gideones et al. explicate the basis on which the redesigned NCATE was built in *Capturing the Vision*: In a professional community, a school of education and the schools with which it collaborates share a vision about teacher preparation and development. 'In a true community effort, higher education faculty view P-12 schools as more than mere sites for student teacher placement . . . the schools are the centers of active learning . . .' (Gideones et al., 1993, pp. 17–19).

This 1980s view of community in teacher development has matured and is evolving into a 1990s view of practice as collegial, joint, characterized by sharing, working in teams, observing peers, and studying with colleagues.

In fact, these practices were recently named by professional development schools as occurring in their settings (Trachtman, 1996, pp. 7–8). Just 20 short years ago, teaching would not have been described in these terms. The concept of professional community is *just beginning* to have meaning in teaching. Practitioners in professional development schools also recently named shared beliefs: that teacher learning requires others; that teaching is collaborative; that teaching is engaging in continuous improvement; that teachers are learners; that teachers are scholar-practitioners.

These practices and beliefs, which focus on community and collaboration, are leading to a new type of teacher, and must also lead to a new kind of administrative leadership based on the concept of the teacher as a full partner in decision making.

NCATE's new draft standards for professional development schools are built on these and like concepts. Certain threshold conditions are designed to be in place before PDS standards would be useful. They could be documented — the existence of a formal partnership; commitment by the partners to the core principles; positive working relationships; commitment of resources. NCATE plans to pilot the standards in a few institutions to learn how they can be helpful in assessing the quality of learning candidates' experience as they progress through these institutions. In this way, NCATE is validating the experience of those institutions that are leading away from the apprenticeship model of clinical training to a full internship with a variety of clinical supervisors.

Technology

Increasingly, technology is poised to revolutionize teaching, learning, and assessment. In keeping with new demands for teachers skilled in integrating technology into instruction, NCATE has implemented new, more demanding standards for the use of technology in schools of education.

As of now, the expectations for use of technology are embedded in various standards as indicators. Indicators are signs of evidence that a school of education is meeting a standard. Faculty are expected to integrate the use of computers and related technology into their teaching and scholarship; candidates are expected to apply 'knowledge of educational technology, including the use of computer and related technologies in instruction, assessment . . .' (NCATE Standards, 1995, p. 24). Resource standards also expect that higher education faculty and candidates have 'training in and access to education-related electronic information, video resources, computer hardware, software, related technologies . . .' and that 'facilities and equipment support computing, educational communications, and educational and instructional technology at least at the level of other units in the university' (NCATE Standards, 1995, p. 24).

Thus far, integrating technology into instruction and assessment has not been a sufficiently high priority in many schools of education. The Office of Technology Assessment, a former arm of the US Congress, issued a report which stated, 'Technology is not central to the teacher preparation experience in most colleges of education. Programs do not prepare graduates to use technology as a teaching tool. Consequently, most new teachers graduate from teacher preparation institutions with limited knowledge of the ways technology can be used in their professional practice' (Office of Technology Assessment, Congress of the United States, 1995, p. 165). The OTA concluded that if information technology is to become an integral part of the teacher preparation curriculum, changes must occur:

1 K-12 and university educators must work together to integrate technology into curriculum and classroom practice;
2 Teacher educators and K-12 staff must receive training and support;
3 Models must be developed with technology supporting specific content areas; and
4 Teacher education faculty incentives need revision to encourage greater use and integration of technology in instruction (Office of Technology Assessment, Congress of the United States, 1995, p. 165).

The study recognized the lack of hardware and software currently available in schools of education, also identified the need for institutions to build continual updating of systems into their resource allocations. Initial expenditures for hardware may be especially difficult for many institutions without external support.

NCATE has initiated a project to assist accredited schools of education to infuse technology into the teaching and learning process, and to assist NCATE in using technology effectively in its accreditation work. NCATE has organized a task force to provide recommendations about:

1 how to direct resources to schools of education (faculty and teacher candidates) so that they understand and are able to use computer technologies in instruction and assessment, and

2   the most appropriate use of resources to facilitate the work of accreditation so that institutions share knowledge and realize saving in direct costs and time.

NCATE's technology task force is focusing on what can be done to close the gap between the knowledge and skills that a graduate of a pre-service teacher preparation program should have and those that programs currently provide. The deficiencies are well-known; NCATE plans to assist institutions in remedying them. Initial priorities are the development of technology plans and a vision of technology integration in the curricula within schools of education; increased faculty development in the use of technology; incentives for faculty to use technology; increased links with the K-12 schools to collaborate on research and use; and increased access to hardware and software.

Technology will also facilitate the use of performance assessment and evidence of it during an accreditation review. NCATE could use electronic communication to examine samples of a candidate's work. The work would include college and external examinations, candidate portfolios, and evaluations of teaching performance. NCATE's work in the area of technology is just beginning. Using technology as a tool in the accreditation process should aid in streamlining the process and make it more cost effective. In addition, the technology should create greater ease of access to valuable information that NCATE collects during the accreditation process. For example, NCATE could develop a list of colleges with exemplary practices in various areas. Colleges that are seeking assistance in a particular area could search for institutions on NCATE's web page that have been cited as having an exemplary approach.

Diversity

NCATE is committed to ensuring that teacher candidates are well prepared to teach all children. In today's pluralistic society, children of color already comprise a large minority, even a majority of seats in classrooms in some states and areas, while only a small percentage of candidates in schools of education are of color.

NCATE has standards on diversity for faculty and teacher candidates, as well as on multicultural curricula and student teaching placement. These standards reflect the values and beliefs that undergird them: that all students deserve a high quality educational experience, and that all teachers should be prepared to help all students learn.

Standard II.B, *Composition of Students*, says that 'the unit recruits, admits, and retains a diverse student body' (NCATE Standards, 1995, p. 21). The standards also contain indicators which are sources of evidence that help teams determine whether a standard is met. Standard III. B, *Composition of Faculty*, notes that 'the unit recruits, hires, and retains a diverse higher education faculty' (NCATE Standards, 1995, p. 25). Diversity in candidates and faculty is valued for its instructive capacity. Studying about diverse cultures does not promote the same quality of understanding as exchange of ideas among individuals who represent a variety of cultural groups. Such interaction has two benefits: improved understanding among specific groups and individuals, and the candidate's expanded capacity to extend such understanding to other groups and individuals.

The diversity standards and indicators have not been without controversy. Accreditation teams are looking for 'plans, efforts, and results' (NCATE Standards, 1995, p. 25) in recruiting minority students and faculty. Recognizing that some institutions are located in remote areas with little diversity, the standards provide *an expectation* for teacher preparation institutions. NCATE has encouraged institutions to take actions they would not have taken without the standards; they have acted to move the field forward.

Linking Preparation and Certification

The National Board's standards embody a vision of accomplished teaching that can become the basis for redesigning advanced teacher preparation programs so that a candidate can obtain a master's degree while preparing for board certification. Accredited universities would offer programs of study designed to prepare teachers for certification assessments. Such a strategy would encourage a meaningful approach to advanced teacher preparation rather than merely requiring candidates to take a series of unrelated courses to renew a teaching license. The National Board standards will serve to motivate the reform of advanced teacher preparation programs by providing a new focus.

Apparatus for Implementation

NCATE is a voluntary accrediting agency, and exists because the field acknowledges the importance of an external quality assurance mechanism to assess the preparation of the nation's teachers. It is the responsibility of the states and state standards boards composed of professionals in the field to determine the consequences of professional accreditation in teacher preparation.

NCATE tailors its partnerships to the needs of individual states. Some states turn the entire review process over to NCATE. In these states, individual programs, such as science education, are reviewed by the professional associations that are members of NCATE (e.g., the National Science Teachers Association), rather than by the state department of education. This procedure saves state resources while ensuring quality. This trend signals a dramatic breakthrough for the teaching profession. States long ago delegated the authority for approving preparation programs to the relevant professional associations in the fields of medicine, law, engineering, psychology, nursing, and others.

As state budgets shrink, more states are relying on the NCATE process to ensure the quality of their teacher preparation programs. They are also beginning to shift available resources from program approval to performance-based licensing. The coming years may see the same level of activity in the licensing area that has been the case in the development of standards for students, teachers, and teacher preparation. Whether the licensing systems will be unique from state to state remains to be seen. It is likely that a system of shared assessments will be developed in the context of a performance-based licensing framework that states use and modify. The work of the National Board is a useful model for states considering performance-based licensing.

As states gear up their reform efforts, they can be informed by studies of the teaching profession. The new report of the National Commission on Teaching and America's Future, *What Matters Most*, represents an unprecedented vision and opportunity to advance teaching as a profession. For the first time in American education history, a comprehensive vision for the creation of a profession of teaching — from recruitment and preparation to induction and continuing professional development — has been advanced by a bipartisan commission of public officials, business and education leaders.

The Commission report contains recommendations relating to every part of the education system. Of those pertaining to preparation, accreditation is addressed directly: 'all schools of education should be professionally accredited' and those found to be inadequate should be closed (National Commission on Teaching and America's Future, 1996). The Commission is providing follow up consultation in selected states to advance the reform agenda outlined in its report, *What Matters Most*. These efforts merge with those of NCATE's New Professional Teacher Project, as NCATE works with seven states to focus efforts on reforms in teacher preparation and licensing. The project is designed to foster collaboration among the stakeholders in each participating state as they build an agenda for reform. The project requires collaboration on the part of all groups involved in education. The NPT coalitions should exert a powerful influence simply because the project participants include virtually all major education stakeholders.

The idea of teacher growth and development as a continuum that spans a teaching career offers a framework to guide the creation of new standards and assessments. In order to move the reforms to the mainstream, educators and policymakers need to commit to change — in existing structures, regulations, and procedures. NCATE is participating in the movement through its efforts to expand the use of accreditation standards in schools of education, and to ensure that preparation standards are aligned with licensing and certification standards.

References

GIDEONES, H. et al. (1993) *Capturing the Vision: Reflections on NCATE's Redesign Five Years After*, Washington, DC: American Association of Colleges for Teacher Education, pp. 17–19.

MURRAY, F.B. and FALLON, D. (1989) *The Reform of Teacher Education for the 21st Century: Project 30 Year One Report*, Newark, DE, pp. 16–34.

NCATE Standards (1995) *Standards, Procedures, and Policies for the Accreditation of Professional Education Units*, Washington, DC: National Council for Accreditation of Teacher Education, pp. 18–29.

Office of Technology Assessment (1995) *Teachers and Technology: Making the Connection*, Washington DC: Congress of the United States, pp. 165–6.

Trachtman, R. (1996) *NCATE PDS Standards Project: Preliminary Survey Findings*, Washington, DC: National Council for Accreditation of Teacher Education, pp. 7–8.

What Matters Most: Teaching for America's Future (1996) New York, NY: National Commission on Teaching and America's Future.

11 The Psychological Dimensions of Teacher Education: The Role of the University

Yvonne Gold

It is well known that teacher education has been a major focus of criticism for a number of years. Factors that contribute to the debate center around the importance of quality teacher preparation, beginning teacher support programs, and ongoing professional development. Those who are the greatest critics propose radical changes in the preparation of teachers. However, throughout the literature the most overlooked and ignored are the critical factors in the education of the teacher — the psychological dimension. The focus has been and continues to be on preparing teachers in the instructional areas. However no matter how competent the individual and their technical skills of instruction, these skills can be severely masked by psychological factors which hinder teachers in carrying out their responsibilities. Those who propose teacher education programs quickly leap to the conclusion that subject matter knowledge is sufficient for teaching competence. It is true that subject matter knowledge and competence in teaching the subject are necessary, however they are not sufficient. What is missing is the psychological maturity and healthy human development of the teacher (Ammons and Hutcheson, 1989).

The characteristics of an effective teacher reflect a multidimensional educator who is balanced in the psychological and instructional domains. Yet, teacher education to date has focused on only one dimension — the instructional. University programs have offered training for teachers in subject matter knowledge and technical skills for effective practice. Clearly, these are necessary for teaching. However, the profession of teaching also includes a critical component that requires the teacher to work with a wide variety of individuals and a multitude of problems where attention must be paid to interactions involved. Challenges faced by teachers today place tremendous demands upon their ability to handle outside pressures such as disrespectful students, as well as internal conflicts and struggles that go far beyond any technical training received. Thus, psychological maturity is endemic to effective teaching and is more critical today than ever before.

Teachers cannot create a learning community for their students without first receiving the necessary skills to meet their own personal — psychological needs (Gold, 1992; Gold and Roth, 1993). In fact, understanding the psychological needs of teachers is an essential factor in helping them identify their individuality, their special interests, and their capacity for growth. As individuals begin their first year of teaching, the major personal problems identified by a large number of them have been physical fatigue, stress, financial worries, loneliness, isolation, and disillusionment (Bolam, 1987). There has been no preparation in learning how to handle the stress that comes from these types of problems.

When teachers are experiencing a great deal of stress during their teacher training and again through their first year of teaching, they begin to lose confidence in their ability to handle difficult situations which affects their capability in the classroom. Lack of self-confidence along with poor coping strategies for handling themselves during a crisis, has undermined many otherwise promising teachers.

An area of grave concern, classroom discipline, has been identified as the number one perceived problem for new teachers (Veenman, 1984), and a major problem for many experienced teachers (Gold, 1996). Many universities offer courses and seminars on how to handle discipline problems and difficult students. Even with this training, teachers who do not possess the stability and self-confidence to face hostile and difficult students experience what is often called reality shock and all of the technical training is lost during the crisis of the encounter (Ward, 1987). What the teacher must have is an understanding of their own psychological needs, as well as a variety of effective coping strategies to meet challenges with confidence and security. Developing this type of psychological maturity goes far beyond the regular teacher training which covers basic strategies for discipline and classroom management. Thus, the need for training in the personal — psychological dimension is essential.

The focus of this chapter is on the role of the university in providing teacher education assistance with the psychological dimension. The chapter begins with a description of the two dimensions needed in teacher preparation programs: The Instructional Domain and the Psychological Domain. Attention then turns to the use of psychological support as part of teacher preparation. Particular notice, in the description, is given to a psychological support program that has been offered to beginning teachers for a number of years. The next section focuses on the role of the university in developing psychological maturity in teachers. The chapter closes with the challenge to include psychological support as part of teacher education programs in the future.

The Two Dimensions Needed in Teacher Training Programs

The Instructional Domain

Learning to be a teacher is a highly complex procedure that is multidisciplinary. It involves the interaction of knowledge, skills, attitudes and behaviors as well as role-expectations, the socialization process and understanding the developmental stages students go through in learning and maturing. Curriculum and learning are essential areas that reflect a major emphasis for most teacher training programs. Teachers must learn to take the curriculum and transform it and adapt it as they plan to meet the needs of their students. They must also learn to pace, sequence, and adapt lessons. The decisions they make are often situation specific. They are required to focus on immediate situations as well as the many complex aspects involved. Teachers need an awareness of pedagogical strategies that they can use to challenge their students' thinking as they seek to develop higher level thinking skills. At the same time, the teacher must know how to establish behavior standards and carry out a plan of action to develop a sense of community within the classroom.

Veenman (1984), in his extensive review of the literature on beginning teachers reported classroom discipline to be the number one perceived problem for them. Many others discussed the importance of training teachers to handle the numerous discipline problems they will encounter (Huffman and Leak, 1986). However, Feiman-Nemser (1992) reported that these types of management and discipline problems frequently arise due to teachers being unclear about their purposes, choosing inappropriate tasks, or not giving their students adequate direction. She encouraged connecting the training of management and discipline strategies with curriculum and instruction issues for teachers. From these reports, many teacher education programs advocated instructional support with attention to classroom discipline as being most important and placed a heavy emphasis on it to offer assistance to new teachers.

In the area of subject matter content, Lee Shulman (1986) wrote extensively regarding the knowledge base for teachers. His reports stated that the emergent research base on teaching and teaching effectiveness lacked one central aspect — subject matter. Shulman strongly urged that this issue needs to be addressed in detail. Thus content standards and developing a knowledge base are appearing more readily in the current literature, especially as connected to new teacher programs.

Essential issues to be considered in teacher training programs are connected with how efficient the new teacher is in transforming their expertise in the subject matter into a form that their students can comprehend, as well as drawing on their expertise in the subject matter in the process of teaching.

Along with these areas, teachers must learn to assess their own actions based on sound theory and research. They must develop the skills of a reflective practitioner, evaluate themselves from an objective understanding of why they are choosing to use the knowledge and strategies they have selected, and they must be able to handle the successes and consequences of their actions.

During their initial training, teachers are developing beginning impressions about what kind of teacher they want to be. These initial experiences of teachers have been identified as being 'imprinted, embedding perceptions and behaviors regarding teaching, students, the school environment, and their role as teacher' (Gold, 1996, p. 548). These imprintings etch impressions and feelings during a critical period of the teacher's life and the feelings are elicited later in their career when they encounter similar experiences. This may well be why teachers have a difficult time changing certain habits and teaching practices and are not aware they are continuing to practice them. Thus the need for gaining awareness into their initial learning patterns.

Along with initial impressions of teaching, new teachers are also being socialized into the profession. The major determinants in the socialization of teachers as reported in the literature are students, parents, and colleagues (Zeichner and Gore,

1990). These factors are interrelated with a new teacher's beliefs and expectations and affect them in a number of ways they may not understand or be able to control (Wildman et al., 1989). The essential role of colleagues and support providers during this critical period has been well documented in the literature (Gold, 1996).

Universities are now increasing their collaboration with school districts in the preparation of teachers in order to make the pre-training period more effective and reality based. New teachers are acquiring the knowledge base from their university preparation, and are receiving more experience in learning how it can be applied in the classroom. As universities and school districts consider their essential roles in the preparation of teachers, a stronger teacher preparation program is beginning to emerge. Although schools can do some of the preparation of teachers, especially in the practical instructional dimension, the educational impact of university faculty on students appears to be most influential in the area of intellectual expertise where the focus on ideas and concepts about their teaching in turn increases their intellectual orientation. Also, according to Pascarella (1994), student involvement at the university level can be shaped by critical thinking and the use of principled moral reasoning which may be enhanced by student discussion at a relatively high cognitive level. Instruction that engages students in problem solving encourages them to transform learning into practical applications.

Providing instructional support for teachers is essential if they are to acquire the necessary subject matter, learn how to prepare a variety of instructional materials, understand the structure of knowledge and how it is transformed into content knowledge, think reflectively and critically about their teaching, and according to Fenstermacher help them 'possess the skill and understanding to acquire the continually expanding knowledge base about teaching and the academic content they impart to students' (1990, p. 169). The Instructional Domain is an essential part of teacher preparation. Teachers must be offered this type of training and support before taking full responsibility of a classroom. However, when teachers begin teaching and attempt to 'put it all together' during their first few months of teaching, the struggle to survive becomes overwhelming (Veenman, 1984), and many dropout (Harris et al., 1992, 1993; Schlechty and Vance, 1981, 1983). Ward (1987) reported that when teachers are personally insecure, lack confidence, or have a sense of not being in control of themselves or their environment, it is not likely they can be successful at teaching, regardless of how strong the technical preparation has been. In fact, incorrectly handled, the impact of this experience may wash out any skills and knowledge these prospective teachers learn in their preparation program. Thus the need for another type of training — the psychological.

The Psychological Domain

During their first experience with teaching, the major personal problems mentioned by a large number of student teachers and beginning teachers were physical fatigue, stress, financial worries, loneliness, and disillusionment (Farber, 1991; Gold, 1992; Gold and Roth, 1993). The existence of stress as an inherent aspect of teaching is clearly documented (Beer and Beer, 1992; French, 1993). Student teachers are attempting to make the transition from student to teacher and may experience a great deal of insecurity in the process (Proctor, Clarke and Mygdal, 1989). When they lack self-confidence, have conflicts between their personal life and professional requirements, teachers feel insecure about who they are as a person and as a teacher. When this takes place, it is not likely that they can be successful in their teaching regardless of how strong the instructional preparation has been.

Pressures of the profession and the inability to handle these pressures are major factors in a teacher deciding to leave the profession (Friedman, 1993). Before they ever leave, what is detrimental for them and for their students is the steady decline of effectiveness as a teacher and as a person. What is needed is a program of knowledge and support that emphasizes awareness of how they are handling pressures as well as recognizing types of strategies they use to cope with the pressures. Teachers must learn how to manage stress through a process of acquiring knowledge and coping strategies that will assist then during this difficult phase of teaching. They need a program of psychological support. However, addressing stress and psychological needs is not a major item on the agenda of professional development programs. When some type of assistance is provided, it is either too little, too late, or misdirected. Too often the assistance is not focused on the real problem.

Psychological support has been defined in a number of ways by a variety of individuals (Gold, 1992; Thies-Sprinthall, 1984; Thies-Sprinthall and Gerler, 1990). It includes emotional support, positive regard, accurate empathy, empathic listening, and meeting psychological needs. Also included are an array of skills and strategies that focus on confidence building, reinforcing a positive self-esteem, instilling a sense of self-reliance, developing a sense of effectiveness, learning to handle stress and manage burnout, and identifying unmet psychological needs of teachers. According to Gold (1992), psychological support is essentially a form of therapeutic guidance where teachers are assisted in identifying psychological, physical, social and intellectual needs that are unmet at the present time (Gold and Roth, 1993). Needs such as security, self-esteem, self-confidence, collegiality, a sense of belonging, safety, and intellectual stimulation, for a few, when unmet create a sense of threat for individuals. Thus causing more stress and pressure on the person. These needs are especially of concern when the individual is not aware that they are unmet and creating stress for them. To be effective in their personal role as they interact with students, other teachers, administrators and parents, teachers must be psychologically stable and in a continuous process of psychological growth and maturity. This is vital in personal interactions in their professional role and has a significant influence on their ability to use fully the instructional and technical knowledge and skills made available to them (Farber, 1991; Ward, 1987). With the increasing demands and pressures placed upon teachers today, the necessity to address personal-psychological needs has become critical. This certainly does not mean that every individual assisting in the training of a teacher must be a psychotherapist or a psychologist. It does mean however, that those who train and assist student teachers and beginning teachers understand the nature of their personal needs and that they have learned how to identify and meet them in their own life. Thus promoting psychological maturity.

We are beginning to see some degree of recognition of the importance of training teachers to recognize and meet their personal and psychological needs. More attention, for example, is given in the supervision literature to working with the teacher's personal concerns, and beginning teacher support programs all have a component that focuses on emotional support. However, offering emotional support through strategies that involve empathic listening and reassurance in difficult situations falls short of providing psychological support to meet personal and psychological needs as long-term life changing strategies. What is available at the present time is some recognition, although limited, with very little being done in this extremely important domain of teacher education.

There are a number of causes that contribute to the lack of a concerted effort to address the domain of personal and psychological needs of teachers. First, there is a lack of a widespread awareness of the relationship of these needs to effective practice. Second, even though there is some recognition, the extent or depth of this influence is not well understood by teacher educators and supervisors in spite of the growing literature and empirical base (Farber, 1991; Gold, 1996). Third, educators are not professionally prepared in areas such as psychology, and often are uncomfortable with psychologically related responsibilities. Even though there is a growing recognition to address this domain, little is being done at the present time. Fourth, educators do not see this domain as their own role. Their charge traditionally has been to develop skills in curriculum and instruction, and not to be as concerned with the personal issues of teachers. What is needed at the present time is a greater understanding of the personal aspects of the teacher's growth and a commitment to the teacher's psychological welfare. All aspects of a teacher's needs affect their performance in the classroom and in their professional role. Therefore, exploring in-depth the nature of personal and psychological needs and how to assist the teacher toward psychological maturity is critical.

A Psychological Support Program

One of the purposes of a university is to educate its students so that they receive an education in varied disciplines, are individuals who analyze, use critical thinking, formulate a belief system, develop their intellectual capability and gain intellectual maturity that will enhance their professional life. Other purposes are to assist students in developing a personal philosophy, to gain a deeper understanding of self that leads to psychological maturity. Thus, the development of the psychological aspects of their life. In order to achieve these purposes, the entire university community needs to participate in the education of its students. It can accomplish this in ways that are more extensive than any other institution. The university provides a wide range of expertise and resources to assist students in developing their personal and professional life, a holistic approach.

In teacher education programs, it is essential that professional competence as well as psychological maturity are provided for. Teachers bring who they are to the classroom and model both their professional expertise and their psychological well being. Teaching is a psychological, social and moral activity that is extremely complex where teachers must coordinate multiple tasks as they simultaneously must deal with their own personality and pressures. Teachers are constantly needing to handle complex dilemmas and make decisions to resolve one problem after another. They often feel that they are forced into situations that demand their decision making even when they are unaware of the final results of their choices. Thus, teaching is highly complex and places tremendous stress on the teacher as a person. The question is, how can teachers, and especially beginning teachers, learn to handle the complexities of their position that contribute to their stress and burnout? This author concludes that when teachers are helped to develop a psychological perspective toward their own well-being, they can use the training received to bring about their own psychological maturity that will affect not only their own mental and emotional well-being, but that of their students as well.

Personal beliefs and behaviors as well as content knowledge and discipline strategies are demonstrated to their students. It has been documented that when a new teacher is overwhelmed with schedules, disruptive students and first year pressures the impact on them emotionally and psychologically affects their ability to retain what they learned regarding subject matter and teaching strategies (Ward, 1987). How they handle themselves emotionally is extremely important. Therefore attention to the psychological development of a teacher is critical to their being prepared to educate the youth of a nation.

A new model program was designed and implemented at the university level (Gold 1992; Gold and Roth, 1993; 1997) to address the issue of developing psychological maturity in teachers. The program includes:

1 identifying personal — psychological needs;
2 acquiring knowledge and coping strategies to handle pressures and problems;
3 gaining self-reliance;
4 learning how to handle stress and manage burnout through life-long skills;
5 developing a sense of psychological maturity, and
6 preparing a life plan for personal and professional wellness.

The personal needs as defined by Gold (1992) and Gold and Roth (1993, 1998) include the physical, social and spiritual areas. The psychological needs represent the emotional and intellectual areas. Within each of these categories, the authors identified specific needs and included inventories where the individual can quickly assess their unmet needs. Once needs are identified, teachers can plan ways to meet them. For example, in a psychological support group facilitated by the author, teachers identified their unmet emotional–physical needs and were given strategies for meeting them. One young teacher explained how she had identified her unmet need for calmness, and now more clearly understood why she was feeling more stress as of late. She shared with the group how her demanding schedule at school left her little time for relaxation. She was feeling pressured and extremely nervous during the past few moths. The facilitator discussed ways the teacher could modify her schedule and plan specific times for relaxation to help bring about a sense of calmness in her life. A number of the teachers in the group expressed that they had high stress levels over the past few months. The facilitator planned a few sessions that included defining stress, learning what causes it, and noting the physical and emotional dangers to an individual. A stress log was kept by all of the teachers during the next week. They monitored their stressors and the ways they handled them throughout the week. At the next weekly meeting of the support group, an analysis was made of their stressors, coping strategies and specific behavior patterns used. A number of insights were gained by the group such as: 'I am more stressed with events over with I have no control.' 'The majority of my stressors are people.' 'I now know why I'm so nervous and tense when I look at all of the stressors I recorded this week. I must do something to reduce my stress.' The facilitator included specific coping strategies to assist them in managing their stress. Discussion then centered on unmet needs identified the previous week and how their stressors were associated with their unmet needs. One teacher immediately shared with the group how her unmet need for self-esteem was connected to all of her stressors. She was highly motivated to work on her low self-esteem which will help her in teaching and in her personal relationships.

This type of psychological support and training equips teachers with specific knowledge and strategies to better manage their life, and grow in psychological maturity which in turn affects their performance in the classroom and their overall professional role.

The critical issue to first be considered is how personal and psychological needs are identified and addressed. A detailed identification of the needs is required along with clearly defined coping strategies for addressing them. Gold and Roth (1993 and 1998) have provided a comprehensive program of psychological support for teachers which has been used extensively with large numbers of teacher support groups, staff development groups, and mentor teacher support groups nationally and internationally. Identification of emotional, physical, social, intellectual and spiritual needs of an individual, along with clearly defined coping strategies for addressing the needs enables teachers to handle the stress they encounter daily (Kieffer, 1994). With the slow wearing away of the morale of teachers (Harris et al., 1992), a carefully planned program of psychological support that encourages and supports teachers as they learn healthy coping strategies is even more essential at the present time to handle the tremendous pressures teachers face every day in their classroom.

Too often teachers in training are so involved in their professional responsibilities that they have little time left for taking care of themselves. This becomes evident during specific periods when pressures are extremely high, such as the month of December. During this busy month many teachers allow their physical health to be neglected. The results are noted in illness, a lack of energy, and overall poor physical fitness. This condition is too often seen during a teacher's first year of teaching. Learning how to develop a physical plan that fits the teacher's schedule and needs is essential for a healthy lifestyle.

The challenge to educators is to provide programs of psychological support for teachers in training and for experienced teachers and mentors (Gold, 1996). A program that includes this type of support for teachers will focus on each of the domains of need through inquiry, reflection on practice, problem-solving, and use of communication skills in sharing concepts and insights learned.

More precisely, educational programs for teachers need to include both the instructional and psychological domains. Thus, teachers can be involved in both personal and professional growth that enhances their life and overall life style which in turn affects their students' personal and academic growth.

The Use of Psychological Support in Teacher Training Programs

The essential need for a program of psychological support has been well documented. Fiske and Chiriboga (1990) believe that life events can have significant influences on the teacher by changing their particular psychological needs. The body of literature on noxious emotions suggests strongly that 'it is not merely the presence of psychologically stressful events that can be life-threatening, but the interpretation one accords them' (Dossey, 1994, p. 75). Life-events that are connected with feelings of hopelessness, helplessness, and despair seem to be particularly dangerous. Goleman and Gurin (1993) discussed Karasek's research on stress and reported his finding that when 'people felt highly pressured but had little or no control over how they met the job's demands, it had a profound effect on their health.' Karasek discovered that the combination of high psychological demands and low decision latitude created 'high job strain' (p. 30). The need for psychological support has always been, and is increasing at a rapid rate. Gold and Roth (1993) refer to psychological support as the 'hidden dimension' (p. 48) of teacher education and professional development. It is the lack of preparation in the hidden dimension that significantly contributes to the high rate of failure of beginning teachers and the burnout of both beginning and experienced teachers.

This entirely new type of support is essential for preservice preparation, new teacher induction, and professional development of all teachers. This type of support concentrates on the growth and development of the individual, rather than focusing on instructional support as the only preparation, which is the present situation. Thus it is imperative that a comprehensive program be implemented into teacher education programs to provide the necessary skills and support to enable teachers to survive and mature throughout their careers. The total growth of the teacher must be addressed.

Psychological support discussed here is a comprehensive program which addresses the psychological needs of a teacher. It also includes the use of individual insight strategies, interpersonal support, and guided group interactions which focus on problem-solving and reflective inquiry to meet personal-professional needs.

The comprehensive aspect of the program can be implemented in a variety of ways. It is comprehensive in that it must deal with all of the fundamental needs: Emotional-Physical, Psycho-Social and Personal Intellectual (Gold, 1992; Gold and Roth, 1993). A comprehensive program will also include stress management and burnout prevention. All of these aspects of psychological support and the underlying needs must be identified and addressed in order for the program to be comprehensive. Most support programs include a type of stress management which provides for short term assistance. These programs deal with symptoms rather than fundamental problems and needs. Therefore, they have short-term effects.

One of the common elements emerging across the nation in the new teacher support and induction programs is that of assigning a mentor to develop a professional relationship with the new teacher. This strategy is helpful in that it provides for interpersonal support. Using it alone however, has been found to be insufficient. What is needed is use of a comprehensive approach with long-term results. When all of the strategies in the psychological support program are combined, it provides a collective effect that works together for a more formidable source of support that contributes greatly to the meaning of comprehensive.

Another aspect of the psychological support program previously discussed deals with both personal and professional needs of teachers. These needs interact and affect each other. By addressing both of these types of needs the program is more successful and has long-term effects. Focusing on essential psychological needs which are also related to professional performance greatly empowers the teacher to solve problems and handle the stress of teaching.

The psychological support program includes strategies that are specifically designed to meet the particular needs of the individual. Practice sessions are included that provide the skills necessary to make life changes. Problem-solving as a focus enables teachers to gain insights and skills to help themselves change specific thinking and behavior that is counter productive to success. This program is in direct contrast to quick-fix workshops that have short-term effects. Goldenberg and Gallimore proposed saying 'good-bye to quick-fix workshops . . . instead, create contexts in teachers' work lives that assist and sustain meaningful changes' (1991, p. 69).

In a psychological support program, teachers experience meaningful changes in their lives. Teachers are engaged in thorough examination of their personal and professional lives, they explore meaningful solutions, and most significant, make long-lasting changes that enhance their lives and the lives of their students.

Psychological support is the hidden dimension of teaching which has been missing from teacher education, induction programs, and professional development programs. It has not been addressed in a concerted fashion in teacher preparation programs, even though the need has been there. However, the need is being magnified by the increasing demands being placed on teachers today.

The purpose of a psychological support program is to focus on underlying problems and needs of teachers, go beyond stress management, develop coping strategies that are life-changing and have long-lasting effects, and develop professional health over the long term. It enables teachers to enjoy their teaching and provides the type of support that enables them to gain self-control over difficult areas of their life (Fennick, 1992). It assists teachers in monitoring their behavior and provides guidance for healthier personal and professional lives.

The psychological support programs developed and used with teachers over the past few years have been extremely successful (Gold, 1992) because they have been designed around the principles and characteristics discussed. They have assisted teachers in becoming aware of areas in their lives that cause them difficulty and affect their teaching in adverse ways. Teachers gain insight into negative feelings and behaviors, identify stressors in their lives, and discover their own abilities to develop effective coping strategies to deal effectively with problems. Specific strategies are developed and supportive environments are provided to resolve immediate concerns. Effective and ongoing strategies are practiced and long-term effects are experienced which bring about life changes.

In working with a wide variety of professionals who were experiencing severely diminished professional effectiveness, identifying psychological needs and designing a psychological support program has been attributed to a clear identification of the problems teachers experience. Highly focused strategies have been used to prepare teachers to meet their personal-psychological needs that if not recognized and met would have had destructive effects on their professional competence. Psychological support as presented here provides a multidimensional approach with practical applications of tested strategies and skills to enhance the teacher's personal growth and professional effectiveness. This type of treatment produces long-term effects, and in many cases life-changing outcomes. Including it in pre-service, induction, and professional development programs prepares teachers to be more successful professionals who develop personal and professional maturity.

The Role of the University in Developing Psychological Maturity in Teachers

A most significant issue discussed in the teacher education literature is the intense debate over who should control the education and training of teachers. Schools of education have received a great deal of criticism from outside the profession (Phillips, 1991; Barr, 1992) and from inside (Holmes Group, 1986; Garnegie Task Force on Teaching as a Profession, 1986; Zeichner, 1993) regarding the preparation of teachers. While alternative school based teacher education programs are on the increase (Darling-Hammond, 1992), there are a number of questions to be considered regarding the role of the university in the educating of teachers. However, the essential question that must be addressed in the preparation of teachers is, what specific conditions can the university provide in preparing teachers? The focus of this section of the chapter centers on and specifically addresses the role of the university in providing personal and psychological support which is best dealt with in a university setting — that is, a multidisciplinary setting. The university is in the best position to assist teachers in the personal-psychological area. Students have an opportunity to interact with faculty from a variety of disciplines with various interests and talents that can help meet their needs from a broader perspective then that which has been the focus of schools — giving instructional support.

One of the important characteristics of an effective teacher is that of possessing psychological maturity. Receiving training to evaluate their strengths and needs regarding their psychological health will also be reflected in the ways teachers encourage their students toward improved psychological health. Teachers of this type continue to assess not only the instructional needs of their students but also their emotional needs, and plan effective programs to accomplish their goals. These teachers are able to manage their stress and the many demands placed upon them in their role as teacher.

When university teacher education includes psychological support programs the teachers they train will enter teaching better prepared to handle themselves and the stress related to teaching, as well as being able to use more effectively the basic skills they learned in their preparation program. When a teacher possesses psychological maturity, they are able to handle their own needs and are thus free of psychological problems that hinder their focusing on the needs of their students. Emotional and psychological mature teachers are better prepared to grow in their knowledge and skill as a teacher.

Thus, programs that prepare teachers who are psychologically healthy will enable these individuals to better demonstrate their proficiency in quality teaching. These teachers will have a positive impact upon the emotional growth of their students as well as their academic competence.

Conclusion

Teacher education at the university level is undergoing intense scrutiny at the present time. Focus centers on who should educate our teachers, what entry standards should be required, are school based teacher training programs superior to university programs, and how effective is alternative certification.

A great deal of attention is centered on these issues which involve the need for control and power and takes the focus away from addressing the needs of individual teachers. All of these concerns are important and need resolving. However, what is essential today is a teacher who is secure and emotionally mature. One who has healthy coping strategies to handle their own pressures. In return they can better cope with changes in society, cultural demands, disrespectful students, and other pressing problems. They can apply the knowledge and research learned in college in meaningful ways for their students with a greater success than will the teacher who has only received training in 'how to teach'.

Who should train our teachers is an essential question that is being addressed by many scholars today and must be intelligently resolved. However, an even more compelling issue centers around the type of teacher needed to teach today's youth. What personal and psychological qualities must today's teacher possess? The university is in a unique position to call upon experts from a wide variety of disciplines to meet this challenge and focus on both the psychological maturity and the academic preparation of teachers. Preparing a teacher who has the psychological maturity and skills to meet the many demands and challenges placed upon them today will not only benefit them but their students as well. To offer less to teachers will hinder their ability to carry out their responsibilities toward their students, the profession and their own well-being.

References

AMMONS, P. and HUTCHESON, B.P. (1989) 'Promoting the development of teacher pedagogical conceptions', *Genetic Epistemologist*, **17**, 4, pp. 23–9.

BARR, R. (1992) 'Turmoil in teacher education in Oregon', in GIDONESE, H. (ed.) *Teacher Education Policy: Narratives, Stories and Cases*, Albany, NY: SUNY Press, pp. 111–31.

BEER, J. and BEER, J. (1992) 'Burnout and stress, depression and self-esteem of teachers', *Psychological Reports*, **71**, pp. 1331–6.

BOLAM, R. (1987) 'Induction of beginning teachers', in DUNKIN, M.J. (ed.) *The International Encyclopedia of Teaching and Teacher Education*, Oxford: Pergamon, pp. 745–57.

CARNEGIE TASK FORCE ON TEACHING AS A PROFESSION (1986) *A Nation Prepared: Teachers for the 21st Century*, Washington, DC, Author.

DARLING-HAMMOND, L. (1992) 'Teaching and knowledge: Policy issues posed by alternative certification for teachers', *Peabody Journal of Education*, **67**, 3, pp. 123–54.

DOSSEY, L. (1994) 'Healing and the mind: Is there a dark side?', *Journal of Scientific Exploration*, **8**, 1, pp. 73–90.

FARBER, B.A. (1991) *Crisis in Education: Stress and Burnout in the American Teacher*, San Francisco: Jossey-Bass.

FEIMAN-NEMSER, S. (1992) *Helping Novices Learn to Teach: Lessons from an Experienced Support Teacher*, Report No. 91–6, East Lansing: Michigan State University, National Center for Research on Teacher Learning.

FENNICK, R. (March, 1992) 'Combating new teacher burnout: Providing support networks for personal and professional growth', Paper presented at the annual meeting of the conference on college composition and communication. Cincinnati, OH, (ERIC Document Reproduction Service No. ED349580 CS213543) pp. 19–21.

FENSTERMACHER, G.D. (1990) 'The place of alternative certification education of teachers', *Peabody Journal of Education*, **67**, 3, pp. 155–85.

FISKE, M. and CHIRIBOGA, D.A. (1990) *Change and Continuity in Adult Life*, San Francisco: Jossey-Bass.

FRENCH, N.K. (1993) 'Elementary teacher stress and class size', *Journal of Research and development in Education*, **26**, 2, pp. 66–73.

FRIEDMAN, E. (1993) 'Burnout in teachers: The concept and its unique core meaning', *Educational and Psychological Measurement*, **53**, pp. 1035–44.

GOLD, Y. (1992) 'Psychological support for mentors and beginning teachers: A critical dimension', in BEY, T.M. and HOLMES, C.T. (eds) *Mentoring: Contemporary Principles and Issues*, Reston, VA: Association of Teacher Educators, pp. 25–34.

GOLD, Y. (1996) 'Beginning teacher support: Attrition, mentoring, and induction', in SIKULA, J., BUTTERY, T.J. and GUYTON, E. (eds) *Handbook of Research on Teacher Education*, New York: Simon and Schuster Macmillan.

GOLD, Y. and ROTH, R.A. (1993) *Teachers Managing Stress and Preventing Burnout: The Professional Health Solution*, London: Falmer Press.

GOLD, Y. and ROTH, R.A. (1998) *The Transformational Helping Professional; A New Vision*, Boston: Allyn and Bacon.

GOLDENBERG, C. and GALLIMORE, R. (1991) 'Changing teaching takes more than a one-shot workshop', *Educational Leadership*, **49**, 3, pp. 69–71.

GOLEMAN, D. and GURIN, J. (1993) *Mind, Body Medicine*, New York: Consumer Reports Books.

HARRIS, L. and ASSOCIATES (1992) *The Metropolitan Life Survey of the American Teacher: The Second Year: New Teachers' Expectations and Ideals*, New York: Metropolitan Life Insurance.

HARRIS, L. (1993) *The Metropolitan Life Survey of the American Teacher: Violence in America's Public Schools*, New York: Metropolitan Life Insurance.

HOLMES GROUP (1986) *Tommorrow's Teachers: A Report of the Holmes Group*, East Lansing, MI, Author.

HUFFMAN, G. and LEAK, S. (1986) 'Beginning teachers' perceptions of mentors', *Journal of Teacher Education*, **37**, 1, pp. 22–5.

KIEFFER, J.C. (1994) 'Using a problem-focused coping strategy on teachers stress and burn-out', *Teaching and Change*, **1**, 2, pp. 190–206.

PASCARELLA, E.T. (1994) 'The impact of college on students: Myths, rational myths, and some other things that may not be true', *Chester E. Peters Lecture*, Kansas State University.

PHILLIPS, N. (1991) 'Teacher preparation woos grads outside education', *The Philadelphia Inquirer* (Sunday, December 1), section A, p. 1.

PROCTOR, T.J., CLARK, C.M. and MYGDAL, W.K. (1989) 'Teacher education students' perceptions of self and the ideal teacher', *Educational Research Quarterly*, **13**, 3, pp. 44–52.

SCHLECHTY, P.C. and VANCE, V.S. (1981) 'Do academically able teachers leave education? The North Carolina case', *Phi Delta Kappan*, **63**, 2, pp. 106–12.

SCHLECHTY, P.C. and VANCE, V.S. (1983) 'Recruitment, selection and retention: The shape of the teaching force', *Elementary School Journal*, **83**, 4, pp. 469–87.

SHULMAN, L.S. (1986) 'Those who understand: Knowledge growth in teaching', *Educational Researcher*, **15**, 2, pp. 4–14.

THIES-SPRINTHALL, L.M. (1984) 'Promoting the developmental growth of supervising teachers: Theory, research programs, and implications', *Journal of Teacher Education*, **35**, 3, pp. 53–60.

THIES-SPRINTHALL, L.M. and GERLER, E.R., JR (1990) 'Support groups for novice teachers', *Journal of Staff Development*, **11**, 4, pp. 18–22.

VEENMAN, S. (1984) 'Perceived problems of beginning teachers', *Review of Educational Research*, **54**, 2, pp. 143–78.

WARD, B.A. (1987) 'State and district structures to support initial year of teaching programs', in GRIFFIN, G.A. and MILLIES, S. (eds) *The First Years of Teaching: Background Papers and a Proposal*, Chicago: University of Illinois State Board of Education, pp. 35–64.

WILDMAN, T.M., NILES, J.A., MAGLIARO, S.G. and MCLAUGHLIN, R.A. (1989) 'Teaching and learning to teach: The two roles of beginning teachers', *Elementary School Journal*, **89**, 4, pp. 471–93.

ZEICHNER, K. (1993, February) 'Traditions of practice in US preservice teacher education programs', *Teaching and Teacher Education*, **9**, pp. 1–13.

ZEICHNER, K.M. and GORE, J.M. (1990) 'Teacher socialization', in HOUSTON, W.R. (ed.) *Handbook of Research on Teacher Education*, New York: Macmillan, pp. 329–48.

12 University as Context for Teacher Development

Robert A. Roth

In considering the role of the university in teacher education, two salient issues come to mind. One is perspective on teaching, and the other is capacity (intellectual, fiscal, etc.) to deliver the program as conceptualized. Program design in large measure determines the nature and extent of required resources. The focus here thus is on the latter issue of conceptualization. Teaching perceived through one lens may be quite different from teaching perceived through another. Teacher preparation, therefore, may be viewed quite differently as well. The intent of this chapter is to illustrate that indeed these differences in the way teaching is conceptualized leads to role differentiation in respect to the education of teachers. This differentiation relates to the respective contributions of the university in comparison with other institutions (e.g., schools, private enterprise) in the preparation of teachers.

In a number of areas the university and other entities make similar or equal contributions to the development of a teacher in the early phases of preparation such as in preservice education. Both school and university teacher education programs can provide excellent teacher preparation in basic areas identified by research as related to effective teaching. These include the following examples: providing sufficient illustrations and concrete examples, providing demonstrations and models; checking for understanding; high level of active practice, guidance during initial practice, and systematic feedback and correction (Rosenshine and Stevens, 1984, pp. 377, 379). Planning, classroom management, and parent relations are other common areas of basic preparation. A number of these are summarized in *What Works: Research about Teaching and Learning* (US Department of Education, 1987.) It is suggested, however, that the university makes significant contributions in unique ways that are endemic to higher education, and particular levels of cognitive functioning are best developed by these unique ways. These premises will be explored in the following sections.

The basic premise advanced here is that there are contributions to the preparation of teachers that are best, if not uniquely, made by higher education. In order to make this case, it is necessary to examine the conceptions of teaching that underlie perspectives of teaching and teacher education. Various dimensions of teaching will be explored to illustrate the need for involvement of the university in the professional education component of teacher education.

Framing the Discussion

Although there is a wide range of issues and factors to consider in conceptualizing teaching, a select number will be analyzed for sake of relevance and economy of space. It is obviously not intended to be an exhausting list. The areas for discussion include:

a teacher belief systems and how they affect instruction;
b teacher dispositions toward certain critical factors in higher order dimensions of approaches to teaching and learning;
c teacher perspectives of efficacy and implications for effectiveness;
d analysis of reflective practice and how particular elements are fostered in a university environment;
e perceptual acuity in the classroom;
f psychological maturity;
g interpretive-predicative processes in managing instruction;
h the knowledge base and its organization for teaching;
i use of research and applications of the knowledge base.

A somewhat basic perspective of the teaching act is that there are specific skills and strategies in the teacher's repertoire that the teacher draws upon as needed. This approach may be identified as either a 'behavioristic' approach, which stresses specified, observable teaching skills identified in advance, or 'traditional craft', which emphasizes the accumulated wisdom of experienced teachers (Zeichner, 1983). These approaches are both limited and limiting and may be categorized as a craft model.

> the model is limited in that it deals only with a prescribed range of activities and a narrow experience with the background and context of the profession. It may lead the apprentice, for example, to see only the classroom or school and may mask the relationship of the school within the community and the role of school in society. It is limiting in that it does not widen the student's perspective to include theory or rationale of practice or the purposes of schooling. (Roth, 1989, pp. 31–2)

A review of several analyses of teaching from a more sophisticated perspective yields a different set of domains that more closely align with an 'inquiry-oriented' (Zeichner, 1983) or reflective practice model. It is this framework that encompasses the more insightful set of domains that will be reviewed here. Teaching is viewed as a composite of these domains which collectively define teaching as an intellectual process beyond the craft model. These conceptions of teaching are those best developed and enhanced in the context of the university setting. Each of these will be explored in the following sections.

Belief Systems

Belief systems form the foundation of teacher practice. Although not always explicit, these values and principles either implicitly or explicitly guide teacher behavior. They influence every aspect of professional practice, including direct instructional behavior (e.g., planning, instructing, modeling, evaluating) as well as conceptualizing new curricula and models of teaching.

Belief systems relate to broader issues such as equity, the school as a social agent, the role of the school in a democracy, individual worth etc. Teachers' beliefs about students, particularly teachers' attributions for the causes of student performance, have significance in relation to students' achievement (Clark and Peterson, 1986, p. 281). The various relationships of the conceptualization of attribution, the teacher's attribution and resultant behavior toward students, as well as the relationship of teacher attribution and planning and decision making have been the focus of research (Peterson and Barger, 1984).

Belief system often is subsumed under the category of the process of conceptual change. Changing beliefs are part of the process of changing conceptual perspectives. As noted by Carlgren et al. (1994), '"conception" has been used interchangeably with ideology, philosophy, personal knowledge, world view, basic principles, belief, perspective opinion, and subjective theory' (p. 233). It consists of 'schemes of concepts, developed as a result of actions and interactions with the world, yet it is anchored in the person's beliefs and its basic assumptions, in a way unknown to us, also influences action' (Gorodetsky, Hoz and Keiny, 1983). Conception of role also reflect teachers' beliefs or basic assumptions about the pupil (learning and teaching); about society or the goals of education; and about knowledge (Carlgren et al., 1994, p. 233). These are fundamental issues more likely to be explored in a university context then a school-based training program.

Dispositions

Teacher dispositions derive from their belief systems. Dispositions relate to a wide range of attitudes and approaches to issues. Dispositions include an attitude toward inquiry, ongoing self development, introspection, principled reasoning, reflection, belief in the child as a learner, etc. These dispositions daily provide guidance to the teachers' performance, how they analyze their instruction, planning and implementation, and their everyday approach to instructional improvement.

Efficacy

A construct of particular importance related to teachers' beliefs and dispositions is that of efficacy. This is an area that is receiving attention in the professional preservice preparation of teachers. In practice, it means the teacher takes personal responsibility for the nature and extent of learning on the part of their students. There is some relationship with what they do and what the students learn and are subsequently able to do which can be attributed to the actions of the teacher. Efficacy appears to have a tandem of beliefs: *I can make a difference, and I know how to make a difference* (Dusek, 1985; Bandura, 1986b). A higher sense of efficacy is associated with one's belief that abilities are growing and increasing in effectiveness, in contrast with the perception of one's abilities as stagnant and static *even if one begins with higher levels of abilities* (Bandura, 1986b).

The manner in which the teacher education student is prepared and the context in which the process is conducted has a significant influence on teacher efficacy. A supportive university environment that helps teachers maintain competence in areas such as instructional problem solving increases teacher efficacy significantly (Hoy and Woolfolk, 1990). Similarly, high teacher burnout schools are correlated with lack of trust in teachers' professional efficacy (Friedman, 1991). The role of the university is to consistently engender a sense that the teacher and factors they control can relate to student achievement. The teacher then attributes the degree of student success in meeting goals to factors within the classroom rather then those beyond it. Teachers thus act on that belief. Students who have difficulties in learning are perceived by teachers with high efficacy as being challenges to their own creativity. These types of teachers are on a continual search for better means to assist students in their learning. Thus, they are not expected to have all the answers in their 'bag of tricks', but rather to have a sense of inquiry and persistence to find alternative solutions. These factors are within the purview of the teacher. It is recognized by these teachers that they are not expected to have the answers to all situations, but rather they are prepared with possible alternatives in a sense of commitment to persisting in the search for effective approaches so all students can learn (Dwyer, 1994).

Reflective and Introspective

A significant characteristic of effective teaching is capacity to look at one's own instructional practices and procedures in an objective manner. Also the capacity to ascertain strengths and weaknesses, as well as view alternatives in order to experiment and find the best alternatives. It is necessary to appraise instruction in context of theory and belief systems, research framework, moral and ethical beliefs, and best practice. This translates to meaning that good teaching is reflective, analytic, and predictive. A reflective teacher is one who assesses the origins, purposes, and consequences of his or her work. The reflective teacher is then one who views knowledge as problematic rather then certain, the role of teaching as a moral craft rather than one of a technician, the curriculum as reflexive rather than received, and the milieu as a topic of inquiry rather than one that is determined in a hierarchical manner (Drener-Hayon, 1994, pp. 51–63). Of importance also is not only that the teacher be reflective, but what they reflect upon. Zeichner and Liston (1987) describe several types of teachers: the technician who is interested in goals that have been decided upon by others; craftsperson interested in rationale in conducting educational activities and quality of the outcome; and teacher as the moral craftsperson who is interested in the moral and ethical implications of educational activities. The relative importance of technical rationality and reflection in action is noted by Schon. According to Schon, 'reflection is action, . . . is of value in of itself' (Kremer-Hayon and Fessler, 1992).

Reflective teachers appraise instruction in context of theory, a research framework, moral and ethical beliefs, and best practice. They see good teaching as analytic, predictive and thus reflective as noted by Schon and others. A salient characteristic is learning to interpret situations and events. There is an organizing framework for viewing episodes, such as the focus of instruction. Related to this is being predictive of classroom phenomenon (Berliner, 1988). Prediction is fundamental to a diagnostic-prescriptive form of teaching. It is analytic in that the teacher must review the possible factors that might influence instruction and learning in that particular situation. It is predictive in that it is intended to project outcomes based on prior practice and success as well as contextual factors that might make the situation unique. The teacher monitors both immediate and continued consequences of instructional behavior. As new knowledge through research and theory emerges, and new insights are gained, these are used as templates to review practice and make modifications. Good teaching is not static.

Perceptual Acuity

Effective teachers are also those who have strong perceptual acuity, recognizing similarities across settings, and intuitively detecting patterns when lessons do not materialize as planned. There is a strong sense of when to adhere to protocols and when to adjust around them, allowing context to aide in guiding practice. Strategies employed involve integration of technical skills into decision-making processes. A necessary element is learning how to be aware of multiple variables in the classroom and process these simultaneously. This 'executive control' relates to an awareness of what is happening in the classroom as well as using instructional time effectively (Dwyer, 1994, p. 142).

Excellent teachers take on personal responsibility for their practice as indicated under efficacy. This leads to personal decision making, in contrast with following rote rules, protocols, and techniques. The teacher makes conscious, informed choices. There is an executive sense of the classroom, knowing what to attend to and of what to take little notice. Evertson and Harris (1992), describe the need for not only routines and rules, but also the necessity to be aware of them and implement them in an equitable manner. This is done not through a rote following of rule-consequence actions, but rather an executive control or sense of the entire classroom and its effect upon the learning environment. The teacher monitors both immediate and continual consequences of instructional behavior. As new knowledge through research and theory emerges, and new insights are gained, these are used as templates to review practice. Psychological Mature Effective teachers also display a degree of psychological maturity. They manage well the stresses and demands of teaching so that these do not interfere with classroom instruction. The psychological needs are reasonably met and burnout is prevented (Gold and Roth,

1993). The university contributes in a variety of ways to the development of the psychological maturity (discussed by Gold in another chapter of this book) of the teacher in ways that the schools are not sufficiently prepared.

The extensive research on university outcomes indicate that evidence from several major syntheses reports that a reasonably consistent set of cognitive, attitudinal, value, and psychosocial changes have taken place among college students. They learn to think in more abstract, critical, complex and effective ways. Progress is made in the development of personal identities and more positive self concepts, and there is an expansion and extension of interpersonal horizons, intellectual interest, individual autonomies, and general psychological maturity and well being (Pascarella, 1994). A significant finding is that individuals who attend college have significantly greater gains in the direction of self-esteem, internal locus of control, intellectual orientation, and personal adjustment and psychological well-being (Pascarella, 1994, p. 51). When teacher education is conducted in the university context, similar gains are extrapolated into the teacher education component, being the same physical environment, intellectual context, same resources, etc. These gains are indicative of not only effective teaching, teacher growth, and characteristics of effective teachers, but also the differential effects of university-based preparation in comparison with other contexts.

Knowledge Base

Assimilation of knowledge bases as a foundation of practice is essential. These include varied disciplines, such as psychology (growth and development), sociology (classroom dynamics as a social unit), anthropology, linguistics, subject matter disciplines, technology, and professional education. Translating this subject matter into a usable format for student learning is a related challenge. The teacher knowledge base has many dimensions to consider in terms of the effective teacher. Each of these plays a role in the development of the teacher and should be considered in the conceptualization of teacher education. For example, same discussion centers around intuitive knowledge of principles gained from experience and empirical knowledge of facts gained through formal instruction. The distinction between knowing *that* and knowing *how* is made by Ryle (1949).

A specific operational description of pedagogical knowledge was proposed by Shulman (1987). The distinction is made between content knowledge of the field to be taught and the pedagogical content knowledge that involves the application of the content knowledge to teaching and involving the representations of that content in a comprehensible relevant manner. Curricular knowledge pertains to the familiarity with the variety of learning materials not only in one's own subject of teaching, but other subjects that pupils are learning as well (Shulman, 1987).

Some studies were attempting to detect differences in the perceptions of university teacher educators and school educators regarding professional education and professional knowledge objectives.

The profile obtained for the university educators entails knowledge about students, about the social context of schooling, and about curriculum. The emphasis was on the theoretical and general knowledge underlying the framework of teacher decision making as well as on skills. The school educators' profile entailed and attached importance to knowledge about teachers and teaching strategies with an emphasis on particularistic knowledge that relates directly to immediate and daily decision making (Schumacher, Rommel-Esham, and Bauer, 1987).

There are several other dimensions of the knowledge base and use of knowledge in analyzing effective teaching. Rather then perceiving the knowledge base and use of research as a direct application to certain situations as if through prescribed protocols, a more complete perspective is to not view it as science alone but rather the scientific basis for the art of teaching (Gage, 1978).

A concept that relates to intellectual capacity of teachers is cognitive complexity. This is a primary consideration of developmental theories such as Carl Glickman et al. (1995) and Art Costa and Robert Garmston (1994). Other perspectives of cognitive complexity are provided by those who have researched the issues of teacher thought patterns (Clark and Peterson, 1986; Day et al., 1990, 1993; Carlgren et al., 1994). Teachers with different cognitive complexity levels may share similar philosophical orientations and beliefs, but are able to analyze at different levels of sophistication. Sergiovanni and Starrett note that teachers who function at higher levels of cognitive complexity are capable of considering the variety of different concepts relating to a specific issue, see their interconnections and relationships, account for a wider range of variables, and are more analytical and reflective about the teaching–learning process (1993, p. 303). Students in classrooms where higher cognitive processes are emphasized and teachers themselves have higher levels of cognitive complexity, in turn, tend to have higher levels of achievement than in classrooms where teachers have lower levels (Harvey et al., 1966). An examination of the theory and research in teacher thought processes reviews a number of ways in which teachers engage themselves intellectually in planning for lessons, in the delivery of lessons, and in the analysis of their lessons as noted by Sergiovanni and Starrett (1993). Teachers who function at higher levels of cognitive complexity have an awareness of several concepts simultaneously, and are able to see their interrelationship as they apply them to a given problem, situation or issue. These teachers are more reflective, aware of, and attend to a variety of subtleties of teaching, and engage in more complex discussions about their instructional practice (Sergiovanni and Starrett, 1993, pp. 302–3).

Another dimension of the knowledge base is the concept of 'schemata', which are knowledge structures or the ways in which knowledge is stored in memory. Studies by Calderhead (1981) and others suggest that more effective teachers may have better developed knowledge structure or schemata of phenomena related to the classroom learning and teaching than less effective teachers (Calderhead, 1983; Doyle 1977; Morine and Vallance, 1975). These teachers have a better sense of the structure of the discipline, and have a sense of how it may be constructed for enhanced meaning on the part of the students as well as the teachers themselves. Barnes (1989) identified information processing during the teaching act through meaningful frameworks (schemata), as an important component of understanding effective teaching. Consistent with a Constructivist point of view, a knowledge of teaching is not static but rather transitory. The notion is that good teachers must maintain a fluid control or a flexible *understanding* of their subject knowledge (Buchmann, 1984, p. 21). They thus see the specific sets of concepts from a variety of view points depending on the range of needs of the students. This has its roots in the continuous integration of learning embedded in the Constructivist perspective as initially described by Piaget (1977) and put forth as Piaget's theory of equilibration. Barnes (1989) identified processing during the teaching act through meaningful frameworks (schemata) as an important component of understanding teaching. She notes that several studies have suggested that schema theory helps explain how teachers are able to use knowledge to guide action and practical situations (Barnes, 1989, p. 15).

A recent perspective of teacher knowledge has to do with pedagogical content knowing (Cochran, Deruiter and King, 1993). It is defined as 'a teacher's integrated understanding of four components of pedagogy, subject matter content, student characteristics, and the environmental context of learning' (Cochran, Deruiter and King, 1993, p. 266). This pedagogical content knowing perspective is in essence 'the expertise of teaching'. An essential component of pedagogical content knowing is making information comprehensible to students (Shulman, 1987). The intersection of content and pedagogy and the variation of ways in which that could be represented to students is pedagogically powerful, yet must be adapted to variations in the ability and background presented by the students (p. 15). Accordingly, this transformation of subject matter in relation to context and students requires adapting and tailoring to the individual student and has roots in psychological schema theory (Glasser, 1984; Floden, 1991). This is essentially a Constructivist orientation that links the knowledge of the students' existing concepts to the interactive process of teaching and learning. Reynolds (1992) and several others have defined techniques that effective teachers employ in making content comprehensible in a variety of contexts. Operationally this has meant well-designed orientation to new information, frequent review, multiple learning tasks, guided practice, use of engagement in appropriate material, and highlighting key concepts in making use of appropriate metaphors. (Brophy and Good, 1986; Conoley, 1988; Druian and Butler, 1987; Osborn et al., 1985; Reynolds 1992; Rosenshine, 1983; Taylor and Valentine, 1985; Williams, 1988; Zigmond et al., 1986.)

Use of Research

Use of research is associated with higher levels of teacher efficacy. Acquiring the skills identified by research as being associated with pupil outcomes is one level of application which enhances teacher effectiveness. A recent trend, however, is the understanding of teachers' use of research findings as 'principles and procedures' within a broader process of decision making and problem solving (Feiman-Nemser, 1990, p. 224). This maintains that 'teachers view teaching as a process of consistently making choices above the means and ends-choices that can be informed by process-product research, descriptive research, experience, intuition, and one's own values' (Zumwalt, 1982, p. 226). Research is best used as a frame of reference, a set of guiding principles to inform practice. These teachers know how to access research, extract key principles, adapt these to particular settings, and in general use theoretical and empirical information as a basis to inform practice.

Approaches to assessment also reveal differences between the more technical orientation to instruction and those characterized by more complexity. In the latter model, the criteria for assessing would include understanding of the developmental level of the learner's performance, the necessary supporting documentation to support the assessment, diagnosis of areas requiring assistance followed by an appropriate plan and a contribution to the group analysis of the evaluation issues. This leads to a variety of insightful questions as proposed by Diez (1996) in another chapter in his volume. These include the teachers' use of frameworks of development, specifically related to the subject of review such as literacy; aspects of the students' performance that the candidate must identify; the use of examples of performance to describe the developmental level of the teacher involved; the development theories drawn upon; use of performance examples and theory that warrant any conclusions drawn; and suggestions for further instruction and practice that make sense in light of the developmental needs of the students (Diez, 1996).

In the remaining section we will examine why the university should occupy a position of primary agent in the preparation of teachers. Also explored are the value-added dimensions of university–school configurations. The concluding section will describe the manner in which the university approach has been utilized.

The University as Prime Agent

The fundamental premise around which the thesis of this article is developed is that the essence of university purpose is to educate in the following mode and domains; and these domains are frameworks which are necessary to understand effective teaching: teacher belief systems; teacher dispositions; teacher efficacy; reflective analytical and predictive aspects of teaching; perceptual acuity; psychological maturity; executive sense of the classroom; knowledge base and schemata and making content comprehensible; use of research; and the understanding of the role of assessment. It is not suggested that most of these ideas are new, however it is important to identify them and provide the context for the respective roles for the university and school-based programs. Although well-documented in most cases, in some instances the information is somewhat speculative and admittedly might require substantial inference beyond the current research. These are easily identifiable in that there is not an extensive reference documentation which accompanies the ideas expressed.

It has been noted that the university purpose is to educate in a variety of modes and domains, such as critical thinking, perceiving, analyzing, reflecting, developing beliefs and values both in varied disciplines and in personal philosophy; understanding the self; and greater intellectual and psychological maturity. Collectively these areas and those described as effective teaching in the preceding pages are what the university is intended for, does best, and accomplishes greater than any other institution.

Belief Systems and Dispositions

Beliefs and disposition form the foundations of practice. The formative nature of the college experience provides significant opportunity for the development of these beliefs and dispositions. This was significantly documented by the work of Pascarella. These beliefs include the nature of the learner, which is required in field studies related to child growth and development, case studies in sociology, multi-culturalism as a pervading influence on American society, and other areas connected to the study of teaching.

Students develop their philosophy of teaching through these varied experiences. Concepts of self renewal, which lead to valuing professional development, are readily acquired in the university environment. Other settings have neither the time nor the resources (fiscal and intellectual) to foster productive and meaningful beliefs, values, and dispositions in a manner comparable to the college/university experience and environment.

The university provides opportunity for testing and exploring hypotheses within low risk situations. This may occur in micro teaching, supervised small group instruction, etc. Within these low-stake environments, teacher education students in higher education have sufficient opportunity to gain experience as well as compet-ence. This contributes to their sense of efficacy in feeling that they can produce changes as a result of their expertise.

Reflection

Acquisition of skills and insights on the values of reflection are related to belief systems, as they are imbedded in dispositions. Reflection is ingrained in the entire higher education process as well, and again is readily transferable to the education of teachers. The processes of the reflective practitioner in education are strikingly identical to reflective processes in higher education. Some 24 reflective practice processes are identified by Roth (1989) that illustrate this point. Some of these are: emphasizing inquiry as a tool of learning; suspending judgment; comparing and contrasting; seeking the organizing framework, theoretical basis, or underlined rationale; identifying assumptions; and initiate after thinking through alternatives and consequences (Roth, 1989, p. 32).

A poignant observation of the colleges' and universities' role as prime agent is provided by Fenstermacher (1990):

> College and university campuses are intended and designed for contemplation and reflection, . . . In a professional school or college, this reflective and contemplative attitude is connected to practice in ways that permit a back and forth between

thought and action, theory and practice, research and decision making. With this dynamic relationship between reflective conversation and considered action the higher education setting is without peer. (p. 181)

Perception

Perception is enhanced through the honing of observation skills, recognition and awareness of the consequential, and acquiring a holistic sense of the environment. These are skills of the social and physical sciences, as well as visual and performing arts and others. Perception is embedded in various disciplines, and the college/ university education experience promotes these techniques. These are the skills and dispositions which are emphasized in field experiences in the disciplines as well as professional education. They are developmentally sequenced from early clinical settings through more extensive field experiences, such as internships and student teaching, leading to intuitive recognition of critical events and subtle cues.

Psychological Maturity

It is known intuitively and empirically that emotional and psychological factors can hinder performance and limit capacity. This impact of the psychological phenomenon has been particularly acute with beginning teachers (Schlecty and Vance, 1983; Gold, 1996). Several works have referred to the crisis in education due to this factor (Farber, 1991). Concerted efforts and new model programs have been designed to address this issue (Gold and Roth, 1993). The university is in the best position to marshal the intellectual and programmatic resources to enhance teacher capabilities to cope and be psychologically prepared. Pascarrella's work (1996) cited earlier also supports this position.

The Knowledge Base

The knowledge base of teaching in varied disciplines resides in the university. More importantly, a deeper sense of learning is envisioned through the development of structural frameworks, or schemata, of the knowledge domains. This is the educative process, not just the facts and statements of the discipline. University processes revolve around the structure of a discipline, which is a critical perspective for the teaching process.

Schwab (1974) explains that the structure of a discipline consists of: a) a body of imposed conceptions which control inquiries into the discipline; and b) syntactical structure or pattern of procedure of inquiry into the discipline. Both of these, the conceptual or syntactical, are different in different disciplines (pp. 172–3).

Schwab (1974) delineates five factors of significance to education which are embodied in the concept of structure of a discipline. He concludes that

In brief, the structures of the disciplines are twice important to education. First, they are necessary to teachers and educators: they must be taken into account as we plan curriculum and prepare our teaching materials; otherwise, our plans are likely to miscarry and our materials, to *misteach*. Second, they are necessary in some part and degree within the curriculum, as elements of what we teach. Otherwise, there will be failure of learning or gross *mislearning* by our students. (p. 163)

Further, there is increasing recognition of the value of interdisciplinary study, as reflected in some of the demonstration lessons required for certification examinations of the National Board for Professional Teaching Standards. A sense of connectedness of the disciplines can be fostered in college and university preprofessional studies, which is capitalized on in professional education. This forms the intellectual foundation for teaching and teacher education. The research community in higher education has recognized this in their endeavors, as noted by Doyle (1990); 'Investigators have adopted . . . theories and interpretive methods from a variety of disciplines — anthropology, linguistics, sociology, literary criticism — to capture the richness and complexity of teaching practices, classroom life, and teachers' knowledge' (p. 19).

The concept of schemata is of particular value to the teaching profession since these organizational frameworks guided development of school curriculum, lesson design, and instructional processes. With this perspective, the teacher enhances students' grasp of subject matter as they construct and reconstruct their knowledge frameworks. In accordance with Constructivist views, the teacher also understands that the student comes with their own personal schemata which influences their learning as they filter and build upon using this framework.

Practical Considerations

A practitioner's inquiry of the preceding rationale might be, 'what of the practical, the utilitarian value? Is it lost in theory and rhetoric?' The nature of teaching is not to be viewed along a theory–practice axis, but theory and practice integrated and imbedded in each other. The several cognitive foundations which characterize intellectual dimensions of teaching and strategies derived from them constitute what is referred to here as the 'paradigm of cognitive processes–imbedded strategies'. This reinforces the notion that teaching is more akin to a profession than a trade, and is not mechanistic or prescriptive. 'Prescriptions such as "ask higher order questions" or "check for understanding" are virtually useless if a teacher does not already know the procedures implied by these directives and the events in which they might be appropriate' (Doyle, 1990, p. 19). Simply stated, training provides for instructing, educating provides for teaching. This is the role of colleges and universities.

The above distinction also may be framed in the contrast between preparation of the apprentice and the reflective practitioner, as noted in the following analysis of the 'craft' metaphor:

There are some benefits of apprenticeship, but the craft model is both limited and limiting. The model is limited in that it deals only with a prescribed range of activities and a narrow experience with the background and context of the profession. It may lead the apprentice, for example, to see only the classroom or school and may mask the relationship of the school within the community and the role of school in society. It is limiting in that it does not widen the student's perspective to include theory or rationale of practice or the purposes of schooling. (Roth, 1989, p. 31)

Conclusion

This conclusion may best be framed with an introduction. Two compelling questions need to be introduced. What is the role of the schools in the college/university primary-agent model? How well are colleges/universities meeting their responsibilities?

First, it must be made patently clear that neither colleges/universities nor schools can prepare teachers in isolation from each other. On the one hand, the culture of most schools is not conducive to learning to teach in the manner of campus settings (Howey and Collinson, 1995), yet the schools are a critical adjunct. What the profession must do is capitalize on university–school factors, strengths, and contributions. The linkage to schools is imperative, and this actually is a means of leveraging the university role in the preparation process. Clinical settings and field experiences, coupled with the knowledge and expertise of school-based practitioners, offers a rich context for professional preparation. Schools are becoming increasingly sophisticated in the knowledge base and current applications. Functioning as prime agent does not mean sole agent.

Second, it is noted that there may be a chasm between what colleges and universities ought to be in teacher preparation, and the manner in which some are now functioning. The conceptions of teaching and related principles of teacher preparation delineated previously should be used as a framework for analysis of teacher education program philosophy and design. In a sense, this is a call for introspection as much as it is a rationale for the centrality of colleges and universities.

References

BANDURA, A. (1986a) *Social Foundations of Thought and Action: A Social-cognitive Theory*, Englewood Cliffs, NJ: Prentice Hall.

BANDURA, A. (1986b) 'Self efficacy mechanisms in socio-cognitive functioning', Paper presented at the American Educational Research Association, San Francisco.

BARNES, H. (1989) 'Structuring knowledge for beginning teaching', in REYNOLDS, M.C. (ed.) *Knowledge Base for the Beginning Teacher*, New York: Pergamon Press, pp. 13–22.

BERLINER, D.C. (1988) *The Development of Expertise in Pedagogy*, Washington, DC: American Association of Colleges for Teacher Education.

BROPHY, J.E. and GOOD, T.L. (1986) 'Teacher behavior and student achievement', in WITTROCK, M. (ed.) *Handbook of Research on Teaching (3rd ed.)*, New York: Macmillan, pp. 328–75.

BUCHMAN, M. (1984) 'The use of research knowledge in teacher education and teaching', *American Journal of Education*, **92**, 4, pp. 421–39.

CALDERHEAD, J. (1981) 'A psychological approach to research on teachers' classroom decision making', *British Educational Research Journal*, **7**, pp. 51–7.

CALDERHEAD, J. (1983, April) 'Research into teachers' and student teachers' cognitions: Exploring the nature of classroom practice', Paper presented at the annual meeting of the American Educational Research Association, Montreal, Canada.

CARLGREN, I., HANDAL, G. and VAAGE, S. (1994) *Teachers' Minds and Actions: Research on Teachers' Thinking and Practice*, London: Falmer Press.

CLARK, C. and PETERSON, P. (1986) 'Teachers' thought processes', in WITTROCK, M. (ed.) *Handbook of Research on Teaching (3rd ed.)*, New York: Macmillan, pp. 255–96.

COCHRAN, K.F., DERUITER, J.A. and KING, R.A. (1993) 'Pedagogical content knowing: An integrative model for teacher preparation', *Journal of Teacher Education*, **44**, 4, pp. 203–72.

CONOLEY, J. (1988, January) 'Positive classroom ecology', *Bios*, pp. 2–7.

COSTA, A.L. and GARMSTON, R.J. (1994) *'Cognitive coaching: A foundation for Renaissance schools'*, Norwood, MA: Christopher-Gordon.

DAY, C., ACALDERHEAD, J. and DENICOLO, P. (1993) *Research on Teacher Thinking: Understanding Professional Development*, New York: Falmer Press.

DAY, C., POPE, M. and DENICOLO, P. (eds) (1990) *Insight into Teachers' Thinking and Practice*, New York: Falmer Press.

DIEZ, M.E. (1996) 'Who will prepare the next generation of teachers?', in KAPLAN, L. and EDELFELT, R. (eds) *Teachers for the New Millennium*, Thousand Oaks, CA: Corwin Press.

DOYLE, W. (1977) 'Learning in the classroom environment: An ecological analysis', *Journal of Teacher Education*, **28**, pp. 51–5.

DOYLE, W. (1990) 'Themes in teacher education research', in HOUSTON, W.R., HABERMAN, M. and SIKULA, J. (eds) *Handbook of Research on Teacher Education*, New York: Macmillan, pp. 3–24.

DRENER-HAYON, L. (1994) 'The knowledge teachers use in problem solving situation: Sources and forms', *Scandinavian Journal of Educational Research*, **38**, pp. 51–63.

DRUIAN, G. and BUTLER, J. (1987) *School Improvement Research Series: Research You Can Use*, Portland, OR: Northwest Regional Educational Laboratory (ERIC Document Reproduction Service No. ED 291 145).

DUSEK, J.B. (1985) *Teacher Expectancies*, Hillsdale, NJ: Lawrence Erlbaum.

DWYER, C.A. (1994) *Development of the Knowledge Base for the PRAXIS III: Classroom Performance Assessments Assessment Criteria*, Princeton, NJ: Educational Testing Service.

EVERTSON, C.M. and HARRIS, A.H. (1992) 'What we know about managing classrooms', *Educational Leadership*, **49**, 7, pp. 74–8.

FARBER, B.A. (1991) *Crisis in Education: Stress and Burnout in the American Teacher*, San Francisco: Jossey-Bass.

FEIMAN-NEMSER, S. (1990) 'Teacher preparation: Structural and conceptual alternatives', in HOUSTON, W.R., HABERMAN, M. and SIKULA, J. (eds) *Handbook of Research on Teacher Education*, New York: Macmillian, pp. 212–33.

FENSTERMACHER, G.D. (1990, Spring) 'The place of alternative certification in the education of teachers', *Peabody Journal of Education*, **67**, 3, pp. 155–85.

FLODEN, R.E. (1991, Fall) 'Putting true scores first: A response to Rogosa and Ghandour', *Journal of Educational Statistics*, **16**, 3, pp. 267–80.

FRIEDMAN, I.A. (1991) 'High- and low-burnout schools: School culture aspects of teacher burnout', *Journal of Educational Research*, **84**, 6, pp. 325–33.

GAGE, N.L. (1978) *The Scientific Basis of the Art of Teaching*, New York: Teachers College Press.

GLASSER, W. (1994) *Take Effective Control of Your Life*, San Francisco: Harper & Row.

GLICKMAN, C.D., GORDON, S.P. and ROSS-GORDON, J.M. (1995) *Supervision of Instruction: A Developmental Approach*, Needham Heights, MA: Allyn and Bacon.

GOLD, Y. (1996) 'Beginning teacher support: Attrition, mentoring and induction', in SIKULA, J. BUTTERY, T. and GUYTON, E. (eds) *Handbook of Research on Teacher Education*, 2nd ed. (In Press) New York: Macmillian.

GOLD, Y. and ROTH, R.A. (1993) *Teachers Managing Stress and Preventing Burnout. The Professional Health Solution*, London: Falmer Press.

GORODETSKY, M., HOZ, R. and KEINY, S. (1983) 'The relationship of teachers' collective conception and school renewal', A paper presented at the International Conference of Science Education in Developing Countries: From Theory to Practice, Jerusalem.

HARVEY, O.J., WHITE, B.J., PRATHER, M.S., ALTER, R.D. and HOFFMEISTER, J.K. (1966) 'Teachers' belief systems and preschool atmospheres', *Journal of Educational Psychology*, **57**, 6, pp. 373–81.

HOWEY, K.R. and COLLINSON, V. (1995) 'Cornerstones of a collaborative culture: Professional development and preservice teacher preparation', *Journal of Personnel Evaluation in Education*, **9**, pp. 21–31.

HOY, W.K. and WOOLFOLK, A.E. (1990) 'Socialization of student teachers', *American Educational Research Journal*, **27**, 2, pp. 279–300.

KREMER-HAYON, L. and FESSLER, R. (1992) 'The inner world of school principals: Reflections on career life stages', *International Review of Education/Internationale Zeitschrift fuer*, **38**, pp. 35–40.

MORINE, G. and VALLANCE, E. (1975) *Special Study B: A Study of Teacher and Pupil Perceptions of Classroom Interaction* (Tech.Rep.No 75-11-6), San Francisco: Far West Laboratory.

OSBORN, J., JONES, B. and STEIN, M. (1985) 'The case for improving textbooks', *Educational Leadership*, **42**, 7, pp. 9–16.

PASCARELLA, E.T. (1994) 'The impact of college on students: Myths, rational myths, and some other things that may not be true', *Chester E. Peters Lecture*, Kansas State University.

PETERSON, P.L. and BARGER, S.A. (1984) 'Attribution theory and teacher expectancy', in DUSEK, J.B. (ed.) *Teacher Expectancies*, Hillsdale, NJ: Lawrence Erlbaum, pp. 159–84.

PIAGET, J. (1977) 'Problems of equilibration', in APPEL, M. and GOLDBERG, L. (eds) *Topics in Cognitive Development: Vol. 1. Equilibration: Theory, Research, and Application*, New York: Pleanum, pp. 3–13.

REYNOLDS, A. (1992) 'What is competent beginning teaching? A review of the literature,' *Review of Educational Research*, **62**, 1, pp. 1–35.

ROSENSHINE, B. (1983) 'Teaching functions in instructional programs', *The Elementary School Journal*, **83**, pp. 335–53.

ROSENSHINE, B. and STEVENS, R. (1984) 'Classroom instruction in reading' in PEARSON, P.D. (ed.) *Recent Research on Reading*, New York: Longman.

ROTH, R.A. (1989, March–April) 'Preparing the reflective practitioner: Transforming the apprentice through the dialectic', *Journal of Teacher Education*, **40**, 2, pp. 31–5.

ROTH, R.A. (1994, September–October) 'The university can't train teachers? Transformation of a profession', *Journal of Teacher Education*, **45**, 4, pp. 1–9.

RYLE, G. (1949) *The Concept of Mind*, New York: Barnes and Noble.

SCHLECTY, P.C. and VANCE, V.S. (1983) 'Recruitment, selection and retention: The shaper of the teaching force', *Elementary School Journal*, **83**, 3, pp. 469–87.

SCHUMACHER, S., ROMMEL-ESHAM, K. and BAUER, D. (1987) 'Professional knowledge objectives for pre-service teachers as determined by school and university teacher educators,' paper presented at the AERA annual meeting, Washington, DC.

SCHWAB, J.J. (1974) 'The concept of the structure of a discipline', in EISNER, E.W., VALLANCE, E. (eds) *Conflicting Conceptions of Curriculum*, Berkeley: McCutchan, pp. 162–75.

SERGIOVANNI, T.J. and STARRATT, R.J. (1993) *Supervision: A Redefinition* (5th ed.), New York: McGraw-Hill.

SHULMAN, L. (1987) 'Those who understand knowledge growth in teaching', *Educational Researcher*, February, pp. 4–14.

TAYLOR, A. and VALENTINE, B. (1985) *Effective Schools. What Research Says about . . . Series, No. 1, Data-search Reports*, Washington, DC: National Education Association (ERIC Document Reproduction Service No. ED 274 073).

US DEPARTMENT OF EDUCATION (1987) *What Works: Research about Teaching and Learning (2nd ed.)*, Washington. DC: US Government Printing Office.

WILLIAMS, P.S. (1988) 'Going west to get east: Using metaphors as instructional tools', *Journal of Children in Contemporary Society*, **20**, 1–2, pp. 79–98.

ZEICHNER, K.M. (1983) 'Alternative paradigms of teacher education', *Journal of Teacher Education*, **34**, 5, pp. 35–44.

ZEICHNER, R. and LISTON, P. (1987) 'Teaching student teachers to reflect', *Harvard Educational Review*, **57**, 1, pp. 23–48.

ZIGMOND, N., SANSONE, J., MILLER, S., DONAHOE, K. and KOHNKE, R. (1986) 'Teaching learning disabled students at the secondary school level: What research says to teachers', *Learning Disabilities Focus*, **1**, 2, pp. 108–15.

ZUMWALT, K. (1982) 'Research on teaching: Policy implications for teacher education', in LIEBERMAN, A. and MCLAUGHLIN, M. (eds) *Policy Making in Education*, Chicago: University of Chicago Press (2150248).

13 Multicultural Education and the University's Mission: Change and Opportunity for Change

Carl Grant

The primary mission of most colleges and universities is excellence in teaching and research. For example, the expressed aims of Cambridge University (1995) include: providing teachers and researchers of the future; encouraging and pursuing research of the highest quality across the whole range of subjects studied at the University; developing new areas of teaching and research to advance scholarship; and meeting the needs of the community.

The mission statement for Michigan State University (1982) is very similar to that of Cambridge University's and is illustrative of many of the mission statements of universities in the United States. It states:

> As a respected research and teaching university, it [Michigan State University] is committed to intellectual leadership and to excellence in both developing new knowledge and conveying that knowledge to its students and to the public. And as a pioneer land-grant institution, Michigan State University strives to discover practical uses for theoretical knowledge, and to speed the diffusion of information to residents of the state, the nation, and the world. In fostering both research and its application, this university will continue to be a catalyst for positive intellectual, social, and technological change.

Implicit, and often explicit, in most universities' mission statement is the goal of providing an education that will enable their graduates to be competent professionals which, in today's world, means being able to successfully serve societies composed of people of different races, socioeconomic backgrounds, languages, and life styles.

In order to make certain that its graduates are prepared to meet society's demands, a university and its faculty undergo frequent evaluations. These evaluations involve examining the three basic pillars of the university's structure: teaching, research, and service. More specifically, colleges and schools (e.g., College of Letters and Science, Law School, School of Education) within universities are often competitively ranked according to the degree of excellence achieved in their teaching and research.

Similarly, a university faculty member is individually judged on the quality of his or her teaching, research, and service. None of these activities, however, are undertaken in a vacuum. It is necessary, in this demographically changing society, to examine these areas to assess how well the universities and their faculty members are preparing their graduates to effectively meet the demands of their clients, who are demographically (i.e., in terms of ethnicity, race, income, language) changing. In one of Cambridge University's (1995) goals, this is explicitly stated: The University's aim . . . [is] to provide an education of the highest quality at both undergraduate and postgraduate level, and so produce graduates of the calibre sought by industry, the professions, and the public service.

There is an increasing belief among a growing number of educators that multicultural education is the instructional philosophy and practice that needs to be infused into teaching and research if a university is to accomplish its mission. Change in the research and teaching to include multicultural education is showing promising results. However, many opportunities to infuse multicultural education are being missed and/or neglected. In order to achieve their mission, these opportunities presented in the areas of teaching and research (as well as other areas) need to be taken advantage of by universities.

In the title of this chapter, a distinction is made between 'change and opportunity for change' because, with multicultural education, rhetoric and action often are not correlated. Thus, it is important that the relationship between the two be clearly understood in order to provide an accurate picture of multicultural education and the university's attention to it in teaching and research.

The first section of this chapter discusses teaching. Discussed here within the broader areas of teaching (i.e., materials, faculty, courses, staff development, policy, and students) are the changes that have been made to include multicultural education and the opportunities available to make changes in these areas in teaching to be multicultural. This section concludes with a critique of the changes and opportunities for change. The second section of this chapter discusses the broader area of research (i.e., conferences, materials, approaches, and globalization of research problems). This section also concludes with a critique of the changes and opportunities for change toward multicultural education. Finally, the chapter ends with some concluding remarks.

Teaching

Teaching is considered a critical area of professional evaluation. At some colleges, teaching evaluations serve as a major criterion in determining promotion. Senior faculty members evaluate the teaching of junior faculty members who are being considered for tenure and promotion. Also, each student registered in a class is expected to complete an evaluation of his/her instructor and, at some universities (e.g., University of Wisconsin-Madison), teaching evaluations are made public for students to read. Although the criteria and questions on the evaluation forms may differ, they usually seek to elicit information about:

1 The instructors' scholarly and professional knowledge. In other words, do the instructors know their field in terms of research, theoretical knowledge, and methodological procedures?

2 The instructors' interpersonal and professional skills. In other words, do the instructors appear to respect their students and make reasonable allowances for individual differences in background and professional goals?

3 The instructors' knowledge of applied skills in education. In other words, do the instructors understand the problems of the working practitioner in education and are they able to give concrete, applicable help and advice relative to their field of specialty?

These questions, interpreted narrowly or broadly, call for the infusion of multicultural education into teaching. Why? Because in order to be consistent with a university's mission, its graduates must be prepared to work with different communities of people. And it is the university's course offerings and the instructor's scholarly and professional knowledge that must prepare them to do so. Simply put, no longer can a university's program and an instructor's approach to teaching use mainly a Burocentric model. Also, the knowledge and skills to critically investigate different perspectives (e.g., positivist, interpretive, feminist, postmodernist, etc.) must be taught. In addition, a university's curriculum and an instructor's knowledge and understanding of the changing world — that is the world students are being educated to live and work in — has to include attention to national and international diversity and social justice issues. What and where then are the changes and opportunities for change in a university's teacher education program and an instructor's teaching? To begin with, in an increasing number of Schools of Education across the United States there is a shift in behavior (procedures) regarding what to do about 'multicultural education'. This shift is taking place in the following areas: offering a course or courses in multicultural education; hiring multicultural consultants to conduct staff development; adopting multicultural textbooks; using reading and audio visual materials that deal with diversity and social justice issues; hiring new faculty members with knowledge about diversity; becoming more aware and sensitive to student experiences and agency in their own education; and implementing multicultural policies and/or mandates. Following is what we know about the changes and the opportunities for change toward multicultural education in these areas.

Multicultural Education Materials

The availability of education texts and journal articles that focus on and/or include attention to multicultural education has increased over the past decade. Between 1984 and 1987, when Christine Sleeter and I analyzed books and journal articles dealing with multicultural education (which also includes descriptors such as 'ethnic studies' and 'human relations'), we located 200 articles and 71 books (Grant and Sleeter, 1985; Grant, Sleeter and Anderson 1986; Sleeter and Grant, 1987).

Today, according to Educational Resources Information Center, there are 2,002 academic journal articles and, according to WorldCat, 749 academic books in the United States on multicultural education. These texts cover a wide range of topics, including the philosophy of multicultural education, and methods and procedures for infusing multicultural education into the curriculum. Instructors for most courses (e.g., curriculum, policy, administration, health, music, reading) are able to locate a text that presents their subject matter specialty from a multicultural perspective. Some of these texts are in their second and third edition. For example, James Banks' *Teaching Strategies for Ethnic Studies* has a sixth edition (1975).

Many educational journals, including those published by subject matter organizations (e.g., math, English, social studies) over the past decade have published a thematic issue on multicultural education and/or articles dealing with social justice, race, class, gender, sexual orientation, and power and equity. Although, for many years, these articles focused on multicultural education in K-12 settings, an increasing number of articles are examining multicultural education at the college level (see, for example, the thematic issue, 'Multiculturalism and Diversity in Higher Education' in the *American Behavioral Scientist*). Also, there are a few journals and other publications (e.g., *Multicultural Education, Urban Education, Teaching Tolerance*, and *Rethinking Schools*) especially devoted to multicultural education and/or issues of equity, power, race, language, and gender issues. Additionally, a good portion of these materials include essays that analyze, offer new visions, and critique multicultural education.

Thus, for the instructors who are interested in multicultural education and who may have had difficulty locating the text they want, there is an increasing quantity of articles addressing subject matter written from a multicultural perspective. Included among these publications are articles that discuss the strengths and weaknesses of multicultural education. These articles can be easily compiled into a course packet, and copying permission of these articles is relatively easy to acquire. Similarly, there is a growing collection of films and videos dealing with issues of diversity. These collections include voices of people of color discussing different political and social issues, examinations of concepts and terms often taken for granted and rarely discussed in relationship to power and equity (e.g., 'assimilation', 'melting pot'), the presence of different writers of color and women writers discussing their work or offering their point of view on different educational issues, revised or corrected versions of history that provide different perspectives on the European American migration (e.g., *The Way the West was Lost* and *The West*).

A major proportion of this material is reviewed and evaluated, and some of these reviews are published in such journals as *Multicultural Education* (see, for example, Professors G. Pritchy Smith and Deborah A. Batiste's monthly column 'Multicultural Resources').

Finally, of all the areas of teaching, materials and resources have seen the greatest change toward multicultural education. Reasons for this include market demands, an increase in the number of scholars in multicultural education, and their publication of multicultural education materials. Nevertheless, there are still other areas that need attention. First, there is a need for more multicultural text and media materials which address the relationships among peoples of color, including their interactions during critical events in history. For example, what were the relationships between African Americans and Native Americans during the 1800s, or between women of color and white women during the suffrage period? Second, although there is an increasing number of faculty members who are beginning to use multicultural materials, this number is still relatively small. Also, much of the multicultural materials do not have accompanying instructor guides. Thus, the use of this material is left up to the instructors, many of whom have not had formal instruction in multicultural education, and to students, many of whom have only very little formal or informal experiences with cultural diversity.

New Faculty

As faculty retire, some of the new hires taking their place seem less threatened by multicultural subject matter, more willing to learn about multicultural education, and more inclined to deal with issues of diversity as they arise in their classes. This occurs in part because, over the past two decades, during the time when many of these new hires were in college, the intellectual paradigm guiding instruction has been shifting. This shift has included movement away from teaching and learning based on a psychological orientation to one that includes the social context of learning and teaching, greater acceptance of feminist perspectives, greater attention to the learning needs of students who are learning English and students who come from gay and lesbian homes, and greater attention on a whole to how schools legitimate inequality. The following statement by Bowles and Gintis (1976) in many ways epitomizes and illustrates the argument about the shortcomings of schools that were becoming increasingly recognized and accepted by scholars over the past decades:

> Schools legitimate inequality through the ostensibly meritocratic manner by which they reward and promote students, and allocate them to distinct positions in the occupational hierarchy. They create and reinforce patterns of social class, racial and sexual identification among students which allow them to relate 'properly' to their eventual standing in the hierarchy of authority and status in the production process. Schools foster types of personal development compatible with the relationships of dominance and subordinance in the economic sphere, and finally, schools create surpluses of skilled labor sufficiently extensive to render effective the prime weapon of the employer in disciplining labor — the power to hire and fire. (p. 11)

Within these new faculty changes and opportunities for change there is still work to be done on such issues as the recruitment and retention of faculty members of color. Although more students of color are attending college, the percentage of students of color who decide on teaching as their profession is no where consistent with the percentage of students of color attending K-12 schools.

Multicultural Education Courses

An increasing number of multicultural education courses are being offered in Schools of Education (Grant and Tate, 1995). The instructors of these courses are often the new faculty hires and proponents of multicultural education who have been members of the faculty for years. One purpose of these courses is to formally introduce and begin the infusion of multicultural education into the teacher education programs. A second purpose of these courses is to prepare the preservice students to work effectively with students of color, students living at or below the poverty level, students with physical and/or cognitive disabilities, and female students in all academic settings.

Instructors of multicultural education courses often point out that when issues about race, class, and gender are brought up in class, tension fills the air and students often stake-out their intellectual turf and hope that the teachers (with the authoritative weight they bring to the discussion) will remain neutral. Alquist's (1992) study of her class is an excellent case in point and illustrates how multicultural education can influence both students and teachers. Alquist states:

> Deeply embedded in these students' world views was the notion that teachers must always be objective or neutral in expressing their views, especially controversial views. . . . I argued that for change to occur, teachers had a responsibility to take a position in support of change and against racism. . . . I was dismayed by their response. This was provocation at the risk of disengagement. . . . I stood my ground. I tried to engage students in a dialogue around partisanship. Many fell back on the so-called 'experts' in the field, teachers who had told them not to take stands. They were divided. I argued that racism and sexism had to be countered. . . . For me to be silent, feign neutrality or claim no perspective would have been dishonest. (p. 100)

Other than the tension among students and between instructor and students, the implementation of multicultural courses has produce additional problems that need attention, especially regarding communication among faculty members. For example, with the inclusion of multicultural courses there is a need to make certain that other instructors do not stop or decrease their attention to include multicultural education in their instruction. Sometimes, when a multicultural course is introduced into a teacher education program, other faculty members believe that they are relieved of their responsibility to teach and or deal with issues of race, class, gender, and homophobia. On the other hand, there is a need to make certain that when more than one faculty member is teaching from a multicultural perspective, the course assignments are not identical or too similar. When assignment overlapping occurs, students become very bored and annoyed and believe that multicultural education has very little conceptual and applied knowledge (Grant and Tate, 1995).

Staff Development

Over the past decade an increasing number of Schools of Education are making multicultural staff development opportunities available to their faculty. These staff development activities take place in a number of ways. One way is to employ consultants to help faculty members sort out what multicultural education is. These consultants can discuss with faculty members about multicultural education's status on other campuses and the barriers and successes to implementing multicultural education, they can help faculty understand what multicultural education could mean to their campus and teacher education program, and they can help faculty members infuse multicultural education into their courses. Another way is to hold minority/feminist lecture series which bring distinguished scholars to campus who have wide appeal and attraction. A third way is to encourage faculty members to attend workshops and conferences dealing with multicultural education, and be involved in faculty exchanges between historically black colleges and predominately white colleges.

Unfortunately, sometimes the opportunities for change do not take place because multicultural staff development is brief and narrow rather than comprehensive and ongoing. Also, some faculty members believe that they already understand multicultural education and/or it is not important enough to their teaching for them to attend the staff development activities. Additionally, academic freedom permits faculty members to ignore learning new ways of teaching and/or including new ideas in their teaching. In spite of these barriers, staff development opportunities need to be made available, and incentives and rewards need to be given to those who participate. The reason for this is to show support to those who participate and let those who do not participate know that multicultural education is not a temporary idea that will fade like the light given off by a fire cracker.

Multicultural Policy

Very little formal multicultural policy exists, although an increasing number of colleges are mandating multicultural education experiences. On some college campuses, ethnic studies course requirements have been instituted. For example, at the University of Wisconsin-Madison, undergraduate students must take one three credit ethnic studies course. Some State Departments of Education mandate colleges and universities in the state which prepare teachers to have the preservice teachers receive multicultural education. Also, in some teacher education programs, students are required to have a field placement in a racially and socioeconomically diverse setting.

Students

Students — that is their curiosity, resistance, previous education, increasing age diversity, ethnicity, and life style diversity — are causing a change and/or presenting opportunities for change toward multicultural education. Many of the students attending college now are members of the post-civil rights generation. On one hand, many come mainly with text book knowledge of the apartheid and blatant racism that has existed in this country for so many years and the conservative rhetoric that argues that the civil rights era has resolved most of the social inequities in the United States. On the other hand, many of the post-civil rights students come with unresolved questions, wondering why the civil rights actions of the 1960s did not solve more problems of social inequities. Also, some of these students believe that they have not been told the whole truth, especially as they continue to observe the failure of the United States to treat all of its citizens fairly and witness this country's rapid movement toward a two-class society of 'haves' and 'have nots'. With students expressing these concerns as questions and statements, instructors are having more encouragement and a greater opportunity to include multicultural issues in their teaching.

Additionally, an increasing number of older students are seeking their undergraduate degrees. Interactions between older students and younger students provide instructors with an opportunity to situate discussions of race, gender, and class in a context which draws upon the life histories and experiences of people in different age groups. Instructors can also learn from these accounts of age and life histories how race, class, and gender issues have personally affected their students, and then plan experiences and activities that will better enable these same students to work with the students they will teach.

Discussion

In this section I have discussed the changes and opportunities for change in teaching to be more responsive to multicultural education. *Change* in teaching to become more responsive to multicultural education has been occurring slowly — most of the attention has been on the call for changes rather than on actual action to bring about change. On the other hand, *opportunities for change* in teaching to become more responsive to multicultural education are plentiful. What we need then is to have more of the opportunities for change to result in real changes. I believe that teacher education programs should include courses which focus on the concepts and practices of multicultural education. Also, faculty development in multicultural education is a must if teacher education programs are sincere about preparing their graduates to be truly qualified teachers for *all* students. Faculty development needs to be comprehensive and systematic. By this I mean there needs to be an overall teacher education program plan, and a plan that each faculty member develops to meet his or her needs. Important to any teacher education program's faculty development plan is the recruitment and retention of faculty members of color, women faculty, and faculty members who are committed to multicultural education. Interviews of new faculty need to include questions that ask the candidates how their teaching and research interests connect with multicultural education. The interview process should also let the potential new hire know and understand that the program's commitment to multicultural education is genuine.

It is difficult to prepare some preservice teachers to work with K-12 students who are different (i.e., in terms of race, class, life style) from them. These students, as we are learning from multicultural research (Alquist, 1992; Gomez, 1991; McMahon, 1997), are very intent on holding on to old traditions and ideas. Haberman (1995) wonders if anyone and everyone can (should) become a teacher just because it is their dream, or because they do well on a battery of exams. This line of reasoning is gaining attention and needs to be given serious thought. Presently the debate on entry into teaching is centered around passing an exam. Although I do not want to debate the pros and cons of this idea, I do believe that having both intelligence and an understanding of issues of social inequities is important to teaching.

There is a great deal of truth in the statement 'You cannot legislate one's attitudes'. Nevertheless, all students on a university campus need to know and believe that the university has a no-nonsense policy and will take appropriate action when it comes to the mistreatment of any student. A policy which explains the university's position on race, gender, disability, and life style bias would help prevent problems.

Research/Scholarship

Most universities have as a mission the engagement in research and/or scholarly activities and some universities are regarded as *research* institutions. Universities acquire their *research* status because they conduct research and contribute to the knowledge learned in the academic and social community. This knowledge is also used to improve teaching at the universities. Similarly, just as a university is judged by its research accomplishments, its faculty members are judged by their individual research accomplishments. Most universities usually require their faculty members to demonstrate some type of scholarly contribution in order to be promoted and receive tenure. The scholarly contribution ranges, depending on the expressed mission of the university. For many research institutions, the publication of articles in refereed journals or a book by a respected publisher, and the presentation of scholarly work at major conferences are necessary for a faculty member to receive promotion and tenure. Since some form of accomplishment in research/scholarship is important to a university's mission and faculty members achieving promotion and tenure, it is reasonable to discuss the infusion of multicultural education into the university's research mission and the scholarly work of their professors.

Over the past decade there has been some change and opportunities for change toward including multicultural education in the traditional research paradigm and even changing the paradigm. Opportunities to learn about how to facilitate change toward multicultural education can be acquired through reviewing research publications, using personally interesting research methods and procedures, and examining research questions from national and international perspectives. Also, whereas the shift with teaching toward multicultural education has taken place on university campuses, the shift with research has taken place on the campus *and* at conferences.

Conferences

The past decade has seen an increase in attention toward multicultural education research at a number of conferences. This increased attention has manifested in the following manner: the organization of special interest groups within national associations; conference sessions devoted to challenging the absence of race, class, and gender as dynamic variables within traditional research; and conference sessions designed to make researchers aware of their responsibility to the people they are studying when conducting multicultural education research. Some examples may be helpful. At the American Education Research Association's annual conference in 1987, several members disenchanted with the Association's lack of attention to race, class, gender, and social justice issues organized a Special Interest Group (SIG) called 'Critical Examination of Race, Ethnicity, Class, and Gender in Education'. This SIG provides a forum for scholars interested in research that integrates race, class, and gender issues and variables, as well as critically examines studies that ignore or fail to analyze the interactions of these variables. The social action by some members within education associations and organizations has increased the opportunity for others interested in doing multicultural education research to have it included at annual meetings or to be featured as an article in the association's journal.

Some organizations, e.g., the National Association for Multicultural Education (NAME), hold annual conferences which focus on multicultural education. In addition to providing a forum which enables scholars to present their multicultural research and an outlet to establish networks with others doing multicultural education research, this organization publishes a magazine (*Multicultural Education*), has a web page, and a national office that scholars can contact for support and assistance.

Research Materials

The availability of research materials that can particularly help those interested in doing multicultural research is both increasing and becoming more varied. Published book-length studies of multicultural education research have become more readily available (e.g., Ladson-Billings' *The Dreamkeepers*, 1994; Grant and Sleeter's *After the School Bell Rings* (2nd ed.), 1996; McLaren's *Life in Schools* (2nd ed.), 1994; Sleeter's *Keepers of the American Dream*, 1992) over the past decade and their numbers are increasing.

Also, the publication of the *Handbook of Research on Multicultural Education* (Banks and Banks, 1995), *Research and Multicultural Education* (Grant, 1992), *The Dictionary of Multicultural Education* (Grant and Ladson-Billings, 1997), and other materials written particularly to help scholars do multicultural education research have added another line of material for those interested in doing multicultural education research.

In addition, PhD dissertations are another line of materials available to scholars seeking information about multicultural education research. According to *Dissertation Abstracts International,* over the past decade the number of dissertations dealing with multicultural education has significantly increased. In 1986, there were seven, from January 1988 to December 1992, there were 52, and from January 1993 to September 1996, there were 151 dissertations that dealt with multicultural education.

These research materials provide educators with a good beginning to help them do multicultural education research. The availability of these materials is increasing in many different disciplines.

Many Methods of Conducting Multicultural Education Research

The increasing use of and acceptance by the academic community of different research procedures (e.g., ethnography, oral narrative, feminist perspectives, action research) is demythifying the research process and making doing research more user friendly to more scholars. Also, the use of these different types of research methodology is increasing the opportunities and understanding of researchers to learn that race, class, and gender are dynamic rather than passive variables. Some scholars are also using multiple theories to investigate research problems. They believe that the combination of non-traditional research procedures and multiple theories better illuminate the complex issues embedded in race, class, gender, and social justice issues.

Globalization of Research Problems

Over the past decade multicultural education as a philosophy and process has crossed national boundaries, encouraging scholars of different countries to learn from one another's research. Collaborative research and writing projects are becoming increasingly easier to locate in the educational literature (e.g., Banks and Lynch, 1986) and at education conferences.

Scholars interested in doing multicultural education research have the opportunity to further their understanding of the problems they are studying by examining the problem in both a national and international context. Many problems related to race, class, gender, and social justice issues cross national boundaries. Thus, insights into problems can be fostered by examining the problem as it is analyzed and discussed in different national and international settings.

Discussion

This section has argued that there have been numerous opportunities for scholars interested in doing multicultural education research to become informed about how to do it. Change in research to include multicultural education in the statement of the problem and to include multicultural education in the methodology is very limited. Organizations need to increase the number of their annual conference sessions that focus on research which takes a multicultural perspective. University's research centers need to reach out to scholars and graduate students conducting research which use different methodological paradigms. With educational research dollars becoming more difficult to acquire, it is important that universities have a research program which strives to serve more than a limited portion of the population. The research reports bearing the name of the university need to be continuously examined to ascertain their attention to multicultural education. Faculty advisors need to encourage their graduate students to use different research methodologies in exploring particular issues. Similarly, they need to encourage their graduate students to read and include relevant research from outside their own country. Travel and technology is allowing researchers to discover that educational problems cross national boundaries. Working together and learning from one another is becoming increasingly important. Cultural differences between countries may suggest that 'solutions' to problems are geographically situated. On the other hand, because of cultural differences, additional insights into a problem may develop or the insights may become sharper.

Conclusion

In this chapter I have argued that the teaching and research mission of a university needs to include multicultural education. I have also argued that, over the past decade, an increasing number of opportunities to include multicultural education in both teaching and research have become available. I pointed out that in some cases these opportunities were taken advantage of but in other cases there was a small and limited response to the opportunities. In the mission statement of Michigan State University, it notes that the mission statement must change as society changes. For example, when the United States moved from an agrarian society to an industrialized society the university's mission statement and teaching and research reflected that change. The statement reads:

> The university's land-grant and service mission first originated in the areas of agriculture and the mechanic arts. While these emphases remain essential to the purpose of Michigan State, the land-grant commitment now encompasses fields such as health, human relations, business, communication, education, and government, and extends to urban and international settings. The evolution of this mission reflects the increasing complexity and cultural diversity of society, the world's greater interdependence, changes in both state and national economy, and the explosive growth of knowledge, technology, and communications. Just as the focus on agriculture and the mechanic arts was appropriate when Michigan State University was founded, the wide range of instructional, research, and public service commitments that now characterize this university is essential today.

Today, as the new millennium approaches, the United States is at another crossroad and changes are taking place. Globalization, technological advances, demographic shifts, international interdependence are some of these changes. These changes demand a new way to live and work with others. They also demand that our institutions of higher education prepare their students to meet the challenges and needs that come with the changes. An education that is multicultural and social reconstructivist seeks to meet these new and rapidly changing demands. As a philosophy it can give direction to both research and teaching, and as a process it can be infused into both research and teaching.

References

ALQUIST, R. (1992) 'Manifestations of inequality: Overcoming resistance in a multicultural foundations course (89–105)', in GRANT, C.A. (ed.) *Research and Multicultural Education: From the Margins to the Mainstream*, Washington, DC: Falmer Press.

BANKS, J.A. (1975) *Teaching Strategies for Ethnic Studies* (6th ed.), Boston: Allyn and Bacon.

BANKS, J.A. and BANKS, C.A.M. (1995) *Handbook of Research on Multicultural Education*, New York: Macmillan.

BANKS, J.A. and LYNCH, J. (1986) *Multicultural Education in Western Societies*, New York: Praeger.

BOWLES, S. and GINTIS, H. (1976) *Schooling in Capitalist America*, New York: Basic Books.

GOMEZ, M.L. (1991) 'Teaching a language of opportunity in a language arts methods course: Teaching for David, Albert, and Darlene', in TABACHNICK, B.R. and ZEICHNER, K.M. (eds) *Issues and Practices in Inquiry-oriented Education*, London: Falmer Press, pp. 91–112.

GRANT, C. (ed.) (1992) *Research and Multicultural Education: From the Margins to the Mainstream*, London: Falmer Press.

GRANT, C.A., and SLEETER, C.E. (1985) 'The literature on multicultural education: Review and analysis', *Educational Review* **37**, 2, pp. 97–118.

GRANT, C.A., SLEETER, C.E., and ANDERSON, J.E. (1986) 'The Literature on Multicultural Education: Review and analysis', *Educational Studies*, **12**, 1, pp. 47–71.

GRANT, C.A., and SLEETER, C.E. (1996) *After the School Bell Rings*, Washington, DC: Falmer Press.

GRANT, C.A. and LADSON-BILLINGS, G. (1997) *Dictionary of Multicultural Education*, Phoenix, AZ: The Oryx Press.

GRANT, C.A. and TATE, W.F. (1995) 'Multicultural education through the lens of the multicultural education research literature', in BANKS, J.A. and BANKS, C.A. *Handbook of Research on Multicultural Education*, McGee. New York: Macmillan Pub, pp. 145–166.

HABERMAN, M. (1995) *Star Teachers of Children in Poverty*, Kappa Delta Pi.

LADSON-BILLINGS, G. (1994) *The Dreamkeepers*, San Francisco: Jossey-Bass.

MAY, S. (1994) *Making Multicultural Education Work*, Bristol, Great Britain: Longdunn Press.

MCLAREN, P. (1994) *Life in Schools* (2nd ed.), New York: Longman.

MCMAHON, S.I. (1997) 'Using documented written and oral dialogue to understand and challenge preservice teachers' reflections', *Teaching and Teacher Education*, **13**, 2.

MEACHAM, J. (1996) *American Behavioral Scientist*, **40**, 2, Thousand Oaks, CA: SAGE Periodicals Press.

MICHIGAN STATE UNIVERSITY BOARD OF TRUSTEES (1982, June 24–5) *Mission Statement* (online) Available at http://web.msu.edu/dig/FACULTY/intro.html.

NASH, R. (1973) *Classrooms Observed*, Boston: Routledge and Kegan Paul.

NIETO, S. (1992) *Affirming Diversity* (2nd ed.), New York: Longman.

SLEETER, C.E. (1992) *Keepers of the American Dream*, Washington, DC: Falmer Press.

SLEETER, C.E. and GRANT, C.A. (1987) 'An analysis of multicultural education in the United States', *Harvard Educational Review*, **57**, 4, pp. 421–44.

UNIVERSITY OF CAMBRIDGE (1995, April) *Mission Statement* (online) Available at: http://www.cam.ac.uk/CambUniv/mission.html.

14 Integrating Educational Psychology into Professional Studies: Linking Theory and Practice

Patricia Ashton

Teaching is more difficult now than ever before. Teachers confront higher expectations and greater obstacles. Students are more diverse and, because of poverty and family and cultural disintegration, are in greater need of teachers' understanding and support. In these difficult circumstances, teachers are expected to meet students' diverse needs while teaching them the complex cognitive and social skills believed to be essential to succeed in the next century — the ability to solve problems, think creatively, regulate one's learning, and collaborate effectively with others (Anderson et al., 1995). Research on the development of expertise clearly shows that extensive knowledge integrated with practice is essential to enable novice teachers to attain expertise in dealing with the challenging tasks of teaching. Ironically, given the difficult conditions of teaching, some policy makers are attempting to deal with the crisis in teaching by eliminating the crucial role of the university in developing teacher expertise.

Teachers have often criticized courses in their preparation programs as 'too theoretical' (Hoy, 1996; Lortie, 1975; Rigden, 1996). In the current political climate of cutbacks in teacher education, an increasingly frequent response to this criticism is to eliminate university courses considered too theoretical. Courses in educational psychology and in social foundations have been particularly vulnerable to this criticism.

In this chapter I describe how beliefs about the relation of theory to practice have changed. Then I describe how educational psychologists are developing innovative experiences that enable teachers to use psychological theory to improve their understanding and practice of teaching.

The Role of Theory in Teacher Preparation

In recent years, the conception of the role of theory and research in the development of expertise has changed dramatically (Donmoyer, 1996). The scientific application of theory to practice is no longer considered a simple matter of directly applying theoretical principles to problems of practice. It has become increasingly evident that teaching is a complex and multifaceted process, and 'theory does not translate overnight into changes in practice, but works indirectly and slowly through the development of the teacher's understandings' (McAninch, 1993, p. 57).

As early as 1892, William James cautioned educators that they cannot deduce educational practice directly from psychological principles and theories: 'Psychology is a science, and teaching is an art; and sciences never generate arts directly out of themselves. An intermediary inventive mind must make the application, by using its originality' (James, 1958, p. 24). In spite of James' cautionary remarks, educational policy makers, researchers, and practitioners throughout this century have believed that they could apply psychological theory directly to the solution of educational problems (e.g., United States Department of Education, 1986). Kohlberg (1983) termed this misconception the *psychologist's fallacy*. Many researchers have pointed out problems with the psychologist's fallacy. Murray (1996) noted that psychological principles and theories are

a   'too imprecise' to provide much help to the teacher;
b   can be used to justify unsound or contradictory practices; and
c   as James pointed out, 'Many diverse methods of teaching may equally well agree with psychological theory' (as cited in Murray, 1996, p. 421).

Kohlberg (1983) pointed out that the misguided efforts to construct teacher-proof and student-proof curriculum were based on the psychologist's fallacy. He argued that these efforts to short-circuit the teacher's point of view doomed them to failure. Fenstermacher (1986) made a similar case for the need to recognize the role of the teacher's perspective in the relation between theory and practice:

> We simplify matters too much if we argue simply that the value of educational research is the improvement of educational practice. That is a misleading construction. The value of educational research when it is done well is to help us know and understand a certain limited range of educational phenomena. This knowledge and understanding gained from the research *may* improve educational practice, if it bears fruitfully on the premises of practical arguments in the minds of teachers. (p. 47)

Similarly, Olson and Bruner (1996) noted that the failures of psychologists to generate laws of learning and theories of abilities are attributable to their failing to take into account the 'goals, purposes, beliefs, and intentions of both the teachers and the learners' (p. 10). Olson and Bruner emphasized the difficulty of applying theory to practice:

> It is never easy to apply theoretical knowledge to practical problems. On the practical art of being a physician, Aristotle wrote in his *Nichomachean Ethics*: 'It is an easy matter to know the effects of honey, wine hellebore, cautery, and cutting. But to know how, for whom, and when we should apply these as remedies is no less an undertaking than being a physician.' Scientific advances increasingly inform us of the effects of various treatments but the art of knowing 'how, for whom, and when' to apply them remains as difficult as ever. (Olson and Bruner, 1996, p. 10)

Because of this difficulty, efforts to improve teaching by reducing or eliminating teacher preparation are foolhardy. Medical educators have not eliminated medical education. Instead, they increased the relevance of theory to practice by integrating theoretical and clinical work through cases and problem-based approaches to education. Similar reforms of teacher education could enable teachers to develop the sophistication necessary to use theory as a legitimate basis for their practices.

Doyle and Carter (1996) and Bolster (1983) have argued that teachers' understanding of their work has a narrative structure organized by stories and images rather than by propositional knowledge. They noted the incongruity between teachers' ways of knowing and psychological theory and research and concluded that the forms in which knowledge in educational psychology is embedded are inconsistent with the ways in which teachers think about their work. McLaughlin (1990) and others have shown that teachers thwart efforts to apply psychological theory to practice when they do not believe in the theory. The answer, however, is not to eliminate theory from teacher preparation programs. Rather, innovative approaches are needed that embed psychological knowledge in contexts that enable teachers to understand the relevance of theory to practice.

Integrating Theory and Practice in Educational Psychology

Anderson et al. (1995) pointed out that 'educational psychology foundations courses were developed in the early part of this century to help upgrade the status of teacher education — to improve the scholarship and rigor of professional programs by posing a scientific basis for further study' (p. 143). Paradoxically, in the postmodern ending of this century, some educators and policy makers uncritically responded to teachers' complaints that such courses are too theoretical, and advocated the elimination of such course work.

Current psychological theory offers insight into why teachers perceive courses that emphasize theory as irrelevant. Historically, educational psychology courses have been placed at the beginning of teacher education programs to provide the foundation of the program. Cognitive psychological theory would predict that the typical educational psychology survey course that exposes prospective teachers to the vast history of psychological ideas in encyclopedic fashion will not have a lasting effect on the beliefs and practices of teachers.

In 1994, the Educational Psychology Division (Division 15) of the American Psychological Association appointed a committee to study the teaching of educational psychology in teacher education programs (Anderson et al., 1995). The Committee based its recommendations on an analysis of the demands of teaching and theory and research on the nature of learning and the development of expertise. Unlike policy makers committed to reducing the role of the university in preparing teachers, the Committee concluded that teaching is a social and moral activity that is highly complex and ill-structured, characterized by the need to coordinate many complex tasks simultaneously: 'The many overlapping events and agendas mean that teachers constantly contend with insoluble dilemmas, in which a decision that resolves one problem may fail to address or even exacerbate another problem' (Anderson et al., 1995, p. 146). Further, teachers must contend with continuous uncertainty, never sure of the results of their actions. Recognizing practitioners' need to reduce the complexity of teaching, the Committee explored how educational psychologists could help novice teachers simplify the complexities of their work. The Committee concluded that if novice teachers could be helped to develop a psychological perspective, they could use that perspective to impose order on their work and to simplify the overwhelming complexity of the classroom.

The Committee identified three principles from the social constructivist paradigm as the theoretical foundation for their recommendations for reform in the teaching of educational psychology:

a   People learn from instruction and experience by constructing personal meaning based on prior beliefs and knowledge;

b   New knowledge is situated in a specific context and transfers to other contexts when the learner has identified common features across the contexts; and

c   Learning is socially mediated by adults and peers.

Entering Beliefs

Emphasizing the importance of learners' prior beliefs, the first principle suggests that educational psychology instructors recognize that instruction will be processed in terms of students' entering beliefs. Beginning teachers typically do not conceive of teaching as a complex activity; they view themselves as ready to teach (Weinstein, 1988, 1989). This naive optimism is a barrier to their professional development. Believing that they already know how to teach, these prospective teachers do not understand the importance of the activities their instructors have designed to engage them in the analysis of teaching. If novices do not conceive of teaching as a complex problem, they are unlikely to become seriously engaged in the preparation process. To dispel this naive optimism, the Committee recommended that educational psychologists create experiences that reveal to novice teachers the 'complex orchestration of subject matter, students, and environments' (Anderson et al., 1995, p. 145) necessary to succeed as a teacher.

Novice teachers' epistemological beliefs contribute to their resistance to the idea of teaching as a complex activity. Many prospective teachers view knowledge as certain. They believe their job is to transmit this knowledge directly to their students. Believing that the role of experts is to convey 'right answers' to their students these novice teachers think that their instructors should simply tell them the correct way to manage their students and to teach effectively. This expectation conflicts with the constructivist epistemological stance that knowledge about effective teaching is uncertain and based on personal judgments informed by knowledge and values. To enable preservice teachers to understand the uncertainties and irreconcilable dilemmas that emerge in teaching, educational psychologists are developing experiences that require prospective teachers to wrestle with the conflict of competing goals. For example, they are designing activities that require novices to consider questions such as how does a teacher reconcile the goal of maintaining firm classroom control with the goal of providing students with activities that encourage exploration and collaboration.

Research on overcoming epistemological misconceptions suggests that changing misconceptions is a difficult process. Humans tend to hold tenaciously to their beliefs and, when confronted with challenges, interpret new information in ways that confirm their prior beliefs. Powerful interventions are needed to enable prospective teachers to overcome their naive optimism and absolutist views of knowledge that lead them to underestimate the difficulties of teaching.

In assessing the role of psychology in the preparation of teachers, Olson and Bruner (1996) also noted the powerful effect of teachers' conceptions about the nature of the learner's mind on their teaching practices. Olson and Bruner recommended that:

> the first step in 'equipping' teachers . . . for their task is to provide them access to the best available understanding of the mind of the child, and to provide teachers as well with insight into what they assume or believe about children's minds and how those beliefs and assumptions are manifest in their own teaching. (pp. 12–13)

Essential to these insights is the recognition that 'explaining what children *do* is not enough: [The focus must be on] what [children] *think* they are doing and what their reasons are for doing it' (p. 13). Therefore, educational psychologists are identifying ways to engage novices in exploring the minds of their students and 'trying to understand the sources and strengths of their conceptions' (p. 13). Bruner and Olson identified four conceptions of mind held by theorists, children, and educators and proposed that an educational psychology with relevance for teachers involves novice teachers in analyzing the implications of these conceptions for educational practice. One way to engage novice teachers in this analysis is to have them describe their conceptions and beliefs about each topic encountered in educational psychology (Shuell, 1996).

The Situatedness of Learning

The second principle proposes that learning tends to be limited to the context in which it occurs. To transfer learning to other contexts requires the learner to see similarities in different settings. This principle offers insight into why prospective teachers have been unable to transfer what they learn in educational psychology courses to their classroom practice. Propositional knowledge learned in a context isolated from practice cannot be expected to transfer to the classroom. Educational psychology experiences and tasks must represent real-life classroom problems if they are to produce learning that can be transferred to the classroom setting. Many practical experiences must be analyzed to enable prospective teachers to see the similarities and differences across situations that affect the appropriateness of transfer. Such tasks should capture as much of the complexity of teaching as possible without overwhelming novice teachers, while at the same time slowing the action so that they can 'practice thinking and acting like a teacher, and later analyze the action' (Anderson et al., 1995, p. 152). These experiences provide novices with the insight that teachers must consider multiple issues simultaneously.

Mediated Learning

Emphasizing the socially mediated nature of learning, the third principle suggests that traditional approaches to educational psychology focusing on students' reading the textbook and listening to lectures do not promote the construction of personal meaning that will influence educational practice. Guided by this principle, the educational psychology instructor recognizes the role of social interaction as integral to learning and acts as a mediator of that learning by promoting novice teachers' dialogue, questioning, and reflection. On the basis of this principle, the instructor constructs experiences and tasks that require prospective teachers to discuss and challenge each other's ideas in a climate of support where they feel free to take risks without fear of failure or humiliation.

In summary, the APA Committee recommended that the goal of educational psychology is to develop teachers' psychological perspective to enable them to make informed decisions about their practice:

> A teacher who holds a contemporary psychological perspective is able and disposed to consider how learners' knowledge, motivation, and development contributes to the meanings they make, the actions they take, and what and how they learn in classrooms. A teacher who holds a contemporary psychological perspective thinks about how the social and instructional contexts of the classroom (e.g., subject matter instruction and assessment, classroom management systems) affect and are affected by individual students' knowledge, learning, motivation, and development. A psychological perspective provides a teacher with a way to 'get hold of' a complex situation and think about its problems and possibilities in light of views of human learning. This advantage is not afforded by mere knowledge about concepts, principles, and theories; it is only manifested when these ideas are tied together as coherent frames that suggest when and how the ideas can be used. (Anderson et al., 1995, p. 145)

The Committee recognized that a single course isolated from practice is incapable of developing a perspective that requires 'learning a new way to analyze, reason, and make judgments' (p. 153). They pointed out that if teachers are to develop a psychological perspective it must become a program-level goal. Educational psychologists must play an integral role in the teacher education program collaborating with other teacher education faculty to develop 'a common discourse for thinking about teaching' that can bring cohesion to the disparate experiences in the program (p. 153). This collaboration would include modeling a psychological perspective in integrated, interdisciplinary seminars and field supervision that focuses on analyses of cases and experiences from multiple perspectives.

Developing Theoretical Perspectives in Educational Psychology

In their deliberations about the role of educational psychology in teacher education, the APA Committee described the pedagogical content knowledge of the educational psychology instructor as including 'knowledge of learners' characteristics, knowledge of what parts of the discipline or field are most useful to learners in various situations; and what methods of teaching the content are most likely to be effective, including what examples, cases, and analogies will represent the content effectively to various learners' (p. 154). Instructors of educational psychology in a teacher education program, they pointed out, 'need to know not only the content defined by the field, but also how that knowledge can be used by teachers' and 'knowledge about prospective teachers as learners' (p. 154).

Researchers have proposed a number of innovative approaches to the teaching of educational psychology that enable prospective teachers to develop a sophisticated understanding of the value of theory to practice. Shulman (1990) described how embedding discussion of psychological theory and principles in the real-world problems of classroom instruction provides novice teachers with an answer to their perennial question: 'What does this have to do with what we are doing in classrooms?' (p. 8). Rather than beginning instruction in his foundations class with general learning theories, he begins with a specific instance of school text used in everyday teaching activities and asks interning teachers to think about what would make it difficult for students to learn the text. The discussion then moves from what would make this text difficult to learn to a discussion of how theories of cognitive psychology offer insight into the specific problem.

Blumenfeld, Hicks, and Krajcik (1996) have used the tasks of teaching, specifically instructional planning, as an organizational framework for teaching educational psychology concepts:

> The problem is how to use psychological perspectives on learning and instruction to design a set of experiences . . . to help a particular group of children develop understanding of the content, under particular conditions and constraints. . . . The benefits are that preservice teachers learn by thinking through what to teach, how to teach it, and how to assess it by anticipating and solving potential difficulties and by justifying their decisions . . . By making explicit what often remains implicit, preservice teachers can confront and reexamine their assumptions and understanding about educational psychology. (p. 51)

From their experiences with this approach, Blumenfeld et al. (1996) have presented 'sobering' evidence of the 'fragility of understanding and how difficult it is to help novices develop robust knowledge' (p. 58). Students who demonstrated adequate propositional knowledge in discussions or writing about a concept were often unable to apply it appropriately or integrate it with other concepts. For example, students experienced difficulties in evaluating high-level thinking, taking into account student diversity, applying developmental theory to the selection and modification of activities, asking questions to foster students' thinking about content, and translating their understanding about learning into effective use of textbooks. These novice teachers tended to focus on what would be fun for students rather than on what students should be learning. Blumenfeld et al. pointed out that these experiences in planning instruction helped these novices overcome their naive optimism about teaching by making them aware of the difficulties in thinking about what and how to teach. By the end of the semester these novices had 'come to appreciate that teaching is complex, uncertain, and situated' (p. 60).

As Shuell (1996) pointed out, however, more than the analysis of practical situations is needed: 'Merely talking about what might be done in a particular situation (e.g., when analyzing a case) does not prepare one to perform the necessary actions' (Shuell, 1996, p. 12). Novice teachers need experiences in taking action on the basis of their developing psychological perspective, assessing the adequacy of that action, and receiving feedback on that action from instructors and peers. Kennedy (1987) noted in her description of professional expertise as deliberate action that 'experiences must entail *both* analysis *and* action, so that students learn the connection between the two' (as cited in Shuell, 1996, p. 12).

These preliminary efforts based on cognitive science offer teachers relevant experiences from which to develop an understanding of the power of theoretical perspectives to inform classroom practice. The ability to examine problems of practice from a variety of theoretical perspectives provides teachers with a powerful tool with which to evaluate and modify their practice. Without such coherent perspectives, teachers are left only with anecdotal folk wisdom passed on in teachers' lounges, unrelated lists of practical maxims like 'Don't smile until Christmas', apprenticeship approaches to teaching that depend on the novice's luck in being assigned an exemplary mentor, and the trial-and-error approach to classroom survival on which teachers have always had to depend because of inadequate preparation for the difficulties of teaching. DeVries and Kohlberg (1990) cautioned us that such practices are based on the *practitioner's fallacy*, that is, the belief that practice can be guided solely by 'what works' as defined by personal experience. Such unsystematic approaches to teacher preparation uninformed by theory, DeVries and Kohlberg pointed out, frequently result 'in practices full of conceptual contradictions and [leave] the child's education at the mercy of the teacher's . . . individual idiosyncrasy' (p. 14).

Conclusion

Evidence of the difficulties of teaching abound. Recent data indicate that education in the United States continues to be inferior to the education offered in other industrialized countries, and the gradual decline in the achievement gap between minority and majority students has slowed or stopped. Teachers need more time in universities — not less — to develop the expertise that would enable them to overcome the inadequacies of current educational practices. Educational psychology grounded in the persistent problems of the classroom — how do students learn, what do they find difficult to learn, how can they be motivated, what is the nature of ability and how can its development be fostered — offers an important source of insights that can inform teachers' decisions about practice. To eliminate this promising avenue for the development of teacher expertise is short-sighted and will further reduce teachers' ability to be effective in the classroom.

References

ANDERSON, L.M., BLUMENFELD, P., PINTRICH, P.R., CLARK, C.M., MARX, R.W. and PETERSON, P. (1995) 'Educational psychology for teachers: Reforming our courses, rethinking our roles,' *Educational Psychologist*, **30**, pp. 143–58.

BLUMENFELD, P., HICKS, L. and KRAJCIK, J.S. (1996) 'Teaching educational psychology through instructional planning', *Educational Psychologist*, **31**, pp. 51–61.

BOLSTER, A.S., JR. (1983) 'Toward a more effective model of research on teaching', *Harvard Educational Review*, **53**, pp. 294–308.

DEVRIES, R. and KOHLBERG, L. (1990) *Constructivist Early Education: Overview and Comparison with Other Programs*, Washington, DC: National Association for the Education of Young Children.

DONMOYER, R. (1996) 'Educational research in an era of paradigm proliferation: What's a journal editor to do?', *Educational Researcher*, **25**, 2, pp. 19–25.

DOYLE, W. and CARTER, K. (1996) 'Educational psychology and the education of teachers', *Educational Psychologist*, **31**, pp. 23–8.

FENSTERMACHER, G. (1986) 'Philosophy of research on teaching: Three aspects,' in WITTROCK, M. (ed.) *Handbook of Research on Teaching*, New York: Macmillan, pp. 37–49.

HOY, A.W. (1996) 'Teaching educational psychology: Texts in context', *Educational Psychologist*, **31**, pp. 41–9.

JAMES, W. (1958) *Talks to Teachers on Psychology; And to Students on Some of Life's Ideals*, New York: Norton.

KOHLBERG, L. (1983) 'Foreword', in REIMER, J., PAOLITTO, D.P. and HERSH, R.H. (eds) *Promoting Moral Growth: From Piaget to Kohlberg*, Prospect Heights, IL: Waveland Press, pp. ix–xvi.

LORTIE, D. (1975) *Schoolteacher*, Chicago: University of Chicago Press.

MCANINCH, A.R. (1993) *Teacher Thinking and the Case Method. Theory and Directions*, New York: Teachers College Press.

MCLAUGHLIN, M. (1990) 'The Rand change agent study revisited: Macro perspectives and micro realities', *Educational Researcher*, **10**, 9, pp. 11–16.

MURRAY, F. (1996) 'Educational psychology and the teacher's reasoning,' in MURRAY, F. (ed.) *The Teacher Educator's Handbook: Building a Knowledge Base for the Preparation of Teachers*, San Francisco: Jossey-Bass, pp. 213–26.

OLSON, D.R. and BRUNER, J. (1996) 'Folk psychology and folk pedagogy', in OLSON, D.R. and TORRANCE, N. (eds) *The Handbook of Education and Human Development: New Models of Learning, Teaching and Schooling*, Cambridge, MA: Basil Blackwell, pp. 9–27.

RIGDEN, D.W. (1996) *What Teachers Have to Say about Teacher Education*, Washington, DC: Council for Basic Education.

SHUELL, T.J. (1996) 'The role of educational psychology in the preparation of teachers', *Educational Psychologist*, **31**, pp. 5–14.

SHULMAN, L. (1990) 'Reconnecting foundations to the substance of teacher education', in TOZER, S., ANDERSON, T.H. and ARMBRUSTER, B.B. (eds) *Foundational Studies in Teacher Education*, New York: Teachers College Press, pp. 2–12.

UNITED STATES DEPARTMENT OF EDUCATION (1986) *What Works: Research about Teaching and Learning*, Washington, DC, Author.

WEINSTEIN, C. (1988) 'Preservice teachers' expectations about the first year of teaching', *Teaching and Teacher Education*, **4**, pp. 31–41.

WEINSTEIN, C. (1989) 'Teacher education students' preconceptions of teaching,' *Journal of Teacher Education*, **40**, pp. 53–60.

15 'Alternative' or Just Easy?

Gary K. Clabaugh

Advances in the knowledge base for teaching now can make teacher preparation meaningfully rigorous and truly empowering. In fact, the knowledge base now permits a fundamental reconceptualization of instruction at all levels of schooling (Preston, 1994). Instead of exploiting this unprecedented opportunity, however, many state officials have paradoxically been fostering lax, disempowering short cuts into teaching. Thirty eight states now offer so-called alternative certification programs (Buck, 1995), and some of them are so undemanding they virtually insure incompetence.

Teach for America

Teach for America is an instructive example. It is touted in the press as a 'revolutionary teacher preparation program' (Phillips, 1991, section A, p. 1), which proves that '. . . bright people who can light up a classroom with enthusiasm and intellect can become effective teachers largely through on-the-job training' (Phillips, 1991). This sort of praise, even the name itself, suggests Teach for America candidates are dedicated altruists who otherwise would have been blocked from teaching by meaningless bureaucratic hurdles.

We should question the altruism of those searching out an easy way into teaching, and if Teach for America is anything, it is easy. After a mere six week crash course in teacher survival skills taught primarily by teachers from their troubled placement sites, Teach for America's 'lively and enthusiastic' novices are turned loose on poverty stricken children. Children who are legally required to be their guinea pigs by state attendance laws.

Once on the job, Teach for America candidates '. . . are assisted by local staff' who are said to, '. . . build a camaraderie through local newsletters and social events, establish resource centers and serve as direct resources during office hours and classroom visits' (Teach for America, 1992). How underwhelming!

Wendy Kopp, Teach for America's founder, claims, 'Amazing things happen when you put creative, idealistic and enthusiastic teachers into the classroom' (Teach for America, 1992, p. 2). Even more amazing things happen when they have to know what they are doing. The plain fact is that no one can go from pedagogical ignorance to even entry level competence in just 30 class days of preparation! Even the notoriously inadequate '90 Day Wonders' given emergency commissions in the military during World War II, received three times that training.

In *Teachers for Our Nation's Schools*, John Goodlad comments on this sort of devaluation of teacher preparation.

> Few matters are more important than the quality of the teachers in our nation's schools. Few matters are as neglected. Most parents exercise considerable care in deciding who should baby sit for their children. But the doors to teaching are unlatched; if the front door is locked, one enters through the back. Those who want to teach in our schools are required to meet no tests of character or commitment.

Corporate Dabblers

How did Teach for America ever lurch to life? Princeton undergraduate Wendy Kopp dreamt up the idea for her senior thesis in Public Policy Studies. Apparently unencumbered by any formal study of teaching or learning, Wendy saw no need for teachers to be less ignorant than she was.[1] Subsequently she sold the same idea to H. Ross Perot and other corporate school 'reform' dilettantes who funded her notion.

What made these business bosses decide Wendy had a good idea? Perhaps they assumed there isn't much to know about teaching and learning, and given the respect shown by top government officials for their own uninformed opinions, that is a perfectly understandable conclusion. Perot, for example, knows nothing about education you couldn't pick up scanning back issues of the *Reader's Digest*. Yet he was appointed czar of school 'reform' for the entire state of Texas. This anointing, may be the basis for Perot's belief that there is nothing of substance in the teacher education knowledge base. How do we know he harbors this conviction? Once in power he immediately sought to disestablish teacher education. Claiming it was a 'Chinese fire drill', he ended up convincing Texas legislators to enact their notorious limit on teacher preparation. No more than 18 credit hours — including student teaching.[2]

More recently, businessmen have gained even greater credibility as authorities on schooling. This past year, for example, 40 state governors brought just their favorite businessmen to the latest National Education Summit. Co-chaired by Wisconsin's Governor Tommy Thompson and IBM's chief executive Louis Gerstner, and held at IBM's conference center in Palisades, NY, this gathering generated still another generation for 'reforming' the nation's schools.

Undermining Legitimate Efforts

Some alternatives to traditional undergraduate teacher certification programs are rigorous and make good use of the powerful new knowledge base. I'm not talking about programs that define their alternativeness in terms of ease of completion. At La Salle University we offer a nationally recognized graduate level teacher preparation program for adult career changers. It's an alternative to traditional programs, but it also is more demanding than our already tough undergraduate training.

Figure 15.1   Instruction in Pedagogy

Teach for America	La Salle
30 class days of instruction in classroom survival taught by a pick-up team of instructors.	900 hours spread across at least one and one-half years of integrated preparation firmly rooted in cognitive science taught primarily by full-time, nationally published faculty who all are veteran teachers.
6 weeks of 1/2 day experience in summer schools.	Three increasingly difficult, widely spaced, carefully mentored practica in which students instruct both 'normal' and special needs children for a total of 20 full-time weeks.

Unlike the usual run of 'alternative' programs, La Salle's graduate level option exceeds state standards in the bargain.

Let's briefly compare Teach for America's 'alternative' training with La Salle's (Figure 15.1).

La Salle is a *responsible* gatekeeper. We take advantage of our students' greater focus and maturity as well as our graduate program's greater flexibility, not to cut standards. We help students gain meaningful mastery of a powerful knowledge base. And after extended observation, including *three* teaching experiences, we know our candidates are disciplined, hard-working, open-minded and trustworthy. Those who are not have been eliminated. Teach for America throws away the advantages mentioned above, substituting some brief survival training and six weeks of half-day teaching in an atypical setting. So far as character is concerned, Teach for America makes do with the following disclaimer: 'Teach for America is not responsible for finding alternative placements for candidates who cannot be hired by their assigned school district because of their criminal records or present involvement in criminal proceedings' (Teach for America, 1992, p. 2).

Special Interests

Collegiate-based teacher educators sometimes are characterized as a 'special interest' just 'protecting their guild'. But the interests of teacher educators are no more 'special' than other human beings who care about what they do. It took guilds, with their rigorous training requirements, to build Europe's great cathedrals and similar enduring masterpieces. These experts certainly didn't invite 'creative, idealistic and enthusiastic' people in off the street to try their hand at stained glass or stone carving. They were unrelenting in their entrance requirements, which is the only way to create competent professionals.

Besides, proponents of 'alternative' forms of teacher preparation have their own special interests too. These interests are very likely at odds with quality schooling. Consider, for example, the corporate types who dabble in school reform. They certainly have special interests, some of which are so obvious one wonders why the media fails to mention them. Consider the policy statement issued by the businessman-led 1996 National Education Summit (The summit co-chaired by IBM's

Louis Gerstner, Jr and held at his firm's facility). It calls for schools to make extensive use of new technologies to improve student performance. Does IBM's chief executive have a special interest in pushing the technology showcased at the Summit (Lawton, 1996, p. 14)? And what sort of employees do these corporate types long for?

a   tough, independent-minded critical thinkers; or
b   compliant 'team players' with strictly circumscribed 'practical' skills.

Liberal arts types, like Lynne Cheney, former Chairperson of the National Endowment for the Humanities, also have their special interests. These stand in direct opposition to quality teacher preparation. Chair of the NEH, Cheney routinely blasted teacher education programs and championed purely academic preparation. An academic degree was, she assured us, both necessary *and* sufficient for teacher preparation. Ask yourself, if education courses are eliminated, who gets to teach those displaced students? And won't liberal arts graduates have a whole new source of jobs?

Public officials also have special interests that are inimical to quality teacher preparation. If they can increase the supply of certified teachers by cheapening requirements, for example, it will drive down salaries and cut the cost of government. If the people entering teaching are less committed, it will weaken teacher unions — a prime goal of those politicians whose opponents were supported by the National Education Association and the American Federation of Teachers.

Then there are the big-city school districts that want to train their own teachers. Guess what sort of teacher they long for. The same sort of coal miners, coal barons longed for. Whatever else happens, you can be very sure that whatever their teachers are trained to do, it won't be to criticize what the school administration is doing. Permitting big city school districts to train their own teachers is, in most instances, the equivalent of hiring a wolf as a sheep dog. Talk about special interests!

Warm Bodies

Many alternative certification programs are just a way of putting warm bodies in front of classrooms. Since women are no longer forced into teaching by a lack of other opportunities, public officials need a new supply of people to teach on the cheap.

This problem is particularly acute in underfunded, often chaotic, city schools and in particularly godforsaken rural schools. In fact, advocates of easy-route alternative certification programs argue their approach is necessary precisely because '. . . the graduates of traditional teacher-education programs do not want to and cannot teach all the children and youth of America' (Haberman, 1991).

Well-trained teachers avoid the nation's educational Calcuttas. However the solution to this problem is realistic salaries and improved teaching conditions, not the hiring of incompetent but 'enthusiastic' candidates who put up with anything in return for being exempted from serious training.

Consider the Mott Hall School in Harlem. They hired four Teach for America teachers, and vice principal Steve Buchsbaum is quoted in the *Philadelphia Inquirer* as saying '. . . they are an asset to our school.' How so? Well when one Teach for America enthusiast showed up for work at Mott Hall, she found she had no desk and, would you believe it, no classroom! Administrators told her there was no money and no space for either. So what did our Teach for America enthusiast do that made her such an asset? She found a space under some stairs and, using her own furniture, set to work in this dingy little niche.

Doctor for America?

Of course, professionals of all types avoid the inner city and the remote hinterlands. So the logic that justifies Teach for America justifies alternative licensure in these professions as well. Graduates of the nation's medical schools avoid practice in these same locales. A few weeks of summer training, some interning in an emergency room and more inner-city or rural physicians. Over time, if they learn from their mistakes, some might even become semi-competent.

There are other possibilities. How about Nurse for America or Dentistry for America? There are plenty of 'lively and enthusiastic' novices who would light up these professions if their entrance requirements were largely waived.

Does this sound silly? Sure. And you know why? Because we take these profession's too seriously to allow such mark downs in the price of entry. What does that tell us about our regard for teaching?

Simpletons with Power

It isn't surprising that counterfeits like Teach for America are taken seriously. Americans have a remarkable tolerance for the trifling of educational amateurs — especially at the very top. Pedagogical simpletons are regularly appointed to positions of enormous educational power and influence. When Ross Perot headed up school 'reform' in Texas he distinguished himself by his total ignorance of research that disproved his mindless proclamations. And what did former Secretary of Education William Bennett know about schooling, teaching or learning that qualified him to become the nation's Secretary of Education? And how about Lamarr Alexander, another Secretary of Education. Wasn't he just an out of work lawyer/politician who dabbled in school 'reform' while governor of Tennessee? The point here is not to attack these individuals personally, but to stress their complete lack of relevant expertise. Would we appoint a blustering businessman as US Surgeon General?

Those who care about schooling can be forgiven a certain indignation at the solemn trifling of incompetents. As the famed philosopher Alfred North Whitehead puts it:

When one considers in its length and breadth the importance of a nation's young, the broken lives, the defeated hopes, the national failures, which result from the frivolous inertia with which (education) is treated, it is difficult to restrain within oneself a savage rage.

Conclusion

Do we really want to improve American schooling? We must respect teaching and recognize that it requires special knowledge and skill. Teachers are *the* key participants in improving our schools, and nothing, or at least nothing good, will happen without strengthening, not weakening, their preparation.

Notes

1　Attempts to ascertain Ms Kopp's pedagogical training came to naught. Teach for America's national office indicated that only one staffer was qualified to comment and on three occasions this individual was unavailable. A Princeton University official also withheld information regarding Ms Kopp's training. The operative assumption, then, is that her major in Public Policy Studies included no meaningful pedagogical studies.

2　For a summary of alternative teacher certification programs in Texas see, 'Alternative Teacher Certification in Texas' ERIC no. ED346093.

References

BUCK, G.H. (1995) 'Alternative certification programs: A national survey', *Teacher Education and Special Education*, **18** (Winter), pp. 39–48.

FEDEN, P.D. (1994) 'About instruction: Powerful new strategies worth knowing', *Educational Horizons*, **73**, 1, pp. 18–24.

GOODLAD, J.I. (1991) *Teachers for Our Nation's Schools*, San Francisco: Jossey-Bass.

HABERMAN, M. (1991, 6 November) 'Catching up with reform in teacher education', *Education Week*.

LAWTON, M. (1996, 3 April) 'Computer technology showcased at summit', *Education Week*, **14**.

PHILLIPS, N. (1991, 1 December) 'Teacher program woos grads outside education', *The Philadelphia Inquirer*, **A1**, 1.

PRESTON, D. (1994) 'About Instruction: Powerful New Strategies Worth Knowing', *Educational Horizons*, **73**, 1, pp. 78–74.

TEACH FOR AMERICA PROMOTIONAL MATERIAL (1992) *Teach for America*, p. 2. P.O. Box 5114, New York, NY.

WHITEHEAD, A.N. (1929) *The Aims of Education and other Essays*, New York: Macmillan, p. 22.

16   Critical Components in the Preparation of Teachers

Mary E. Diez

Abstract

The author argues that effective preparation of teachers requires a set of components that can best be delivered through a college or university program linked to local schools, including a clear conceptualization of what teachers need to know and be able to do, a coherent curriculum based on the conceptualization, performance assessment used to support candidate development, and collaborative relationships among liberal arts faculty, teacher education faculty, and teacher educators in K-12 schools. Because of its impact on both the development and documentation of development, performance assessment is seen as a key component. Examples of the components are drawn from the teacher education program at Alverno College in Milwaukee, Wisconsin.

For teacher educators, the last 10 years have been a puzzling period. At the same time that groups like the National Board for Professional Teaching Standards (NBPTS) and the Interstate New Teacher Assessment and Support Consortium (INTASC) have been undertaking major work to make clear what teaching requires in terms of knowledge, dispositions and performance, some in the alternative preparation movement have been arguing that a teacher needs little more than a bachelor's degree in a subject area to be ready for the classroom. At the same time that Goodlad's National Network for Educational Renewal, the Holmes Group, and others interested in the reform of teacher education have been creating models for teacher education that parallel those in other professions, some in state legislatures have been marshaling forces to argue against the need for professional preparation of teachers. At the same time that states have increased requirements for undergraduate teacher education, they have created quick routes to by-pass those requirements for persons with degrees. And at the same time that advocates for children are calling for teachers to have expertise in the subjects that they teach, some responsible for school district hiring policies are working to make entry into classrooms more flexible.

The tension between these conflicting views invites exploration. Clearly, teaching requires knowing a discipline, e.g., mathematics, science, history, English, etc. What counts as *teaching* and *knowing*, however, is at the heart of the matter. For many people, *teaching* is telling, i.e., disseminating information or presenting lectures that incorporate the received view of a discipline. While some take comfort in the 'right answers' that such an approach to teaching suggests, thinking of teaching as disseminating information may preclude consideration of multiple perspectives. Such an approach may omit attention to the skills that involve how to use that information. And it also may create the problem of distancing the teacher from the students, with a focus on information or 'content' taking priority over a focus on students. And so, it is not likely to lead one to consider the differences among students, including special learning needs or prior knowledge.

For those who assume that teaching is telling, what might *knowing* mean? Is having an undergraduate major in the field or a respectable score on the GRE sufficient evidence of knowledge? Unfortunately, for many college graduates in the United States, an undergraduate major may require little more than a collection of courses. That the typical major of studies does not necessarily imply the completion of a coherent program, nor the mastery of the central concepts of the discipline, is a serious concern raised by *An American Imperative* (1993).

The positions outlined above most closely resemble a positivist or behaviorist view of teaching and knowing, where knowledge is viewed as external to the knower (Case and Bereiter, 1984; Jonassen, 1991). Alternatively, teaching may be viewed in a constructivist frame, where knowledge is viewed as an interaction between the knower and the known. Constructivists see teaching as providing learners with the opportunity to develop knowledge, believing that *knowing* must go beyond the discipline or subject area to connect with the world of the learner (Brooks and Brooks, 1993; Bruer, 1993). INTASC's first principle suggests this added level of knowing, or what Shulman (1987) calls 'pedagogical content knowledge':

> The teacher understands the central concepts, tools of inquiry, and structure of the discipline(s) he or she teaches *and can create learning experiences that make these aspects of subject matter meaningful for students.* (my emphasis)

The further description of this principle suggests that knowing 'is not a fixed body of facts, but is complex and ever-evolving'. It describes the teacher as appreciating 'multiple perspectives' and as committed to 'continuous learning'. It identifies skills that the teacher needs, e.g., the ability to use 'multiple representations and explanations of disciplinary concepts that capture key ideas and link them to students' prior understandings', and to 'represent and use differing viewpoints, theories . . . and methods of inquiry in his/her teaching of subject matter concepts' (INTASC, 1992). Clearly, this goes well beyond the expectation many hold of an undergraduate major in a subject area.

Developing this kind of *knowing* requires a well-designed, coherent program linking disciplinary learning with frameworks from developmental and cognitive psychology. It calls for an interactive approach to knowing, through questioning and exploring and comparing diverse viewpoints. And it invites a focus on learning as making meaning.

Where do the potential teachers best learn to link their subject matter to students' prior understandings? For many, on-the-job experience is the answer, where new teachers can use trial and error to discover what works with their students. The problem with a 'trial and error' approach is that the new teacher may not come up with what works, and the students will fail to learn. For new teachers whose high school and college experiences were largely limited to attending lecture presentations and experiencing multiple choice testing, 'teaching as they were taught' is almost guaranteed to lose their students' attention. Moreover, in the absence of a structured mentoring program, they may not be able to learn from mistakes, may in fact become so discouraged that quitting is the only viable option.

Perhaps a better alternative, adopted by many teacher preparation programs, is requiring teacher education candidates to participate in significant field experiences over several semesters where they can try out teaching strategies under the guidance of accomplished classroom teachers. Ideally, college/university supervisors from both the discipline area and professional education also provide feedback on the teacher candidate's performance — either on site or after reviewing videotapes of a candidate's work with students. This approach has the advantage of limiting the harm that can be done to the classroom full of students, as well as providing the benefit of counsel to the teacher candidates from their mentors.

There are probably few who would argue that a teacher can be prepared in the absence of subject area preparation in the liberal arts and connectedness to K-12 schools. And, as I've illustrated above, philosophical and political differences underlie opinions about where best to locate teacher preparation. My thesis in the remainder of this chapter will be that the effective preparation of teachers requires a set of components that can best be delivered through a college or university program linked to local schools:

- A clear conceptualization of what teachers need to know and be able to do;
- A coherent curriculum based on the conceptualization;
- Performance assessment used to support candidate development;
- Collaborative relationships among liberal arts faculty, teacher education faculty, and teacher educators in K-12 schools.

I will further argue that assessment-as-learning is a most critical component in making teacher preparation effective. I will use the experience of teacher educators and particularly my colleagues at Alverno College to illustrate these components.

A Clear Conceptualization of What Teachers Need to Know and Be Able to Do

The last eight years have seen enormous efforts to build a conceptualization of the knowledge, skills, and dispositions required for effective teaching. NBPTS, beginning in 1987, set out to create not only a clear statement about expectations for accomplished teacher performance, but also a means to recognize performance through the process of board certification. Their work has sparked continued discussion about the roles and responsibilities of teachers; for example, in 1990, INTASC began to develop a set of NBPTS compatible standards to guide state licensure. INTASC represents another pioneering effort in the conceptualization of what teachers need to know and be able to do, focused on what needs to be in place when the teacher candidate is ready to take over a classroom as the teacher of record.

Similar work has been engaged in at the state level, through state standards boards or special commissions, by the National Association of State Directors of Teacher Education and Certification (NASDTEC), and by Education Testing Service through the development of its PRAXIS III Performance Assessment Criteria.

The National Council for the Accreditation of Teacher Education (NCATE), in its 1987 'redesign' process, mandated similar work on the part of colleges and universities seeking national accreditation. While the development of a 'conceptual framework' to guide their work with candidates needs to be grounded in defensible knowledge bases, it may, of course, draw upon models provided by NBPTS, INTASC, and NASDTEC. Consistent with a constructivist philosophy, the expectation of NCATE is that, while teacher educators may not have to reinvent the wheel, they do need to make the wheel their own.

NCATE's standards require a major change for many college and university-based teacher educators, who too often in practice have conceived of a program as a collection of courses. Even though courses may continue to be a major vehicle for organizing the development of candidates, these standards make clear that the program should be conceptualized in terms not only of what teachers need to know but also what they are able to do. For the teacher education faculty at Alverno College, that means describing the abilities of the teacher, where an 'ability' is defined as 'a complex integration of knowledge, behavior, skill, disposition, attitude, and self-perception' (Alverno College Faculty, 1994).

Alverno's Conceptualization

In the late 1970s, Alverno College formed a Teacher Education Study Group composed of education faculty as well as faculty from different liberal arts and professional disciplines. Working with literature reviews in teacher education, the analysis of their own experiences as educators in a variety of fields and at various levels of the education system, and a set of empirical studies of professional abilities required of practitioners in the field, the group identified abilities as essential to the preparation of teachers:

1 Conceptualization: Integrating content knowledge with educational frameworks and a broadly based understanding of the liberal arts in order to plan and implement instruction.
2 Diagnosis: Relating observed behavior to relevant frameworks in order to determine and implement learning prescriptions.
3 Coordination: Managing resources effectively to support learning goals.
4 Communication: Using verbal, non-verbal, and media modes of communication to establish the environment of the classroom and to structure and reinforce learning.

5   Integrative Interaction: Acting with professional values as a situational decision-maker, adapting to the changing needs of the environment in order to develop students as learners.

The group went on to create detailed conceptual maps of these five abilities, making explicit the professional commitments, dispositions, and values that support the development of the teacher (see Figure 16.1). The maps also define the ongoing professional growth of the teachers, moving from a description of what is expected when they are licensed and first employed, to what is expected when they have gained some classroom experience, to what is expected when they become a master teacher. For example, the model of ongoing teacher development in the ability of coordination shows the experienced teacher 'building skills in collaborating in order to enhance the levels/fronts of student learning' and the master teacher as extending that 'collaboration across the institution and with the wider society in systemic network'.

Alverno's five teaching abilities are not merely professional ideals or statements of principles. The faculty's adoption of them expresses a commitment to structure and implementing the curriculum in such a way as to make it possible for all graduating teacher candidates to perform at the level of beginning professional practice. These five abilities are further delineated in both a conceptual handbook provided to teacher education students and faculty and in course syllabi across the program. On a regular basis, the teacher education faculty examines the conceptual framework of the five abilities, analyzing them in relationship to other documents, e.g., the NBPTS propositions and the PRAXIS conceptualization.

A Coherent Curriculum

It's one thing to set forth a description of what a teacher should know and be able to do. It's quite another to design a set of experiences that will help teacher candidates develop the knowing and doing required by the standards implicit in such a description. Whether a teacher education program works with the INTASC standards, the NBPTS standards, or state standards alongside their own conceptual framework, such statements need to be mined for the knowledge and experiential bases implied. These bases should not be conceptualized, however, as isolated or serial 'bits' that can be strung, clothesline fashion, across the years of a program. Rather, once they are identified, a program's faculty needs to think about how to integrate them in order to provide candidates with a coherent, developmental, integrative process of learning.

Coherent

One of the challenges to teacher education in the past — and indeed to all of undergraduate education — has been coherence, i.e., the connectedness of experiences within a course and across courses. The source of coherence for a teacher education program is the conceptualization of what teachers need to know and be

Figure 16.1 Coordination: Managing resources effectively to support learning goals

Expectations for the Beginning Teacher

Developing the use of resources toward learning goals
- Helping learners to make sense out of resources for learning
  - Identifying ⎤ varied resources, including
  - Allocating ⎟ time, space, activities, concepts,
  - Organizing ⎟ framework, media and technology
  - Managing ⎦ and community resources

Structuring the learning environment
- Creating a climate of acceptance and willingness to learn
- Shaping the environment to provide for data gathering, reflection, practice, etc.
- Integrating uses of technology into daily learning
- Creating variety in learning activities
- Dealing with both individuals and groups

Collaborating with learners and others for the sake of the learners
- Making links with the learners' other environments
- Drawing upon professional colleagues
  - Coordinating the effect all members of the system have in all the learning taking place
  - Trying out new ideas with the goal of reaching all learners
  - Sharing plans, problems, ideas
  - Infusing diversity throughout the learning experiences

Monitoring the processes of learning
- Linking practice with data base
- Linking frameworks in an ongoing way to allow ongoing evaluation, adjustment, and adaptation in practice
- Maintaining effective records of learning, including portfolios that include examples of performance
- Using appropriate technology
- Teaching in a manner that supports assessment as learning

Establishing an initial confidence in self as teacher
- Developing skills of self-assessment
- Effectively drawing upon resources
- Flexibly dealing with change

Expectations for the Developing Teacher

Integrating the use of resources in focused learning experiences
- Focusing strategies to effect movement to learning goal
- Stimulating skill building in learners
- Initiating student involvement in managing resources
- Implementing media and technology resources
- Integrating multimedia and technology throughout learning experiences

Building skills in collaborating
- Developing relationships to enhance the levels/fronts of student learning
- Seeing the learner as self-teacher
- Seeing that all the 'worlds' that learners bring with them into their relationship with you are other arenas in which learning is going on
- Establishing consistent interaction lines with other teachers
  - Actively seeking and giving feedback and sharing experiences and ideas with colleagues in same system and across systems
  - Using media to support cooperative learning

Developing skills in monitoring student growth
- Moving back and forth easily from action to reflection to action

Acting with increased confidence in self as a tool of learning
- Practicing self assessment
- Seeing self as informed with knowledge
- Seeing self as interacting with much experience
- Seeing self as comfortable and flexible in action

Expectations for the Experienced Professional Teacher

Practicing as teacher within institutional framework
- Structuring environments to make effective use of institution as resource
- Assisting learners to identify resources
- Managing and integrating varied resources toward learning goals
- Collaborating across the institution and with wider society in systematic networks
- Monitoring impacts of large and small aspects of learning environments
- Collaborating with those inside and outside the school to implement technology

Demonstrating highly-skilled adaptation to changing situations
- Responding to needs quickly
- Handling multiple levels of interaction and understanding

Merging elements of autonomy and collaboration in working in an effective, productive style

Actively continuing one's own ongoing, experiential learning

Acting with developed professional values
- Practicing self-assessment in all aspects of the teacher role
  - Articulating a philosophy of teaching, learning and assessment
- Committed to processes that lead to goals and seeing self as part of the process that leads to goals
- Making choices out of professional values
- Co-creating with others to make the whole institution a learning environment

able to do. Coherence is created when courses and experiences and assessments within a program are integrally connected and mutually reinforcing of the conceptual frameworks that make the expectations of teacher knowledge, disposition and performance explicit. Significant concepts need to be threaded through the courses, recurring whenever their contribution to the developing understanding of the candidate is needed. Similarly, faculty need to model what is taught in courses, for example, faculty employing cooperative group activities in their own courses when they promote the use of group work in K-12 teaching.

Developmental

Related to coherence is the developmental nature of learning to teach. When candidates can take courses in any order, the assumption is that they are separate and isolated experiences, not intended to build one upon the other. If the abilities describe what the faculty expect candidates to demonstrate upon graduation and licensure, then developmentally designed courses need to provide practice that leads to the development of those abilities. Courses, experiences, and assessments need to become successive approximations of the role that the candidates are preparing to carry out. Making a program developmental requires faculty communication and collaboration, not just as the program is being designed, but across time.

Integrative

The nature of teaching requires connections — between theory and practice as well as between subject area knowledge and instructional knowledge. Where normal schools may have erred in emphasizing practice to the exclusion of theory, more recent teacher preparation programs often failed by disconnecting theory from its application in practice. If candidates are to experience an integrative curriculum, they need to be able to make connections between significant theoretical frameworks and perspectives and the way teachers draw upon understandings from such frameworks in their practice. They need to be able to see their content specialization in a new light, by thinking about how its representations are useful in teaching and developing what Shulman (1987) has called 'pedagogical content knowledge'.

Alverno's Work in Developing a Coherent Curriculum[1]

The integration of knowledge, skill, and dispositions described in the five abilities provided the Alverno faculty with a clear picture of the beginning teacher. As they worked to revise the courses and field experiences across the four years students spend within their undergraduate program, they identified central concepts, such as the developmental needs of learners or the effective use of media and technology in the classroom. They designed courses in such a way that these concepts are addressed again and again, rather than relying on single courses in developmental psychology or educational computing to prepare candidates in these areas. They saw that with each course, candidates deepened their understanding of the knowledge bases of teaching, as well as their ability to apply that understanding in action.

The faculty members designed coursework and field experiences to build developmentally, across the years of the program. Candidates begin, for example, with coursework and field experiences that require them to apply the frameworks they are learning with individual students or small groups in tutorial settings. They progress to more complex tasks with larger groups and whole class instruction. Across their assignments, they add levels of complexity, gradually becoming able to attend to a variety of factors in their analysis of a classroom and in their own planning and implementation of learning experiences.

The field experiences are also designed to promote the constant interrelating of knowing and doing. Faculty have developed a set of reflective logs that guide students in each of four semester long field experiences prior to student teaching. These logs direct students to make links between theoretical knowledge and practical application (conceptualization and diagnosis), to observe processes and environments of learning (coordination), to translate content knowledge into suitable short presentations or learning experiences (communication), and to begin to translate their philosophy of education into decisions regarding all aspects of teaching environments and processes (integrative interaction).

Also considered a part of the curriculum is the modeling of faculty in their own teaching and interaction. Alverno faculty believe that it is critically important to create experiences that model the kind of learning environment they expect teacher candidates to create for their students.

In addition, they seek to provide a broad range of experiences in schools that model effective practice with diverse populations. They believe that effective teaching with diverse students is an area where knowing and doing are critically linked. Joining efforts with schools and teachers who are working effectively with students from different racial and ethnic groups, from a range of socioeconomic groups, and with a range of learning styles and needs, is a priority in the Alverno program — as is modeling effective supports for students on campus, who bring a diversity of backgrounds and needs.

Performance Assessment

Given a clear conceptualization of what teachers need to know and be able to do, and a coherent curriculum designed to provide what candidates need to develop as teachers, the next logical question is how will we know if they have, indeed, developed to a sufficient degree to become the teacher of record in a classroom? In the past, completion of a set of courses with an adequate g.p.a. (as a kind of global assessment) qualified candidates for the initial license in most states. Today, most states have added a basic skills test for admission to teacher education, and many require additional testing at the completion of the program. Darling-Hammond, Wise, and Klein (1995) criticize much of teacher testing as either unrelated to teacher knowledge and tasks or inaccurate in the application of research.

At the national level, the NBPTS is developing performance assessments for approximately 30 certificates, and INTASC is also using portfolio and assessment center methods to assess candidates' readiness for licensure. These assessments are developed to tap into the knowledge, dispositions, and performances that the NBPTS and INTASC standards describe. Using performance assessment in teacher education would provide a similar coherence between the conceptual framework and the assessments used to determine candidate progress.

But teacher educators have a second, and perhaps equally powerful, reason to incorporate performance assessment as an essential component in preparing teacher candidates. Not only do such instruments provide documentation of the development of the abilities, but the experience of the assessment process in itself can contribute to candidate development. When candidates *practice* the abilities that will be demanded of them as teachers and when those responsible for preparation use assessment and feedback to help candidates *develop*, assessment is a powerful guide to growth. In this way, assessment becomes integral to learning.

Alverno's Work in Developing Assessment-as-Learning

Again, it is useful to look at the experience of the Alverno teacher education program — which, it must be pointed out, is grounded in Alverno's pioneering work in performance assessment across the undergraduate curriculum for the past 20 years (Alverno College Faculty, 1994; Diez, 1994; Loacker, Cromwell and O'Brien, 1986). The Alverno faculty's use of the term 'assessment-as-learning' is intended to highlight the importance of the process for candidates and distinguish it from institutional and program assessment. Essential to their concept and practice of assessment-as-learning are these characteristics:

1 Expected learning outcomes or abilities

With a focus on the development of the five abilities, candidates are aware of the goals they are working toward. Alverno faculty believe that making the conceptual frameworks of the program explicit makes learning more available to students. In each course syllabus, the five abilities are integrated with specific course content in the design of course goals. For example, in an 'Integrated Reading Curriculum' course, focused on working with learners in grades 3–6, candidates know that they are expected to 'assess the literacy development of intermediate students and prescribe appropriate teaching strategies', as a goal focusing on Diagnosis and Coordination.

2 Explicit criteria for performance

For each performance assessment, candidates can review the criteria to guide their work and to provide a structure for self assessment. In an assessment developed using materials from a local school district's writing assessment process, candidates develop and use a rubric to assess actual intermediate grade writing samples. They analyze samples for strengths and areas of need and plan appropriate teaching strategies based upon that analysis. Students collaborate in formulating a teaching plan for the teacher to use with this group of students. Among the criteria for this assessment, students are expected to

- Assess the developmental level of the learner's performance and provide sufficient evidence to support the judgment;
- Diagnose areas requiring attention/instruction and provide an appropriate teaching plan;
- Contribute to the group discussion of the process.

3 Expert judgment

Alverno faculty members assess the candidates' performance thoughtfully. They gather evidence from the candidates' performance and weigh it against the criteria they have developed. For example, in the assessment described above, the faculty members examine the candidates' use of frameworks of development, specifically related to literacy. What aspects of the students' performance do the candidates identify? How do they use examples of performance to describe the developmental level? Do they make explicit the development theories they draw upon? Does their use of performance examples and theory warrant the conclusions they draw? Do their suggestions for further instruction and practice make sense in the light of the developmental needs of the students? Is their plan likely to be effective?

4 Productive feedback

The faculty member's work is not aimed at judgment alone. His or her careful examination of the candidate's reasoning is the first step in developing feedback to guide the candidate's next stage of development. Feedback, keyed to the criteria for a quality performance, is given in various modes — sometimes oral, sometimes written, sometimes individually, and sometimes in a group. Often, peer feedback is incorporated in the process, assisting candidates to learn the meaning of the criteria by having the experience of examining another's performance and finding evidence of strengths and weaknesses.

5 Self assessment

Throughout the program, Alverno faculty have designed all assessments to include the experience of reflective self-assessment. The program's success in helping candidates develop abilities of reflective practice hinges on performance assessments that not only elicit the habits of mind and the skills of the reflective practitioner, but also clearly frame what candidates need to reflect upon. Because performance assessments are situated in authentic contexts and teaching roles, with criteria specifying the expected level of performance, candidates can more easily focus on specific ways they need to improve their teaching than if they merely learned about reflective practice. Moreover, in coming to see assessment as integral, they overcome whatever tendencies toward defensiveness with which they may have started their studies. Most important, developing skill in self-assessment prepares candidates to make habitual the disposition to examine and refine their practice so that, when they leave the supportive environment of their teacher preparation program, they are ready to work as autonomous practitioners.

6 Assessment as a process involving multiple performances

Alverno teacher education candidates will experience hundreds of assessments in their undergraduate program. Rather than seeing assessment as separated from learning, they come to see it as part of learning. Rather than seeing any one assessment as the 'whole story', they recognize that any assessment is a *sample* of performance. The cumulative picture that they draw through experiencing assessment-as-learning across their courses provides an ever deeper and richer portrait of themselves as teachers-to-be. Likewise, assessment in multiple modes and methods and times provides the faculty with confidence in their judgment of the candidate's development of the abilities of the teacher.

Alverno faculty believe that performance assessments are most beneficial when they come as close as possible to the realistic experiences of the practicing teacher. In developing the curriculum for teacher education, they have identified a number of roles that teachers play, including but going beyond the primary role of facilitator of learning in the classroom. Therefore, performance assessments of the abilities of the teacher may be simulated to focus on parent–teacher interaction, multidisciplinary team evaluation, the teacher's work with district or building planning, or the teacher's citizenship role, as well as on actual classroom teaching performance in the field experience and student teaching classrooms. In this way they provide candidates with successive approximations of the role of the teacher.

Collaborative Relationships among Teacher Educators

The fourth component in my thesis is that the preparation of teachers needs to happen in collaborative ways, not only across the various discipline and professional programs in a college or university, but with higher education faculty joining their colleagues in K-12 schools.

Again, NCATE standards (1995) describe the range of types of collaboration required for quality practice in teacher education. Within the college or university itself, the links between liberal arts faculty and teacher educators are critical for the candidates' ability to integrate their discipline learning and their preparation for teaching. Collaborative work across these disciplines in a teacher education program is essential in the development of a coherent and developmental curriculum.

But of utmost importance is the relationship between those responsible for the integration of theory and practice. In the past, teacher education has been weakened by a serious 'disjuncture' between teacher preparation programs and the world of practice. This disjuncture is the focus of John Goodlad's call for the 'simultaneous renewal' of K-12 and teacher education and of the Holmes Group's design of professional development school models of teacher preparation. NCATE standards require clinical experiences in schools with whom the teacher preparation program maintains a relationship.

The *kind* of relationship is critical as well. For too many teacher education programs, schools are sites *used* by candidates, but the teachers and administrators at the sites do not see themselves as being equal partners in the process. New approaches, most visible in the emergence of professional development schools, are changing that picture. These approaches are generally marked by factors like the following:

- clear agreements between college/university and school or school district;
- presence of groups of candidates at the school site, working with teachers and college/university personnel;
- focus on the professional development of the teachers at the site;
- participation in collaborative research undertaken by K-12 teachers, teacher education candidates and college or university teacher educators.

The role of the college or university is critical in creating the circumstances in which teachers are prepared — both in their experience of the liberal arts as connected to their development as teachers and in the consistent linking of theory and practice in their placements in schools and classrooms.

Alverno's Work in Developing Collaborative Relationships

As part of the reconceptualization of its undergraduate degree in the early 1970s, the Alverno faculty developed new means of communication across discipline departments. Most faculty belong to interdisciplinary groups focused on eight general education abilities (Communication, Analysis, Problem Solving, Valuing in Decision Making, Social Interaction, Global Perspective Taking, Effective Citizenship, and Aesthetic Responsiveness) or other cross cutting issues, like international study, technology and teaching, and experiential learning. These interdisciplinary groups are one visible sign of a culture that supports collaboration and communication across disciplines; another is found in the criteria for promotion, which include an explicit expectation of collaborative work.

Moreover, each discipline — not just teacher education — has developed a conceptual framework outlining the abilities that mark, for example, an historian, a psychologist, a biologist, etc. Finally, because the college's mission is focused on the development of the students, the faculty engages in dialogue on a regular basis about ways to improve teaching and learning. Because liberal arts and teacher education faculty have both formal and informal channels for collaboration; the result is curriculum and teaching practice that supports the integration of subject area studies and professional education.

Alverno teacher education faculty see our relationships with practitioners as modeling the ability of coordination for our students. In particular, our efforts to 'establish consistent interaction lines with other teachers' with whom the candidates work are keyed to this ability.

Our relationships with teachers and schools do not follow a single pattern. We seek cooperating teachers for work with candidates in many ways, and while our first choice would be a school where all professionals model the five abilities to an exemplary degree, we also work with a team of teachers from a school and individual teachers whose practice makes them models. We have several partner schools, where groups of candidates may be assigned with a college faculty member.

Our work with professional development in the local schools has been focused by the needs of the Milwaukee Public Schools, an urban system with 150 schools and 102,000 students. The reform effort underway in the district builds on the development of 10 interdisciplinary teaching and learning goals to guide K-12 curriculum. The district is also developing performance assessments of those 10 goals, across content areas. Alverno has become a partner with the district in this reform effort. At their request, and with the support of the Joyce and Bader Foundations, we are working with 9–10 teams of teachers from the middle and high schools each year (over a five year period), to assist them to develop assessment-as-learning approaches in their classrooms. In the Assessing Learning Project, each team attends a two week summer institute and then participates in a year long follow up, during which Alverno faculty work with them on action research projects at the school site. Teachers from the first years of the project have become staff for the succeeding years; the institute is currently co-directed by Alverno teacher education faculty and teachers from the district. Another project now underway with 21 of the elementary schools has a similar focus. The links become ongoing as many of the teachers who have participated in the program become cooperating teachers or portfolio assessors for Alverno teacher education candidates.

While our approach to a professional development relationship with this urban district may strike some as very different (and perhaps not worthy of a more narrowly defined 'PDS' label), we believe that it is having the kind of positive impact sought by those who propose PDSs as important for teacher education. The focus on a joint interest in performance assessment as promoting student learning has led to true collaboration work — for example, in the joint design of the Assessing Learning Project summer institute, joint work on the development of district-wide performance assessments, and the support of specific classroom projects incorporating assessment. In the latter example, groups of Alverno teacher education candidates are assigned in field experiences with teachers from the Assessing Learning Project who want to incorporate new modes of teaching and assessment in their middle or high school classes. One group assisted a team of teachers to establish a 'Socratic Seminar' for sophomore students, with a focus on group discussion and critical thinking. Other candidates have been assigned individually to teachers who are piloting the MPS performance assessments in the arts, oral communication, and problem solving in mathematics and science. These candidates bring their own experiences with performance assessment as well as their understanding of the theory; they work as partners with their cooperating teachers in the pilots.

In our work with teachers, collaborative research is carried on in several ways. First, the incorporation of assessment-as-learning in the classroom provides a rich source of data for a teacher to learn — both about the students and about the teaching/learning process. In some cases, teachers are trying out assessments of their own design in their classrooms. In others, the pilots of district wide assessments are part of a larger study of the impact of these forms of assessment. And, because we are also engaged in an 'archiving process' to document the impact of the Assessing Learning Project, we are working with teachers across classrooms to create videotapes that will assist other teachers to enter into the process of changing the picture of assessment in their classrooms.

We are aware that in many institutions, efforts like the Assessing Learning Project might distract faculty from teacher education, rather than contribute to it.

That's why we choose to focus on collaborative relationships as central, rather than professional development *per se*. The kind of collaboration we describe in the description of our ability of coordination guides our work both on campus with our liberal arts colleagues and in the schools, with our K-12 colleagues.

The Four Components Revisited

It is possible to picture teacher preparation outside of the college or university setting drawing upon the conceptualization of the abilities of the teacher, using as a guide the work of either NBPTS or INTASC. It is less possible to envision ways to develop a coherent, developmental, integrative, reflective process outside of the college or university context. But the kind of assessment-as-learning that both develops and documents the development of candidates is hard to imagine outside of an institution dedicated to the development of its students. Cynics will say it's hard to imagine it happening *in* higher education, but models like Alverno College, Hope College (MI), Clayton State College (GA), the University of Northern Colorado, and Winston-Salem State University (NC) provide 'existence proofs' to the contrary.

And, while the movement toward professional development schools highlights the importance of connecting teacher education with practicing teachers and schools, to provide experiences that are essential in the preparation of candidates, their success depends upon the clarity of the conceptualization of what it means to teach, the coherence of the experiences at the college and at the school site, the quality of assessment that provides documentation of the candidate's development, and the quality of collaboration among all the parties to ensure the prior three.

Performance assessment is key. Without it, we run the risk of leaving the conceptual framework or knowledge bases for teacher education programs abstract and ethereal. Without it, the focus can remain on *what is delivered* to the candidate, as in a collection of courses and experiences, without examining *what happens* to the candidates as a result of their interaction with those courses and experiences. Without it, even the best of relationships with K-12 teachers and administrators will lack the support of data on candidate performance to guide adjustments in collaborative practice.

Yet, clearly, all four components are needed to provide the professional preparation of a teacher. These components need to work in harmony, each influencing the others in a process of continuous improvement. When the Alverno faculty began work to reconceptualize teacher education at Alverno in the late 1970s, we began a process that we now recognize is both ongoing and recursive. As our experience and reflection spark changes in the articulation of the education abilities and concepts that guide the curriculum, we reexamine and refine courses and assessments. As we make changes in courses to respond to needs identified by our colleagues in the schools (most recently in relationship to increase application of technology and to more complex integration across the curriculum), we also look at the descriptions of the abilities and redesign field experiences and assessments. Thus, the four components — which are, together, critical in the preparation of teachers — are also critical to each other.

Note

1 For a more complete description of the development of the Alverno teacher education program, see Diez, 1990.

References

ALVERNO COLLEGE FACULTY (1994) *Student Assessment-as-learning at Alverno College*, Milwaukee, WI: Alverno Productions.

WINGSPREAD GROUP ON HIGHER EDUCATION (1993) *An American Imperative: Higher Expectations for Higher Education*, Racine, WI: The Johnson Foundation.

BROOKS, J.G. and BROOKS, M. (1993) *The Case for Constructivist Classrooms*, Alexandria, VA: Association for Supervision and Curriculum Development.

BRUER, J.T. (1993) *Schools for Thought: A Science of Learning in the Classroom*, Cambridge, MA: MIT Press.

CASE, R. and BEREITER, C. (1984) 'From behaviourism to cognitive behaviourism to cognitive development: Steps in the evolution of instructional design,' *Instructional Science*, **13**, pp. 141–58.

DARLING-HAMMOND, L., WISE, A.E. and KLEIN, S.P. (1995) *A License to Teach*, San Francisco: Westview Press.

DIEZ, M.E. (1990) 'A thrust from within: Reconceptualizing teacher education at Alverno College,' *Peabody Journal of Eduction*, **65**, 2, pp. 4–18.

DIEZ, M.E. (1994) 'Probing the meaning of assessment,' *Essays on Emerging Assessment Issues*, 5–11, Washington, DC: American Association of Colleges for Teacher Education.

HOLMES GROUP (1991) *Tomorrow's Schools*, East Lansing, MI: The Holmes Group.

INTERSTATE NEW TEACHER ASSESSMENT AND SUPPORT CONSORTIUM [INTASC] (1992) *Model Standards for Beginning Teacher Licensing and Development: A Resource for State Dialogue* (Working draft), Washington DC: Council of Chief State School Officers.

JONASSEN, D.H. (1991) 'Objectivism versus constructivism: Do we need a new philosophical paradigm?,' *Educational Technology Research and Development*, **39**, 3, pp. 5–14.

LOACKER, G., CROMWELL, L. and O'BRIEN, K. (1986) 'Assessment in higher education: To serve the learner,' in ADELMAN, C. (ed.) *Assessment in Higher Education: Issues and Contexts* (Report No. OR 86–301, pp. 47–62), Washington, DC: US Department of Education.

NATIONAL BOARD (1994) *What Teachers Should Know and Be Able to Do*, Detroit, MI: National Board for Professional Teaching Standards.

NATIONAL COUNCIL FOR ACCREDITATION OF TEACHER EDUCATION (1997, revision of the 1995 standards) *Standards, Procedures, and Policies for the Accreditation of Professional Education Units*, Washington DC: NCATE Standards.

SHULMAN, L. (1987) 'Knowledge and teaching: Foundations of the new reform,' *Harvard Educational Review*, **57**, pp. 1–22.

STANDARDS PROCEDURES AND POLICIES FOR THE ACCREDITATION OF PROFESSIONAL EDUCATION UNITS (1995) Washington, DC: National Council for the Accreditation of Teacher Education.

17 The Role of the University in Teacher Learning and Development: Present Work and Future Possibilities

Alan J. Reiman

Teacher preparation and development have become increasingly important foci for the process of school reform and educational excellence. A spate of national reports (Carnegie Forum on Education and the Economy, 1986; Commission on Teaching and America's Future, 1996; Holmes Group, 1986; National Governors' Association, 1986) have reaffirmed the importance of quality teacher preparation, induction, and ongoing professional support and development. The National Commission on Teaching and America's Future, for example, in a recent report 'What Matters Most: Teaching for America's Future' (1996) acknowledges that teaching and quality preparation of teachers are the linchpins of real reform. Endorsing an even more significant role for colleges and universities, this report also admonishes policymakers to confront several 'fatal distractions' — myths that hamper thoughtful, coherent, and long-range solutions to teacher development. Among the myths are assertions that anyone can teach, that teachers don't work hard enough, and that teacher education is not of much use. This enduring set of beliefs substitutes 'bromides and platitudes for the hard work required to improve teaching' (1996, p. 51) and teacher preparation in the higher education arena.

In this chapter philosophical and theoretical considerations and practical applications for college- and university-based teacher education are addressed. Because teacher education programs borrow from both the liberal arts traditions and the professional schools traditions *vis à vis* rationale and practice, both traditions are reviewed briefly. In each case, however, the reviews will go beyond a descriptive account. The traditions are analyzed from the standpoint of adequacy as they relate to teacher education and higher education visions. What are the basic tenets of the liberal arts tradition and is it necessary to teacher preparation? How extensive is the research base for the professional schools tradition? And how broad is the evidence base for specific claims as generalized explanations of learning and development? Finally, do any of these programs actually relate to performance? Certainly no theory or practical application, no matter how reasonable and cogently stated, will have utility for teacher development if the connections to performance cannot be determined.

The second section reverses the question. How does university- and college-based teacher education offer anything that can take novices beyond the naive or 'natural teaching skills', like for example, the tendency to talk about what one knows (Bereiter and Scardamalia, 1985; Murray, 1996, p. 3) that some persons argue is a naturally occurring human tendency (Stephens, 1967). Do novice teachers (preservice and induction) perform differently and more effectively after such educational experiences or is such professional development just another time-wasting endeavor that has no consequence in improved learning and/or psychological development? What conditions are most needed for vital college- and university-based teacher education programs that are developmental in orientation?

Obviously the second set of questions are more complex and require an inquiry into the aims and processes of education. In fact, Bruner (1966) suggests the need for a different epistemology to understand professional practice. Although basic research and theory are vital, the practical questions require a theory of instruction or, in this case, a theory of adult learning and development that addresses the unique dimensions of teacher education. The main difference is between describing and prescribing. In the latter case the issue is programmatic and educative. Arranging formal and informal educational experiences that produce learning and development requires an entirely different set of questions, that have only recently been explored in teacher education (Houston, 1990; Murray, 1996; Sikula, 1996). At the conclusion of this examination, a summary and synthesis are presented. The goal will be to frame an emergent framework for college-based teacher learning and development at a point of parsimony between the overly abstract and the narrowly reductionistic.

Higher Education as a Purposeful Learning Environment

Fundamental to colleges/universities is educational purposefulness. Ideally, a commitment to purposeful learning is pervasive on a campus. Anyone who has participated in higher education knows that classroom lectures, participation in research, campus-wide forums, informal discussions and debates, theater productions, concerts, interaction with many international cultures, the student radio and newspaper, literary journals, visual arts programs, volunteer services, student government, and residence living, all contribute to a potentially rich, diverse, intellectual, and aesthetic experience. Further, within the academic arena, colleges and universities have supported intellectual learning in the liberal arts tradition, and later through professional schools. How effective are these academic traditions in promoting purposeful learning environments?

Liberal Arts Tradition

At one end of the continuum is the expert liberal arts framework as a basis for learning and development. The main assumption is that true education is liberal education. Thus expert academicians, without any necessary experience or exposure to the professional aspects of teaching, instead offer exposure to the older traditions, typically through the lecture method. The idea is to develop an inquiring or reflective mind-set by the college students through academic expert knowledge. This approach is a favored learning mission for higher education.

At the highest level of abstraction within the liberal arts approach, higher education assumes substantial gaps in students' knowledge base and the expert professor selects the area for educational learning. Naturally the aim is intellectual learning rather than any immediate connection to professional learning or personal development. In fact, the liberal arts tradition attempts to steer clear of anything that resembles vocationalism. Instead, the liberal arts tradition prefers to stay on the high ground, maintaining that 'great works' can provide illumination on the problems of greatest human concern.

However, scholars of higher education learning and teaching increasingly argue for better connections of traditional teaching to student experiences and personal development. For example, two forthcoming reports from ASHE-ERIC (Student Learning Outside the Classroom: Transcending Artificial Boundaries and Enhancing Student Learning: Reintegrating Intellectual, Social, and Emotional Development) advocate an integration of academic learning to life to enhance both academic learning while promoting intrapersonal/interpersonal, cognitive, and ethnical development.

Admittedly there is some evidence the college- or university-based environment does promote more than intellectual development. For example, studies by Spickelmier (1983) and Deemer (1987) indicate that students with an academic orientation in college grow in ethical reasoning as measured by the Defining Issues Test (Rest, 1986, p. 55). These students follow a 'high road' to development characterized by an educational orientation, an interest in intellectual stimulation, a regard for civic responsibility, and a political awareness. The good news is that ethical reasoning as measured by the DIT, and other developmental assessments, may serve as indirect indicators of undergraduate and graduate interpersonal, intrapersonal, intellectual, and ethical development. The bad news, however, is that studies of programs that emphasize the academic content of humanities, social studies, literature, or contemporary issues show little impact on ethical reasoning development, in particular, or social or intellectual development in general (Rest, 1986). Unfortunately, the liberal arts tradition eschews the empirical, preferring to rely more on the global assumptions of intellectual inquiry, reflection, and illumination through challenge and exposure to leading academic minds.

The Professional Schools' Tradition

The professional schools' tradition is at the opposite end of the higher education continuum. Whereas the liberal arts tradition focuses on content learning and illumination through exposure to great works and great minds, the professional schools' model assumes that educational learning and development are connected more directly to real life problems. Preparation for *action* rather than *content learning/ illumination* is the primary goal of professional schools. In the early decades of this century, for example, the professions of engineering, medicine, and law began to appropriate the prestige of the university by situating their professional schools within it. The prevailing mission of these programs is to build an epistemology of practice (Shils, 1978a). And the major strategy for fulfilling this mission is to prepare prospective practitioners as problem solvers who apply knowledge, theory, and research to solve particular problems in their respective professions. However, the trend has been joined-at-the-hip to an emphasis on learning scientific knowledge, with little attention given to other domains of psychological development such as problem-solving and problem-finding (Arlin, 1984), self-understanding (Loevinger, 1976), ethical reasoning (Rest, 1986), and interpersonal or social perspective-taking (Selman, 1980). Schon's critique (1987) argues that contemporary colleges and universities gave a privileged status to the tradition of expert knowledge in professional schools, bolstering science and technique as the curricula core. Thus, although the professional schools tradition is situated on the opposite end of the knowledge/ practice continuum, it has not, until recently, addressed the need to promote thoughtful and caring practice *vis à vis* psychological development in the interpersonal, intrapersonal, and ethical domains.

Recent scholars like Boyer (1990) suggest the universities must reconceptualize scholarship. Rather than it being a one way street, with basic scientific discoveries first occurring, and then applied, the process should be far more dynamic. As Boyer relates, 'New intellectual understandings can arise out of the very act of application — whether in medical diagnosis, serving clients in psychotherapy, shaping public policy, creating an architectural design, or working with the public schools. In activities such as these, theory and practice vitally interact, and one renews the other' (Boyer, 1990, p. 23). The univesity's role in supporting professional schools is central to learning and development. Such an enterprise contributes to both application and basic discovery, both particularly needed in a world in which complex, almost intractable problems warrant new insights and skills.

Preparation for Indeterminate Zones of Practice

Just mentioned, the professional schools of the modern college or university continue to be grounded in systematic, scientific knowledge with practica as the final opportunity to apply research-based knowledge to the problems of everyday practice. Yet educators worry that something is missing in college-based professional schools. Although they provide more applied experience that can be connected to theory and research, still missing are wisdom, ethics, and 'problem finding'. As a dean of an engineering school put it, 'we know how to teach people how to build ships but not how to figure out what ships to build' (Schon, 1987, p. 11).

Reflecting this Zeitgeist, scholars of the university and student life have called for integration not only of theory and practice, but traditional learning and intellectual, social, and ethical development (Astin and Leland, 1991; Block, 1993; Bryson and Crosby, 1992). For example, they argue that when students learn to collaborate and to treat their peers with civility during controversial discussions they are learning firsthand a core dimension of citizenship. They also point out that the university environment offers a singularly unique setting for this larger vision of integrating learning and personal development. A special report of the Carnegie Foundation for the Advancement of Teaching (1990) spoke to this very issue in Campus Life: In Search of Community. The main thesis of the work is that universities offer a unique and powerful environment for intellectual and moral learning. However, such potential is diminished when an ethos of thoughtful teaching, learning and open, just, caring, and disciplined community is not pervasive.

Such an eductional mission would provide a *neo-in-loco-parentis* framework for higher education, 'a framework that not only could strengthen the spirit of community on campus, but also provide, perhaps, a model for the nation' (Carnegie, 1990, p. 8). Clearly, colleges and universities need to play a central role, not only in academic learning, and more adequate professional practice, but also in developing future leaders. One implication is that college and university learning and development, in the broadest sense, would be defined by student productivity, not faculty productivity. Further, every effort would be made to create 'human scale' settings, characterized by ethics and caring.

Development as a Complementary Goal for Higher Education and Teacher Education

Perhaps the question of the relationship between practical competence and academic learning in college-based teacher education needs to be turned upside down. We should start, not by asking what the proper association is between traditional arts and sciences and professional schools, but rather by asking what we can learn from a careful examination of the role that learning and development play in professional and humane practice and leadership. Murray (1996) makes a similar point when he calls for teacher education scholarship to be organized around children's learning and developmental needs and teachers' responses to them. He adds, 'To connect the curriculum to real student problems is an exceptionally demanding task for the teacher, which is another reason why teachers need specialized knowledge and skill' (Murray, p. 9, 1996). Following this line of thought, colleges and universities (and teacher education) would connect the curriculum to the current learning needs and developmental dispositions of students — educating for understanding and thoughtful and moral practice.

A Developmental Conceptualization of Learning

During the past 20 years, the cognitive science literature unequivocally demonstrates that understanding is dependent upon, and shaped by a person's experience and developmental dispositions. Several lines of theory suggest that understanding is best viewed as mental constructions. These mental constructions are qualitatively different from each other over time. Further, an older student reasons in ways that are new and unavailable to the younger student. A new area of research similarly has examined how young adults construct meaning from experience, and how these

Alan J. Reiman

Figure 17.1   Three faces of teacher development

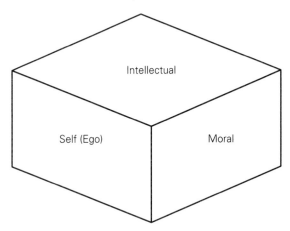

Source: NC State Mentor Curriculum, 1993.

mental constructions are qualitatively different and novel from earlier reasoning. Baltes and Schaie (1976) liberated the field of cognitive psychology with their findings on adult plasticity. Likewise Piaget (1972) suggested the possibility of adult cognitive growth in his later works, a theme examined in detail by Arlin (1984). In a similar vein, Loevinger (1976), Selman (1980) and Kegan (1994) have studied interpersonal and intrapersonal development in adults, and Rest (1986) has summarized research on the growth of ethical reasoning in adults (see Figure 17.1).

What the just cited researchers find is that there is the potential for cognitive, interpersonal, intrapersonal, and ethical development for adults. Persons do not have to initiate a slow slide into senility beginning sometime after adolescence. A meta-analysis by Lee and Snarey (1988) confirms the wisdom of this revision with longitudinal growth patterns for both ego and moral development. They found that the process of ego (self-understanding) and moral development continues into adulthood but not at the same rate. Thus, during early adulthood, ego development is somewhat in advance of moral development, both domains are in parity in the middle phase, and moral development is in advance during later adulthood. Both Kegan's (1994) and Arlin's (1986) work demonstrate the possibility of cognitive-developmental growth beyond the early Piagetian formulations. Further, persons at more complex stages are more empathic, principled, more tolerant of ambiguity, and more flexible in resolving complex human-helping problems (Sprinthall, Reiman and Thies-Sprinthall, 1996).

Wisdom has been conceptualized as a hallmark of adult development (Arlin, 1986, 1990) and is strikingly similar to Erikson's (1982) theory of generativity in the adult life span. These lines of inquiry have examined how adults construct and use their knowledge and how such reasoning is associated to persons' sense of self (including how they relate to others) and to ethical reasoning. The process by which persons attempt to make meaning of their experiences (knowledge construction, self-understanding, and ethical understanding) is developmental and improves over time under certain conditions. Perkins (1992), who summarizes a developmental sequence for knowledge acquisition: retention of knowledge — understanding of knowledge — thoughtful practice with knowledge, cites research on the importance of generative experiences.

Thus, the current period in teacher development research can be considered as a time of transition. Old models of adult and teacher learning have given way to a new series of research initiatives that have been appearing since the mid-1980s. The goals are broad, namely, to create a firm basis in theory and research for the practice of professional teacher development as it first unfolds at the university, and later as the new teacher enters the classroom. It may be premature, however, to suggest anything more than the possibility of a growing consensus. Can the emergent developmental paradigm, for example, also explain idiographic and individual differences? Certainly the dilemma of the broad gauge versus the narrow gauge theory also creates difficulties.

Katz and Rath (1985) have stated the problem cleverly with their 'Goldilocks Principle'. Some theory for teacher development is extremely broad and abstract. Certainly some of the psychoanalytic and humanistic theories represent such excessively broad propositions. Yet, Katz and Raths also note the other side of the problem. Theory can be so focused on specifics that the framework becomes too narrow. The process–product behavioristic approach represents just such an example of reducing human complexity to a few simple-minded propositions. Thus the behavioristic model creates a theoretical bed that is far too small. Goldilocks serves as a metaphor for professional teacher education schools within the college or university. It potentially wanders from place to place seeking a better fit as the field itself tries to build theory, research, and practice.

In fact, several studies have observed that there are often 'loose linkages' between the three strands of teacher preparation programs — liberal arts education, professional study, and practical experiences (Goodlad, 1990; Schwartz, 1988; Zeichner, 1986). For example, the fact that colleges have been unable to exert much influence on the nature or quality of the student teaching experience is but one example of fragmentation. Principals often choose cooperating teachers 'based on administrative convenience rather than educational value' (Darling-Hammond and Goodwin, 1993, p. 37). Further, cooperating teachers who can potentially have a remarkable positive or negative effect on the student teacher, often receive little or no training for their roles. Given that college supervisors average only six visits to a student teacher per semester (American Association of Colleges for Teacher Education, 1987), the cooperating teacher is very influential in the student's clinical experience. However, without the careful integration of theory, research, and practice, Goldilocks will continue to traverse from fad to fad — never appreciating the differences between the cosmic and the trivial.

The challenge for teacher education, then, is complex. There is no neat linear equation from theory to practice nor the other way from practice to theory. And there are no simple formulas for integrating academic learning, professional practice, and developmental goals. Yet, as Griffin (1987) found, effective university and college teacher education programs are based on a conception of teacher growth and development; acknowledge the complexities of classroom, school, and community; are grounded in a substantial and verifiable knowledge base; and are sensitive to the ways teachers think, feel, and make meaning from their experiences. With these considerations in mind, a closer look is given to the relationship between teacher education and college/university.

As mentioned previously, the liberal arts tradition and the professional schools tradition have had an important but uneasy alliance. Teacher education programs are a case in point. As studies just mentioned illustrate, there are often 'loose linkages' and lack of continuity between the three strands of teacher preparation programs — liberal arts education, professional study, and practical experiences (Goodlad, 1990; Schwartz, 1988; Zeichner, 1986).

Some policy-makers have responded by calling for the elimination or reduction of teacher education programs. Clabaugh and Rozycki (1996) describe the devaluation of teacher preparation in stark terms. One example given is Perot's persuasion of the Texas legislature to restrict required teacher preparation coursework to no more than 18 credit hours including student teaching. Those who would abandon teacher education often leap to the conclusion that subject matter knowledge is both necessary and sufficient for teaching competence. Subject matter knowledge is certainly not sufficient. As a counterpoint, the authors point out that in order to treat foot disorders in Texas, one must have studied graduate-level biomedical and clinical pediatry for four years and, as of 1995, serve a year's residency — the equivalent of 240 credits, which is more than 13 times the study it now takes to become a Texas teacher. Both academic knowledge and professional practice are needed. Additionally, prospective teachers must learn, recognize, and understand the ways the students learn and develop intellectually, socially, and morally. Less discussed or understood, however, is that such an understanding of student learning and development requires the prospective teacher to be at sufficiently complex plateaus of intellectual, social, and ethical reasoning, so as to be able to recognize and promote such development in students.

Does Development Make a Difference?

But do higher developmental stages make a difference in the real world of adult (and teacher) behavior? Over the past 20 years there have been a series of studies and meta-analyses which validate the question yet only under certain circumstances. Hunt (1974) had shown that conceptual complexity interacted with teacher tasks. At more complex stages, teachers were more flexible, more adaptive, and more effective (Sprinthall, Reiman and Thies-Sprinthall, 1996). Blasi (1980) also had shown a steady positive relationship between justice reasoning levels and behavior in a meta-analyses of 80 studies. Miller (1981) in his review of a large number of conceptual level studies and performance in teaching, reported a consistently positive relationship. The same findings were reported by Holloway and Wampold (1986) for professional counselors. In each case the task, providing help to another person in a humane atmosphere where the goal is to enhance the other person's professional knowledge, skills, and growth toward automony, allocentrism, and conceptual complexity required more complex developmental dispositions by the teacher or counselor. As O'Keefe and Johnston (1989) found, teachers who process experience more complexly have a greater ability to 'read and flex' with pupils, to take the emotional perspective of others, and to think on their feet and find alternative solutions (less 'functional fixedness'). It is important to note that 'higher is not happier' (Loevinger, 1976). At greater levels of cognitive complexity an adult is more aware of the plethora of barriers to growth.

In general then, higher plateaus of cognitive development predict performance in complex human-helping tasks like teaching. Other more conventional indices such as grade point average, standardized intelligence/achievement measures, or static personality traits do not (Sprinthall and Thies-Sprinthall, 1983). With the research base outlining the advantages of developmental dispositions as predictors of behavior, can college teacher education programs promote such development? A review of adult base rates in the three domains discussed here: interpersonal/ intrapersonal, intellectual, and ethical development would not inspire such a sense of accomplishment. For example Hunt (1974) found student teachers functioning just below the midpoint on his scale of conceptual complexity. Loevinger (1976) reported that the modal stage for adults was between Stage 3 and Stage 4 on her levels of ego development (intrapersonal and interpersonal), between conformity and autonomy. Similarly Rest (1986) reports that most adults function at the midpoint of his scales as well. And, as was noted earlier, research has shown that standard academic instruction has marginal effect on ethical reasoning. Likewise, conceptual development studies and subsequent reflections have led to the following observations:

1 Cognitive-developmental theory can be applied to adults.
2 There is a consistent predictive relationship between more complex stages and performances in complex human helping tasks like teaching.
3 The intellectual, interpersonal/intrapersonal, and ethical complexity of teachers is necessary for teaching in today's schools.
4 The general developmental levels of preservice teachers and adults in general are modest, about the mid-point on various indices of development.
5 Traditional university education appears to assume rather than promote development.
6 College or university teacher education programs should examine how the professional education strand of students' experiences might bolster development across the three domains described (i.e., intellectual, interpersonal/ intrapersonal, and ethical).

Bridging Learning to Practice: A Role-taking/Reflection Framework

A series of field-based studies has shown that cognitive-structural growth along the intellectual, interpersonal/intrapersonal, and ethical domains requires five elements in teacher education programs (Sprinthall, Reiman and Thies-Sprinthall, 1996).

These elements could be aligned in unique and powerful ways by teacher education programs, liberal arts programs, and public school partners. The conditions
included the following:

1   Role-taking (not role playing)

This element is based on Mead's concept of social role taking. It requires a person
to undertake a complex new human helping role such as tutoring, student teaching,
or working in a community internship. The role-taking (action) precedes and shapes
the intellectual consciousness (reflection) that grows out of it.

2   Reflection

'All reflective thought arises out of real problems present in immediate experience'
(Mead, 1934, p. 7). For Mead, reflection did not have value in and of itself, rather
it is inherent in lived experience and the dialogue between persons participating in
new experiences. Thus sequenced readings, journaling, and discussions of the role-
taking experiences are necessary. However, one cannot assume a sophisticated
fluency with reflection. It has become obvious, for example, that cooperating teachers and mentors need help in learning how to guide the reflections of novice
teachers (Reiman and Thies-Sprinthall, 1993).

3   Balance

It is important that action and reflection remain in balance or as praxis. Usually, this
means that the complex new role is sequenced with guided reflection each week.
Too great a time lag between the action and reflection or the other way around halts
the growth process.

4   Continuity

There is a learning truism that spaced practice is vastly superior to massed. We
have found that the complex goals of promoting cognitive-structural growth in the
interpersonal, intrapersonal, conceptual, and moral/ethical domain requires a continuous interplay between action and reflection. A one or two-week workshop
followed by actual helping has not caused shifts in the cognitive structures of the
participants. Typically, at least one semester and preferably two semesters are
needed for significant structural growth. Thus, the university or college provides an
optimum setting for student development.

5   Support and challenge

Essentially, we rediscovered Vygotsky's zone of proximal growth (1978). The
condition requires educators to provide support and challenge that is appropriate to
the learning and developmental needs of students. Vygotsky's zone or what Hunt
(1976) calls the arena for the constructive mismatch requires substantial 'reading
and flexing' on the part of the instructor. Support must be provided when dis-
equilibrium is great, however, as the learner becomes more confident, challenge or
mismatching is provided. This is the most complex pedagogical requirement of the
developmental approach.

Bridging Learning to Practice: Coaching and Laboratory Experiences

As just noted, teacher education, like other fields, can benefit from a theory of instruction. Such a theory would enable faculty to elaborate delivery systems within teacher education. However, without a clear view of the why, what, and how of a theory, it can end up as directionless — shades of J. Abner Peddiwell's Saber Tooth Tiger. Do we educate specific skills as a latter-day version of paleolithic skills with Peddiwell's clubs and hand-fishing? Or do we educate for understanding and thoughtful, caring, and moral practice? In the author's view, one avoids such a choice. It is not an either/or question. Instead, university and college-based teacher education must be guided by a theoretical framework that is sufficiently comprehensive to address specific skills as well as humane practice. In other words, it may be possible to have a dual focus on specific behavioral teaching skills (e.g., learning models of instruction) on the one hand, and addressing human development on the other. The cognitive-developmental framework just described addresses human development. But what about the learning of specific pedagogies that promote student learning and development?

During the 1980s Joyce and Showers organized the components of an effective coaching framework. These components have been studied and data is accumulating in support of the framework (Joyce and Showers, 1995). The four components in the approach are:

a   describing and understanding the model;
b   viewing the model;
c   planning and/or peer teaching the model with opportunities for sustained feedback; and
d   adapting the model to new situations.

When the model can be adapted to new contexts, Joyce and Showers identify the person as having 'executive control' of the instructional model. In our own research and program development, however, two additional components have been added to strengthen the overall framework. Before describing the model, prior knowledge and experience with the model should be assessed. This pre-assessment offers an opportunity to create generative experiences (Perkins, 1992) as part of the introduction of the model. Additionally, a step is added after the fourth component (adapting the model). This final step is post-assessment. Thus, the student is able to maintain a portfolio of their learning performances throughout their teacher education experience.

A related area of importance are college laboratory-based experiences which have been supported by research (Allen and Ryan, 1969; Berliner, 1985; Metcalf, 1992; Winitsky and Arends, 1991). Although field-based experiences represent an important and increasing proportion of the teacher preparation curriculum, there is increasing concern that experiences of longer duration have resulted in saturation of field placements and overwhelming supervisory loads (Guyton and McIntyre, 1990).

Figure 17.2 *Teaching/learning framework*

Conditions for Instructional Coaching	Conditions for Development
* Pre-assessment	1 Significant New Role
1 Rational/Theory	2 Guided Reflection
2 Demonstration	3 Balance between Experience and Reflection
3 Practice with Feedback	4 Support and Challenge
4 Adapt and Generalize	5 Continuity
* Post-assessment	

A meta-analysis of 60 studies of laboratory experiences showed that such experiences produce consistent and positive results in terms of teacher affect, knowledge, and behavior (Metcalf, 1996). There is no consistent diminution over time in the changes produced by the laboratory experiences. 'Furthermore, there is no evidence indicating that a series of laboratory experiences must culminate in natural classroom practice. Rather, work with school-age learners is likely to be most efficacious when simulated, on-campus experiences precede and follow it' (Metcalf, 1994, p. 110).

Colleges and universities offer an ideal setting for further research and development of microteaching, case-based instruction, interactive computer simulations, and other laboratory-based experiences. It is important to point out that laboratory experiences had the least impact on the affective or interpersonal development of preservice students. However, on-campus laboratory experiences hold the potential to provide effective, highly efficient professional experiences, and may be superior to extensive and extended field-based experiences, particularly when the cooperating or clinical teachers have had minimal training for their roles.

Similar findings have been reported in the developmental literature. For example, a quasi-experimental study by Exum (1980) found the amount of field-based experience each week was less important than the analysis and reflection on the experience. Experience by itself, as Dewey noted (1938), can be educative or miseducative. It is not simply the adding-on of new experiences and new systems to process meaning. Instead, new learning requires cognitive structural change. And significant educative experiences require high quality analysis and reflection that is appropriately matched and mismatched according to the needs of the adult learner. Both the roletaking/reflection framework and the coaching framework have been synthesized as an overall theoretical construct for teacher education (see Figure 17.2).

The Case for Differentiated Teacher Education

New findings in cognitive science and human development have confirmed the ingenuity of Piaget and his methods. However, these new findings also have shown that the story of human development is more complex than originally hypothesized by Piaget. In particular, contrary to Piaget's notion that stages have a universal cross-disciplinary character, it now appers that the progression to more sophistic-ated patterns of abstract or formal reasoning is often discipline specific. Growth is asynchronous. Therefore one cannot assume that complex reasoning skills in math-ematics transfer to science. Or that complex intellectual abilities imply the person also possesses high complexity in interpersonal, intrapersonal, or moral domains. Thus the educator must be prepared to 'read and flex' instruction and experiences according to the needs of the adult learner. Developmental theory based on the assumption of growth is a result of appropriate interaction in facilitating environ-ments. The theory, by the way, does not suggest static personality states.

For teacher education, such a transfer would move toward the creation of different learning atmospheres for prospective teachers — a teacher education cur-riculum differentiated by learning components (prior knowledge, explanations, demonstrations, practice, roletaking experiences, reflection/analysis, types of feed-back, adaptations, and assessments). A case in point is a college program developed and studied by Widick, Knelfelkamp, and Parker (1975) which found that a differ-entiated curriculum could stimulate conceptual development and that different strategies work only for particular groups. More recent examples of successful researched programs that differentiate instruction include Sprinthall and Scott (1989) and Reiman and Thies-Sprinthall (1993). Also, research is being conducted on innovative support programs for first-year college students (Bulletin, 1996). Findings converge on one main point. The college setting provides a powerful environment for coordinating such experiences.

Needed Vision of Teacher Education Excellence

Should teacher educators expand their university and college-based programs to include more than academic excellence and subject-matter expertise or does aca-demic excellence predict future success in today's classrooms? A careful analysis of relationships between academic excellence and human excellence, finds almost no relationship (Heath, 1994; McClelland, 1985). Academic grades do not predict who will and who will not fulfill their adult roles successfully, and they only modestly predict an adult's job status. Further, academic aptitude scores predicted no positive adult outcomes, including measures of occupational success. This said, no one would dispute the primacy of basic academic skills and knowledge. What is missing, however, is a conception of healthy human development or psychological maturity and the development of teachers' pedagogical conceptions and actions (Ammons and Hutcheson, 1989).

Can we create teacher education programs that produce students who are problem solvers, ethically driven, and other-centered? Perhaps. Selected colleges and universities have demonstrated some success in helping future leaders become more interpersonally aware, reflective, and principled. For example, Alverno College selected interpersonal maturity and value maturity as two of the most important competencies that students need for the future, and have organized their curric-ulum to promote the growth of these competencies. Studies of the Alverno College program demonstrate that enhanced interpersonal awareness can be taught (Much and Mentkowski, 1982). Studies have also demonstrated that intentional interventions in teacher preparatory programs to promote growth of self-understanding, allocentrism, and principled reasoning can be successful (Black, 1989; Newman, 1993; Reiman and Parramore, 1993; Zeichner, 1986).

Putting such a vision into action, however, requires teacher education programs and the larger college or university institution to work collaboratively toward such a vision. Referring back to the theoretical conditions of human development mentioned earlier (see Figure 17.2), a series of questions could be asked by institutions hoping to invent or reculture a teacher education program that hopes to promote human excellence. Some theory-based questions follow:

1 Complex new helping experiences

How can complex helping experiences be integrated into the college learning environment? How might such experience be graduated or sequenced? Are there new roles within teacher preparation that might encourage student reflection on social and environmental justice issues? How might growth from such experiences be assessed?

2 Guided reflection

How can faculty be prepared to guide student reflection? How are instructor written responses to student reflections differentiated according to student developmental levels? What role should journals play in the university setting? How might a developmentally coherent curriculum be implemented across the student teachers' teacher education program? How should students of teaching be educated to initiate high quality student–teacher, parent–teacher, and teacher–teacher relationships that are characterized by authenticity, empathy, and regard?

3 Support and challenge

How can accrediting and legislative groups be mobilized to recognize the importance of psychological maturing outcomes like interpersonal understanding? How can faculty be rewarded for promoting mind, character, and self in the student body? How can large institutions be made more human scale, in order to promote a more caring ethos? Should teacher education programs forge closer relationships between students and faculty like, for example, having faculty participate in non-age-graded experiential and flexible classes and curriculum over the entire four-year college experience? How can future teachers assume mentoring roles while they are participating in their teacher preparation program?

4 Continuity

How can future teachers be encouraged to appreciate the connectedness they have with students, parents, and peers? How might the transition from preservice teacher education to the beginning years be made more seamless? In what ways might the university and teacher education program be aligned so that future teachers experience frequent exemplars of high quality teaching? How might new teaching skills be monitored to assess how easily they are transferred to classroom settings?

Teacher Education for Democracy and Full Human Competence

As Dewey (1938) illustrated, the full human development of students ensures that civic participation is experienced by everyone. Democratic education means learning to contribute to the common good through the daily decisions we make and the problems we solve, to love and care for others, and to have good character. These competencies are indispensable in a democratic society.

Dewey's vision of a genuinely democratic school as an institution remains as an ideal and compass for both teacher education and the larger colleges/university settings. Unfortunately, and all too frequently, the curriculum of these institutions promotes partial human competence. Academic curriculum is no guarantor for students to reach their intellectual, interpersonal, and character potentials. Needed are learning environments (persons, experiences, and curriculum) that are consistently organized to be just beyond the students' current preferred ways of solving problems. As one colleague puts it, we need an academic world inhabited by peers and adults who think about the world and behave in it in a 'zone of next development' (Mosher, Kenny and Garrod, 1994, p. 168). Teacher educational goals must reach beyond simply matching the intellectual developmental tasks of future teachers. While intellectual development is important, our future teachers do not need to go to the university or college merely for development from the neck up (Oja and Reiman, 1996). Development as the aim of education does not happen in a one or two week experience. Full human development takes time. For Dewey, the growth of the individual involves an enlargement of both his or her social perspective and socio-moral commitments, while the person is simultaneously acquiring the skill and knowledge to resolve complex problems. The conclusion is inescapable: Dewey meant to create in schools the social, governmental, curricular, and instructional conditions that could support persons' full development.

In our future, all teacher education programs and the college or university institutions that support them, must create curriculum and instruction of human scale, priding themselves upon creating learning environments that draw upon the life-experience of future teachers. Schools are democratic to the extent that they contribute to the all-around growth of every student. Directing the nature and quality of future teachers' experience to enhance their learning and growth must become our *raison d'être* and the initiation of these efforts must be a continuous reflective process with experiences that model consecutiveness and planned order. The true measure of our success is when those student teachers in turn promote the full development of their own students.

Universities and colleges provide a unique role in the education of future citizens and the education of future teachers. As an academic community, they provide an ideal place for laboratory experiences. They also have unmatched potential for creating learning environments that promote full human competence. Astin's multi-institutional longitudinal study of more than 20,000 students, 25,000 faculty, and 200 institutions in *What Matters in College? Four Critical Years Revisited* (1993) is a vivid and exhausting examination of universities as learning centers. However such environments must be deliberate, organized for the 'next zone of development'. Dewey's central view was to promote a balance between experiential learning and careful, rational examination. He did not want students simply to experience in a vacuum. What Dewey didn't know was what characterizes development, whether it be intellectual, social, or moral, at particular stages. A generation of research in genetic epistemology and developmental psychology now offers educators relatively clear blueprints of what people are like at various stages of their lives and what stimulates their intellectual, moral, and personal-social growth. A challenge for college-based teacher education is to find the right balance between reflection, analysis, and experience.

Kohlberg (1980) believed the American Revolution was unfinished; that the moral and rational capacity for full democracy and justice was latent in human thought and must be stimulated by experiences such as complex new roles, or living in a democratic community such as the college. This objective is undertaken when real moral issues of justice, rights, and obligations are decided by all. Colleges and universities, and the teacher education programs that reside within, offer an extraordinary means of setting free and developing the capacities of future teachers, without respect to race, gender, class or economic status. And the future test of this enlarged vision will be the extent to which they educate all future teachers into the full stature of their possibility. Our third president, Thomas Jefferson, said it best: 'If a nation expects to be ignorant and free in a state of civilization, it expects what never was and never will be' (1816).

References

ALLEN, D. and RYAN, K. (1969) *Microteaching*, Reading, MA: Addison-Wesley.

AMERICAN ASSOCIATION OF COLLEGES FOR TEACHER EDUCATION (1987) *Teaching Teachers: Facts and Figures (RATE I)*, Washington, DC: American Association of Colleges for Teacher Education.

AMMONS, P. and HUTCHESON, B.P. (1989) 'Promoting the development of teachers' pedagogical conceptions', *Genetic Epistemologist*, **17**, 4, pp. 23–9.

ARLIN, P. (1984) 'Adolescent and adult thought: A structural interpretation', in ARMON, C., COMMONS, M. and RICHARDS, F. (eds) *Beyond Formal Operations: Late Adolescent and Adult Cognitive Development*, New York: Praeger, pp. 258–71.

ARLIN, P. (1986) 'Problem finding and young adult cognition', in MINES, R.A. and KITCHENER, K. (eds) *Adult Cognitive Development: Methods and Models*, New York: Praeger, pp. 22–32.

ARLIN, P. (1990) 'Wisdom: The art of problem finding', in STERNBERG, R.J. (ed.) *Wisdom: Its Nature, Origins, and Development*, New York: Cambridge University Press, pp. 230–43.

ASTIN, A.W. (1993) *What Matters Most in College?*, San Francisco: Jossey-Bass.

ASTIN, H.S. and LELAND, C. (1991) *Women of Influence, Women of Vision: A Cross-generational Study of Leaders and Social Change*, San Francisco: Jossey-Bass.

BALTES, P. and SCHAIE, K.W. (1976) 'On the plasticity of intelligence in adulthood and old age: Where horn and donaldson fail', *American Psychologist*, **31**, 10, pp. 720–5.

BEREITER, C. and SCARDAMALIA, M. (1985) 'Cognitive coping strategies and the problem of inert knowledge', in CHIPMAN, S.S., SEGAL, J.W. and GLAZER, R. (eds) *Thinking and Learning Skills (Vol. 2): Current Research and Open Questions*, Hillsdale, NJ: Erlbaum, pp. 65–80.

BERLINER, D. (1985) 'Laboratory settings and the study of teacher education', *Journal of Teacher Education*, **36**, 6, pp. 2–8.

BLACK, A. (1989) 'Developmental teacher education', *Genetic Epistemologist*, **17**, 4, pp. 5–14.

BLASI, A.G. (1980) 'Bridging moral cognition and moral action: A critical review of the literature', *Psychological Bulletin*, **88**, 1, pp. 1–45.

BLOCK, P. (1993) *Stewardship: Choosing Service over Self-interest*, San Francisco: Berrett-Koehler.

BOYER, E. (1990) *Scholarship Reconsidered: Priorities of the Professoriate*, Princeton, NJ: The Carnegie Foundation for the Advancement of Teaching.

BRUNER, J. (1966) *Toward a Theory of Instruction*, New York: Norton.

BRYSON, J.M. and CROSBY, B.C. (1992) *Leadership for the Common Good: Tackling Public Problems in a Shared-power World*, San Francisco: Jossey-Bass.

BULLETIN (1996) 'First-year college officials report results of inaugural year', LXVIII **14**, pp. 1–3, NC State University, Raleigh.

CARNEGIE FOUNDATION FOR THE ADVANCEMENT OF TEACHING (1990) *Campus Life: In Search of Community*, Princeton, New Jersey.

CARNEGIE FORUM ON EDUCATION AND THE ECONOMY (1986) *A Nation Prepared: Teachers for the 21st Century*, New York: Carnegie Foundation.

CLABAUGH, G. and ROZYCKI, E.G. (1996) 'Foundations of education and the devaluation of teacher preparation', in MURRAY, F. (ed.) *The Teacher Educator's Handbook*, San Francisco: Jossey-Bass, pp. 395–418.

COMMISSION ON TEACHING AND AMERICA'S FUTURE (1996) *What Matters Most: Teaching for America's Future*, New York: Rockefeller Foundation and Carnegie Corporation.

DARLING-HAMMOND, L. and GOODWIN, A.L. (1993) 'Progress toward professionalism in teaching', in CAWELT, G. (ed.) *Challenges and Achievements of American Education*, Alexandria, VA.: Association for Supervision and Curriculum Development.

DEEMER, D. (1987) 'Life experiences and moral judgment development', Doctoral dissertation, Minneapolis, MN: University of Minnesota.

DEWEY, J. (1933) *How We Think: A Restatement of the Relation of Reflective Thinking to the Educative Process*, Chicago: Henry Regenery.

DEWEY, J. (1938) *Experience and Education*, New York: Collier Macmillan.

ERIKSON, E. (1977) '*Cross-age and peer teaching*', Unpublished doctoral dissertation, University of Minnesota.

ERIKSON, E. (1982) *The Life Cycle Completed*, New York: Norton. Exum, H.

EXUM, H. (1980) 'Ego development: Using curriculum to facilitate growth', *Character Potential*, **9**, pp. 121–8.

GOODLAD, J. (1990) *Teachers for Our Nations Schools*, San Francisco: Jossey-Bass.

GRIFFIN, G. (1987) 'Clinical teacher education', *Journal of Curriculum and Supervision*, **2**, 3, pp. 248–74.

GUYTON, E. and McINTYRE, J. (1990) 'Student teaching and school experiences', in HOUSTON, R. (ed.) *Handbook of Research on Teacher Education*, New York: Macmillan, pp. 514–34.

HEATH, D. (1994) *Schools of Hope*, San Francisco: Jossey-Bass.

HOLMES GROUP (1986) *Tomorrow's Teachers: A Report of the Holmes Group*, East Lansing, Michigan: Holmes Group.

HOLLOWAY, E. and WAMPOLD, B. (1986) 'Relation between conceptual level and counselling related tasks', *Journal of Counselling Psychology*, **33**, 3, pp. 310–19.

HOUSTON, R. (1990) *Handbook of Research on Teacher Education*, New York: Macmillan.

HUNT, D. (1974) *Matching Models in Education*, Toronto, Canada: Ontario Institute for Studies in Education.

HUNT, D. (1976) 'Teachers' adaptation: "Reading and flexing" to students', *Journal of Teacher Education*, **27**, 3, pp. 268–75.

JEFFERSON, T. (1816) 'Letter to Colonel Charles Yancey'.

JOYCE, B. and SHOWERS, B. (1995) *Staff Development for Student Achievement*, New York: Longman.

KATZ, L. and RATHS, J. (1985) 'Disposition as goals for teacher education', *Teaching and Teacher Education*, **1**, 4, pp. 304–7.

KEGAN, R. (1994) *In Over Our Heads: The Mental Demands of Modern Life*, Cambridge, MA.: Harvard University Press.

KING, P.L. and MAGOLDA, B.M. (1996) 'A developmental perspective on learning', *Journal of College Student Development*, **37**, 2, pp. 163–73.

KING, P.M. and KITCHENER, K.S. (1994) *Developing Reflective Judgment: Understanding and Promoting Intellectual Growth and Critical Thinking in Adolescents and Adults*, San Francisco: Jossey-Bass.

KNEFELKAMP, L.L. (1974) 'Developmental instruction: Fostering intellectual and personal growth of college students', Unpublished doctoral dissertation, University of Minnesota.

KOHLBERG, L. (1980) 'High school democracy and educating for a just society', in MOSHER, R.L. (ed.) *Moral Education: A First Generation of Research and Development (Chapter I)*, New York: Praeger.

KUH, G.D., DOUGLAS, K.B., LUND, J.P. and RAMIN-GYURNEK, J. (In Press) 'Student learning outside the classroom: Transcending artificial boundaries', *ASHE-ERIC Higher Education Report*.

LEE, L. and SNAREY, J. (1988) 'The relationship between ego and moral development', in LAPSLEY, D. and POWER, C. (eds) *Self, Ego and Identity*, New York: Springer-Verlag, pp. 151–78.

LOEVINGER, J. (1976) *Ego Development*, San Francisco: Jossey-Bass.

LOEVINGER, J. (1987) *Paradigms of Personality*, New York: Freeman.

LOVE, P.G. and LOVE, A.G. (In Press) 'Enhancing student learning: Reintegrating intellectual, social and emotional development', *ASHE-ERIC Higher Education Report*.

McCLELLAND, D. (1985) *Human Motivation*, New York: Scott Foresman.

MEAD, G.H. (1934) *Mind, Self, and Society*, Chicago: The University of Chicago Press.

METCALF, K. (1992) 'The effects of a guided training experience on the instructional clarity of preservice teachers', *Teaching and Teacher Education*, **8**, 3, pp. 275–86.

METCALF, K. (1994) 'Laboratory experiences in teacher education', in POSTLETHWAITE, T. and HUSEN, T. (eds) *International Encyclopedia of Education* (2nd ed.) Oxford: Pergamon, pp. 3197–202.

METCALF, K. and KAHLICH, P.A. (1996) 'Laboratory experiences as transition from campus to field', in McINTYRE, D. and BYRD, D. (eds) Teacher Education Yearbook V, Reston, VA: Association of Teacher Educators, pp. 97–114.

MILLER, A. (1981) 'Conceptual matching models and interactional research in education', *Review of Educational Research*, **51**, 1, pp. 33–84.

MOSHER, R., KENNY, R.A. and GARROD, A. (1994) *Preparing for Citizenship*, Westport, Connecticut: Jaeger Press.

MUCH, N. and MENTKOWSKI, M. (1982) *Student Perspectives on Liberal Learning at Alverno College: Justifying Learning as Relevant to Performance in Personal and Professional Roles*, Milwaukee, WI: Office of Research and Evaluation.

MURRAY, F. (1996) 'Beyond natural teaching: The case for professional education', in MURRAY, F. (ed.) *The Teacher Educator's Handbook: Building a Knowledge Base for the Preparation of Teachers*, San Francisco: Jossey-Bass, pp. 3–13.

NATIONAL GOVERNORS' ASSOCIATION (1986) *Time for Results: The Governors' 1991 Report on Education*, Washington, DC: National Governors' Association.

NEWMAN, L. (1993) 'The beginnings of expertise: A neo-Piagetian perspective on student teachers representation of the problem of adapting differences among learners', *Learning and Individual Differences*, **5**, 4, pp. 351–71.

O'KEEFE, P. and JOHNSTON, M. (1989) 'Perspective taking and teacher effectiveness: A connecting thread through three developmental literatures', *Journal of Teacher Education*, **40**, 3, pp. 20–6.

OJA, S.N. and REIMAN, A.J. (1996) 'Describing and promoting supervision for teacher development across the career span', in FIRTH, J. and PAJAK, E. (eds) *Handbook of Research on School Supervision*, New York: Macmillan.

OJA, S.N. and SMULYAN, L. (1989) *Collaborative Action Research: A Developmental Approach*, London: Falmer Press.

PERKINS, D. (1992) *Smart Schools: From Training Memories to Educating Minds*, New York: Macmillan.

PIAGET, J. (1972) 'Intellectual evolution from adolescence to adulthood', *Human Development*, **15**, 1, pp. 1–12.

REIMAN, A.J. and PARRAMORE, B. (1993) 'Promoting preservice teacher development through extended field experience', in O'HAIR, M. and ODELL, S. (eds) *Teacher Education Yearbook I: Diversity and Teaching*, Fort Worth: Harcourt Brace Jovanovich, pp. 111–21.

REIMAN, A.J. and THIES-SPRINTHALL, L. (1993) 'Promoting the development of mentor teachers: Theory and research programs using guided reflection', *Journal of Research and Development*, **26**, 3, pp. 179–85.

REIMAN, A.J. and THIES-SPRINTHALL, L. (In Press) *Supervision and Mentoring for Teacher Development*, New York: Longman.

REST, J. (1986) *Moral Development: Advances in Research and Theory*, Westport, Connecticut: Praeger.

SCHMIDT, J.A. (1985) 'Older and wiser? A longitudinal study of the impact of college on intellectual development', *Journal of College Student Personnel*, **26**, 5, pp. 388–94.

SCHON, D. (1987) *Educating the Reflective Practitioner*, San Francisco: Jossey-Bass.

SCHWARTZ, C. (1988) 'Unapplied curriculum knowledge', in TANNER, L.N. (ed.) *Critical Issues in Curriculum* (87th yearbook of the National Society for the Study of Education), Chicago: University of Chicago Press.

SELMAN, R. (1980) *The Growth of the Interpersonal Self*, New York: Academy Press.

SHILS, E. (1978a) 'The order of learning in the United States from 1865 to 1920: The ascendancy of the universities', *Minerva*, **16**, 2, pp. 159–95.

SHILS, E. (1978b) 'The order of learning in the United States from 1865 to VYGOTSKY, L. (1978)', *Mind in Society: The Development of Higher Psychological Processes*, Cambridge, MA: Harvard University Press.

SIKULA, J. (1996) *Handbook of Research on Teacher Education*, New York: Macmillan.

SPICKELMIER, J.L. (1983) 'College experience and moral judgment development', Doctoral dissertation. Minneapolis, MN: University of Minnesota.

SPRINTHALL, N.A., REIMAN, A.J. and THIES-SPRINTHALL, L. (1996) 'Teacher professional development', in SIKULA, J. (ed.) *Second Handbook of Research in Teacher Education*, New York: Macmillan, pp. 666–703.

SPRINTHALL, N.A. and SCOTT, J. (1989) 'Promoting psychological development, math achievement and success attribution of female students through deliberate psychological education', *Journal of Counseling Psychology*, **36**, pp. 440–6.

SPRINTHALL, N.A. and THIES-SPRINTHALL, L. (1983) 'Teacher as an adult learner: A cognitive-developmental view', in GRIFFIN, G. (ed.) *Staff Development (82nd Yearbook of the National Society for the Study of Education)*, Chicago: University of Chicago Press, pp. 13–35.

STEPHENS, J.M. (1967) *The Process of Schooling: A Psychological Examination*, Austin, Texas: Holt, Rinehart and Winston.

VYGOTSKY, L. (1978) *Mind in Society: The Development of Higher Psychological Processes*, Cambridge, MA: Harvard University Press.

WIDICK, C., KNEFELKAMP, L. and PARKER, C. (1975) 'The counselor as a developmental instructor', *Counselor Education and Supervision*, **14**, pp. 286–96.

WINITSKY, N. and ARENDS, R. (1991) 'Translating research into practice: The effects of various forms of training and clinical experience on preservice teachers' knowledge, reflectivity, and behavior', *Journal of Teacher Education*, **42**, 1, pp. 52–65.

ZEICHNER, K. (1986) 'Social and ethical dimensions of reform in teacher education', in HOFFMAN, J.V. and EDWARDS, S.A. (eds) *Reality and Reform in Clinical Teacher Education*, New York: Random House.

Notes on Contributors

Patricia Ashton is Professor of Educational Psychology in the Department of Educational Foundations at the University of Florida. She received the M.A. from Washington University and the Ph.D from the University of Georgia. Her research interests include cognitive and socio-emotional development, teaching, and motivation. She co-authored with Rod Webb *Making a Difference: Teachers' Sense of Efficacy and Student Achievement*, a report of research in middle and high school classrooms. She served as Editor of the Journal of Teacher Education from 1990–92 and co-editor of the *American Educational Research Journal*, Section on Teaching, Learning, and Human Development from 1996–98.

Gary K. Clabaugh is a Professor of Education at La Salle University and Director of their Graduate Program in Education. Author of three books and numerous lesser publications, Clabaugh also serves on the Publications Board of *Pi Lambda Theta* and is active in professional organizations. His column, 'The Cutting Edge,' appears regularly in *Educational Horizons*. Clabaugh's major professional interest is the role of foundations of education in teacher preparation. To that end he recently chaired the Council of Learned Society's Task Force on Accreditation and Academic Standards. This body revised the CLSE's standards for review by the profession. Clabaugh also is a Board Member of the Society of Professors of Education and recently co-authored 'Foundations of education' a chapter in *A Knowledge Base for Teacher Education*, published by the American Association of Colleges for Teacher Education.

Linda Darling-Hammond is the William F. Russell Professor in the Foundations of Education at Teachers College, Columbia University, where she is also Co-Director of the National Center for Restructuring Education, Schools, and Teaching (NCREST) and Executive Director of the National Commission on Teaching and America's Future. She is currently a visiting fellow at the Stanford Center for Advanced Studies in Behavioral Sciences. She is actively engaged in research, teaching, and policy work on issues of school restructuring, teacher education reform, and the enhancement of educational equity. She is author or editor of seven books, including The Right to Learn: A Blueprint for School Reform. Professional Development Schools: Schools for Developing a Profession, A License to Teach: Building a Profession for 21st Century Schools, and Authentic Assessment in Action. In addition, she has authored more than 150 journal articles, book chapters, and monographs on issues of educational policy and practice.

Mary E. Diez is Professor of Education and Graduate Dean at Alverno College in Milwaukee, Wisconsin. A 1995 winner of the McGraw Prize in Education, she is a past president of the American Association of Colleges for Teacher Education and currently serves on the Board of Examiners for NCATE, the technical advisory committee for INTASC, and is a member of the National Board for Professional Teaching Standards.

Edward R. Ducharme is the Ellis & Nelle Levitt Distinguished Professor of Education at Drake University, Des Moines, Iowa, where he has taught for the past six years. He is also Professor of Education Emeritus at the University of Vermont where he taught and chaired academic departments for 19 years. He holds degrees from Colby College, Harvard University, and Teachers College, Columbia, where he received his doctorate in 1968. He taught secondary school English in New York State for seven years prior to beginning his career in higher education. Ducharme has published widely on teacher education, higher education faculty development, public education, and secondary teaching. In addition to publishing over forty articles, he has authored or co-authored nine chapters in books or handbooks. He currently serves, with his spouse Mary K. Ducharme, as co-editor of the *Journal of Teacher Education*. Ducharme has been actively involved in the American Association of Colleges for Teacher Education (AACTE) for 25 years; for seven years he was a member of the Board of Examiners of the National Council for the Accreditation of Teacher Education (NCATE); he has presented frequently at AACTE and the American Educational Research Association (AERA).

Mary K. Ducharme is Professor of Education at Drake University, Des Moines, Iowa, where she has taught for the past six years. She holds degrees from the University of Dallas and the University of Nebraska-Lincoln, where she received her doctorate in 1983. She taught elementary school in Nebraska and California, worked as a program planning consultant for the Nebraska Department of Education, and directed a federal curriculum project in a junior–senior high school prior to beginning her career in higher education. She was a Kellogg National Fellow from 1987 to 1990. Ducharme has taught courses in teaching methodology, qualitative research design, and curriculum studies. She has been major adviser for numerous doctoral students in Iowa. She has published articles on teacher education programs and faculty, public education, and elementary teacher preparation. Ducharme has been actively involved in the American Association of Colleges for Teacher Education (AACTE) since 1980 and the American Educational Research Association (AERA) since 1982. She has presented frequently at the annual meetings of both organizations. She was instrumental in founding the Nebraska Consortium for the Improvement of Teacher Education, an organization devoted to collaborative reform and improvement of teacher education in the state.

Dr Calvin Frazier serves as a Senior Consultant for the Education Commission of the States and a Senior Associate for the Center for Educational Renewal.

He has consulted with school districts, institutions of higher education and states for the last nine years on policy issues around the renewal of teacher education. He was Colorado Commissioner of Education from 1973–1987, held various teaching and administrative positions in the public schools, and worked for 13 years in faculty positions in 3 major universities. He served as president of the Council of Chief State School Officers from 1983–1984; has been a member and chairman of the Board of Trustees for the Education Testing Service; and was vice-chairman of the U.S. delegation to UNESCO in 1983. He has represented the U.S. in meetings in Poland, England, Sweden, West Germany, People's Republic of China, and Australia.

He received his Masters and Ed.D in Educational Administration from the University of Oregon and his BA from the University of Puget Sound.

John I. Goodlad is Co-director of the Center for Educational Renewal at the University of Washington and president of the Institute for Educational Inquiry. In addition to advancing a comprehensive program of research and development directed to the simultaneous renewal of schooling and teacher education, he is inquiring into the mission of education in a democratic society to which such renewal must be directed.

Yvonne Gold is a Professor in the Department of Teacher Education, California State University, Long Beach and a psychotherapist in private practice in Los Alamitos, California. Her research interests and publications focus on teacher stress and burnout, psychological support, and beginning teacher and mentor support programs. She has worked extensively with local school districts, university teacher induction programs and graduate programs in education. She has published numerous articles, book chapters and monographs on these and related areas including *Teachers Managing Stress and Preventing Burnout: The Professional Health Solution* (Falmer Press), and *The Transformational Helping Professional: A New Vision* (Allyn and Bacon). She was recognized as University Distinguished Faculty Scholar (1990–91), Named University Outstanding Professor (1991–92) and received the University Distinguished Faculty Teaching Award (1992–93) from California State University, Long Beach. Dr Gold is a director and program evaluator for one of the Beginning Teacher Support and Assessment programs in California where she uses her psychological support and stress management strategies with beginning teachers and mentors.

Carl A. Grant is a Hoefs-Bascom Professor of Teacher Education in the Department of Curriculum and Instruction at the University of Wisconsin-Madison. He has written or edited eighteen books or monographs in multicultural education and/or teacher education. These include Research and Multicultural Education, 1993; Multicultural Research: A Reflective Engagement with Race, Class, Gender and Sexual Orientation, 1998; Making Choices for Multicultural Education (3rd edition) (with Christine Sleeter), 1998; After the School Bell Rings, (2nd edition) (with Christine E. Sleeter), 1995; Educating for Diversity, 1993. He has also written more than 100 articles, chapters in books, and reviews. Several of his writings and programs that he directed have received awards. Professor Grant was a Fulbright Scholar in England in 1982–1983 researching and studying multicultural education. In 1993 Professor Grant became President of the National Association for Multicultural Education (NAME) and in 1997, he received the School of Education Distinguished Achievement Award.

Mary M. Kennedy is a Professor at Michigan State University. Her scholarship focuses on the relationship between knowledge and teaching practice, on the nature of knowledge used in teaching practice, and on how research knowledge contributes to practice. She has published two books addressing the relationship between knowledge and teaching and has won four awards for her work. Prior to joining Michigan State University in 1986, her work focused mainly on policy issues and on the role of research in improving policy. She has authored numerous journal articles and book chapters in these areas, and has authored reports specifically for policy audiences, including the United States Congress.

Dr Barry Munitz is currently President and Chief Executive Officer of The J. Paul Getty Trust in Los Angeles. From 1991–1998 he served as Chancellor of the California State University, the largest system of postsecondary education in the United States. Dr Munitz has been chairman of the American Council on Education and chair of the California Education Round Table. He presently is vice chair of a commission studying the costs of higher education in the United States.

Frank B. Murray is H. Rodney Sharp Professor in the School of Education and Department of Psychology at the University of Delaware and served as dean of the College of Education between 1979 and 1995. Currently, he is Executive Director of the Holmes Partnership and was chair of the National Board of its forerunner, the Holmes Group. He was president and co-founder of the Project 30 Alliance, an organization of faculty in education and the liberal arts. Recently he served as co-editor of the *Review of Educational Research* (1994–97). In 1996 he edited *The Teacher Educator's Handbook* for the American Association of Teacher Education. For his contributions to the fields of child development and teacher education, he was awarded an honorary doctorate from Heriot-Watt University in Edinburgh, Scotland in 1994.

Dr Rosemary Papalewis is currently Executive Director, Inter-Institutional Relations, and Assistant Vice Chancellor of Academic Affairs for the California State University. She is also an active instructor in educational administration. Dr Papalewis has been president of the National Council of Educational Administrators (NCPEA) and president of California Professors of Educational Administration (CAPEA). Dr Papalewis presently serves as the California State University's representative to the California Citizens Commission on Higher Education.

James Raths is currently Chair of the Department of Educational Studies at the University of Delaware. He has had extensive experiences in teacher education administration, serving variously as executive secretary of a campus-wide council on teacher education at the University of Illinois, Dean of Education at the University of Vermont. He has also participated in the early days of the Holmes Group and in planning the re-design of NCATE. His publications are directed at research and evaluation of candidates and teacher education programs.

Alan J. Reiman is an Assistant Professor in the Department of Curriculum and Instruction at NC State University and served as a clinical assistant and clinical associate professor between 1988 and 1995. Before that he was a classroom teacher for 10 years. Currently, he directs the NC State Model Clinical Teaching Program and the Mentor Network. He also is the coordinator of a 12-university consortium called the Model Clinical Teaching Network which sponsors research and development in innovative clinical teacher education practices.

Robert A. Roth is Professor of Education and Chair of the Department of Teacher Education at California State University, Long Beach. He is author of more than 100 publications and research studies. He is past national president of the Association of Teacher Educators (ATE), National Association of State Directors of Teacher Education and Certification, and the Interstate Certification Compact. He has been named Distinguished Leader in Teacher Education in the United States by ATE, Distinguished Teacher Educator by the California ATE, Distinguished Member by ATE, and University Distinguished Faculty Scholar at California State University, Long Beach. His areas of interest include teacher education program structure, interpersonal communication, new teacher induction, and teacher stress and burnout.

Gary Sykes is a Professor in the departments of educational administration and teacher education, Michigan State University, where he specializes in policy related to teacher professionalism and to school choice.

Arthur E. Wise is President of the National Council for Accreditation of Teacher Education in Washington, DC. At NCATE, he has directed the implementation of rigorous accreditation standards, and initated efforts to develop a system of quality assurance for the teaching profession. He previously served as director of the RAND Corporation's Center for the Study of the Teaching Profession.

He currently also serves as chair of the board of directors of the National Foundation for the Improvement of Education, is a member of the National Commission on Teaching and America's Future, and serves on the board of directors of the National Board for Professional Teaching Standards.

Index

0195